BERNARD OF CLAIRVAUX

Detail from a 1496 altarpiece depicting the crucifixion, from Esrum Abbey in Denmark. The detail is a scene based on Bernard's vision of the Amplexus, his embrace by Christ while praying before a crucifix. Photo: Jens Bruun, altertavler.dk. Courtesy of the National Museum of Denmark. Used by permission.

BERNARD OF CLAIRVAUX

AN INNER LIFE

BRIAN PATRICK MCGUIRE

CORNELL UNIVERSITY PRESS

Ithaca and London

First published 2020 by Cornell University Press

Printed in the United States of America

Library of Congress Cataloging-in-Publication Data
Names: McGuire, Brian Patrick, author.
Title: Bernard of Clairvaux : an inner life / by Brian Patrick McGuire.
Description: Ithaca [New York] : Cornell University Press, 2020. | Includes bibliographical references and index.
Identifiers: LCCN 2020005651 (print) | LCCN 2020005652 (ebook) | ISBN 9781501751042 (hardcover) | ISBN 9781501751554 (pdf) | ISBN 9781501751547 (epub)
Subjects: LCSH: Bernard, of Clairvaux, Saint, 1090 or 1091-1153. | Christian saints—France—Biography.
Classification: LCC BX4700.B5 M2538 2020 (print) | LCC BX4700.B5 (ebook) | DDC 271/.1202 [B]—dc23
LC record available at https://lccn.loc.gov/2020005651
LC ebook record available at https://lccn.loc.gov/2020005652

To my Cistercian friends

❧ CONTENTS

Acknowledgments   ix

Chronology of Bernard's Life and Times   xi

Note to the Reader   xv

Maps   xvi

Introduction: In Pursuit of a Difficult Saint   1

1. A Time of Hope and Change   7

2. A Saint's Origins   13

3. From the New Monastery to the
   Valley of Light, 1115–1124   30

4. Monastic Commitment and Church
   Politics, 1124–1129   54

5. Toward Reformation of Church
   and Monastery   68

6. Healing a Divided Church, 1130–1135   79

7. Victory and Defeat: A Conflicted
   Church, 1136–1140   110

8. The World after the Schism: One
   Thing after Another, 1140–1145   141

9. Preaching a Crusade and Leaving
   Miracles Behind, 1146–1150   181

10. Business as Usual in Preparing
    for Death   215

Fifteen Questions about Bernard: The Background for My Portrait   251

1. *What are the primary sources for the life of Bernard?*   251

2. *What can previous biographies of Bernard tell us?*   255

3. *How did Bernard relate to women?*   266

4. *How did Bernard relate to the body?*   269

5. *Can Bernard's sexual identity be defined?*   272

6. *How did Bernard express his commitment as monk and abbot?*   273

7. *What was Bernard's involvement in the Second Crusade?*   277

8. *Did Bernard show tolerance toward the Jews?*   282

9. *How did Bernard relate to Cîteaux's abbot and to the Cistercian Order?*   284

10. *Bernard the monster? Returning to Peter Abelard and Gilbert de la Porrée*   289

11. *Bernard and Peter the Venerable: Friendship or rivalry?*   291

12. *How could Bernard praise monk-knights?*   295

13. *Can Bernard's liturgical sermons be used as sources for his inner life?*   297

14. *Did Bernard contribute to "the persecuting society"?*   301

15. *Was Bernard "a sick man living on his nerves"?*   304

Notes   309

Sources and References   315

Index   351

✿ Acknowledgments

This volume is the result of years of reading and thinking about Bernard of Clairvaux, and it would not have been possible without the support and inspiration of scholars such as Dom Jean Leclercq and Sir Richard Southern. Leclercq was kind and generous to me, while Sir Richard became a friend whom I will always miss. But I have also benefited from visits to Trappist-Cistercian abbeys, especially in the United States, but also in Ireland, England, Scotland, and Hong Kong. I think especially of the Cistercian brothers of Myrendal on the Danish island of Bornholm. Monks and nuns have made me welcome in their world and have shared their prayers and thoughts with me. The first to do so was Thomas Davis, formerly abbot of New Clairvaux in California, and he is one of many brothers who have been willing to share their thoughts and lives with me.

I am also grateful to Bernard McGinn, professor emeritus of the University of Chicago, who was one of the readers of the original manuscript and here as in so much else in our friendship has provided me with helpful criticisms and suggestions.

I am in debt to Michael West Oborne, friend since the third grade at Saint Augustine's School in Oakland, California, in 1956. Michael has taken me to innumerable medieval Cistercian sites and has an unfailing interest in monastic history.

To my spouse of more than fifty years, Ann Kirstin Pedersen, I am thankful for her infinite patience with a distracted husband and her love of Cistercian life and spirituality.

I am also indebted to my friends E. Rozanne Elder and James France, who are fellow Cistercian scholars.

Finally, I want to thank Peter Potter, formerly editor in chief at Cornell University Press, and his successor, Mahinder Kingra, for their support in seeing this manuscript grow from thought to fact. Also thanks to Mary Kate Murphy, for her superb editing.

Kandestederne, Skagen, Denmark, 20 August 2019
The feast of Saint Bernard

1073–85 Gregory VII pope. The Gregorian Reform. In a broader sense, the first medieval reformation.

1090 Bernard is born in Fontaines-lès-Dijon, Burgundy, as son of the knight, Tescelin, and his wife, Aleth de Montbard. He has five brothers and one sister.

1098 A group of monks, together with their abbot Robert, leaves the monastery of Molesme to establish a more strict observance at the "New Monastery," which comes to be called Cîteaux. Robert is called back to Molesme and the prior Alberic is abbot until 1109.

c. 1100 The youth Bernard is sent to the canons at Saint Vorles in Châtillon-sur-Seine, where his family has property; here he is given instruction in the humanities.

1106 or 1107 Bernard's mother, Aleth, dies while he is at Châtillon.

1108 The prior at Cîteaux, Stephen Harding, is elected abbot and remains in office until 1133.

1111 Bernard leads an informal monastic community at Châtillon. He seeks out some of his brothers and other relatives, and they join the community.

1112 or 1113 Bernard, together with several friends and all of his brothers, except for the youngest, seeks entrance at Cîteaux.

1113 Cîteaux sends out monks to found a new monastery, La Ferté.

1115 Cîteaux's abbot, Stephen Harding, sends Bernard and some of his brothers and friends to found Clairvaux as a daughter house in the county of Champagne. Bernard is abbot here until his death in 1153. He regularly preaches sermons, many of which he transcribes and circulates.

1118 Bernard sends monks to establish Clairvaux's first daughter house, Trois Fontaines, about fifty miles to the north. During Bernard's abbacy, Clairvaux gains sixty-five daughter houses.

1119 The abbots of Cîteaux's four first daughter houses come to the mother abbey for a General Chapter to approve a constitution for the Cistercian

Order, *Carta caritatis*, the Charter of Charity. The same year Clairvaux establishes its second daughter house, Fontenay, on land belonging to Bernard's family. Bernard is ill and has to stay away from Clairvaux for a year. He probably does not attend the Chapter.

1120 The Benedictine abbot, William of Saint-Thierry, visits Bernard and becomes his friend and later contributes to his hagiography, the *Vita Prima*.

1121 A third daughter house for Clairvaux, Foigny, is founded in Picardy, about 175 miles to the north.

1124 Bernard challenges Arnold, abbot of Morimond, because he has plans to bring his monks to Palestine. Bernard's letters on the subject are incorporated in his letter collection.

1125 Bernard writes his *Apology to William* for his friend William of Saint-Thierry, concerning art and architecture in the monastery.

1128 Church synod held at Troyes, close to Clairvaux, to found the Knights Templar. Bernard presents the new order in his *In Praise of the New Knighthood*. Probably at this time Bernard also writes *On Grace and Free Choice*, a brilliant response to the question of grace and freedom as found in Saint Paul's Epistle to the Romans.

1130 Disputed papal election. Innocent II has to abandon Rome to his rival Anacletus. In France Bernard attends a church synod at Étampes, where he gives his support to Innocent. Bernard then plays a decisive role in the schism and travels three times to Italy and twice to Aquitaine in dealing with the matter.

1135–1153 Bernard's eighty-six Sermons on the Song of Songs given to his monks in chapter in Clairvaux and afterwards revised for a European audience.

1138 Back in Clairvaux with the papal schism behind him Bernard laments the loss of his brother Gerard, who had been his main practical support. Bernard's lament for Gerard is contained in Sermon 26 on the Song of Songs.

1139 The Second Lateran Council, called by the victorious Innocent II. Bernard apparently does not attend.

1141 William of Saint-Thierry convinces Bernard to declare Peter Abelard's teaching on the Trinity and the Redemption to be heretical. Church synod at Sens, where Bernard has Abelard's writings condemned. Abelard appeals to Rome but stops on the way at Cluny, where Abbot Peter the Venerable protects him and helps arrange a reconciliation with Bernard, made possible by the abbot of Cîteaux.

1140 or 1141 Bernard writes *On Precept and Dispensation*, concerning obedience and freedom in the monastery.

1141–1147 Bernard opposes the election of William Fitzherbert as archbishop of York and in the end one of Bernard's own abbots, Henry Murdach, gains the office in 1147.

1146 (31 March) Bernard addresses the knights of his feudal world outside the pilgrim church of Vézelay. From here he travels for several months in the Rhineland seeking support for the Second Crusade, which will be a fiasco. The detailed record of his travels gives a sense of how he had become sought out by the masses as a miracle maker.

1145–1153 After a succession of three popes who had each lasted a year or less, a Cistercian abbot, Bernardo Paganelli, is elected and takes the name Eugenius III. He has great problems with the Roman population. Bernard assumes that he now has a close bond with the pope, but he is disappointed.

c. 1148–1152 Bernard writes what can be called his testament in a declaration of what is important in the life of the Church, for the sake of the pope: *On Consideration*, good advice on the contemplative life.

1148 (March) Council of Reims where Bernard has no success in having Gilbert de la Porrée's teachings on the Trinity condemned.

1148 (8 September) Bernard's friend and contributor to his hagiography, William of Saint-Thierry, dies.

1148 (2 November) Malachy, archbishop of Armagh and Bernard's friend, dies at Clairvaux. Bernard writes his hagiography.

1150 (Spring) Attempt to launch a new crusade with Bernard its leader, but he declines.

1150 (December) Bernard writes to the dying Suger, abbot of Saint Denis and once the most powerful figure in France next to the king.

1151 Archbishop Eskil of Lund visits Clairvaux and becomes close to Bernard. He brings monks back with him from Clairvaux to found Esrum Abbey in Denmark.

1153 (Spring) Bernard makes his final journey, to bring peace to the citizens of Metz.

1153 (20 August) Bernard dies at Clairvaux. Soon after, his secretary and author of his hagiography, Geoffrey of Auxerre, writes to Archbishop Eskil to inform him and thus the entire Church of the loss.

1174 (18 January) Pope Alexander III canonizes Bernard.

✍ NOTE TO THE READER

I have avoided footnotes or endnotes in this book—except in the section Fifteen Questions about Bernard: The Background for My Portrait—in order to maintain the integrity of the text. In the Sources and References section, I indicate the primary and secondary sources I have used in writing this life of Bernard.

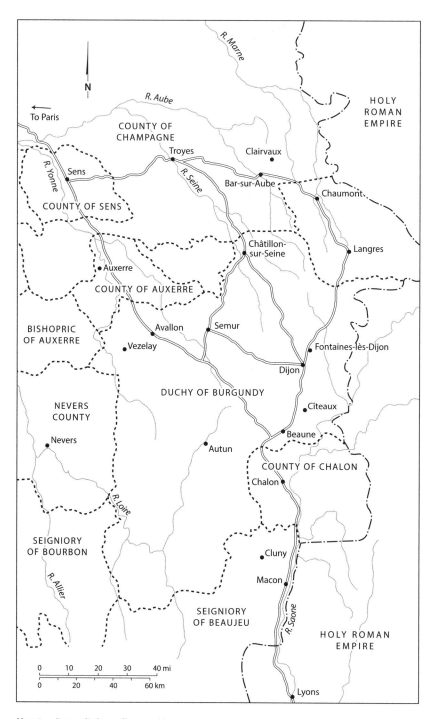

MAP 1. Bernard's immediate world.

MAP 2. The Europe of the Cistercians at the death of Bernard (1153). Adapted from a map by Johnny Gøgsig Jakobsen. Used by permission.

Introduction

In Pursuit of a Difficult Saint

Bernard of Clairvaux (1090–1153) almost defies characterization. Monk, abbot, adviser of kings and popes, author of some of the finest Latin prose to emerge from the Middle Ages, he was a man of many talents. At first glance he can seem abrasive, overconfident, almost arrogant. But as the following pages will show, he is a point of departure for European culture in its search for faith, meaning, and community. Any history of Western Europe in the twelfth century has to include Bernard and his almost frenetic activities. And yet he was literally cast on the trash heap of history when French revolutionaries attacked his monastery of Clairvaux and mutilated his tomb. In 1793 his bones, together with those of Malalchy of Armagh and other saints, were rescued by local peasants and taken to the parish church of Ville-sous-la-Ferté, where they are to be found today. We do not know, however, which remains are Bernard's.

I am not the first to call Bernard a difficult saint. Years ago, the great monastic historian David Knowles used the term in trying to define Bernard's identity. In visiting Trappist-Cistercian monasteries in the United States and speaking about Bernard, I have time and again met monks who told me they found Bernard's life and writings difficult to appreciate. If a saint is supposed to be a person who invites imitation in seeking God and embracing others, then Bernard's words and actions can easily be intepreted as devoid of charity.

1

His reputation today sharply conrasts with that of his theological opponent, Peter Abelard (1079–1142), whose writings Bernard considered heretical. After the French Revolution the remains of Abelard and his former lover Heloise were brought to Paris and reinterred in an elegant tomb in Père Lachaise cemetery. To this day flowers are left at the place of burial, while Bernard's resting place has been all but forgotten.

Abelard has been embraced by modernity, while Bernard is often dismissed as an unenlightened relic of the Middle Ages. However much Abelard is to be admired for his theological insights and sense of self, Bernard does not deserve to be dismissed as an evil genius. Bernard received such treatment from the Italian author Umberto Eco, who is said to have used him as his model for the vicious murderer Jorge in his best-selling novel from 1980, *The Name of the Rose*. In fact Bernard represents the same Christian humanism that Abelard personifies. The two became enemies partly because they were so close in what they sought from life and learning, though they diverged in how to achieve these goals.

Bernard deserves reevaluation as a person and participant in the history of Christian life and spirituality. His inner life and external actions illuminate his own time and provide a context for ours. In addition to his sophisticated theology, his moving sermons, and his influence among kings and popes, Bernard can plausibly be considered the first European. Through his vision and talent for inspiring people to work together, he helped build Christianity's first continent-wide monastic order, the Cistercians, whose monasteries extended from Ireland to Sicily and Norway.

The first time I contemplated writing a biography of Bernard was in early 1975, on a walk through the early spring garden at St Johns College, Oxford, England. My doctoral supervisor, Sir Richard Southern, who had become president of the college, told me that he wanted me to write a new biography of Bernard: "The last good one was written by the Abbé Vacandard in 1895 and we have needed another one ever since." I felt flattered that Southern, whom I admired as a medieval historian and had come to love as mentor and friend, tendered such an invitation. My answer, however, showed all the confidence of arrogant youth: "I can't write such a biography, Dick, for I hate the man." Sir Richard reacted with disappointment but also a kind of resignation: "I know what you mean." Southern understood that I found Bernard to be intolerant and unsympathetic. He had his own doubts and never came to write extensively about Bernard. He did not mention the subject again, even though in later years when I visited Oxford, we had many good and memorable conversations. But Bernard remained a closed subject between us.

I never forgot Southern's invitation and could not keep away from Bernard. In 1978 I discovered the fruitful environment of Cistercian scholars who meet each May in connection with the Congress on Medieval Studies in Kalamazoo, Michigan. I got to know living Cistercian monks and nuns. They encouraged me to take a second look at the medieval sources. The Bernard I discovered in the following years was not visible in his own writings but in stories about him, usually recorded after his death, *exempla*. These brief moralizing anecdotes cast a more sympathetic light on how Bernard was remembered, both at Clairvaux and in the Cistercian Order as a whole. Sometimes these anecdotes contain remarkable narratives not otherwise found in contemporary sources for Bernard's life or his own writings. For example, there is a description of how Bernard in prayer before a statue of Mary received drops of milk from her breast, memorialized in art and text as the "Lactation of Saint Bernard." This story is first indicated in art, in a late thirteenth-century altarpiece of the Knights Templar from Majorca. Not much later, the lactation is described in a French collection of moralizing stories, *Ci nous dit*.

Closer in time to the living Bernard is a narrative of how a brother at Clairvaux who came upon Bernard praying before the crucifix was overwhelmed by a vision of the figure of Jesus bending down to embrace the abbot. Herbert, monk of Clairvaux, recorded this story, known as the *Amplexus*, in a collection of miracle stories from the late 1170s, almost twenty years after Bernard's death. The vision aptly summarizes Bernard's devotion to Jesus as a human being. Cistercian spirituality as found in Bernard's writings seeks union of body and spirit in moving toward an incarnate God. The body is not denied but rather is joined to the soul in a wholeness that cries out for the totality of union with the divine. Bernard in one of his Sermons on the Song of Songs (71.10) quoted the Psalm verse "For me it is good to cleave to God" (Ps 72:28) and described how "when God and man cleave wholly to each other, it is when they are incorporated into each other by mutual love [. . . so] God is in man and man in God."

Bernard's Mastery of Prose and His Inner Life

Is it possible to write a new biography of Bernard that does justice to all his roles? What about Bernard the maker of miracles? How can we in our skeptical times incorporate this aspect of his legacy? My goal is to seek insight into Bernard's inner life, insofar as this is possible, and in so doing, I will be considering how Bernard understood himself and conveyed himself to the world around him. Miracles were part of his worldview and of his world;

as such they can tell us as much about Bernard's inner life as do his writings and other actions. I will not be investigating whether he really did perform miracles. Certainly those around him generally believed he did, though, as we shall see, there also were skeptical voices. Whatever we think of miracles, many ordinary people in the second quarter of the twelfth century looked to Bernard for divine help with their pains and illnesses.

Bernard on Bernard is our best source on his life and thoughts. But the observations of Bernard's closest friends and companions can be just as helpful. I realize that in making use of Bernard's own writings, I am dealing with a master of prose whose command of the Bible in its Latin translation, the Vulgate, was total. He was also familiar with classical writers and the Church Fathers. Hardly a sentence in Bernard's corpus appears without a direct or indirect biblical quotation, and sometimes it is impossible to separate what Bernard himself wrote from what he incorporated from elsewhere. While being aware of these borrowings, I think it is necessary to make a leap of faith and to assume that Bernard meant what he said, regardless of the means he used to make his statement. He cannot be reduced to a purely literary figure, for his writings were meant to contribute in a dynamic, forceful way to the direction of his world according to Christian principles. This is the great paradox of Bernard: he chose to withdraw from society and isolate himself from human concerns and yet ended up being completely involved in the world. As he wrote in an oft-quoted passage, "I have kept the habit of a monk but I have long abandoned the life."

I have entitled my work *An Inner Life* because I intend to look at Bernard from within, in his intellectual, emotional, and spiritual interior life. I offer no sophisticated methodology, only a desire to see Bernard as a human being with hopes, dreams, frustrations, and moments of pure joy. Well-known stories of his temptations by women suggest that he was heterosexual in his orientation, as does his assertion that a man cannot be alone with a woman for long without sexual intercourse taking place. [For Bernard and women, see question 3 in the Fifteen Questions about Bernard: The Background for My Portrait section.] So much for spiritual friendships between the sexes! He harbored doubts about the company of women but enjoyed very much the companionship of men. If we can speak of gender affectivity, it was all focused on men, without there being the slightest trace of homosexual attraction. The absence of this element does not, of course, rule out the possibility that Bernard was physically attracted to other men. Whatever the case, he had no qualms about expressing great fondness for other men and asking them to reciprocate.

I make no attempt to "liberate" Bernard or to make him more palatable for our time. He belongs to the twelfth century, not the twenty-first. But his faith in God and involvement in a community of men invite our attention, living as we do in an age when faith is difficult, if not suspect, and viable, affectionate human communities are thin on the ground. My approach to Bernard in preparing this book has been old-fashioned monastic *lectio*, careful meditative reading of his writings in an attempt to get to know the man, as it were, from the inside. At times I have had to sit back and absorb the beauty of his Latin prose in all its rhymed complexity and simple variety. At other times I have felt, at least for a moment, that I have been able to look into the depths of his affective life. There are, of course, traps. When Bernard mourned the loss of his brother Gerard in the twenty-sixth Sermon on the Song of Songs, he was announcing his situation not only to his Clairvaux brethren but to a European audience. He clearly meant what he wrote, but his readership was imagined as public and not private. Similarly his letters, as we have them, were intended to be read by their recipients but preserved for everyone who could benefit from their contents. The medieval letter is a public document, a precious manifestation of the author's message to the world, and as such only an indirect reflection of the writer's private state of mind.

The word that appears repeatedly in Bernard's writings is *affectus*, a word that has no exact modern equivalent but indicates a deep-seated attachment. Cistercian *affectus* unites intellect and feeling in a spiritual life that for Bernard was deeply monastic but at the same time broadly Christian. It is this kind of attachment that enabled an abbot and twelve monks to leave their familiar surroundings and establish a religious community in a new place, with all the demands involved in clearing and cultivation of the land, constructing buildings, and clarifying the monks' right to be in that place. *Affectus* involves hard work but also bonds of attachment among the monks to each other in living a disciplined life that required waking in the darkness and stumbling down the night stairs to the church for vigils. This devotion was only possible because the brothers had learned to trust and depend on each other, whether in the forest, the fields, or the monastery.

This aspect of Bernard's life, as of any monastic life, is all but hidden from us. His everyday existence in the monastery is almost taken for granted by his biographers. Instead they focus on his periods of illness, his travels, his political involvements, and especially his miracles. We might wish to know what Bernard did and thought and felt when, as became increasingly rare, he was home at Clairvaux and not receiving important guests. But we can only guess.

The first part of this biography will be very much indebted to the description of Bernard found in the first book of the so-called *Vita Prima* (First Life) of Bernard, written by his friend, William of Saint-Thierry shortly before William's death in 1148, five years before Bernard's death. [See question 1 for more background.] To anyone objecting that a modern biographer should not rely on a medieval work of hagiography, I would answer that William's closeness to Bernard makes him a witness who deserves appropriate consideration. By contrast, the second book of the *Vita Prima* was composed by a Benedictine abbot, Arnold of Bonneval, who had been asked by the Cistercians to write an account focusing on Bernard's involvement in the papal schism of the 1130s. Books III–V were written by Bernard's secretary, the monk Geoffrey of Auxerre, who was conscientious but did not attain the intimacy with Bernard that William did. The first chapters of this biography remain close to William's account, for when the historian finds a credible and useful source, it is imperative to make good use of it.

In what follows here I do not intend to eulogize Bernard. Certainly he has had his share of praise. Nor do I mean to expose him for falsehood. Somewhere in the middle between excessive praise or blame, I seek to find Bernard as man, monk, abbot, political figure, and central actor in Christian Europe in the first half of the twelfth century. But Bernard is not only the past. He lives on today in the monks and nuns who belong to the two Orders of the Cistercians, the Trappists (O.C.S.O.) and the Regular Cistercians (O.Cist.). They are his descendants, even though some of them have confided in me that they have difficulty reconciling Bernard's thoughts and actions with their own spiritual journeys. They are hesitant about incorporating Bernard into their spiritual lives. For them, as for myself, Bernard requires patience. Difficult saint and founder of a spiritual empire, Bernard of Clairvaux, as I have discovered, can still surprise us.

❧ CHAPTER 1

A Time of Hope and Change

The world into which Bernard was born in 1090 was full of hope and promise. From the ninth to the eleventh century, Western Europe had been the object of Viking plundering. Today, some Danish archaeologists claim that the Vikings were more traders than pirates, but monks along the coasts and rivers of Europe knew better. Nothing they had built was safe from these marauders. Nevertheless, the salvation for the West was the fact that sooner or later Vikings settled in some of the areas they had previously molested: Normandy, eastern England, Ireland, and Sicily.

Travel, once dangerous, became possible and even attractive. In the middle of the eleventh century a troubled young man, Anselm of Aosta, traveled north to Normandy, one of the regions that previously had been so unstable. There he found a teacher, Lanfranc, who had also come north from Italy and had joined a new monastery, Bec. Anselm sat at Lanfranc's feet and experienced the joy of discovering the liberal arts and the way to Sacred Scripture, as the Bible then was called. In the 1060s, when Lanfranc joined his lord, Duke William of Normandy, in the conquest of England, Anselm remained behind and composed prayers and meditations redolent of a new spirit within the Christian religion.

What do Anselm and his life have to do with Bernard? When Anselm died in 1109, Bernard was nineteen and seemed destined for the life of a wandering scholar that had characterized Anselm's first years. But in the years to come Bernard would profit from a new interiority that had been born in Normandy in the decades prior to his birth. Anselm was not the only monk who was writing prayers and spiritual reflections that gave Christian belief greater intensity. John, of a neighboring monastery at Fécamp, was also rethinking religious language. Bernard along with many others in the first decades of the twelfth century would benefit from a theological language that called upon God to be present and immediate. Bernard did not come to write prayers as Anselm did, yet prayers are lodged in the sermons that Bernard left behind for his monks.

For much of its first millenium Christianity had been a religion that concentrated on external manifestations of belief. In a turbulent world it was sufficient to care for the baptism of pagans. Once this was done, a superficially Christian population was left to attend to its inner life and thoughts. Besides baptism there was the crucifixion itself, but almost as meaningful was the division of a tunic in two for a beggar on a freezing winter's day. The Roman soldier Martin who shared his clothing with a beggar became the first popular saint in Western Europe besides Mary, the apostles, and the martyrs. Martin's act of charity imitated the selflessness of Jesus himself, and according to legend it was Jesus who appeared to Martin and told him that the beggar he clothed was indeed himself, the Lord.

What mattered was to perform the external act, whether it was the pouring of water and invoking the Trinity in the sacrament of baptism or the division of one's possessions. The Church rarely asked about motives, and so it was the dawn of a new age when monks like Anselm and John of Fécamp began questioning their own motivations. They spoke to God, Jesus, Mary, and the saints, telling them that they not only were in need of their help but felt driven to consider their inner lives. Anselm and his contemporaries cried out for the Lord. The language they used was derivative of what is found in the Psalms of David, the prophets of the Old Testament, and the Gospels, but they offered an immediacy and a personal element that represented a new form of Christian life.

This search for intimacy would come to characterize Bernard's life and helps explain why he joined a monastery. At the same time, however, he benefited from other factors in creating his life. A few decades before Bernard was born, the Western Church had experienced the upheaval of what many history books call the Gregorian Reform, after Pope Gregory VII (1073–85), who is best known for defying the German king and Roman emperor Henry IV. I prefer to call this movement the first medieval reformation, for it brought about a genuine reformation or restructuring of the Christian Church. It meant that rich families no longer could buy church offices for their younger sons: the old sin of simony, which had been with Christianity since the Acts of the Apostles, was outlawed. Eventually this reformation brought about a new orientation of monastic life, which until then had been dominated by the care and upbringing of children.

From the time of Bernard onwards, children were excluded from monasteries, at least in the new reformed monasticism. Children had to grow up first and make their own choices, instead of being brought to the monastery at the age of six or seven when their parents chose to hand them over. Bernard came to the monastery as an adult, and the new monasticism that he joined insisted on individual choice. Once again, inner motivation and personal intention came to the fore, instead of exterior actions and choices made by others. In this sense Bernard and his contemporaries would discover the meaning of Christianity as manifested in the words of Jesus, emphasizing the consent that comes from the heart instead of the gesture's symbolic assent.

The first reformation of the Church also brought conflict between kings and emperors, on the one hand, and popes and bishops, on the other. The secular arm, as it was called, was used to calling the shots, and certainly this arrangement seemed necessary at a time when society was fragile and the Church needed protection from all the diabolical forces at loose in society. But now it was a question of giving God what was rightly his, and the reform party in Rome, led by Gregory, insisted that their spiritual power was superior to the worldly power of kings. For a long time kings had in fact often thought of themselves as endowed with priestly authority, but Gregory insisted on an absolute separation between the secular and the sacerdotal. Bernard of Clairvaux would benefit from this new regime and would consider it to be a right of his to lecture kings on the limitations of their power. With him begins a new period in European history that sought a balance of power, an arrangement lost in the sixteenth century when Catholic and Protestant sovereigns took over the churches in their realms and tried to run them. Bernard and his contemporaries would have been horrified at this development, for they considered spiritual power far superior to temporal.

The first reformation of the medieval Church unleashed an almost limitless energy, for now popes, bishops, and abbots found it possible to turn to the laity, which until that time had been left to its own devices. The reform meant not only cleansing the Church but also preaching Christ in a new manner, as happened at Clermont-Ferrand in what today is central France. Here in 1095 Pope Urban II called upon the knights of the Christian world to take part in what was called an "armed pilgrimage" (*peregrinatio armata*) and to go the the Holy Land and deliver its sacred places from the Muslim peoples who were making it impossible for Christian pilgrims to pray and recall Christ's life. What we call the First Crusade was then known as a pilgrimage, but a journey with the sword of vengeance, not the pilgrim's staff.

The pope described the sufferings of pilgrims and called for a new kind of pilgrimage, one that would unite not only the crowned heads of Europe but also ordinary soldiers and knights. As a young abbot he felt called upon to criticize one of his fellow abbots for taking his monks to the Holy Land. Bernard rejected this form of monasticism, but he soon succumbed to a relative's plans to form a new order of knight-monks. And later in life he found it necessary to preach what we call the Second Crusade, which, as we will see, turned into a fiasco with great loss of life.

The Crusades promised salvation: the very act of going on crusade provided an indulgence that showed the way to the kingdom of God. But for the thousands of men and some women who went to the East, the Crusades brought death and destruction. Throughout the first decades of the twelfth century, after the remarkable conquest of Jerusalem in 1099, Bernard had to live with the attraction of the armed pilgrimage to Jerusalem. He had to tell his monks that it was better for them to remain in their monasteries seeking the heavenly Jerusalem than to head for the earthly Jerusalem. But, finally, in 1147 he preached the necessity of saving the earthly Jerusalem from those who threatened it. For Bernard and many other sincere monks of his time, it was a dilemma to seek to imitate Christ and encourage others to find him in what often turned out to be not salvation but perdition.

Over its history in the West, Christianity has attempted time and again to realize the challenge of the gospel by bringing men and women to a new awareness of the presence of God. In Bernard's half century, this awareness could be achieved in one of two ways: by going on crusade or by going into a monastery. There were still traditional ways of seeking Christ: by going on a conventional pilgrimage to one of the holy places or simply by living a decent life as a peasant, merchant, or knight. Those men and women who entered the monastery of their own free will knew that the choice they made was for a lifetime and could not be undone, except in exceptional circumstances. In an earlier time, powerful relatives could intervene to reverse this choice, but in Bernard's time, the monastic vow was forever.

We will never know why Bernard chose to become a monk, but that choice was much more "ordinary" in his time than in ours. He grew up in a family that was quite conventional for the knighthood of the time. Bernard's brothers played knights as children and looked forward to following in the footsteps of their father. The fact that they did not do so was due to Bernard's example, but they did not reject their original vocation because they came to question its worth. To be a knight was to be a member of Christ's army, a *miles Christi*, and knights had every opportunity to achieve eternal salvation.

In our time there is still a deep-seated prejudice that sees medieval people as manipulated by the Church and forced to live in a certain way. But in point of fact many people of the twelfth century saw the Church as their mother, giving them access to God's grace and looking after them in the drama of life, at birth with baptism, in adulthood with confirmation and marriage, and in sickness and death with the sacrament of the sick. The Church opened the way to Mary and the other saints, and the lives of peasants and knights could be happy and peaceful. There were exceptions, of course, but ordinary life in the medieval period was calm, after all the fear and disruption of the centuries when Western Europe had been under siege.

It is almost impossible for the historian of medieval Europe to penetrate the surface of everyday life of that time, for there is so much we do not know. But thanks to chronicles written at the time and to evidence found in excavations, it is possible to assert that the medieval period was a time of hope and change. The fear of losing everything as a result of Viking invasions was receding, and change was coming thanks to new methods of cultivating the land, improved types of plows, and the clearing of areas that for centuries had been left as marsh and forest. There is a sense in some written sources that things were improving, and the many parish churches and cathedrals built during this period attest to this. For merchants, whose lives depended on the presence of people in their towns, churches that attracted pilgrims helped guarantee prosperity. If nothing succeeds like success, then Europe was succeeding admirably in the twelfth century.

At the same time, however, Bernard's Europe had a shadow side: there was no police force, no standing army, and only a rudimentary judicial system. In his time murders took place in Paris, the very heart of Christian Europe, and although Bernard and his contemporaries lamented this, they could not control events. Similarly, the French king could get away with invading the territory of his vassal, the Duke of Champagne, and with putting a torch to a whole town, which came to be called Vitry-le-Brulé. However much Bernard condemned such an action, he could not stop it. Naked force continued on its hideous way and led to loss of life. For all the good intentions of churchmen and knights, life could be sacrificed as the result of grudges and enmities.

Bernard did not join the monastery in order to quell such disputes, but in the course of his life he dealt with many such confrontations. We will see, ironically, how a man who sought contemplative distance from the world rather quickly became absorbed in the affairs of the world. In Bernard I find an example of a classic dilemma in Western Christianity: the choice between seeking peace and quiet and making a loud impact on his surroundings. For this reason Bernard has remained controversial, from his own lifetime to the present. Indeed, many of my medievalist colleagues have no love for Bernard. In what follows I will not present Bernard as someone who is easy to understand. Long ago I called him "the difficult saint." He remains difficult to accept in all his pursuits, but this biography will attempt to show how his life developed and changed as he came to believe that he was called upon to influence and even shape his surroundings. [For more information about previous biographies of Bernard, see question 2 in the Fifteen Questions about Bernard: The Background for My Portrait section.]

🍏 CHAPTER 2

A Saint's Origins

Fontaines-lès-Dijon

The site of Bernard's birth is a hill on the outskirts of Dijon, the capital of Burgundy. In the twelfth century, Fontaines had a fortification that has long since disappeared, and today one finds a ninteenth-century chateau-like building there whose foundations may be much older. Nearby is a Gothic church. Bernard was the third of seven children born to Tescelin Sorus ("The Red") and Aleth of Montbard. He got his name from Aleth's father, Bernard of Montbard, a relation of the dukes of Burgundy. Aleth came from the high nobility, while her husband was of a humbler, though respectable, noble line. Tescelin's parents are not known, but he was related to Josbert de la Ferté, vicomte of Dijon and seneschal of Count Hugh of Champagne. Josbert would play a central role in the foundation of Clairvaux.

Apparently Aleth had originally intended (or been intended by her parents) to become a nun, but when she was fifteen years old Tescelin appeared and asked for her hand in marriage. We gain this information from the *Vita Quarta*, probably thanks to Bernard's cousin Robert. He is the very man who in youth created trouble for Bernard by abandoning Clairvaux for Cluny (as we shall see in looking at the first entry in Bernard's letter collection). But the *Vita Quarta* shows how he turned out to be a loyal relative who late in life provided details about Bernard's background that we otherwise would lack.

William of Saint-Thierry in the first book of the *Vita Prima* and the *Vita Quarta* are in agreement in describing Aleth's home life as that of a nun, and we might wonder how a woman could have brought seven children into the world and at the same time lived like a virgin. Our problem, however, is not that of the medieval biographers. For them marriage was a necessary condition for most women, but it was best to keep a distance to its sexual side. For the devout woman genuine piety in itself created an atmosphere of purity. Aleth as she was remembered by Bernard and by Robert was an ascetic and pious person.

On the basis of what the *Vita Prima* says about Bernard's brothers, his first years were spent in the company of youths who loved playing war. His brother Gerard, for example, is described as "a knight active in combat, prudent in counsel, and loved by all for his remarkable courtesy and kindness." There is no hesitation here about a knight's way of life. He loves to fight but can also show gentleness. The Latin term *benignitas* implies more than kindness. Gerard would have bent over backwards to help someone in need. His knightly virtues come close to the expression of Christian charity. We meet Gerard and his brothers only through the mirror of William of Saint-Thierry and Geoffrey of Auxerre, his first biographers, but for these monks, a knight's life could be commendable.

Bernard's father and brothers took their place in the world in order to serve secular lords, especially the Duke of Burgundy. Later in life Bernard seems to have shown no aversion to the military persuasion. As we shall see, he helped invent a way of life that combined monasticism and knighthood. Praying at night and fighting during the day became, thanks to Bernard, a commendable religious vocation. Bernard's attachment to knights, in the hope of their becoming monks, is also shown in a story about how some young knights found their way to Clairvaux. He made an exception to normal discipline and regaled them with ale. Bernard wanted them to cease from participating in tournaments, but did not otherwise criticize their lives. After they left the monastery, the knights "were converted from their normal ways and enlisted themselves in the spiritual struggle." This story was later altered and the guests were made into students, not knights, and they were given wine instead of beer. By the time this version appeared, Cistercians were more likely to be budding academics than future knights. Wine had replaced beer as the appropriate drink with which to entertain. Bernard and his biographers accepted fighting, the shedding of blood, and the sacrifice of life as necessary functions in a society where the best men were good fighters, whether for secular lords or for the good Lord. Or for both.

Bernard's arrival in the world is remembered as being something special, for his mother Aleth had a dream in which she saw a dog inside of her. It was white, except for red hair on its back, and it was barking. She was told that the dream predicted her child would be "the guardian of God's house," a guard dog and an outstanding preacher. Such dreams became almost fashionable in the annals of the saints. The best-known is that of Dominic and the Order he founded, playing with his name and making the Dominicans *Domini canes*, the Lord's dogs, barking away in their preaching. We can ask if the Dominicans stole from the Cistercians. Bernard's mother's dream announced that he would be different from his brothers in their military vocation.

William of Saint-Thierry has information about Aleth that is not found in Geoffrey of Auxerre's *Fragmenta*, normally his source for Bernard's origins. Aleth, he tells us, insisted on nursing her own children. An upper-class woman of the twelfth century would normally have found a wet nurse to take care of her children's needs, but instead "she gave them a mother's goodness in a natural way." On the one hand, she nourished them individually. On the other, however, she withheld from them "sweet delicate foods" and according to William taught them "the way of life of a hermit." Her homelife is described as "monastic . . . rather than that of the court." Clearly the composers of the *Vita Prima* sought to find monastic roots for Bernard and his brothers in their mother's way of life, while the father is hardly mentioned. To what extent the portrait of Aleth is accurate we cannot determine, but she emerges in these first chapters of the *Vita Prima* as a woman of strong opinions and regular habits.

The description of Aleth, however, is complicated by the fact that she must have allowed having a soothsayer woman come to Bernard when as a boy he was ill with a splitting headache. The woman was meant to play musical instruments and soothe him, but Bernard would have nothing to do with her and sent her away. Subsequently the pain disappeared.

The language used to describe the episode does not make it clear who exactly the woman was, but Bernard's rejection is clearly intended to show that he instinctively refused having anything to do with people who claimed forms of magic to provide cures. The story is meant to indicate that even at such a young age, Bernard had a sense of what was right and wrong, but it also indicates that Aleth, like most mothers, was willing to try almost anything for the sake of her sick child.

Châtillon-sur-Seine

When Bernard was about eight years old, he moved with his family to a property they owned in the town of Châtillon on the Seine River, near the boundary of the duchy of Burgundy. They occupied a house on the southern slope of the bluff above the town, the same promontory that was crowned by a church and a castle. The latter belonged to the dukes of Burgundy, the former to the secular canons of Saint Vorles. They were known as outstanding educators. Certainly in what has been written about Bernard, these canons are often described as such, but if we return to the *Vita Prima*, it is simply stated that Bernard "gave himself up to his studies" and made great progress in little time. Since we have no other information about this school, we can only conclude that Bernard's outstanding ability as a writer and theological thinker came from within and not necessarily from his teachers at Châtillon. But there could have been a memorable teacher or two who helped stimulate his talents.

In the segment of the *Fragmenta* we have from Raynald of Clairvaux, we are told of a vision that the boy Bernard had at Christmas and which took place at Châtillon. This vision is also mentioned in William of Saint-Thierry but without reference to Châtillon. Bernard was waiting for the night office and its first celebration of the Nativity of the Lord. He dropped off to sleep and saw the Christ child: "Bernard was taken out of himself so that his childlike love was transformed by the holy boy." He thought he was present at the moment of the Lord's birth. William comments that Bernard frequently spoke about this event, and then he mentions Bernard's *Homilies in Praise of the Blessed Virgin Mary* as further manifestations of this devotion.

Bernard's perception of Jesus as an infant anticipates by more than a century Francis of Assisi's crib scene at Greccio. For both Bernard and Francis, the mystery of the Incarnation invites us to understand the presence of Christ in the world. Their emphasis on the innocent, naked child and the meeting of humanity and divinity provides a point of departure for centuries of devotion to Jesus. Our sources provide no explanation for the source of Bernard's spiritual experience. Being there "at the very moment of the Lord's birth" means participating in the act, just as Saint Bridget of Sweden two hundred years later experienced being present. There is nothing in Bernard's background that would have encouraged him to see the Christ child in this manner, but with this vision begins a humanization of Christ in Western Christianity.

The story of Bernard's participation in the mystery of Christ's birth indicates that as a child he took part with great intensity in the liturgical year and made Christian symbols an integral part of his life. But for anyone who visits Châtillon today, it is remarkable that right beneath the hill on which the family lived is the Douix Spring, for centuries a site of Celtic ritual. I wonder if the woman whose magic powers were intended for Bernard in his headache could have been connected to this place. At least it must be remembered that Burgundy in the early twelfth century had been Christian for only a few hundred years. Just beneath the surface of Christian society were remains of pagan life. Bernard is shown as having rejected any resort to this culture, but it remained geographically close by. In the hagiographical literature there was no conflict for Bernard, for Christianity triumphed over paganism, but in his family and upbringing there could have been remnants of old layers of belief.

The key person in Bernard's life was his mother. According to Robert of Châtillon, who was her nephew and Bernard's cousin, Aleth on the feast of Saint Ambrose would gather all the clerics she could find and eat and drink with them. She realized that she would die on this day (7 December) and prepared herself and her family for the event. Even though she was dying, she still had clerics brought together for the usual meal. She sang with them until she died.

This whole story is not included in William of Saint-Thierry's description of Bernard's youth, but he does tell how Aleth in her last hours gathered the clergy around her to sing hymns. When she no longer could sing, she was seen to move her lips. She raised her hand for the sign of the cross but did not complete the action. Her hand remained elevated above her. Aleth is thus described as a saint, but one who for William had shared a good life with Tescelin: "For many years before her death, she brought up her children, insofar as a woman could who is obedient to her husband's authority and does not have rights over her own body." William thus combined for Aleth an ascetic life (fasting, vigils, and prayers) with family existence in obeying her husband and looking after her children. Aleth is seen as a kind of nun, but since she could not make monastic profession, she made up for a lack of vows, especially chastity, by "almsgiving and various works of mercy."

Thanks to the *Vita Quarta* it is possible to imagine Aleth enjoying herself with the clerics she would invite to her home. The *Vita Prima*'s account is much more ascetic, but both descriptions make it clear that Aleth was a strong personality. For Bernard the loss of his mother must have been traumatic. If her death took place in 1106 or 1107, as has been assumed by modern biographers such as Watkin Williams, the teenage Bernard must have keenly felt his mother's loss. There is no need to use Freudian language to explain a medieval person, but the disappearance of his mother must have been a terrible blow for a young man who later in life would characterize himself as being mother to his monks.

Bernard was not forgotten at Châtillon. Well after his death, the story arose that one day when he was praying before the statue of Mary in the church of Saint Vorles, she pressed one of her breasts and sent a flow of milk into his mouth. This was seen as a sign of the wisdom he partook from Mary, but for us it is perhaps more an indication of the fact that the child who once received his mother's milk later found a spiritual mother to make up for the one he had lost. Mary became his mother, and Bernard's writings certainly contributed to the special Cistercian devotion to Mary. There is no evidence that he composed the hymn "Salve Regina," which to this day is sung in every Cistercian house at the end of Compline. But certainly Bernard made a significant place in his own life and that of his Order for his devotion to Mary. One mother took the place of another.

Uncertain Years (1107–1111)

For William of Saint-Thierry the teenage Bernard was impressive in his surroundings: "Gracious and pleasing to look at, of charming manners, and a keen intellect and polished in speech." His friends would have tempted him into a way of life where sexual freedom apparently was considered the right of the young male from the knightly class. Here we are told of Bernard's temptations. There are three incidents making women out to be tempters. After looking at a woman, Bernard had to jump into a pool of freezing water. A naked girl came to his bed, and he three times cried "Thief," for she was trying to rob him of his chastity. A third temptress entered his bed naked and is said to have been "stroking and stimulating" Bernard, who rolled over on his side and went back to sleep. The woman is said to have been "filled with dismay and amazement at his persistence," and so left him.

Years ago the Australian Trappist-Cistercian monk and authority on Bernard, Michael Casey, surmised that these incidents may have taken place after Bernard's entrance to monastic life and not before. There is no way of establishing any precise chronology, and the historian might claim that such stories are the stuff of hagiography, the triumph of the future saint over the wiles of the flesh. But we do have other indications that Bernard, like his contemporaries, could have cultivated a sensual side. One of his enemies accused him of having written erotic poetry when he was a youth. Berengar of Poitiers began an attack on Bernard for his treatment of Berengar's master, Abelard, by asking rhetorically whether Bernard was not trying to outdo his brethren in his poetic competitions. He mentioned *cantiunculas mimicas* (poems of imitation) and indicates they were pornographic, for he claimed he could not write down any of them because "I fear to fill the page with the placement of filthy comment."

Berengar had every reason to blacken Bernard's reputation, but his accusation cannot be dismissed as pure polemic. The young Bernard, like his male clerical contemporaries, could have fantasized about women. Certainly the Goliard poetry of the period indicates an enjoyment of erotic imagery. It is hard to know whether the semiclerical culture in which Bernard was brought up emphasized male bonding alone or also relationships with women. For the historian John Boswell, "gay clerical culture" was rife in the first decades of the twelfth century. Our sources for Bernard, however, indicate an exclusive orientaton toward women. Yet he lived in what must be called a homoerotic world. With his mother gone and his father hardly visible, his friendships were all with other young men. Eventually he would bring the friends of his youth into his new monastic sphere and continue cultivating them as friends. Homoeroticism could manifest itself in purely spiritual terms.

Playing Monks (1111–1112)

Bernard's conversion away from the world and toward monasticism came when his brothers tried to send him away "to literary studies." According to William he could not escape the memory of his mother. He imagined her telling him that it was not for such "trifling . . . that she had educated him." The decisive moment arrived when Bernard's brothers were together with the Duke of Burgundy in besieging a castle. Bernard passed by a church, turned aside to enter, and then came a flood of tears: "That was the day that saw his purpose firmly fixed in his heart."

According to William, Bernard had decided to enter Cîteaux because it was so strict. But he did not intend to come by himself to the New Monastery, as he would have called it at the time. First he gathered together his brothers and friends and encouraged them to stick together in an experimental form of monastic life. William writes that "they had their own house in Châtillon" but does not specify if this was Bernard's family home. The group remained together for six months, without putting on monastic garb, and during this period its members were to have sufficient time to prepare themselves for monastic entrance. William describes the little community as living like the first Christians: "It became like the early church," where there was one heart and one soul (Acts 4:32).

Even today, potential recruits to a Cistercian house are encouraged to stay in the monastery only for some months and then go home and settle their affairs. Thus the arrangement made by Bernard is not surprising. He apparently wanted his confreres to have an opportunity to prepare themselves not only spiritually but also materially for making their commitment. This period has been seen by the great monastic scholar Jean Leclercq as an indication that Bernard already at this point functioned as abbot. This claim

exaggerates what took place during the Châtillon months. Bernard was trying to determine if it would work to bring together his family members and
his school friends into a monastic community. His goal was not to become
abbot but to join Cîteaux.

Apparently the first to choose the ad-hoc community of Châtillon was
Bernard's uncle, Gaudry, Aleth's brother. Maternal uncles were often central
figures in medieval church life, and Gaudry was important for Bernard. He
had a solid position in feudal society as castellan or keeper of the castle of
Touillon, a few miles from the future abbey of Fontenay. By accepting Bernard's invitation, Gaudry was confirming what he must have considered to
be his sister Aleth's desire. Her memory remained strong not only for Bernard but also for his brothers and for his uncle.

Next to join was the second-youngest brother, Bartholomew. He was not
yet a knight and so had no commitment to any secular lord. But his brother
Andrew had just become a knight and apparently found it hard to leave his
new profession. Suddenly he cried out, "I see my mother," and so "another
recruit left the ranks of the world for the army of Christ." William points
out that Andrew was not the only brother to see Aleth. Bernard too had such
a vision.

The eldest brother, Guy, was already married and had infant daughters.
His wife would have to give her consent for Guy to leave her, but Bernard
told Guy that she would either accept his departure or else soon die. Here
we find what only can be called ruthlessness in Bernard: nothing was to stop
his plans for the new way of life. It was not yet a question of formal monastic
entrance, only of imitating the monastic life. But as far as Bernard was concerned, all his male family members were to join him.

Guy ostensibly respected his wife's refusal but told her that he instead
would have to live the life of a peasant, cultivating the soil with his own hands
in order to keep her. The poor woman fell quite ill and came to accept
her husband's vocation, begging Bernard's forgiveness. She in turn asked
to become a nun. Such a story emphasizes the fact that for Bernard there
could be no compromise. Monastic life required total commitment from all
those whom he thought belonged in it. We are not told what happened to
the infant daughters, who were probably handed over to some other family
members (but not one of Bernard's brothers). In spite of the valiant efforts
of Jean Leclercq to demonstrate Bernard's attachments to women, I find
hardly any place in his world for women, unless they joined a nunnery. They
might find inspiration in the Cistercian way of life, but in Bernard's time
no women's house was formally accepted as part of the Cistercian Order.
Women had to give up their own desires and accept the necessity of mens'

monastic vocations. Besides Aleth and the Virgin Mary, the women in Bernard of Clairvaux's life remained peripheral.'

The most spectacular conversion story among those of Bernard's brothers concerns the next eldest, Gerard, who is described as a knight loved by all. At first he refused Bernard's counsel that he become a monk, but he was warned that he would be struck by a lance. Soon after, Gerard was taken prisoner and a lance cut his side, on the same spot where Bernard had pressed his finger. Gerard cried out, "I am a monk, a monk of Cîteaux," but his protests did no good. The rest of the story makes up the kind of monastic *exemplum* tale in which the Cistercians of Clairvaux came to excel. Gerard made a spectacular escape from his imprisonment, with the bolt to his cell door falling away. This story is like something out of Saint Paul (Acts 16:26), but there is also a touch of humor, with Gerard being told by one of his captors that he had better hurry lest he miss the whole of Mass. The man at first failed to recognize his prisoner.

Some readers might ask why I have repeated well-known stories that are better told in the original source than in my summaries. I want to emphasize how vivid these narratives are, not only the one about Gerard but also that concerning his married brother, Guy. These men come across as individuals who were happy with their vocations as knights and prior to Bernard's intervention had no intention of becoming monks. They must have told their stories to Geoffrey of Auxerre when he was collecting material for his *Fragmenta*, which in turn were converted into William of Saint-Thierry's smooth narrative. Such tales were meant to shed light on the strength of Bernard's person, and they also remind us that in the twelfth century marriage was very much a contractual obligation and not an alliance especially blessed by the Church. Bernard could in good conscience break up a marriage. We are reminded how Heloise once wrote Abelard about how marriage is a burden and for the intellectual a distraction.

A classic story of conversion to the monastic life is supplied by that of Hugh of Macon, a school companion who is said to have lamented the fact that Bernard had left him for the monastery. Bernard managed to persuade Hugh that he should join also, but then Hugh's companions convinced him to hold back. They physically surrounded him so that Bernard could not get close, but then there was a terrific downpour that made everyone run for cover. Except for Bernard and Hugh. Now they could converse in peace in the open, and without getting wet: "The pact they had made was renewed and their proposal confirmed." The language here is that of friendship, for Hugh is said to have looked upon Bernard as "dear friend and companion" (*socii et amici carissimi*). There is tenderness and affection here, but behind them is Bernard's iron determination to make sure that the men he loved followed him into the monastic calling. It is not by accident that Hugh's story is followed by a generalization that sums up Bernard's impact: whenever Bernard appeared "mothers hid their sons from him, wives kept their husbands away from him, and friends fended off their friends from him." Bernard's speech had such "power. . . . that hardly any other love could withstand its force."

The only other figure in the history of Cistercian monasticism who has had such an impact on his surroundings and attracted hundreds of men to the monastery is the monk of Gethsemani Thomas Merton (1915–68). But in his case it was not personal contact that brought so many converts to the monastery. It was his writings, especially his account of monastic conversion, *The Seven Storey Mountain* (1948). At the time of Bernard's own conversion to monastic life, he had apparently written nothing, but he had a reservoir of personal relationships on which he drew to make sure that his entrance involved not just himself but a whole crowd of the men who meant the most to him.

Not everyone who was called by Bernard came and stayed. William describes a sad case, "a miserable sight, down and out and, to look at, pathetic." This is William's own observation and not a story he took from Geoffrey of Auxerre. The fellow ended up returning to Clairvaux but was apparently just tolerated by the community, where he died not as a brother but more as a beggar. We find here a classic warning against abandoning the monastic life, a theme already found in the literature of the Desert Fathers in late antiquity and which will appear regularly in Cistercian accounts.

At this point Bernard is said to have been ready to leave Châtillon and to join what then was still called the New Monastery. William calls him "a father among his brothers," indicating not only the Rule of Saint Benedict's emphasis on the abbot's role as father but also the way Bernard appropriated to himself a paternal instead of a fraternal role with his own brothers. William adds an anecdote of how the youngest son, Nivard, was left behind at the family home as he was playing in the road with his friends. His brother Guy told him that the family inheritance was now his, and Nivard was to have answered that this was not fair, for his brothers had gained heaven while he only had been given earth. In the original version of this story in the *Fragmenta*, Nivard is supposed to have commented that he had been cursed with this division of inheritance.

William mentions the fact that Bernard's one sister, Humbeline, was also left behind with their father. Later, after she was married, she came to visit Bernard at Clairvaux, and we are given a not-too-edifying story of how the abbot refused even to consider seeing her. The other brothers from her family also would not go out to their sister, apparently because she was dressed to the teeth and scandalized them by her appearance. But Humbeline insisted that since she was a sinner, Christ had also died for her. She promised that she would carry out whatever Bernard ordered. He subsequently made an appearance and ordered his sister to dress and live more modestly. She returned home and for two years continued in her marriage, but in a more ascetic way of life. Eventually she convinced her husband to let her go and joined the monastery of Jully.

The story is one more tale of conversion to the monastic life, but Bernard's initial response to his sister is disturbing. He seems to have been repelled by her physical apearance, "calling her vile, like a snare of the devil trying to capture souls." Her brother Andrew was even more outspoken, calling her in Costello's translation "wrapped-up crap." This type of response to the presence of a woman indicates a revulsion in Bernard and his brothers toward the female sex. For them it was a question of keeping themselves from feminine attractions, and such stories indicate that the first generation of Cistercians did its best to keep women at a distance. Later in life Bernard could write with great affection to a few women, but he still preferred to remain in an almost all-male world. It is only decades after his death that the Cistercians began officially to welcome women into their Order.

These stories of conversion are intended to show that all the men who came into contact with Bernard ended up being persuaded that the monastery was the best way of life for them. At this time in the history of Western Christianity there was a general view that few people would attain salvation and most of these would be monks or nuns or those who made possible their way of life. Thus for Bernard it was imperative to get his friends and relatives to join the monastery. He could not stand living or dying without them. It is only later in the twelfth century and especially in the first decades of the thirteenth that the need for a pastoral Christianity to offer salvation to all the baptized became recognized. Bernard did not dismiss the rest of humanity as the devil's prey, but he concentrated on those near and dear to him. He desired fiercely that they share with him the life of the cloister.

Geoffrey of Auxerre remembered Bernard as being physically and spiritually irresistible, with "a certain grace that was more spiritual than fleshly and in his face there was a radiance that was bright not in an earthly but in a spiritual way." His eyes were those of an angel. Geoffrey added details about Bernard's stomach troubles, for he had great difficulty in digesting food. His description presents us with a medium-sized man with reddish hair like his father's and usually showing a warmth and charism that could win over many. This son of a knight and a nun-like mother wanted to convert to the monastic life all those he loved. The Bernard we find here had a great capacity for generating enthusiasm. What he considered to be good for himself had also to be good for others.

Entering Cîteaux (1113)

There were a number of what could be called monastic experiments in the first years of the twelfth century, made up of men who wanted to live more strictly according to the Rule of Saint Benedict. Among them were the brothers who in 1098 left their monastery at Molesme and established the New Monastery. The monks who remained behind felt cheated of their abbot, Robert, and they appealed to Rome that he be returned to them. At the time the pope hardly exercised universal power over the Western Church, but with the pope making himself available for such a complaint, Rome was on the way to the "fullness of power" (*plenitudo potestatis*) it would come to exercise in the Western Church in the course of the twelfth century.

It is important to be aware that Robert and his brethren did not intend to found a new monastic order. Their goal was to establish a monastery that was in harmony with the practices they felt Molesme had abandoned: distance from secular powers and an ascetic way of life. The pope's recall of Robert to Molesme could have ended the experiment, for Rome's decision included any monks who wanted to go with Robert. The remaining community at the New Monastery made the prior, Alberic, their abbot, and at his death in 1109 the prior Stephen became abbot.

It is this man who received Bernard and his companions one day in 1113. According to William of Saint-Thierry, the brothers of what would become Cîteaux were discouraged "because of the lack of vocations, and their hopes for future numbers were fading." This assertion is modified by the later summation of the beginnings of Cîteaux, the *Exordium Parvum*, which indicates that it was under Abbot Alberic that there was a lack of vocations, while numbers increased under his successor Stephen. The Dutch historian Adriaan Bredero has pointed out that Cîteaux already in 1113 sent out monks to establish the first daughter house, La Ferté, so Stephen Harding must have had a surplus of monks in order to be able to establish a new house. We can thus ask why William of Saint-Thierry, writing in the mid-1140s, would have remembered so differently how it all began. One answer might be what the Australian Trappist-Cistercian monk Michael Casey has called the "Cistercian propaganda machine." The people around Bernard remembered the past in the light of his outstanding achievements and could not imagine the Cistercian Order without him. Thus it may not have been deliberate manipulation of the historical record that made William "forget" about La Ferté. That monastery did not come to have the many daughter houses that Clairvaux created and could have been all but forgotten by the 1140s. So its foundation was not remembered as a turning point. This was the arrival of Bernard and his companions.

Bredero has accused the *Vita Prima* of providing a "biased account" of events, but any hagiographical text is biased, for its purpose is to show that the person described was an extraordinary human being with great virtue and an impact on his surroundings. The person of Bernard is meant to overwhelm the reader of the *Vita Prima*, so much so that we hardly hear about his first abbot, Stephen. Stephen deserves a place as the central founder of the Cistercian Order and thus was an essential figure in the monastic vocation of Bernard. But we can only give Stephen his due by going outside the sources we have for Bernard and turning to the foundation documents for the Order. Here we find Stephen's imprint.

Most of what William of Saint-Thierry wrote about Bernard's entrance at Cîteaux is his own composition and not taken from the *Fragmenta*. Cîteaux is described as "at that time still hidden away and of no importance," and Bernard is said to have wanted to disappear "from the hearts and memory of mankind." William makes a direct comparison between Bernard and Jesus himself. Both of them began to provide examples in order to teach others: "He himself began to do what he would later teach other people." Bernard's ascetic way of life is summarized by what he would tell his novices when he became abbot of Clairvaux: "Leave your bodies outside." Bernard's absorption in the spirit is expressed by the fact that he was unaware of his physical surroundings. He did not know, it is said, that the novitiate roof was vaulted, and he saw only one window at the east end of the church, not the three that were there.

These examples have been cited time and again in descriptions of Bernard, sometimes to show his saintliness, sometimes to indicate that he went too far in his asceticism. William was convinced that "his mind was totally occupied with God," and so he registered hardly anything with his bodily senses. Clearly William looked at his friend in terms of the ascetic practices of the Desert Fathers of late antiquity, as well as the Gospel narratives of Jesus's fasting in the desert and refusing to be tempted by the devil. But there are relatively unusual aspects to this asceticism, such as the attention given to Bernard's revulsion to sleeping: "He used to complain that he wasted no time more than when he was asleep." As abbot he would object to a brother's "sleeping in an unbecoming or worldly way," apparently from the position in which he lay or his snoring.

William reserves the greatest detail for his description of Bernard's eating habits. He would eat only because he had to do so, and eating was "agony for him." William describes how painful the passing of food was for Bernard, "and that part of his body was so obsessed with distressing sickness that it discharged only with great pain." Food for Bernard was not intended to give him life but to put off his death. Years ago the Oxford historian Beryl Smalley responded to one of Jean Leclercq's works about Bernard and pointed out that we are well informed not so much about Bernard's sexuality as we are about his consumption of food: "Rashly indeed, I suggest that the psycho-historians might switch their attention from sex and aggression to food." I think that Smalley, who herself in the last years of her life hardly consumed any food, detected an element of anorexia in Bernard's habits. William explained that even though Bernard at times would have liked to eat a little extra, "he finds he can hardly do so."

In the history of Christianity there have been many such men and women who have denied the impulses of their bodies in order to make room in themselves for seeking God's presence. For the historian with a natural skepticism, it is difficult to know when we are looking at the genuine article or an attempt to imitate it. In Bernard's case what speaks for the veracity of his commitment is William's assertion that Bernard assumed that the other brethren were "holy and perfect but himself to be still no more than a beginner." This lack of awareness of self in the context of a community ethos is certainly a sign that the novice Bernard was absorbed with his own world and not in touch with his surroundings. But William did not conceive of him as a dreamer. Bernard wanted to imitate the others by engaging in hard physical labor. He would pray and meditate inwardly while he used his body outwardly. Here we meet an assertion that became vintage Cistercian idealism: our best teachers are the trees and fields. Nature tells us what to do, as Bernard himself asserted in one of his letters: "Woods and stones will teach you what you can never hear from any master." The same sentiment appears in a letter to his pupil Aelred of Rievaulx: "You will have experienced sometimes under the shade of a tree during the heat of midday what you would never have learned in the schools."

In these lines I think we find the key to the success of the early Cistercians and especially of Bernard. They embraced manual labor as a means of reaching out for God. They saw nature as a place to encounter God, not in inspiring walks but in cutting down trees! Bernard apparently found a way of life at Cîteaux that suited his temperament and in which he believed that other brothers were far more advanced than he. William described him as being physically unsuited to perform the work of the other brothers: "He was so close to tears that he asked God to give him the grace for harvesting." But as soon as the work was done, he would pray or meditate, making "solitude of heart his own, and so he was everywhere alone with God."

This description of Bernard is William's own and not an expansion of a chapter from the *Fragmenta*. William could have based it on his conversations with Bernard, or on the words of Bernard's family members. These passages are vivid in conveying to us how the young Bernard lived at Cîteaux, but we also notice that there is virtually nothing about how he fitted into the monastery's shared life. In William's view, Bernard lived like a hermit in community, seeking to order his own spiritual life, contributing to the physical needs of the monastery, but keeping to himself. We hear nothing about his relationship to Abbot Stephen Harding, and on this matter we have to move to the witness of the *Liber Miraculorum* by Herbert of Clairvaux and the later *Exordium Magnum*, both compiled well after Bernard's death. They tell how the young Bernard at Cîteaux had vowed to say daily prayers for his deceased mother but one day forgot to do so and had to be reminded by his abbot. Stephen apparently kept tabs on Bernard, and the story indicates that Bernard was not always the perfect monk. This is the only such story we have, however, and otherwise we have no indication of how Stephen and Bernard related to each other.

Stephen was a brilliant administrative innovator who developed the structure of the first monastic order in Europe, as can be seen from the text of the *Carta Caritatis* drawn up in 1119 at one of the first General Chapters. What did he think in 1113 of this remarkable youth who had managed to convince so many other young men to come with him to the New Monastery? We do not know, but he must have noticed how Bernard spent his time reading and imbibing Scripture. Later in the *Vita Prima* Geoffrey of Auxerre describes how Bernard absorbed the whole of the Bible and made it, as it were, a part of the very fabric of his being: "When he was meditating and praying, the whole of the Sacred Scripture appeared to him as if it were placed open before him." Certainly the writings of Bernard bear witness to this ability, for they resonate with scriptural language, which became his mode of communication. Anyone who reads him today can only marvel at Bernard's attention to Scripture, especially because he makes it seem almost natural and easy to function in this manner. The language of the Bible in Jerome's Vulgate Latin translation became the very ground of Bernard's thought and being.

In manual labor, meditative reading (*lectio*), and participation in choir, Bernard was alone, off by himself, even in the midst of the Cîteaux community. We know his school friends and brothers were nearby, but we hear virtually nothing about his interaction with them. Later in life, in one of his Sermons on the Song of Songs, Bernard recalled the beginnings of his monastic vocation and indicated that he could suffer from an inability to involve himself and even had to deal with what in monastic parlance is *acedia*, something that today might be called depression:

> I am not ashamed to admit that very often I myself especially in the early days of my conversion, experienced coldness and hardness of heart, while deep in my being I sought for him whom I longed to love.

The phrase Bernard used is *corde durus et frigidus*, and here he was not quoting or paraphrasing a biblical passage. He was consoling his brothers by using his own life as an example for them: what they might experience in terms of a sense of alienation from God he too had felt. He added that he in his discouragement could gain help from the sight of a good or holy man, or else in remembering a dead or absent friend. What Bernard did not add here is that he could gain a sense of comfort in being part of a community. We get the impression that the young Bernard—at least as the older man remembered him—separated himself from the other monks. Other men could be important for him, but only when they were dead or absent. It is not at all clear what an impression those present in choir or manual labor made on the young Bernard at Cîteaux.

In another Sermon on the Song of Songs, Bernard did speak of community, but not necessarily of how he had experienced it in his youth. He told the brothers to maintain peace and not to offend each other. He warned that a brother who gives himself over to anger and spite can become obsessed with his injury: "He cannot pray, he cannot read, nor meditate on anything holy or spiritual." Bernard may have been remembering the past, but he may as well have been describing what he found at Clairvaux when he was abbot. The question remains how Bernard functioned as a member of Cîteaux before he became abbot, and the answer is that we do not know.

These seminal three years of his life are almost completely hidden, for William, who knew Bernard so well, had little to tell his readers. The chapter about Bernard at Cîteaux ends with a paean to his ability as a preacher, how all who listened to him "are struck with astonishment at his teaching." William apparently filled in the gaps from Bernard's early years by telling his readers how his absorption in the Scriptures from that time later paid off when he began to preach. This conclusion is understandable but does not shed light on how Bernard fitted into his first monastic community. What we can say is that Bernard was privileged to experience one of the most brilliant abbots of the twelfth century. Stephen Harding created the Cistercian Order by giving it the Charter of Charity, inventing the General Chapter and the visitation of daughter houses by father abbots. This structure was just beginning while Bernard was a monk at Cîteaux, but the sources for his life say nothing about his participation in these innovations. Bernard and Stephen seem to have existed in different spheres.

🍂 CHAPTER 3

From the New Monastery to the Valley of Light, 1115–1124

Founding Clairvaux

When Stephen sent out a group of monks to found the second daughter house of the New Monastery, he chose Bernard as their abbot. Apparently this decision was made at the last minute: "As they were going, Stephen appointed Bernard." The reaction among the older and more experienced monks was one of surprise and even skepticism: "They feared for Bernard because he was a youth of tender age and subject to sickness." Also he was not suited for hard physical labor.

William of Saint-Thierry dismissed the matter with these remarks, but we can ask why the abbot of Cîteaux chose a twenty-five-year-old sickly fellow to take on the difficult task of establishing a new monastic community. One possible explanation is that Stephen felt crowded by Bernard, who even at this relatively early age could have been difficult to live with. Here I am only guessing, for there are no extant sources, but on the basis of how Bernard later in life manifested such self-assuredness, Stephen might have felt that the best thing he could do with such a dynamic youth was to give him the overwhelming task of fathering a new monastery.

In the original deed of gift for Clairvaux, Bernard's relative Josbert de la Ferté is mentioned. He came from the village of Ville-sous-Ferté, four miles from the site of Clairvaux. Thus we might have a reason why Bernard was chosen as abbot: he was being sent to a place that had belonged to a member of his biological family. But Bernard's elder brothers or his uncle might seem to have been just as qualified for the position of abbot. Did family members already at this point consider Bernard to be their spiritual and moral leader?

According to William of Saint-Thierry, Clairvaux was called the Valley of Wormwood and was a den of robbers. In the Cistercian literature about new foundations, it is often asserted that the monks came to "a place of horror and vast solitude," as described in the Old Testament book of Deuteronomy (32:10). This phrase was used both by William and in other early Cistercian literature. In recent years historians have pointed out that the sites of new abbeys were seldom deserted. There were often peasant communities on site that had to be removed in one way or another. Thus William's description of Clairvaux may have been purely literary. Nevertheless, the monks who came from Cîteaux faced a great challenge in erecting temporary buildings and beginning to cultivate the land.

William claims that Bernard was not particularly concerned with the physical challenges of the new environment. His desire was to save souls by bringing them to the monastery and keeping them there. Bernard confided in William that his only concern was "to have a mother's love for every soul." The theme of motherhood returns time and again in Bernard's writings and shows his attention to his brothers, something recognized in the early work of the historian of religion Caroline Walker Bynum. Twelfth-century spiritual writers captured the image of Jesus as mother but also saw the abbot as mother to his monks, thus expanding the traditional view of the abbot as father figure from the Rule of Saint Benedict.

This description of early Clairvaux provided William with a platform for making a statement about Bernard, an observation that has not gotten the attention it deserves. William described how Bernard could be discouraged "that his efforts cannot show any results" but then he would "forget himself" and find comfort in the souls he was helping to save. Bernard's "charity gives birth to confidence, yet humility keeps it in place." Behind this commendation there may be an indication of what we now call bipolar behavior: the abbot could be discouraged but then went to the other extreme of joy. He was clearly afraid that his monastic life was not succeeding, for in the next anecdote William describes how Bernard in the middle of the night went outside the monastery and saw a great number of men coming down from the hills. The valley could hardly hold them all. Bernard found comfort in this vision, but it also shows how he had feared as a young abbot that his monastery would not survive.

In these anecdotes about the beginnings of Clairvaux it is possible to see who Bernard was becoming. The isolated figure of the New Monastery was now father abbot and mother caregiver of a community of men. He expected his foundation to grow and prosper. But he was also afraid of failure. Like every monastic founder from the Desert Fathers onwards, Bernard faced the possibility that his way of life would come to nothing. But Bernard was attached to a movement where the individual monastery gained sustenance from a network. Bernard takes his place here as part of a monastic institution, even though William says little about the support that Cîteaux must have given early Clairvaux.

Early Days

According to the Cistercian *instituta* or statutes, a new foundation was supposed to be based on twelve monks and an abbot, as with the apostles and Jesus, and to bring with it whatever was needed for the liturgy and everyday life. No new foundation, however, could have enough resources to get through the first year before a harvest provided necessary food supplies. Every monastery had a cellarer, in charge of supplies, especially food, and this office was given immediately to Bernard's brother Gerard, who kept it until his death in 1138. Bernard in his lament at the time on Gerard's death made it clear that his brother was superb in his job and made it possible for Bernard as abbot to concentrate on spiritual matters while Gerard took care of the material requirements of the house.

In the autumn of 1115 Gerard told Bernard that they were in trouble: "Their needs were so pressing that he could not accept mere verbal encouragement." It is then that a woman from Châtillon appeared and asked for prayers for her sick husband. The material help she in turn provided for Clairvaux enabled the monastery to get through the winter. The husband was healed, and we have here the beginning of a string of miraculous events associated with Bernard. William adds, however, that thoughtful men were careful about going to Bernard with "unimportant matters because they knew his mind was tender and still fresh from the delights of heavenly secrets." They sought out Bernard for spiritual concerns and those of conscience.

What in a traditional work of hagiography would be a straighforward miracle story here becomes a point of departure for an attempt to capture the meaning of Bernard's life. Bernard lived his Cisterican life in "solitude" and "the sublime height of contemplation." The result was that the brethren of Clairvaux "were almost all estranged from him." The Latin verb here is *absterruit*, "to drive away by terrifying," and so the meaning is even more powerful than in Hilary Costello's otherwise superb translation. Bernard spooked the brothers! When he spoke to his monks they could hardly understand what he was saying. He treated them as if they were angels, but when they went to him to confess their sins, he came to realize that they were ordinary human beings. He wrongly believed that his monks were safe from temptation and that if they succumbed, then they were not true monks.

I look carefully at these passages about Bernard's first period as abbot of Clairvaux because their content may reveal a great deal about how he perceived his functions and responsibilities. Most of what is written here comes from William and is not found in Geoffrey's *Fragmenta*, and what we find probably reflects what Bernard had told William. Bernard was apparently in a quandary about how to deal with his monks, and he got to the point where he "regretted having to speak at all since he did not know what to say." His concern was that he might "harm the conscience of his hearers" because he would overwhelm them with what he said. What he preached might hinder them in advancing in their own spiritual lives. At this point Bernard had a vision of a boy bathed in a great light, telling him that he should just go ahead and utter whatever words came to him. This vision is included in the *Fragmenta*, but not in the description of Bernard's quandary I have given from the *Vita Prima*. But the result was that Bernard now could take part "in ordinary conversation and act in a more humane fashion."

The person described in hagiographical literature is often made out to have been more or less born a saint. In this genre there is rarely any attempt to show development of the person. Thus William's portrait of Bernard is unusual in showing how he had to learn how to live with other people, to be aware of their abilities and limitations, and to treat them with kindness, insight, and tolerance. There is an implicit criticism here of the young Bernard, and perhaps an explanation of why we hear virtually nothing about Bernard as monk at Cîteaux. He could have been insufferable, lost in his own meditations, refusing to accept the limitations of his body, and believing that others were far more pious than he. When this difficult young man became abbot, he had to learn how to listen to others and tolerate their limits. He had to extend to his brothers the paternal and maternal affection necessary in any viable human community, especially one based on the Gospels.

Here William says that Bernard's father, Tescelin, now came "to live with his sons and become one of them." The language implies that Tescelin took the monastic habit. Why is Tescelin's choice mentioned at this point in the *Vita Prima*? For William, Tescelin's arrival may have been part of Bernard's humanization project. He felt a responsibility for his father and wanted him to take part in the Clairvaux community. He could not leave him behind.

Here, as in so much else, Bernard departed from the Desert Fathers' insistence on leaving behind everything and everyone who had taken part in their lives, especially close relatives. Bernard took it for granted that he needed his family members with him in his new way of life, and this inclusion also covered his father. In the Gospels we hear Christ saying that in order to follow him, one must leave "brothers or sisters or father or mother" (Mt 19:29), but here we have a monk, later an abbot, who brought his brothers and eventually his father with him to the monastery.

At about this time (1118) Clairvaux founded its first daughter house, Trois Fontaines, but this fact is not mentioned here but only much later in the *Vita Prima*. William's purpose was not to provide a history of Clairvaux but to trace Bernard's life, and Trois Fontaines eventually got attention because it provided the setting for a story about Bernard's concern and affection for the monks he sent there. But already in the first years of Clairvaux there are letters from Bernard that give us an idea of his concerns. He wrote to Prior Guy and the monks of the Grande Chartreuse—a letter that until recently was dated to the mid-1120s but is now thought to have been as early as 1116. Thus the very year after Clairvaux was founded Bernard found the time and energy to reply to a letter from Guy, for his "warm and kind greeting." He rejoiced in what was taking place at his monastery, showed affection for the fledgling community, and mentioned the law of charity. Bernard wrote how he had come to realize that since we are flesh and blood, "our desire or affection must take its point of departure in the flesh." This is an amazing concession from a young man who already had done much to kill the instincts of his body. [For Bernard and the body, see question 4 in the Fifteen Questions about Bernard: The Background for My Portrait section.] Now he wanted to admit its needs in accepting what "belongs to earth and afterwards that which is heavenly." In this life we move from the physical to the spiritual. For a young man of twenty-six, this is a remarkable statement and the first indication of how Bernard was to address the monastic world.

In completing this rather long letter Bernard stated that he had three reasons compelling him to finish. One of them was that he was busy with his duties. He did not specify which specific tasks were pressing him, only "the cares of my monastery." In his Sermons on the Song of Songs Bernard at times referred to his obligation as abbot to guests who had arrived. One could easily dismiss such a reference as literary window dressing, but perhaps Bernard really meant what he wrote.

Is the text of this and other letters what Bernard originally wrote? Certainly the letters included in his collection were revised and edited at a later point. But this letter, which turns into a mini-treatise on love, anticipates what Bernard would write in his *On Loving God*, where he described in great detail the stages of love.

Illness and Treatment (1119–1120)

The young abbot was sent to Clairvaux without having been ordained to the priesthood. The bishop of Châlons-sur-Marne, William of Champeaux, was contacted and agreed to take care of the matter. Bernard was accompanied by an older monk, Elbodo from Cîteaux, who is said to have been tall and strong, while Bernard was in a bad physical state. There was a discussion at the bishop's court concerning which of the monks was the abbot, and most of the retainers were in favor of Elbodo. William, however, knew his man. His insight reminds one of the situation much later when Joan of Arc was able to pick out the true dauphin and reject the false one. In such a moment of revelation, God's will is made manifest and human judgment put aside.

William of Saint-Thierry provides a detailed description of the friendship that grew up between William of Champeaux and Bernard. It was not long before the bishop took charge of his affairs. He realized how ill Bernard was, and insisted that the abbot change his ways and take better care of his body. Bernard apparently refused to listen, and so William of Champeaux went to the fledgling Cistercian General Chapter. If this was the Chapter of 1119, it was the decisive one when the Charter of Charity was adopted and the new Order was given a constitution. Bernard as abbot of Clairvaux apparently did not attend because of his illness and thus missed the actual founding of the Cistercian Order. For William of Saint-Thierry, however, the development of the Order was not a concern. It was Bernard's physical health.

William of Champeaux got what he wanted at Cîteaux. Bernard was to leave the monastery compound and live for the time being in a hut on the outskirts of the property. He was not to follow the usual regime for food and drink, nor was he to be burdened by the monastery's business. A few chapters later, William of Saint-Thierry provides an almost graphic description of Bernard's physical state after he returned from his yearlong exile outside the monastery. He refused to allow himself to be exempted from the workload of the monastery and his office. His stomach rejected food, which he vomited undigested, something that made it impossible for the brothers in choir to concentrate. So a container was dug into the spot next to where he stood, presumably so that he could retch into it. Eventually, Bernard had to give up on community life and remained by himself, unless he came to meetings or was to provide spiritual guidance or take care of monastic discipline.

William does not make Bernard's situation attractive, and he even indicates that the brothers could not handle his vomiting in choir. It is not clear from this narrative whether Bernard's condition was the result of his youthful excessive asceticism or if it was a congenital weakness. In describing his eating habits (or lack of them), William mentions "bread dipped in milk or water, cooked vegetables, or the soft mash made for babies." He could not handle anything more solid, but then William adds that he "refused other things for the sake of frugality." In spite of his situation Bernard apparently still tried to maintain the ascetic practices of the cloister.

William's description precludes any modern medical conclusions, but it is worth considering the possibility of gastroparesis, which is the inability to digest food, possibly as a result of diabetes. So far as I know, diabetes was unknown to twelfth-century Europeans. The ancient Egyptians and the Greeks had described the disease, but much medical knowledge was lost in the first centuries of our era. Bernard could have inadvertently dealt with his illness by living on such a sober diet. His asceticism may have prolonged his life. Sixty-four years is actually quite impressive in view of the illnesses that William describes. But what matttered for William was the fact that in spite of pain and nausea, Bernard succeeded so well in bringing many men into the monastery. William mentions the number of monasteries that Bernard founded: "Just think of the many houses he has set up throughout the whole of Christendom." These were just one of his many accomplishments, which included ending schisms, opposing heresies, and bringing peace "to discordant churches and people."

William of Saint-Thierry's Attachments

William's paean to Bernard ends by pointing out what he had done for individuals in terms of their own needs. Clearly William was to some extent speaking about himself. As abbot of the Benedictine house of Saint-Thierry, William enjoyed a certain amount of freedom to travel. In 1119 or 1120, he came to Clairvaux together with another abbot and met Bernard in his little hut. William uses the sensual language of the Song of Songs to describe what he found: "I was admitted into that royal bedchamber" (Sg 1:3–4). He claimed that he had such a powerful desire to spend time with Bernard that if he had been given the opportunity he would have dropped everything and stayed with him forever.

The Bernard whom William found, however, was not content with his situation and complained that he had to obey the primitive person who was supposed to be taking care of him. This man had been entrusted to Bernard

by William of Champeaux, other Cistercian abbots, and the Clairvaux brothers themselves. But William of Saint-Thierry noticed that the food given
to Bernard was inedible. He could only enjoy the taste of water because it
soothed him. William contrasts Bernard's sorry physical state with his awareness of the glory that was to come at Clairvaux. One night Bernard was
praying and heard voices as if from a great number of people passing. He
followed them to a spot that was overgrown with bushes. Here there were
choirs of men singing, and it was on this same spot that the church of Clairvaux was later built.

Bernard anticipated what Clairvaux was to become after it was moved
to a more suitable location. As in the earlier vision, Bernard seems to have
needed reassurance that his monastic way of life would receive God's blessing in terms of numbers. But when his brothers later argued for the expansion of the monastery in moving it to a more spacious site, he objected and
was worried what people would say if the project failed or ran out of money.
Bernard, who in history books is the great monastic success of the twelfth
century, was in doubt and needed to be encouraged, sometimes even from
above.

William's description of Bernard's vision of the future church building
at Clairvaux is followed by what is perhaps the most frequently quoted passage in the *Vita Prima*, his characterization of the monastery in its "golden
age" (*aurea secula*). He tells of the silence the visitor would find at Clairvaux,
whether at midday tasks or midnight rest, "save for the brothers occupied in
the praise of God." When the brothers did speak, it was to describe whatever
was befitting for their vocations. The picture is so ideal that the historian
almost itches to expose it as an exaggeration, and recently one eminent Cistercian scholar, E. Rozanne Elder, has pointed out that William was praising
the Clairvaux that he remembered from his first visit. William was comparing this vision of monastic joy and sobriety with a later Clairvaux, which had
become almost too big and unwieldy for his taste.

Golden ages are seldom what they are made out to be. William did his
best to pay tribute to the men "who made Clairvaux ready to be the place of
plenty and peace that it is today." But by praising so highly the monastery of
1119, he was implicitly passing judgment on the community of 1145, when
William wrote. He drew on the Life of Saint Benedict found in the *Dialogues*
of Gregory the Great, making early Clairvaux like the cave at Subiaco where
Benedict first lived. William lamented Bernard's double standard, for he
showed understanding for the weaknesses and limitations of his own monks
but made endless demands on himself: "If only he had shown these same
qualities toward himself." But Clairvaux under Bernard was remembered

as "a school of contemplation and spirituality" (*spiritualium scola studiorum*). William wrote these lines while Bernard was still alive, and I wonder how the abbot of Clairvaux may have reacted to such praise. Certainly William was not the only churchman to elevate Bernard to the skies, but here we find a close friend who knew him well.

First Literary Productions

Bernard's period of illness and forced isolation from the community in 1119–20 enabled him to write his *Homilies in Praise of the Blessed Virgin Mary*. He claimed in his Preface that there was no need for him to write such sermons for the sake of the brothers. They could apparently do without them, but Bernard wanted to write in order to "satisfy my own devotion." We could almost speak of a work of "private spirituality," except for the fact that Bernard's work was copied and distributed—the beginning of his literary reputation. His intended audience was not only monks, for he ended the first Homily with an appeal to the married to "reverence the integrity of [Mary's] flesh amid frail flesh." Bernard addressed also women who were consecrated to a life of virginity. They should "admire the Virgin's fruitfulness." At the same time he considered the role of Joseph, to whom it was given, with the Christ child, "to carry him, to take him by the hand, to hug and kiss him, to feed him and to keep him safe." Joseph was for Bernard neither husband nor father, and yet he assumed these roles because he was called upon to do so. In so doing he gained the privilege of intimacy with Jesus.

Bernard here renewed traditional language and the imagery of the Nativity, and he was applying the vision he had apparently experienced as a child. The tenderness of God as revealed in his Son is manifested in these sermons, but it is Mary who is the center, with Bernard addressing her: "My lady, say this word which earth and hell and heaven are waiting for." Bernard was not formulating a new theology of the Incarnation, but he was making Christ more accessible through his mother and foster father.

Perhaps just prior to this period of illness, Bernard succeeded in converting homilies that he had used for his monks into what we call *The Steps of Humility and Pride*. He dedicated the work to his relative Geoffrey, who in 1119 became abbot of Clairvaux's second daughter house, Fontenay. Geoffrey later returned to Clairvaux as prior and finally became bishop of Langres. Bernard's relatively brief treatment of the topic takes its point of departure from Saint Benedict's description in the Rule of the steps of humility in monastic life, but Bernard provided a matching description of the steps of pride. Here Bernard could draw on his own experience of monastic life and provide warnings against a descent into sin, as in warning against the fifth step, singularity. The monk who manifests this trait is "more complacent about fasting for one day when the others are feasting than about fasting seven days with all the rest." Such a monk prefers his own personal devotions to sharing the night office with his brethren: "After sleeping through the night office while the others were singing psalms, he stays to pray alone in the oratory." *Singularitas* means singling oneself out and neglecting the practices of the community as a whole. Bernard's examples show that he knew what he was talking about. The final step toward self-destruction is revolt: "He has already shown his contempt for his brethren by insolence, and now his contempt for superiors flashes out in open revolt."

Certainly there were open revolts by monks or lay brothers against abbots in the twelfth century, and Bernard knew what every abbot risked with undisciplined monks. He apologized to the monk Geoffrey in concluding his work, for he had concentrated on the steps of pride rather than those of humility. Bernard said he knew the way down into pride better than the one up into humility, but it was necessary to look to Benedict to find the ascent. The work became one of Bernard's most popular and appeared in English already in 1940 and was among the first to be translated into English by Cistercian Publications when it was established in the 1970s. One generation of monks and nuns after another has been able to see itself in Bernard's descriptions of how monastic life can turn into a nightmare. At the same time, however, Bernard provided a pattern for genuine monastic humility.

A Distant Daughter: Foigny (1121)

In 1121 the bishop of Laon offered Clairvaux a site for a daughter house in his diocese. Bishop Bartholomew, however, was offering the same site he had promised to Norbert and the first Premonstratensian canons, and so another location had to be found. Twelve monks arrived with their abbot Rainald on 11 July 1121. We are not told of this event in the *Vita Prima*, which generally mentions new foundations exclusively in terms of miracles associated with them. But Bernard's decision to found a monastery 175 miles to the north of Clairvaux indicates a changed sense of what he imagined monastic life could embrace. Until now the fledgling Cistercian Order had largely limited itself to the the duchy of Burgundy and the county of Champagne, but by adding distant Picardy Bernard took a step that was to anticipate the Order's expansion into a European network, the first international organization in Europe, after the Western Church itself.

We have three, possibly four, letters addressed to Rainald by Bernard, and the first indicates that the new abbot was homesick for Clairvaux. The salutation of the letter says everything in terms of what Bernard wanted to be for Rainald: "All that a devout brother and a trustworthy servant could desire to give another, is given by Bernard, his brother and fellow-servant, and not his father or lord." Rainald could not have been in doubt that Bernard was his father abbot, but Bernard insisted on another role, that of brother. He asked him not to look up to him: "When you lift me up, cast me down; by overdoing who I am, you lessen me." Rainald had apparently written a very adulatory letter to Bernard, who now insisted that "we are all brothers, for we share one heavenly father." Bernard accepted the role as Rainald's father in terms of a father's affection, "but I will not accept a father's authority."

Here as elsewhere in his writings Bernard juggled roles and their obligations, in asking for equality instead of hierarchy. It is only in the final section of the letter that he addressed what probably was Rainald's main concern: he was homesick for Clairvaux. Bernard's answer was quite clear. The will of God "gains priority to what we feel and need." He praised Rainald as "my dearest companion, whom I greatly need," but Rainald was to remain at Foigny "and show obedience in whatever you do." In spite of Bernard's generous concern for his friend, he made no concessions concerning Rainald's duties.

The second letter continues in the same vein. Bernard shared in Rainald's sorrow. It was hard for him not to have Rainald nearby. But he found that the abbot of Foigny had become almost a burden in telling him of his troubles: "Why do you allow yourself to let me become even more concerned, when I am already sufficiently concerned about you?"

The next section of the letter gives an idea of what had been going on. There were brothers at Foigny who were complaining about their conditions, perhaps because of the rigors of a new foundation. For Bernard it was Rainald's responsibility as abbot to do his duty: "You must comfort, encourage and provide admonishment in carrying out your duty and bearing your burden. . . . I have no doubt that whoever shares in your work will also be able to share the reward you gain." Bernard promised that when Rainald had an opportunity to see Clairvaux's prior, who was being sent to Foigny, then the prior's words would provide encouragement, and so a letter's consolation was superfluous. This "living voice" would be far better than to "pour forth words onto dry pages." Bernard is more direct in this letter than in the first one. His tone is still affectionate, but firmer, and in the dispatch of Clairvaux's prior to deal with the problems of Foigny, we see the beginnings of the Cistercian administrative network. But Bernard was not immediately involved: he left the task to his second-in-command.

The third letter is much briefer. Bernard indicated that he formerly had grieved about what Rainald had told him. Now he was worried about what he had not been not told: "I am unclear about what is happening and so am worried about it all." Rainald had apparently stopped informing Bernard about his situation: "I beg you to cease concealing from me everything happening to you." The letter ends, however, with a practical request: Rainald was to return the books that he had borrowed from Bernard. In the midst of what look like great problems at Foigny, Bernard remembered his books.

A fourth letter is usually interpreted also as a missive to the abbot of Foigny but can only be dated sometime between 1121 and 1131. The letter concerns Rainald's treatment of a monk who in some way had injured him. He had been sent to Clairvaux, and now Bernard returned him. Also involved in the matter was a novice. The letter is too brief to allow us to determine the exact situation, but it shows that Bernard continued to involve himself in the affairs of this daughter house.

Bernard's letters to Rainald demonstrate his concern for his monks, also after he sent them off to found daughter houses. Rainald clearly expected comfort and encouragement, so much so that he apparently became a burden to Bernard. But Bernard maintained contact and used the epistolary genre to provide consolation. He also at one point found the situation so complex that he chose to send his prior to deal with it.

Letters to Errant Relatives (Early 1120s)

Bernard's letter to his cousin Robert of Châtillon occupies first place in traditional collections of Bernard's letters. Chronologically it may not be the first letter he wrote, for datings vary from 1121 to 1125. But the letter fully deserves pride of place, for it sums up many of Bernard's concerns: monastic vocation, loyalty to one's promises, duty to one's abbot, and bonds of friendship. In this letter we find almost every aspect of Bernard's personality: how he could be gentle, kind, forgiving, and then turn angry, vindictive, threatening. I am of course aware that the letter is a rhetorical tour de force: Bernard must have written it in the expectation that its content would be read and admired or reviled by a European audience, and so he invested time and energy in creating its language. This letter needs to be seen together with the others placed at the head of the collection; they deal with commitment to the monastic life: what it meant to become part of a monastery and what was involved in leaving it behind.

Robert's exact relationship to Bernard is a matter of dispute, but there is no doubt that he was a cousin, though because he was considerably younger than Bernard he is often called a nephew. As a child he was promised by his parents to Cluny. The practice of oblation (giving away a child to a monastic institution) had then existed for centuries, and powerful abbeys like Cluny regularly took on sons of the nobility. The Cistercians would refuse to take on children in this manner and required in their statutes that their recruits come of their own free will, as adults, and not as offerings (oblates) of their parents. The Cistercians thus represent a watershed in monastic history, and their emphasis on free will and individual choice marks a point of departure in Western culture as a whole, away from a society based on obligation and toward one emphasizing individual choice.

Robert did not follow the decision of his parents but joined the Cistercians. We do not know if he first was at Cîteaux or if he came directly to Clairvaux after its foundation, but he decided at one point that his true vocation was at Cluny. After all, his parents had promised him there. Bernard wrote to Robert with every possible argument to bring him back to Clairvaux, and we find here the fullest expression of Bernard's arguments for a monk's stability of life. Thus began a debate that would continue for the rest of Bernard's life. Time and again Bernard felt called upon to pass judgment on a monk who had left one monastery for another.

With Robert, however, there seems to have been no doubt in Bernard's mind. He had made a commitment to Cîteaux and could not renege on it. Instead of describing this promise in legal terms, however, Bernard began by emphasizing how he personally had been hurt by Robert's departure to Cluny: "I can conceal my grief no longer. I cannot hold back my anxiousness nor check my grief." Bernard constructed an imaginary dialogue with Robert: "But you state that you have not harmed anyone nor rejected anyone." Bernard claimed he was not concerned with the reason why Robert left, but only grieved that he had not returned. He even considered the possibility that it may have been his own fault that Robert did not return. He assured Robert that he had nothing to fear from him, "for although you are not here with me, I have thrown myself with all my heart at your feet. I have done so because all my affection has brought me there. I prostrate myself before you, declaring my love to you. Are you still afraid now?"

Bernard comes across here as a loving father—or mother—who would do everything possible to get back the prodigal son. He pointed out other examples of how a youth betrayed a trust and then blamed Robert's decision on the grand prior of Cluny, who came to Clairvaux "clothed as a sheep but inside was a hungry wolf." This man had told Robert that what he endured at Clairvaux was not necessary for a genuine monastic vocation: "He recommended feasting and forbade fasting." Thus the fault lay with this untrustworthy figure who seduced Robert to Cluny, where he was divested of his crude Cistercian habit and instead "dressed with a fine and new one." Everyone congratulated him on his choice, but Bernard lamented to Christ himself because of what had taken place: "O dear Jesus, how much trouble was made in order to destroy a single poor soul!"

The Cluniacs contacted Rome and made the case that Robert was given as an oblate by his parents. Bernard turned aside from this judgment and appealed to an eternal one: "The day of judgment will come and then a clean heart will prevail, more than sly talk, and a good conscience more than a purse full of money." He implied here that the papal chancery could be bought for money and appealed from Rome to the judgment seat of Christ. The tone of the letter has changed from a tender appeal to Robert and excuses for him because of Cluniac manipulation to excoriation for what he had done. Robert himself well knew that he entered the Cistercian Order from the world and not from Cluny. He had spent his year in novitiate and had taken his vows. He now deserved to be called a "foolish boy." Bernard asked who had "bewitched" Robert "to violate the vows which your lips had given?" He would be called to "render account" a term taken from the Rule of Saint Benedict. Bernard left open the possibility that if Robert left Clairvaux in order to embrace a harsher and more perfect way of life, then it could have been acceptable. But this was not the case.

The tone changes again with Bernard's description of his bond to Robert as that of father to son: "I grieve in sadness not because of the effort I have wasted, but for my lost son's hapless state of being." Robert must get up, cast aside the luxuries that surround him at Cluny, and act as a true soldier of Christ: "Shake off the dust and go back to your battle." A military image has made its entrance in the last sections of the letter.

It is remarkable how Bernard combined almost every emotional and intellectual argument: Robert made a free choice, he was seduced by the Cluniacs, his parents' oblation of him does not count, Roman church officials were bribed, Robert was in danger of going to hell if he did not live up to his obligations, he must fight like a true soldier. Behind all these rational arguments is the emotional appeal of father to son, expressing a bond that cannot be broken: "I conceived you in the monastic vocation by word and by example." The lost child must return: "My heart refuses to forget you, for half of it has gone with you." This language borders on romantic love, the kind of attachments Chrétien de Troyes would memorialize in his verse. Clairvaux and Troyes are only about forty miles apart. As Jean Leclercq pointed out in the memorable chapter "Champagne as a Garden of Love," in his book *Monks and Love in Twelfth-Century France*, Bernard was appealing to a love that was close to the loves of the troubadours. At the same time he claimed that his monk was a knight, a fighter in God's cause. As *miles Christi* he could not desert the army he had joined. Years ago the great medieval scholar Etienne Gilson in his seminal book on the theology of Bernard denied that there could be any connection between the romantic love ethos of the troubadours and the spiritual love sought by the Cistercians. But Leclercq later made it clear that the two loves are quite close, even if different.

The second letter in the collection was probably written before the one to Robert. It is dated to about 1120 and was intended for Fulk, who was also a cousin of Bernard's. He had been professed as a canon regular of Saint Augustine but had been convinced by his uncle to return to the world. He does not get the gentle treatment that characterizes the opening of Bernard's letter to Robert. Fulk is said to have violated charity, to which he had been committed. His uncle had taken his nephews away from Christ's army so that he could drag them down to hell! Fulk could not undo his profession. What a cruel uncle! He would die soon, but first he had to kill the soul of his nephew. "What do you have to do in towns when you have chosen the cloister? What are you doing in the world when you have given up the world?" The last section of the letter uses military language: "I beg you to make yourself known and engage first in the battle."

Bernard did not here imply the kind of closeness he had with Robert, who after all had been his monk at Clairvaux. His involvement in Fulk's vocation must have been a result of family bond, but apparently his appeal did not have the desired effect. Fulk became archdeacon of Langres, a fine position, but he remained in the secular clergy. Robert apparently did return to Clairvaux and late in life provided invaluable information about Bernard in what became the *Vita Quarta*. These two letters with their spectacular language reveal something of the passion and commitment Bernard already as a young abbot could express toward the monastic life. Clairvaux was just getting started as a monastery and must have required all of Bernard's attention, except for 1118–19, when his health restrained him. Somehow he found the time and energy to write these letters.

A third letter, quite brief, to otherwise unknown canons, is included in the collection, and it is apparent that the three letters belong together. Bernard made the point that it was acceptable to transfer from the Rule of Augustine to that of Benedict because the canons in question would be adopting a stricter way of life. In the years to come there would be multiple cases in which the Cistercians would claim that they could accept men from other monasteries if it was a question of their taking up a vocation that was more demanding. We can see how the letter collection was shaped so that it begins with Bernard's conception of the obligations of monastic life. A commitment to Clairvaux/Cîteaux was absolute (Letter 1), regardless of the outmoded practice of oblation. A canon who had obligated himself under the Rule of Saint Augustine could not put this vow aside in order to enjoy a less demanding position as a member of the secular clergy (Letter 2). Finally Bernard responded (Letter 3) to the request of William of Champeaux, bishop of Châlons-sur-Marne, to accept that canons living under the Rule of Augustine join Clairvaux. By following the Rule of Saint Benedict, they would observe a stricter way of life and require more of themselves.

The letters brought together at the head of this collection demonstrate Bernard's view of monastic life. Later letters fulfill other purposes, such as showing Bernard's involvement in the affairs of the Church in general or in individual churches. Historians are notorious for complaining about lack of sources, but when it comes to materials that cast light on Bernard's activities, we have a wealth of material, so much so that a history of his inner life is hard-pressed to account for all the ways in which he expressed himself and became involved in the world of his day.

An Apology Attacking Cluny (1122)

An indication of Bernard's growing involvement in monastic affairs outside of Clairvaux is found in his work known as the *Apology*, probably completed in 1122. Apparently he and William of Saint-Thierry had discussed Cluny when they had been together during William's visit to Clairvaux. Now Bernard claimed that these conversations did not include anything "that I am afraid to lay before the eyes of all." Thus even though the little treatise is dedicated to William, it was clearly Bernard's initiative to compose it. At the same time he insisted he was a great friend of Cluny: "I am always delighted to see any of its members." He pointed out that he had attended community meetings there and had never tried to encourage someone to leave the Order. He conceded that "no one order is suitable for everybody," and he appealed against division in the Church. Different gifts are given to different people. There follows a long paean to unity, followed by a warning against those who speak unfavorably of other Orders. Cistercians are not to point their fingers at other monks because they are not as strict: "We fill our stomachs with beans and our minds with pride."

Finally after all his cautions Bernard launched into a harsh attack against Cluniac practices. This section of the *Apology* is the one usually quoted, and it certainly is quotable, with his description of how a "little wine" had become a great amount, and how monks were allowed to enjoy the comfort of staying in the infirmary without being ill. Here Bernard the polemicist came to the fore: "Did the Fathers in Egypt adopt such a manner of life?" He spoke of the early abbots of Cluny, known for their asceticism, and compared their regime with what he now heard took place at the monastery.

Art historians and most medieval historians are aware of Bernard's caricature of the grotesque images to be found in monastic cloisters: "Filthy monkeys and fierce lions, fearful centaurs, harpies, and striped tigers." Here Bernard has moved from a reasonable and thoughtful reflection on the various types of monastic life to a polemic against Cluniac practices. At the same time he may have implicitly been attacking the love of manuscript decoration that manifested itself at Cîteaux under Abbot Stephen. In the words of art historian Conrad Rudolph, it may have been "public knowledge that Bernard and Harding did not see eye to eye on the subject of art within the monastery." Cluny may have been a foil for Cîteaux, though it is clear that Bernard's main object of criticism was Cluny. Already at this time he may have been smarting from the departure of his cousin Robert to that monastery. In any case he was using his friend Abbot William in order to express his concern that Cluny had lost its monastic vocation: "The walls of the church are aglow, but the poor of the Church go hungry."

The Boundaries of Friendship: Abbot William

Why did Bernard address his polemic against Cluny to a Benedictine abbot of a relatively distant monastery? He reveals something of his motivation in a letter to William that must have been composed at about the same time as the *Apology*. Bernard complained that he had not known how to fulfill William's request. But he did not see how he could criticize the Cluniacs without creating scandal. So he asked William whether he wanted Bernard to present the case differently: "And so that I can do what you want, in the manner you want, ask me directly." Bernard ended this brief letter by telling William how the composition of the work was distracting him from his devotions and prayers. But he nevertheless spent a great deal of time on the project. One can only imagine the reaction in monastic houses when the polemic reached them.

At about this same time William wrote Bernard a letter that has disappeared, but Bernard's response gives us an idea of its content. William had apparently accused Bernard of not loving him as much as he, William, loved Bernard. Bernard's response was more or less an admission of William's complaint, but Bernard insisted that we cannot know what is going on inside each other. Only God knows our hearts. So he asked William how he could imagine that he knew what was within Bernard's heart. But the matter is much more complex: "Perhaps you are correct in saying my affection for you is less than what you have for me, but I am surely certain that you cannot be sure." Bernard challenged William to explain how he could be certain. He asked his friend what proof he expected to be given of his love: "Woe is me if . . . this man loves me more than I should be loved or if my love for him is less than what he deserves." William would have to be satisfied with the fact that Bernard loved him "as much as I can do so in accord with the ability I have been given."

This is a remarkable letter that cannot be dismissed as a display of rhetoric. Clearly William wanted to get closer to Bernard. He even offered to give up his abbacy so he could come and join the Clairvaux community, but Bernard refused to let him do so. William's reproach inspired Bernard to write about the limits of love. He insisted that we are ignorant of the inner lives of those we love, but we still are obliged to love as much as we can.

Bernard and William were not alone in seeking to plumb the depths of their interior lives. Time and again in the twelfth century monks and churchmen found ways of expressing their affective bonds. Bernard was willing to describe the depths and limitations of his love. He did not give William what he wanted, but the two of them remained friends for life.

The theme of friendship introduces the next letter in the collection, with Bernard recalling to William how the latter had given him the salutation "To his friend everything a friend could wish." Bernard assured William that in making use of the same expression, he felt closeness to William. His letter had come on the solemnity of Mary's Nativity (8 September), and so Bernard with his liturgical duties did not have leisure to provide a full answer. William's messenger, however, was in a hurry and could not wait until the next day, so now Bernard had to drop everything else and compose a brief letter. There was also the matter of a runaway monk, whom Bernard was sending back to his own abbot. Apparently the fugitive wanted to stay at Clairvaux, but Bernard insisted on following normal procedure, but in a humane way. As he instructed William, "You also should correct him harshly . . ., then comfort him with a letter to his abbot on his behalf." In other words, the poor fellow should be given some support and understanding.

Another letter, probably composed at an earlier point, begins with news of Bernard's health, about which William apparently had inquired: "I have been sick and remain so, but not much more than I usually am nor much less." Finally Bernard replied to what must have been William's main concern.

William wanted to come and be a monk at Clairvaux. He had asked Bernard what he thought of his proposal. Bernard advised him not to carry it out: "Keep to what you have got, remain where you are, and try to do good for those over whom you have charge." William should not try to extricate himself from the responsibility of his office.

This is a real letter that deals with a genuine exchange between two abbots. Bernard made a conventional statement that William as abbot was obliged to those under him. Years later William would disobey Bernard's advice and in 1135 leave his position at Saint-Thierry and join a newly founded Cistercian monastery, not Clairvaux but Signy in the Ardennes. We can ask why Bernard did not want his friend to come to Clairvaux on a permanent basis. It may have been a question of the scandal that would have arisen if an abbot of a prominent Benedictine house gave up his position in order to become a humble monk under Bernard. But the abbot of Clairvaux may have had more personal reasons to want William to keep a distance. After all, William had challenged Bernard's sense of self by telling him outright that his love for William was not what it should be. Bernard met his match in William, and some experts in medieval theology would today assert that William was a more profound thinker than Bernard. But I think the main reason for Bernard's insistence on physical distance was his conviction that he and William could not coexist in the same monastery. He could visit Clairvaux when Bernard was ready for him and in need of him, but otherwise he was to remain at his post as abbot of Saint-Thierry.

A final letter to a certain W, who could be William, sums up the entire ethos of friendship. Bernard was unable to tell his friend on paper what he perceived in his heart (*ut affectus est animus*). He expressed confidence that he had never lost his friend: "I cling to him, and no one can take him from me." Bernard made use of Church Father Jerome's adage that a friendship that ends was never a friendship. But in Bernard's case, "true friendships do not grow old, or they were not true." Bernard claimed that he lacked the holy leisure of his friend, but because the friend considered Bernard to be worthy, then "I am yours and shall remain as yours so long as I live." The letter does not end here: Bernard mentioned the sermons for which the friend had asked. They were not finished, but Bernard promised to send them when they were completed.

Thus a practical matter was meant to seal the friendship between the two men. William of Saint-Thierry would have been an apt recipient for such a letter, but it could as well have been meant for another W. There were certainly other friendships in Bernard's life. The language he used borders on that of romantic love as it developed in the Western tradition, and it is apparent, as Leclercq so well pointed out, that the court at Troyes and the monastery at Clairvaux shared a similar ethos: "I am yours and will be yours as long as I live" meant lasting friendship and eternal love. What more could two who love each other say or write? We thus have a paradox of love, if the letter was intended for William of Saint-Thierry, that Bernard both loved him and desired to keep him at a distance. Surely many human love relationships are of this type, where two people seek each other out and yet keep a distance from each other.

Disciplining a Wayward Abbot (1124)

In the spring or early summer of 1124, Arnold, abbot of Morimond, one of the four daughters of Cîteaux, left his monastery with a group of monks. Arnold came from a distinguished family. His brother Frederik was archbishop of Cologne. He had founded Morimond in 1115 as its first abbot but now nine years later had decided to take some of his monks to Palestine, perhaps to reinvigorate their enthusiasm for the monastic life. Whatever the reason, Bernard strongly disagreed with the decision and composed a number of letters warning against what was happening. In the first of them, he admitted that as abbot of a daughter house to Cîteaux, he had no right to involve himself in the affairs of another daughter foundation. His excuse was that the abbot of Cîteaux, under whose jurisdiction Morimond belonged, was traveling in Flanders, "so he has not gotten the letters you asked he be given and remains ignorant of this new adventure in which you are engaged."

In criticizing Abbot Arnold for his scheme, Bernard used the same language of affectivity that we find in his letters to William of Saint-Thierry, but here he was perhaps even more expressive in what he formulated: "I would cast myself at your feet, take your knees in my embrace, put my arms around your neck and kiss your beloved head." Bernard pointed out that he and Arnold had shared "during many years Christ's sweet yoke." They must have once been together as monks at Cîteaux. But once he made this emotional plea, Bernard allowed himself to lecture his fellow abbot: "Great support of our Order, are you not the least afraid that when you fall, then the entire structure will collapse?"

For anyone who claims that the Cistercian Order as such did not exist in the 1120s, surely Bernard's language indicates an awareness of a well-organized entity, but one that he feared would collapse if an abbot from one of Cîteaux's first four daughters could pull out of the construction. Bernard warned of the scandal that would arise, but he also questioned what might happen to the monks who remained at Morimond: "Who will be with them in order to keep at bay prowling wolves?" Also what about the houses that Morimond had already founded? "Unhappy and wretched are they, especially because they will lose their father while he is still alive." Near the end of the letter, Bernard pointed out that Arnold had acted "without your brethren's and brother abbots' advice and without the permission of your father and master." The Rule of Benedict requires that all important decisions be discussed by the entire community. The Cistercian statutes, adopted just a few years before, in 1119, referred such matters to the General Chapter, and the very core of Cistercian life was the presence and consent of the father abbot, the abbot of Cîteaux, who according to Bernard, had no idea of what was happening.

Bernard thus took it upon himself to carry out the function of Cîteaux's absent abbot, and we can rightly ask if it was correct for him to do so. In terms of the Cistercian constitutions, he was out of line, but Bernard's sense of righteousness usually did not limit itself to purely legal considerations. He continued to pursue the matter and subsequently wrote to the pope to tell him how "a brother abbot of ours, called of Morimond, has made the bad decision to leave the monastery . . ., and driven by a lack of seriousness, has chosen to set out for Jerusalem." So far as Bernard was concerned, what was needed in the Holy Land was "soldiers as fighters, not monks to sing and pray." The passage is remarkable in view of the fact that a few years later Bernard was to help invent a new monastic order, the Knights Templar, which both fought and prayed. But at this point he could not conceive of such a symbiosis. His tone to the pope is harsher and more legalistic than in the original letter to Abbot Arnold.

There are several more letters from Bernard on this matter. He addressed a monk Adam after the death of Arnold, who apparently could not handle the pressures on him in his attempt to leave Morimond. Adam had taken over the project, and Bernard sent him a long letter that is a small treatise on obedience in the monastic life. It is not enough, Bernard wrote, for Adam to claim that he was merely following the command of his abbot: "It is quite wrong to profess obedience by disobeying what is higher for the sake of what is lower." In other words, God's law is elevated above "a man's commands." Bernard proceeded into what can only be called a scholastic division among what is "wholly good," what is "wholly evil," and that which is in between. The question is where the boundary lies for these different types of actions. More concretely, the abbot of Cîteaux must complain "that you have ignored him in order to favor your own abbot." Bernard imagined that Adam might reply that he had gotten papal permission for his action. But the pope could not allow what is wrong. He must have been deceived about the truth of the matter so that he could be tricked into giving his permission.

Bernard was on dangerous ground, for papal authority by the eleventh century had become a foundation of the reformed Western Church. In order to avoid questioning a papal decision, Bernard assumed that the pope had been misled. At the same time he challenged a fundamental principle of the Rule of Saint Benedict: the abbot's decision is always to be accepted. If Adam claimed he could not go against his abbot, then he must remember that he was obligated by prudence and had freedom to ignore orders that were wrong. The vow of obedience had its limitations. When a monk made his profession in the abbot's presence, it was done "only in his presence, but not in accord with his whim."

In this mini-treatise on obedience, its requirements and limitations, Bernard reveals how far he had advanced. He was in his midthirties and had been abbot at Clairvaux for less than ten years. Yet he was taking on disciplinary and ethical matters that involved not only the fledgling Cistercian Order but also the Church as a whole. The result was the kind of breathtaking and rather disturbing certitude that he would manifest the rest of his life. Bernard was questioning the authority of the pope when it was based on misinformation. He was himself taking on an authority that belonged exclusively to the abbot of Cîteaux, his father abbot. He was addressing a European audience in hanging out the dirty linen of the Cistercian Order for all to see, so that it could be laundered in what Bernard considered to be the purity of his own intentions. Bernard was taking a great risk in challenging his surroundings and insisting on his own sense of what was right.

How Could He?

By the year 1125 we find Bernard on the verge of European fame or notoriety. His early sermons were being copied and admired for their beauty of style and spiritual depth. His treatises may have caused consternation not only at Cluny but also at Cîteaux. His letters defined statements of his understanding of the Rule of Saint Benedict and the Cistercian constitutions. At the same time, his missives expressed friendship, affectivity, and love. Centuries earlier, Carolingian authors such as Alcuin had tried to capture the same humanity in expressing mutual bonds, but no one since Cicero and Seneca had managed to capture so intensely the importance of friendship as lived experience. Bernard had by his midthirties become a master of prose and a champion of the affective life.

At the same time, Bernard revealed himself as a practitioner of invective. Writing to Bruno, Count of Berg and Altena, who in 1131 would become archbishop of Cologne, Bernard warned him about Abbot Arnold, who "has illegally left his monastery and caused great scandal for our Order." Bernard accused Arnold of gathering a "great crowd of monks" "not for the sake of Christ but for his own." Bernard's purpose in writing Bruno becomes clear here: some of the monks who had gone astray with Arnold were from Cologne. Now Bernard had heard that these men were in the vicinity of Cologne, and so he considered it to be Bruno's duty to get hold of them "so that they may grasp the fact that they do not owe obedience to someone who himself is disobedient." Bernard's language is direct and uncompromising. There is not the slightest grain of sympathy for what Arnold had done. He had taken the best and strongest monks of Morimond and left behind "the more simple and least devout."

In the opening of the letter Bernard explained how he recently had met Bruno at Reims, and because of this encounter he could now contact him as "an old friend." Bernard's method is apparent here. He made the acquaintance of fellow churchmen, as at Reims, a center for theological studies, and later turned to them for assistance. Bernard was a consummate networker and did not hold back in asking his correspondents to listen to his case and act as he thought best.

How could the abbot of a monastery that prided itself on being hidden away from the world already at this time of life involve himself so eagerly in matters that in point of fact were none of his business? It would be interesting to know how Abbot Stephen of Cîteaux reacted when he returned from his travels and was told that Bernard had begun a campaign against the abbot of Morimond. [For Bernard, Stephen, and the Cistercian Order, see question 9.] Stephen reveals nothing in the sources, except for his contributions to the constititutions of Cîteaux and a very few letters. In one he wrote to the monks of the Benedictine house of Sherborne in England, where he once had been a monk before he had gone to the Continent and his new life. He told the brothers there that he valued them and what they had been to him. Here is the antithesis of Bernard's combativeness, for we meet a gentle, loving man.

Bernard could also be gentle and loving, but his affection came at a price. His self-assurance can be misunderstood and interpreted as arrogance, but much of the time he was trying to live in accord with the principles found in the Gospels, the Rule of Saint Benedict, and the Cistercian constitutions. It would be wonderful if we had a firsthand account by a monk of Clairvaux of how he experienced Bernard as abbot, especially during these years, when he for the most part remained in his monastery. But William of Saint-Thierry's loving portrait will have to suffice, and we will have to remember that William was not allowed to stay at Clairvaux as a monk.

William does not explain how Bernard could have dared to challenge so many authorities and assert his own. Only Bernard can tell us, and his certitudes belong to the twelfth century and not to our own time. He became a figure of immense authority and spread his knowledge and insights far and wide.

The monk of Cîteaux who became abbot of Clairvaux and arbiter of monastic and church life in a European context could tell his own monks that he could experience moments of discouragement. In one of his Sermons on the Song of Songs, Bernard described how he was plagued by "languor of soul" and "dullness of mind." He specified that he found in himself "barrenness of my spirit and the resourcelessness of devotion." He used the language of the book of Job (6:2) to describe how his heart had withered. The result was that his prayers got nowhere: "The psalms are stale, reading is disagreeable, prayer is devoid of joy, the accustomed meditations irretrievable." Consequently he had difficulty working, fell asleep at vigils, had trouble curbing his temper, let go of his tongue and his appetite, and felt "indifference and dullness in preaching."

Such a list of aberrations must clearly have been meant for the brothers, who would have heard the oral version of this sermon. Bernard knew that some of them were thinking that other brothers received God's grace and help, while they were left behind. In the typically Cistercian manner of using one's own experience as an example to others in order to provide encouragement, Bernard took his point of departure from his own limitations. Such a passage can be seen as more than a moralizing example. Bernard indicated here that he knew what it was like to lose courage and find the ascetic life unbearable. He shared with his brothers a sense of limitation and mutual need: "I have applied these things to myself, for your sake, that you may do likewise." The lesson was to stand before God "in awe rather than yield to pride." Fear of the Lord is the beginning of wisdom (Prov 9:10). In fear and trembling Bernard struggled to reach out for the presence of God.

 CHAPTER 4

Monastic Commitment and Church Politics, 1124–1129

Looking outside Clairvaux

Until he left for Italy in the early 1130s and became involved in resolving the papal schism, Bernard spent most of his time at his monastery of Clairvaux. These years before he dedicated himself to defending the papacy might at first seem rather tame by comparison with what came afterwards. But a closer look especially at the letters composed at this time shows that Bernard was already committing himself to causes that had nothing to do with Clairvaux or even with Cistercian monasticism. We have to remind ourselves that Bernard got up before dawn together with his brothers and stumbled down the night stairs to a darkened church in order to intone vigils. The words of the Psalms tell all: waiting for the dawn, keeping watch, reciting the Psalms that tell of pain, hope, anger, and praise of the Lord. I assume Bernard already at this early (or late) hour began to consider the texts of the letters that he intended to send off the same day. He would have tried to concentrate on the meaning of the words, but they became his own, his way of expressing to the world who he was and what he believed in. In such a way his inner life took on integrity. In the messages he sent, Bernard sought to express what he thought was God's will. Here he reached out to influence the troubled world around him. In this way we can imagine how Bernard at home in Clairvaux shared his mind and heart with those who would listen to him. And to some who would not.

Probably in the autumn of 1124 Bernard wrote to Jorannus, abbot of the Benedictine house Saint Nicaise at Reims. He comforted the abbot for the loss of his monk Drogo, who had left the monastery to become a Cistercian. Bernard insisted that he would never have advised Drogo to leave his monastery. He admonished the abbot to control his anger and referred to his own experience with his cousin Robert: "I regretted [his departure for Cluny] but kept quiet and asked God that those who had taken him away from me might bring him back, and also that he might return of his own free will."

The same autumn Bernard wrote to Hugh, abbot of Pontigny. Hugh and Bernard had been friends in their youth. They had studied together, and Hugh's noble parents and well-connected friends had done what they could to keep him from becoming a monk. Now he was abbot of a successful monastery with ten daughter houses. The letter is seemingly Bernard's attempt to show that he did not try to encourage Hugh to accept Drogo at his monastery: "I did my best to remove any suspicion that I had been involved in the matter." But Bernard's declaration of innocence in arranging for Drogo to come to Pontigny ends with a statement that reveals his involvement: "If you [Hugh] want to put up with all this trouble rather than losing him, then it is up to your devotion and you must see the matter through."

The Latin text reveals Bernard's duplicity, and so I translate quite literally: "This devotion will teach you best." Bernard was bending over backwards to show that he was not manipulating the question. He insisted that he had not told Drogo that he would gain permission from Rome so that he could leave his monastery at Reims.

We are fortunate in having a third letter in this case, and it was directed to Drogo himself. Bernard praised him for having left his monastery "as a layperson would leave behind the world." Drogo had embraced "a new discipline's observances." Thus Bernard approved of his choice, and here we find in embryo what became Bernard's teaching: it was permissible for a monk to leave one monastery for another if by so doing he was embracing a stricter way of life. By considering the Benedictine house at Reims as equivalent to the life a layperson led, Bernard was guaranteeing the virtue of choosing the Cistercian discipline. His only advice was that Drogo stand firm in the face of the devil's temptations, presumably the inclination to return to Reims and a less demanding way of life. Apparently Drogo did not persevere and returned to Reims, so Bernard's efforts were in vain. He cannot be accused of trying to attract Drogo to the Cistercian Order, but he did speak with two tongues in these letters: the one praising Drogo for leaving his monastery, the other insisting he was not trying to convince him to do so.

Perhaps the most important aspect of these three letters is what they indicate about Bernard's continuing relations with a friend of youth whom he had convinced to become a monk together with him. His letter to Hugh, abbot of Pontigny, is as intimate as one can be with a close friend. Of course such a missive was not a private affair: hardly any letter was such in the twelfth century. But Bernard wrote in expectation that Hugh would understand him. In spite of Bernard's insistence on not luring Drogo to Pontigny, he left the matter in Hugh's hands. He trusted his old friend.

As a parallel to Bernard's relations with other monastic figures, we can consider his letters to a central layperson, Count Theobald of Blois, later of Champagne. During the autumn of 1124 Bernard wrote to the count and thanked him for his concern for his health. This attention Bernard interpreted as an indication of Theobald's love of God: "For why else does a man of your greatness have concern for an unimportant person like me?" After this introduction comes the body and purpose of the letter: for a second time Bernard asked Theobald to take pity on a certain Humbert. He assumed the man's plight was known to the count, so he did not go into detail. But in another letter, dated to the spring of 1125, Bernard reminded the count of promises made first to Dom Norbert of Xanten and then to Bernard himself, to restore to Humbert and his wife and children their possessions.

It is significant that Bernard would have taken time out from monastic obligations to compose letters on a purely secular matter. His argument is formulated in such a way that the count had to listen to him: "I am afraid my many letters will offend you, but I am more afraid of offending God . . . if I do not pay attention to the situation of an unhappy man such as Humbert." Bernard felt a moral obligation to intervene, and at the same time he made it imperative that the count show mercy.

Probably a few years later, in 1127 or 1128, Bernard again turned to the count and asked him to be receptive to a number of people: "I cannot remember a single time when you have rejected me." First he appealed on behalf of some canons, that they be granted an audience with the count. This favor would mean that their neighbors would then show respect for these churchmen. If the count's ministers or soldiers tried to grab the canons' property, then they would have to face the count's reaction.

The same letter describes how Bernard had recently met a woman at Bar-sur-Aube, a town about ten miles from Clairvaux. She was married to a man who had displeased the count, but now Bernard asked that the count show mercy. Also at Bar, the defeated party in a duel had his eyes put out. This was done at the count's orders, and his servants also confiscated the man's possessions. Bernard insisted that they be returned to him. Finally

Bernard asked that the bishops who were meeting in Troyes, the count's capital, be well received. Good treatment should especially be extended to the bishop of Langres: "my bishop, as he is yours."

The letter can look like a grab bag of special requests, and its concerns were probably not unusual for an influential abbot in the face of a powerful count. But we only have to remember the portrait of Bernard in the first book of the *Vita Prima* as a solitary man seeking the isolation of a monastery far from the madding crowd. Here we find Bernard coming to a town and meeting men and women who believed that he could help them with the count. He did not turn them down but risked his own position with the count by speaking on their behalf. There is a political dimension in Bernard. Here is a man who used his contacts in order to improve the lot of unfortunate people who apparently had nothing to do with the Cistercians.

Two final letters in this series to Theobald indicate that Bernard felt he had access to the count. In one letter he recommended a person to the count because of the man's poverty and holy way of life. If Theobald did not have pity on his poverty, then at least he should show respect for his holiness. Perhaps Theobald could do without the man's poverty, but he could not be without his holiness. By the logic of language Bernard succeeded in turning a request into a demand. The next letter apologizes for Bernard's ceaseless letter writing, "But the love of Christ presses me and the need of friends also." The man in question was aged, came from a religious house of good reputation, and now needed a letter to Theobald's uncle, who was Henry, king of England. We know nothing more than what is found in these letters, but they both show that Bernard did not hesitate when it was a question of helping his friends. Theobald's response is unknown, but these letters point to the creation of a network of power and influence reaching outside the monastery of Clairvaux.

The Duties of Bishops—and Abbots

In 1127 or 1128 Bernard drew up a statement about how bishops should behave. The work is constructed as a letter sent to Henry, the archbishop of Sens, but because of its length (about thirty pages in the Latin edition of Bernard's works), it is usually considered to be a treatise, *On the Conduct and Office of Bishops*. Bernard chose Henry as the recipient of his work probably because the archbishop of Sens was known for having had a change of heart after his election in 1122. Prior to this time he had lived at the court of Louis VI of France and had gained a reputation for self-indulgence.

Bernard was certainly aware that the First Lateran Council, held in 1123, had emphasized the powers and functions of bishops. What can rightly be called the first medieval reformation of the Church had set forth a program according to which bishops would serve primarily ecclesiastical interests and not secular ones. Canons in cathedral chapters were expected to organize into communities living according to a rule, and bishops were expected to encourage them.

This was the final letter included in the first version of Bernard's letter collection, made in the late 1130s. A longer recension was made in a later collection from 1145, and then the final collection, known as *perfectior*, was made at about the time of his death. Despite the later changes, the first version of what we might call a letter treatise has two central themes: first, a distinction between the lives of bishops and monks, and, second, the importance of contemplation and its virtues, such as humility, in a prelate's active life. The second theme will appear again in Bernard's late treatise *On Consideration*.

Humility is a major concern of this work, which ends with Bernard's rejection of the need for exemptions of monasteries from episcopal power: "Abbots who desire papal exemptions from episcopal control and who claim the right to wear episcopal regalia have abandoned the twelve steps of humility." Bernard was referring to the Rule of Saint Benedict and warning abbots against taking on the privileges of bishops without showing the humility that the Rule required. Bernard criticized abbots of his own Order who "make a vexatious point of infringing this rule of humility, showing themselves so proud that they . . . disdain to obey their own bishop." Monks are to work, to live in seclusion, and to practice poverty. They are not to seek privileges or exemptions from episcopal authority.

It may seem surprising that Bernard at such a relatively early point in his monastic career chose to write to the most important ecclesiastical figure in France in order to criticize developments in his own fledgling Order. By doing so he was once again usurping the authority of his father abbot, Stephen of Cîteaux. He was using a public platform to reshape Cistercian discourse about the Order's charism and practices. At the same time he was also directing larger criticism at ecclesiastical abuse, as in pointing to the way "schoolboys and beardless youth" were being given high positions in the Church because of their noble backgrounds. Such people "chase after ecclesiastical charges" whose attainment released them from all responsibilities.

Once again it is possible to see the beginning of the polemic against abuse of office in the Church, which will return in the 1140s with the much better-known *On Consideration*. What is remarkable here is not Bernard's concern with the state of the Church. It is his public statement about what was happening in his own Cistercian Order. Instead of addressing the General Chapter concerning his opposition to exemption for Cistercian monasteries from episcopal authority, Bernard made a declaration that clearly was intended to reach not only abbots but also bishops: "I am amazed that some abbots of monasteries in our order infringe on this rule of humility."

To the same archbishop, Henry of Sens, Bernard wrote in about 1128 to defend the cause of the monks of Molesme. Thus Bernard chose to help out the very monastery that had originally broken into two factions with the foundation of Cîteaux and had created problems for the first Cistercians. In a second letter he reminded the archbishop how the prelate previously had abandoned his charges against the monks of Molesme. But now these monks had gone to Bernard with the complaint that the archbishop was making new demands on them. "I implore you to give up these claims of yours and I trust you will not turn me down," Bernard wrote, pointing out that the archbishop in the past had been generous with him, and so "I am certain you will not deny me this small matter."

Was the abbot of Clairvaux trying to win over the powerful archbishop by flattery? Bernard's rhetoric indicates a high degree of self-confidence, but this attitude is surprising in view of the fact that Clairvaux was still a relatively unknown monastery, while Henry was one of the most prominent churchmen of his time. Bernard apparently did not hold back, and he had no qualms in defending a monastery that only a few decades earlier had challenged the first Cistercian foundation. Molesme's monks had complained to the pope about their abbot, who had left them to found what became Cîteaux. The brothers who had remained at Molesme got their abbot, Robert, back, and for the next century Cîteaux refused to count Robert as its first abbot. For Bernard, however, there were no hard feelings.

A third letter on behalf of the monastery of Molesme was sent to the bishop of Langres, Guilencus, and is dated to 1125 or 1126. Bernard insisted that the monastery was asking only for recognition of its own rights. He added that Count Theobald was on his side, thus threatening intervention. Bernard appealed to the bishop's generosity and claimed he was asking only for what was "reasonable." This letter is found in a section of the collection that includes a number of missives to bishops. They demonstrate that by the second half of the 1120s Bernard felt comfortable in addressing bishops not only for Cistercian causes but also for other matters that had gained his attention.

To the bishop of Chartres, Geoffrey, Bernard wrote, probably in 1127, on behalf of a recluse who had been enclosed in a cell. He had broken his vow and left the enclosure, but now he wanted to return. Bernard asked the bishop to show pity on the "poor creature" and let him continue the life to which he had originally dedicated himself. Apparently the same case is considered in a second letter, where it was also a question of a vow to go to Jerusalem. Bernard's argument is that a lesser vow should not block a greater one. The logic is apparently that the vow to Jerusalem was of less significance than the vow to live in enclosure, for "God does not require that a promise be carried out if something better instead is done."

To the same bishop of Chartres, Geoffrey, Bernard expressed reservation about Norbert of Xanten, whom we know as the founder of the Premonstratensian Order. Norbert was supposed to go to Jerusalem but had failed to mention the matter when Bernard a few days earlier had spoken with him. He had told Bernard that the Antichrist was about to come, but Bernard was not convinced: "I did not feel that I had to agree with him." The second part of the letter is dedicated to the cause of the same Humbert on whose behalf Bernard had appealed to Count Theobald. He mentions his appeal to the count: "But not gaining favor from him, I obtained nothing." Bernard reminded the bishop how at Troyes he had begged him to intercede for Humbert with Count Theobald. It is likely that this contact took place at the count's court, and so the abbot of Clairvaux must have made the journey to the count's residence, where bishops and other abbots probably also were present. Once again it is remarkable how the abbot of a monastery that chose to establish itself far from human settlements could justify making his way to a town and its courtly milieu.

While Bernard was willing to tell bishops what to do, he in turn could be reluctant to carry out their wishes. He wrote Ricuin, bishop of Toul, that he was sending back to him a man whom Ricuin had put in his trust so the individual could do penance. It was not his function as abbot to care for the souls of laypersons. Pastoral care belonged to the bishop, not to the abbot. Bernard tried to formulate his point of view in an attractive manner. Whenever he had to deal with serious questions with which he could not cope, he wrote, it was natural for him to refer them to the bishop's authority: "I am not at ease about the matter until I have been strengthened by [the bishop's] decision or his counsel." Once again it is noteworthy how Bernard could take on responsibility for non-monks but in cases like this one turn them over to the bishop.

To another bishop, Henry of Verdun, Bernard appealed for a woman who had gone to him for counsel about the state of her soul. She had followed his advice, and now Bernard asked the bishop to look after her with a shepherd's care. He used a phrase here that comes from the Rule of Saint Benedict: the abbot is to render account (*rationem reddere*) for his monks. In this case, Bernard told the bishop he was to render account before God for this woman. Thus Bernard claimed that he had done what he could: "It was our task to correct the sinner; it is yours not to despise her but to receive her back." The last few lines of the letter indicate that the woman had been separated from her husband. Now it was an open question if she could be reconciled with him and if he was willing to take her back. Otherwise he was to live alone, without a wife. In this case Bernard seems to have taken on a pastoral role and to have given a penitent absolution. But in the end he turned the woman over to the bishop's care and discretion.

There was nothing in the early Cistercian documents that forbade abbots from involving themselves in pastoral care, but these statutes exclude the possession of parish churches and thus would seem to rule out contact with parishioners. Bernard might have defended his behavior by pointing out that people such as the penitent woman came to him. He did not seek them out. The journey from Clairvaux to Troyes would have made it possible for troubled people to approach the abbot, who apparently already had a reputation as a man of insight and charity. The moment Bernard left the perimeter of the abbey, he became visible and thereby available to the lay world. In some cases he was willing to listen to its needs.

More conventional is Bernard's celebration of a conversion to Clairvaux. To Alexander, bishop of Lincoln, he wrote to tell that a canon of that diocese, Philip, had stopped at Clairvaux on his way to Jerusalem. He had decided to remain there: "He is no longer a questioning onlooker but has become a devoted dweller and citizen belonging to Jerusalem." For Bernard Clairvaux was Jerusalem, bound to the heavenly Jerusalem "by heartfelt devotion, conformity in its way of life, and a spiritual relationship." Bernard could hardly emphasize more strongly his belief that conversion to the Cistercian Order and especially to the monastery of Clairvaux was the best way to heaven.

The letter reveals that Bernard's rejoicing over the canon's conversion was not his only reason for contacting the bishop. He asked that Philip's arrangement with his creditors that they keep his prebend be honored. Apparently Philip had outstanding debts when he left home. At the same time Bernard asked that the dwelling Philip had built on church land for his mother, as well as the surrounding property, be kept for her during her lifetime. Once again Bernard was willing to involve himself in matters that at first glance would seem quite irrelevant for a Cistercian abbot. But his purpose seems to be clear: to ensure that his new convert to Clairvaux could trust that his affairs were being taken care of. His old mother would be looked after, so long as the bishop respected his wishes and those of Bernard.

A long letter, probably from 1127, summarizes Bernard's involvement with church figures outside the Cistercian Order. It was written to Suger, abbot of Saint Denis, the great royal foundation outside Paris where French kings were buried. Suger was well known as a political figure who had become invaluable to the king, but Bernard rejoiced that the abbot had had a change of heart: "I can tell you that even though I hoped to hear of such a transformation, still I hardly hoped ever to do so." Bernard's directness is disarming, and he was blunt about how he had looked upon the monastery as a secular institution, which soldiers frequented as much as monks, where business transactions took place, and where even women gained entrance. "But now it is all quite different. God is called upon, continence is the rule, discipline is kept, spiritual reading is encouraged, for the silence that is maintained is not disturbed."

Bernard went so far as to say that the brothers' sense of shame for their past faults encouraged their new way of life in its austerity. I wonder how the mighty Suger reacted to such unveiled criticism of the monastery that he had led. Bernard stated that there had been two abuses. The first was the state of Saint Denis: the arrogance (*insolentia*) of its former way of life. This problem had now been solved. The other, however, was still acute, the fact of a man's being both churchman and military figure. Bernard was referring to Stephen of Garland: deacon, archdeacon, provost, and at the same time seneschal to the king. In 1127 he lost all his offices and was driven from the court. In 1131 the king gave him back his title of chancellor. Bernard's condemnation had some effect, but not a lasting one.

It is apparent from what Bernard wrote that Suger had protected Stephen, but now Clairvaux's abbot insisted that the reform of the monastery lead to the removal of a figure who had combined secular with ecclesiastical preferment. Such a demand is ironic in view of the fact that Suger himself came to combine both ecclesiastical and secular functions. He would end his career as regent for King Louis VII while the king was on crusade. For Bernard such a dual role was unthinkable, and yet we find him time and again intervening in the affairs of princes.

In ending his letter to Suger, Bernard insisted that if Suger was a true friend of Stephen, then he was obliged to make the man a friend of the truth. Genuine friendship can only exist between two persons who are bound together in loving the truth. The letter concluded in providing a warning to end well what had been begun. Suger's change of heart and reformation of his monastery should lead to his ridding it of Stephen of Garland.

As in so much else in his career Bernard took it upon himself to tell powerful people how to behave. Saint Denis was among the most prestigious monastic houses in the French kingdom, while Clairvaux was still a relatively new little foundation in the county of Champagne. Bernard did not care about precedence or royal favor. He spoke out directly to Suger in praising his reform and demanding that it be completed by the removal of a powerful official.

Seeking a New Consensus

Bernard's early ascent to fame is indicated not only in his writing the powerful abbot Suger but also in his answering a query by perhaps the most prominent theologian of Paris, Hugh of Saint Victor. In 1125 Hugh wrote to Bernard and asked his view concerning the necessity of baptism. Hugh was critical of an unnamed theologian who apparently was claiming that anyone who failed to be baptized after the time when Christ spoke of baptism's necessity would automatically be condemned to eternal damnation. Bernard replied in what is included in the letter collection as a letter but is more a short treatise. He claimed he was not seeking verbal contests or novelties of expression. Bernard was certain that faith alone can be sufficient for salvation. The anonymous theologian (who may well have been Peter Abelard) was keener to profess what was new rather than being eager for the truth: "He shows a total lack of discernment, preaching a God who is either exceedingly niggardly or excessively bountiful."

Bernard was convinced that they who lived before the time of Christ could obtain salvation by living good lives. After Christ came and had his conversation with Nicodemus about the necessity of salvation, it still took a long time before his words were revealed to humankind. Bernard anticipated what later theologians would call baptism of desire. He argued here in a manner close to what we today call scholastic theology. Bernard's point of departure was monastic theology, with its careful meditation on sacred texts. But in using logic and argument, Bernard followed the procedure of the cathedral schools of his time.

In a superb article, "*Bernardus scholasticus*: The Correspondence of Bernard of Clairvaux and Hugh of Saint Victor on Baptism," the American monk and scholar Hugh Feiss has shown how Bernard expressed his thought and belongs to what can be called "nascent scholasticism." It would be wrong, however, to make a watertight division between the theology of the monasteries and that of the cathedral schools. The two could complement each other, as in this letter treatise.

At about the same time as Bernard composed his first polemic against Peter Abelard, he completed the work *On Grace and Free Choice*. He dedicated

it to his friend William of Saint-Thierry and asked him to make any necessary corrections: "to amend it yourself or else to return it to me for emenda-
tion." Bernard opened the work by telling how he once had spoken of his
own experience of God's grace. "Some bystander" challenged him in asking
what role the individual plays if all that comes about was God's doing.

I would like very much to locate the exact situation in Bernard's life when
he began to question the role of grace. His opening discussion could well
reflect his own inner doubt and uncertainty, or it could be a result of his
conversations with William of Saint-Thierry. In any case we are confronted
once more with the fact that the meditative and contemplative content
of Bernard's monastic life opened new perspectives: outside to the larger
church, and within to a rethinking of theological questions. Bernard's point
of departure is free choice (*liberum arbitrium*) as the basis of human action.
He saw it as cooperating with grace, and found "voluntary consent" to be a
"self-determining habit of the soul." He proceeded from here in emphasizing
the freedom exercised by the human person. Each person who has the use
of reason has freedom of choice. But grace is still necessary, and only with
Christ can the individual be restored to the divine image present in us. The
grace that is given by God does not remove freedom of choice.

Bernard here did his best to combine grace with individual free choice.
He saw this tension in terms of God's creation. There is no polemic here,
no opponent to be attacked, as in the work on baptism. Bernard could be
serenely self-sufficient, but we of course can ask why he took the time to
deal with such an abstract topic. He did not need to show his academic cre-
dentials, as a master in the schools had to do every time he engaged in debate
with a colleague. Bernard here challenged a central theological question that
he may have felt was being neglected by the masters of cathedral schools.
As so often, he was not a scholastic theologian and yet could argue as if he
had been trained in the schools. He revealed a knowledge of the Bible and
the Fathers and a willingness to pursue intellectual inquiry. Once again we
are far from the contemplative monk's vocation, and yet Bernard's life these
years in the monastery may have given him the time and energy he needed
to take up such questions.

Bernard McGinn in his introduction to the Cistercian Publication translation of *On Grace and Free Choice* calls it "the most mature dogmatic product"
to come from Bernard. He shows how the work was read and commented on
beyond the Middle Ages and into the Reformation. Bernard carefully defined
consent and saw a threefold freedom in human life: in nature, grace, and
glory. Both good and evil rational creatures enjoy freedom from necessity.
Everyone who uses reason has freedom of choice. Grace is necessary so that

we can will that which is good, but even after sinning, the human person has not lost free choice. In the image and likeness of the creator, there is a freedom that makes it possible to enjoy free counsel and free pleasures. Thanks to Christ the likeness of the divine image is restored in the human person. But there is always freedom of choice, regardless of grace or of temptation.

I have touched briefly on the main points of this important treatise that emerged from Bernard's own meditations on a subject that has concerned theologians before and after him. But the most central element for future consideration would be his insistence that human merits are the result of God's free gifts. We cannot earn grace, and yet free choice is active in the work of salvation. Bernard thus saw the human person not as a helpless victim of his or her own weakness, nor as a strong conqueror of death and sin. Through Christ there is hope and salvation. Bernard turned to Paul, "who attributes to God, and not to his own choosing power, everything susceptible of good" (Phil 2:13).

A third work of theology belongs to these years and can be tentatively dated to 1129 or soon afterwards: *De laude novae militiae* (In Praise of the New Knighthood). [For background, see question 12 in the Fifteen Questions about Bernard: The Background for My Portrait section.] On 13 January 1128 Bernard attended a council at Troyes where the institution of the Knights Templar was given ecclesiastical approval. The master of the new Order was Hugh of Payens, a relative of Bernard, who had founded the company of knights in 1118. The concept of combining monastic and knightly vocations was quite new. After all, medieval people conceived society in terms of the three orders, each with its different functions. But now it became acceptable for a man of prayer also to be a man of war, for the knights would be stationed in the Holy Land and defend it at the same time as they would lead lives of prayer.

Bernard's support of the new Order is remarkable in view of the fact that a few years earlier he had condemned the idea of establishing Cistercian monasteries in the Holy Land. But now he altered his way of thinking, perhaps in making concessions to a close relative, perhaps simply in developing his own conception of prayer and fighting. There was a tradition in Christian thought that praised fighting for the Lord, and Bernard latched onto this understanding in his defense of the new knighthood. He saw monks as waging war "against vices or demons," and so the conflict could be transferred to the new knighthood: "Rejoice, brave athlete, if you live and conquer in the Lord; but glory and exult even more if you die and join your Lord."

Bernard's praise of the new knighthood combined with an excoriation of the traditional knight who fights for glory and gain. Such knights, he claimed, were full of vanity in dress and habits: "Why do you blind your-selves with effeminate locks and trip on long and full tunics?" The knight of Christ is "not a mankiller" but can be described as "a killer of evil." Bernard did his best to justify violence and killing for a necessary cause. He described the Templars as living lives that were the antithesis of the self-indulgence of secular warriors: "They forswear dice and chess and abhor the chase; they take no delight in the ridiculous cruelty of falconry." Bernard accepted that such men were both monks and soldiers: "They lack neither monastic meek-ness nor military might."

These sections of Bernard's treatise are often quoted, while the last chap-ters, comprising more than half of the work, are generally ignored. Here he imagined Jerusalem, Bethlehem, Nazareth, and other holy places, on the basis of descriptions found in the Old and New Testaments. The defense of the Templars thus turned into a visualization of the Holy Land that the knights would be defending, and military images give way to scenes from the life of Christ and his sufferings. These chapters indicate that the Holy Land to which Bernard was sending the Templars was more the product of his biblical imagination than a description of the physical places themselves. In this manner it is possible to understand how Bernard in 1146 could have encouraged an entire generation of knights to head for Jerusalem. What he saw was the city of God and not an earthly city, and he hardly conceived of the carnage that would come about in these places.

It might be objected that Bernard came from a family of knights and must have known what knightly behavior would involve. However much he heard about fighting when he was growing up, he did not himself engage in it, nor did he experience the loss of anyone close to him because of war or conflict. For Bernard the knightly station was an ideal that could be translated into a monastic commitment: "They dwell united in one family with no personal property." Bernard was something of a dreamer, and it was only in the wake of the disastrous Second Crusade that he had to face the dire consequences of war. In the 1120s he could imagine a happy band of men living in har-mony with each other, defending Jerusalem, and praying together. There must have been some meaning in the concept, for the Knights Templar lasted until the early fourteenth century, when a French king disbanded them in order to grab their material resources. But that was a different and perhaps more cynical world, in contrast to that of Bernard's hopeful early twelfth century.

These three works—on baptism, grace and free will, and the new knighthood—might at first seem to have nothing in common except chron-ological proximity. But together they provide an indication of how the still young abbot of Clairvaux was developing. First of all he was already in contact with one of the finest theologians of the schools of Paris. Secondly, thanks to his friend William of Saint-Thierry, he was concerned with letting a European learned audience know his thoughts about how grace is bestowed without revoking free will. Finally, he was devoted to the idea that a good monk could also be a good knight, at least in certain circumstances and in a monastic order quite different from the Cistercians. In all three areas Bernard was seeking a new consensus in the Church about what it meant to become a Christian, to receive God's grace, and to offer oneself to a life of prayer and fighting. Bernard was, as it were, testing the frontiers of Christian life. He set about his task with immense confidence and an almost naive lack of concern for making major errors. In today's Christian West it is inconceivable that a man of prayer can also engage in combat, but Bernard lived in another world and wanted to sanctify a new form of knighthood: "What can we say of this, except that this has been done by the Lord, and it is marvelous in our eyes?" The words evoke Psalm 117:23 in the Vulgate, a celebration of the new knighthood.

🍂 CHAPTER 5

Toward Reformation of Church and Monastery

Addressing the Church's Place in Society

From the time of Charlemagne the Western Church lived in the shadow of kings and emperors. They were its protectors in a society where violence was common and church institutions vulnerable to attack. Medieval rulers continued the tradition of the last Roman emperors, who from the time of Constantine considered it to be their right and duty to look after the interests of the Church. From the middle of the eleventh century, however, a party of reforming clerics based in central Italy tried to free themselves from secular power. They insisted that kings and emperors had no right to decide who would be bishop—or pope—while at the same time being born into a powerful family did not give one an automatic right to be chosen as bishop. The Church had its own spiritual realm, and this was inviolable, as Emperor Henry IV came to learn under Pope Gregory VII (1073–85).

Bernard was born in the aftermath of the first medieval reformation of the Church and grew up in a world where royal, ducal, and other secular figures had to respect the prerogatives of the Church. His actions in defending what he found to be ecclesiastical interests reflect his attachment to this reformation, even though he by no means was extreme or radical in his view of how Christian society should function. Like other church figures, he took it for granted that there would be a great amount of cooperation between ecclesiastical and secular powers. They could strengthen each other, and only in extraordinary situations was it necessary for churchmen to distance themselves from kings and other lay authorities.

In 1129 Bernard joined with other Cistercian abbots, including his father abbot, Stephen Harding, and addressed King Louis VI of France concerning a quarrel between the king and the bishop of Paris, Stephen of Senlis. The bishop had tried to reform the chapter of Notre Dame cathedral in Paris, but the canons had objected and had gone to the king for his support. Louis backed them and forbade the bishop to change the canons' customs. We have here a classic case of the old regime, where king and churchmen supported each other, in the face of a new world where the Church reformed itself and kept secular authority at a distance.

The bishop reacted to King Louis's intervention by putting his diocese under interdict. There could be no saying of Mass and no distribution of the sacraments. This measure led to violent resistance, and the bishop had to flee his diocese. The king reciprocated by confiscating the bishop's possessions. It is at this point that the Cistercians intervened, addressing the king as "Stephen abbot of Cîteaux and the entire assembly of Cistercian abbots and brethren." This is one of the rare occasions when we get a chance to see Bernard working together with his fellow Cistercian abbots and under the abbot of Cîteaux. He seems to have joined with Hugh of Macon, abbot of Pontigny, and the archbishop of Sens in meeting the king. But the king upstaged the bishop and abbots by going to Pope Honorius II and convincing him to remove the interdict. At this point Bernard and Abbot Hugh of Pontigny wrote to the pope and told him that the king had fooled him. The pope had made his decision after hearing only one side of the conflict.

Bernard and Hugh opened their appeal to the pope with the assertion that the bishops and the Church in general wept at what they experienced. Now "a great crisis has taken us away from our monasteries and into the public sphere, and we are speaking of what we there find." They insisted that the papal order to lift the interdict was the result of a lie. The abbots here asserted not only that the pope was being manipulated. They claimed that their king (or at least his representatives at Rome) were liars! Bernard seems also to have written another letter to the pope, this time on behalf of the bishop of Chartres, Geoffrey. They complained that the king was still holding the property of the bishop. "How long does it seem right to your holiness that this situation should continue?" Bernard was ghosting a letter for the sake of a bishop.

If Bernard had been a bishop, it would seem to have been right and just for him to compose such documents. But he was not, and yet he was drafting letters to the pope for a bishop involved in the controversy. Bernard also wrote to the pope on behalf of the arcbishop of Sens. He had been known as a worldly prelate, interested in wealth and luxury, but had altered his way of life. Bernard pointed out that his former existence had been acceptable to the king, while now in his religious devotion, he offended the monarch. Bernard's language is extreme, but it expresses the reformed church's dilemma: it was in opposition to secular powers that required churchmen to follow their lead. Now "Herod is out to destroy Christ in the diocese of Sens!" The archbishop was a Christ figure, while King Louis had become a Herod.

For anyone who believes that medieval society was based on compulsion and lack of freedom of expression, such a letter should be a lesson. Bernard spoke out powerfully and nakedly, telling off the king and lecturing the pope. But he had to pay for such openness. He felt obliged to write the papal chancellor, Cardinal Haimeric, to defend himself against charges that were being made against him. Bernard conceded that he had involved himself in a number of cases that had nothing to do with his own monastery: "Can I be blamed for being present on those occasions, since I am only suited to live in hiding? I am my own judge and bear witness to my life." Bernard conceded the gap between his actions and his vocation. He was indeed present for various cases: "This I do not deny, but I was summoned and compelled to go there." Bernard claimed that he had been forced to become involved in the type of disputes that had characterized the canons of Paris. He appealed to Haimeric to take care of the matters that belonged to his jurisdiction and not to Bernard's. He conceded that he had no right to leave his monastery unless he was ordered to do so by his bishop or a papal legate. For a moment it looks as though Bernard handed the conflict between king and bishop over to papal discretion. But the letter ends on a quite different note: "Do not imagine that because I am off in a corner and keep silent that the Church's problems will end, so long as the papal court keeps passing judgments that harm those who are absent, so that it can satisfy those who are present." Thus Bernard signaled that he would not retreat in silence to his monastery but would continue to defend the bishops of Paris and Sens.

This letter was probably sent in January of 1130 and indicates a breach between Cardinal Haimeric and Bernard. But their estrangement would end with the papal schism the following month, when Bernard quickly forgot that he resented Haimeric for being so pliable with the French king. We shall see in the next chapter how Bernard seems to have swallowed his concerns and dedicated himself to the defense of the papacy. But his point of departure here, as in the defense of the bishop of Paris, was an insistence that the Church was sovereign and not to be subjected to royal policies.

An indication that Bernard's relationship to Haimeric was not purely political is found in a slightly earlier letter, dated to 1128. Bernard wrote that he had sent the cardinal many letters on behalf of various people, but now he said: "Look, I am present. It is I who have spoken." In the two envoys Bernard sent to Haimeric, he should see three persons, for he was with them: "I will always be present in their hearts and be safer and more grateful than in my own heart." Bernard conceded that anyone who fails to see the power of friendship and that of love would find such an assertion unbelievable. Such a person does not accept that "in the company of the believers there was one heart and one soul." Bernard borrowed from a well-known assertion in the Acts of the Apostles (4:32) about the unity among the members of the first Christian communities. But he was not only speaking of community. He was asserting the bond of friendship, *vis amicitiae*. He developed this idea further: we are one person even if we occupy three bodies. The result was unity of spirit.

Bernard proposed that Haimeric share in this love, as a fourth person, "if you consider it appropriate and agree in the same unity of love." Was Bernard trying to flatter Haimeric and make him do his will? There is certainly an element of church politics here. At the same time Bernard in so carefully formulating his concept of love was offering himself to Haimeric. Such language might be dismissed as pure flattery, but for Bernard it was possible to combine Christian idealism with political realities.

Monastic Discipline and Commitments

Well before Bernard became involved in papal and royal politics, he was already writing letters on behalf of purely monastic institutions. Thus we have from shortly after 1121 a letter of consolation to Simon, the abbot of Saint Nicholas in the diocese of Laon. Bernard wrote of the evils of the world against which Simon strove. He encouraged Simon nevertheless to moderate the rigor of his actions. This was probably a reference to the fact that Simon was trying to give up parishes that may have been acquired through simony. Here as in so many other instances the reformation of the Church in its separation from secular interests came at a cost. At the same time the monks from the Order of Cluny, whose monastery Simon had taken over, should not be forced to live a stricter way of life. Bernard provided a number of suggestions about how Simon was to take the brothers' needs and desires into consideration. Apparently Simon had left the monastery in order to establish peace with the community, but the monks had asked him to return. What is surprising here is that Bernard did not offer a single solution to the splits within the monastery. He did not try to force the brethren to accept a unitary reformation of their way of life. Instead he recommended that different factions within the monastery should have an opportunity to go in their chosen directions.

Bernard remained in contact with Abbot Simon, for in the spring of 1125 he wrote that he had kept one of the abbot's stray sheep with him for a time. The monk in question had apparently sought a stricter way of life. Bernard claimed that the situation showed a truth that he had once before expressed to Simon, that a monk who is discontented with his monastery can change his mind and accept its life once he has had the opportunity to experience a stricter discipline elsewhere. In other words, the monk had found Clairvaux too demanding and was now ready to return to his former monastery. This monk, called Nicholas, provides an illustration of what I have previously shown became a general principle for Bernard: it is legitimate to leave one's monastery for a stricter way of life. But a monk who converts to this more demanding discipline can also return to his former monastery, as Nicholas had done.

The question of receiving monks at Clairvaux from other monasteries also appears in a letter dated to before May of 1125 or 1126. Bernard wrote to the monks of Flay, a Benedictine house in the diocese of Beauvais, and said he understood from their letters that they were upset with Clairvaux for receiving one of their monks. They took it for granted that their monastery was well known and thus it was wrong for Bernard to take over their member. But he replied: "Your monastery may be well known, but not so to us." Bernard found no obligation to return the monk to an obscure monastery. The monks claimed that their house was known all the way to Rome, but Bernard replied: "It does not follow that your fame has reached us. We are, after all, far from Rome!"

Bernard might seem here to be ironic, but he claimed to be telling the truth. He had never heard of this monastery, which was "separated by a great distance, in a different province and speaking another language." In any case he had been quite careful with this brother, whose name was Benedict. He had been told to return to his own monastery but then pleaded that his abbot had forced him to work as a doctor "in order to gain favor with the world's princes," and so he had to care for thieves and for the excommunicated. When Benedict pleaded with his abbot that his soul was in danger from associating with such people, the man refused to listen. Thus he had left not so much a holy way of life as an unholy one. Bernard accepted the truth of this story and considered Benedict now to be a monk of Clairvaux. He refused to be intimidated by the abbot's insults and threats: "We have every confidence that we have acted according to the law in receiving this monk of yours."

This is a complex letter, which begins with a legal defense of Bernard's actions and ends with harsh accusations against the monks of Flay and especially their abbot. In another letter from the same time, Bernard indicated his lack of respect for the abbot already in the salutation, for he first mentioned the brothers of Flay, and secondly their abbot Hildegard. Such a put-down must have been noticed, as the salutation of a letter was supposed first to mention the most important person addressed, and here Bernard did not even try to be rhetorically correct. He defended opening the doors of his monastery "to a monk who was lonely, apart, poor and unhappy" and who was fleeing his monastery because his soul was in danger. The abbot nevertheless accused Bernard of violating the Rule of Saint Benedict, and Bernard only repeated what he had written in the previous letter: Flay was totally unknown to Clairvaux. His tone became sarcastic when he insisted that if one of his Clairvaux monks came to Flay in order to live a stricter life, then Bernard would not complain, but "I would beg you" to receive him.

Here is the key argument, that Clairvaux offered a more trustworthy path to monastic improvement than Flay. But there was also the question of a brother using his medical skills. Brother Benedict claimed he had been forced to do so by the abbot, while the abbot insisted that he practiced medicine of his own free will. This is a sore point in the reformed monasticism of the twelfth century: Cistercian brothers with medical knowledge were to be prudent in using their skills outside the monastery. Bernard could vouch for the fact that brother Benedict during his stay at Clairvaux remained at the monastery and did not wander about among questionable laypersons. His defense ends with a declaration of love: he invited the brothers of Flay to reproach him as much as they liked, while Bernard from this point onwards would love them with "pure love, treat you with reverence and consider you to be friends."

Why did Bernard change his tone? I assume he knew such a letter would be noticed and copied. If he only expressed vitriol toward Flay, then he would be looked upon as an arrogant abbot who considered his monastery to be superior. Bernard wanted to show bonds of affectivity in monastic life, even with a house and an abbot whose behavior he censured.

In another letter, Bernard encouraged Guy, abbot of Trois Fontaines, a Clairvaux daughter house, not to be angry with an acolyte at Mass who had spilled some wine from a chalice. He explained that it is right to be upset when there is a righteous cause, but it is wrong to be more angry than is appropriate. Bernard made the point that what matters is one's intention. It is motive that is the primary concern, and not the outcome from an action. In other words, it is what we seek to do that counts (*intentionis propositum*), that makes for guilt or merit. This is a remarkable statement because it is more or less what Peter Abelard was expressing at about the same time in his *Ethics*: what matters in a moral act is intention. Perhaps the Mass servers were careless, but they had no intention of spilling the wine. Bernard decided to ease the conscience of his abbot by giving him a penance.

Bernard turned here to a theological query: do all the elements of bread, water, and wine have to be present for the sacrifice of the Mass? Would the lack of one make the ritual invalid? His answer is surprisingly human: in such a question each person is required to believe "as it seems best for himself." Bernard belonged to a period in the history of Christianity when theologians were seeking universal answers to questions of behavior and were defining the content and meaning of church rituals. He, nevertheless, refused to give any final answers. He asked instead what he would have done at Mass if he had found there to be no wine in the chalice. One possibility was to go ahead and complete the ritual. Bernard did not doubt that in such a situation the bread was duly consecrated, even though the proper order was not followed: "I cannot deny that bread and wine with water ought to be prepared together." But there is a great difference between blaming negligence if the ritual is not carried out correctly and denying the validity of the sacrament. In other words, the transformation of bread into the body of Christ was not affected by the fact that there was no wine. The sacrament of the Eucharist was valid, even if both elements were not present.

This is a surprising letter in what it reveals about Bernard. His concern was not the correct manner of performing a sacred ritual. It was the intention of the celebrant and the grace of God that could compensate for what may have been missing in human action. In responding to the abbot of a daughter house, Bernard was showing pastoral care and concern for the man's situation. He was sharing with Guy his own lack of certainty about some of the questions and saying that each peson "must believe as seems best to himself." We have a tendency to look upon medieval theology as fixed and rigid, but here is a different way of believing, taking human weakness into consideration and assuming that God will take care of what may be lacking in human action.

Another letter to Abbot Guy of Trois Fontaines concerns a brother who had left the monastery but apparently wanted to return. Bernard reflected on the role of pity in human behavior: it cannot be created by the will and is not liable to reason. Reason and will cannot stifle pity. Thus pity for such a brother is understandable, and the brother should be given every opportunity

to reintegrate in the community. But Bernard was not optimistic. He coun-
seled Guy to call the brothers to a meeting and there remove any previous
sentences issued against the former renegade. In this way, the brother's pride
would be healed by the brothers' humility and the Rule of Saint Benedict,
which encourages the abbot to seek the advice of the brethren, would be
maintained.

For Bernard, however, providing a general principle was not sufficient. He
referred to his own experience at Clairvaux with a wayward monk, a brother
Bartholomew. One day the man so upset Bernard that the abbot in his anger
told him to leave the monastery. Bartholomew retreated to one of the Clairvaux granges. When Bernard realized where he was, he wanted to bring him
back to the monastery, but Bartholomew refused to return unless Bernard
promised that he would regain his former position in the community and not
be demoted as a runaway to the most inferior rank. Bartholomew blamed
Bernard for turning him out of the monastery without giving him a chance
to have his case heard.

Bernard conceded that he could not depend on his own judgment in
the case because he had become so emotionally involved. So he handed
the matter over to the brothers of Clairvaux. When he was away from the
monastery, they decided that Bartholomew should not be disciplined, for
his expulsion had not been in accord with the Rule of Saint Benedict. Bernard thus concluded in the letter to Guy that if such concern should be
shown for a monk who only one time had left the monastery, then all the
more consideration was owed to the monk of Trois Fontaines, who was
much worse off.

This is a remarkable letter. Bernard no doubt wanted to place himself in
a favorable light and show that he was forgiving and acted according to the
Rule. But he did not need to conclude the letter with a personal anecdote.
He had made his point for Abbot Guy, but it is as if he needed to emphasize
that abbots are not dictatorial figures and have to listen to the voices within
their communities. They can act too quickly and forget that they are obliged
to show kindness and understanding.

Bernard made himself and his own experience available not only to Guy
as abbot of Trois Fontaines but to the entire community, for we can assume
that such a letter was read aloud to all the brothers. Another letter, probably
from 1127, was sent to the same monastery's brothers but addressed one of
them in particular, who is not named. Bernard apologized for not coming to
the monk: "Don't imagine that my failure to come and visit you means that
I do not care for you. I care for you as if you were a son of mine." Bernard
insisted that he was a mother concerned for her child, and once again we

see how Bernard, like other Cistercian abbots, saw himself as a mother to his monks.

In this section of Bernard's letter collection, which includes many letters addressed to abbots, he made it clear that he was still beholden to the men whom he had known at Cîteaux or Clairvaux and who now headed other monasteries. To Artald, abbot of Preuilly, he mentioned the bonds that existed "not only because we share the same Order and have made the same vows, but also because of the debt shared in our old friendship." Thus the letter opens with a classical expression of goodwill (*captatio benevolentiae*), but then comes a warning: Artald was thinking of making a foundation of his monastery in Spain, and Bernard considered it to be too far away from the Cistercian heartland of Champagne-Burgundy. Why did Artald want to exile "your sons to such a far away place," where it would be expensive to find a suitable site and erect buildings? Instead Bernard suggested a place much closer. This was Vauluisant, near the border of the Ile-de-France, where Artald on Bernard's advice in 1127 founded a daughter house.

We know that the Cistercians eventually extended their monasteries to Spain and to virtually every corner of Europe. But the Bernard we meet here is a conservative abbot who did not want to expand the buildings of Clairvaux and relocate to a site with more room. He could write to Artald as a fellow monk who had been with him at Cîteaux and now had gone on to found Cîteaux's fifth daughter. Artald reminds us that the expansion of the Cistercian Order did not owe itself exclusively to Clairvaux and Bernard. The abbot of Clairvaux was networking here, reminding the abbot of Preuilly that the abbey of Pontigny had a suitable spot for a daughter house that he would happily hand over to Preuilly. There was nothing wrong with the site, Bernard insisted, but Pontigny did not need it.

Bernard was able in this case to make use of being well informed and could provide an ambitious abbot with an alternative to a distant daughter house. At times, however, he showed total disagreement with what he considered to be a dangerous plan. This was the case with Stephen, abbot of Saint John at Chartres. Bernard had heard that the man intended to leave his monks and go to Jerusalem "in order to spend your life there only for God." It might be useful for someone who sought perfection to leave behind his own land, "but," Bernard wrote, "I cannot agree that it follows that you have the right to abandon those who have been given over to your care." He asked rhetorically if Stephen was attracted by the idea of casting off responsibility. Bernard warned him against the allurements of Satan. Stephen apparently did go to Jerusalem and in fact ended up as patriarch of the Church there. Bernard had made his point, as he had in dealing with the Morimond monks and their plans. He insisted on stability of life, but he belonged to an Order that had begun, after all, with a break from stability. And as we have already seen, Bernard's own life was anything but limited to his own monastery.

Anyone who follows the content of Bernard's letter collection will wonder at the diversity of his correspondents. One to whom he seemed genuinely devoted was Oger, canon regular of Saint Nicolas des Pres in Tournai. Bernard's letters to him are dated between 1124 and sometime after 1140. Oger was superior of his house for fourteen years but when he resigned his post, he incurred Bernard's criticism. Oger seems to have been an important recipient of Bernard's writings, including the *Steps of Humility and Pride*. It was to Oger that Bernard entrusted his *Apology*, discussing the right kind of monastic life. "It was not my intention that you should send it to the abbot of St. Thierry, but I am not bothered." Bernard insisted that he would be glad if William of Saint-Thierry saw the work, and he encouraged Oger to go see William. The two of them could go through Bernard's composition and make any necessary corrections.

In another letter, which can be dated more precisely to 1125, Bernard apologized for answering Oger's letter with a short note, but it was Lent and a time for silence. It was a burden to have to express one's thoughts in writing, Bernard remarked. If two friends were together, they could say just what they wanted, while in absence "we have to compose with difficulty what we wish to ask or answer." The letter turns into a reflection on how to express oneself in writing and how one's desire can be frustrated: "When words come forth in the mind, the very word one desires disappears."

Bernard claimed to prize the silence of Lent but was breaking it with his own thoughts on how to write. He complained to Oger that it was his duty as a monk not to teach but to mourn. He admitted that in the very act of writing he was abrogating the silence he sought.

In a briefer letter to Oger, perhaps some months earlier, he complained that friendship could not be expressed by written language: "I am sure you express less than you feel." It was the same for Bernard. But he went right ahead and spoke of his friendship. When he got hold of Oger's letter, his friend was already present in his heart. As he now wrote his letter, he was certain that Oger was present to him, and he was sure he would be present to Oger when Oger read it. Nevertheless, he suggested that they stop writing to each other and find rest "in those we love." Bernard continued in this vein, expressing his devotion to Oger's abbot, then praising Guerric, a mutual friend.

At times it is amazing how Bernard could play with language in order to express its limitations and then would turn around to state that he did not want to use language but instead sought the real experience of love and friendship. These letters indicate a circle of monastic friends who for Bernard were recipients of his writings and to whom he conveyed his conception of the monastic life. Bernard is slippery in his quest for meaning and definition. But there is a surprising sense of tolerance here, an enjoyment of the presence and absence of friends and a respect for friendship as an integral part of monastic life.

❦ CHAPTER 6

Healing a Divided Church, 1130–1135

A European Figure

In the first years of the 1130s Bernard became a European figure, involving himself in the ecclesiastical and secular politics of his time and influencing them to a greater or lesser degree. He dedicated himself to solving the perilous situation in which there were two popes at the same time in the Western Church. By 1138 he had been to Italy a number of times and had traversed what today is France—journeys that must have been grueling for an individual with gastric problems and with a firm commitment to the prayer life of the monastery. At the same time as Bernard missed the daily office, he was separated from the brothers he loved in Clairvaux, both his brothers in the flesh and his spiritual brethren, who looked to him for spiritual guidance and inspiration.

It must have been difficult and even hazardous to travel from town to town, monastery to monastery, in a landscape where forests could house robbers and there were great stretches of land that were uninhabited and thus provided no shelter. Yet we hear practically nothing about how Bernard experienced such journeys. We have only the well-known anecdote about how though he rode "beside the Lake Lausanne [also called Lake Geneva] the whole day, he did not even see the lake." Bernard's ability to turn inward and sense the presence of God may have been his salvation on his travels, but even an ascetic and mystic must eat and drink, and here he would have had to live with many different types of nourishment. For better and worse for his physical state of being.

Where did he spend the night? It seems likely that Bernard made use of the fact that the Rule of Saint Benedict required monasteries to receive guests as if they were Christ, but Bernard could not count on getting lodging at Cistercian monasteries, at least in Italy where at his time they were still few and far between. So he had to be in debt to more traditional Benedictine and Cluniac houses, and since his relationship to the abbot of Cluny, Peter the Venerable, was problematic, he could not expect always to be welcomed as a friend at places attached to the great monastic headquarters of Cluny.

The narrator of the second book of Bernard's hagiography, the *Vita Prima*, was a Benedictine abbot, Arnold of Bonneval, who was probably chosen by Bernard's secretary, Geoffrey of Auxerre. As a non-Cistercian Arnold could gain more credibility in providing an account of Bernard's dealings especially with the papal schism that for nine years split the Western Church. Arnold had not known Bernard as closely as William of Saint-Thierry. The external events that Arnold narrates can only be a point of departure in looking for Bernard as a human being. Bernard must have had his moments of fatigue and near despair. If we assume that he was not interested in power for its own sake but was willing to exercise his spiritual and intellectual abilities in order to influence events and heal the schism, then Bernard is an unusual figure in human history: the contemplative who came to play a central role in the political life of his times. He did not withdraw into solitude, nor did he sacrifice his monastic vocation in trying to shape church and society. He found a middle ground. His insight and power of persuasion somehow managed fruitfully to combine. There would be church figures similar to Bernard, such as Bonaventure, who shaped the Franciscan Order and at the same time wrote seminal works of theology. But Bernard has a special place, for he insisted on being apart from the world and yet regularly involved himself in its concerns.

At the same time, however, it is necessary to take into consideration the way Bernard became connected with miraculous events. The second book of the *Vita Prima* narrates one miracle after another. Healings and other supernatural events reveal how Bernard was perceived by his surroundings. Certainly part of his impact in the 1130s was his ability to attract crowds of people, among whom were many who hoped that Bernard would relieve them of their ills. Arnold's descriptions imitate the Gospel narratives of Christ's miracles, and at times the miracles can almost seem to get in the way of Arnold's narrative of how Bernard used persuasion to deal with the schism. Arnold's focus, of course, is not on the schism as such but on Bernard's impact on it, and for a twelfth-century church author, brilliant words and actions naturally included miracles.

Arnold was writing hagiography, and everything in his account was intended to portray Bernard as a saint. The account of the 1130s needs to be supplemented by Bernard's own writings, and especially by his letters. However stylized they are, they reveal his concerns and show how he tried to influence events. The letters reveal how Bernard wanted to be remembered, but also how his secretary, Geoffrey of Auxerre, wanted Bernard to be appreciated. We could use the letters, as Adriaan Bredero does in his important work on Bernard, to reveal inconsistencies and manipulation of the facts. But the letters remain the best source we have for understanding Bernard's attempts to have an impact on his surroundings.

Explaining His Absences to the Brethren

At least twice in the 1130s Bernard felt obliged to convey to the brethren of Clairvaux his feelings about spending so much time away from them. The first letter is usually dated to 1135, and its first section expresses Bernard's sense of loss in his absence from Clairvaux. He claimed that if the brothers missed him, then for him it was all the more the case. They experienced the absence of one person, while he had to cope with the absence of many. He had as many sources of anxiety "as I do have sons at Clairvaux." He formulated this idea in different ways: "You have but a single reason for your grief, while I have many because I feel pain for each of you." Bernard admitted that his activities were not in harmony with his vocation as a Cistercian monk: "I have to deal with matters that upset the peace of my soul."

In the letter's next section Bernard expressed the hope that his participation in the affairs of the Church would soon be over. In the meantime he wanted his monks to be in good spirits, for God was with them, and so the physical distance that kept them apart from him should not matter. Any monks who lived life with attention to prayer, reading, and acts of charity "can be assured that I am at no great distance from them." Bernard was joined to his monks in spirit, for he was close to them "in my heart and in my soul." At the same time, however, he warned that certain of the brothers might make trouble and be rebellious. Thus his vision of Clairvaux was not of a place in total harmony. He saw the possibility that his absence could allow difficult brothers to undermine the unity of the community. Perhaps he had heard about dissension from correspondents at Clairvaux. He is not specific enough to provide exact information, but his reference saves the letter from being saccharine.

The third section is an exhortation to the monks of Clairvaux to serve God. In this service charity will set them free. Through this bond of service Bernard promised to be present to his brothers, "especially in those hours when you are at prayer."

The letter is thus divided into three almost equal sections. In the first Bernard claimed that his sorrow and grief in missing each of the brothers was far greater than their pain in missing him alone. In the second section he expressed how he needed their sympathy and that they were not to be angry with him for staying away. He asssured the brethren that he was always present to them in the spirit. The third section provided encouragement to serve God, a dedication that would provide a necessary bond between himself and the brothers.

Bernard must have spent time and energy in composing this letter, for he wanted to acknowledge an unpaid debt to the brothers at Clairvaux. He did not apologize for his long absence, but he admitted that his actions were not in harmony with his vocation as a Cistercian monk and abbot. At the same time he warned his monks not to get out of line.

Probably two years later, in 1137, Bernard wrote again to the monks of Clairvaux. He began this letter by claiming that he felt sorrow, a sorrow that would not disappear until he returned to them. The only consolation he had in his troubles was the thought of his monks, but meanwhile he was living in what he called a state of exile. He claimed it was hard enough to live in exile from God, as we all do in this life, "but on top of this I must suffer exile from you." He indicated that this was the third time he had been separated from his brothers at Clairvaux: "I am forced to leave behind those who belong to me in order to deal with the needs of others."

The language of this letter has more pathos than that of the earlier one. Bernard wrote of his coming death and burial. He also referred to what consoled him: the thought of his life in Christ "who has paid for my life by offering his own." In the final section he gave the brothers a brief account of what he was doing. He had acceded to the request of the emperor and the pope and allowed himself to be "dragged" to Apulia. He asked the brothers to pray for their Cistercian brother Baldwin, who was the first monk in the Order to be made cardinal and who took down Bernard's dictation. Bernard also asked for prayers for the pope and for others, including brothers Bruno and Gerard, a reminder that Bernard's brother-in-the-flesh Gerard traveled with him during these years.

This is not as compact and succinct a letter as the first one to the monks of Clairvaux. It is as if Bernard at this point felt unable to collect his thoughts in the same clear manner as he had two years earlier. Certainly he had a great deal on his mind. He was facing the greatest enemy of Pope Innocent, Roger of Sicily, and the outcome of the confrontation between Roger's forces and those of Pope Innocent was uncertain. At the same time, however, the emotional language of this letter reminds us that it was composed in the midst of the affective awakening of the twelfth century. Bernard's attachment to the monks of Clairvaux resembles the expression of love in the world of Chrétien de Troyes. The thought of dying for the loved one is very much in harmony with the new romanticism of the twelfth century, here transferred to the soul's yearning for God.

Did Bernard really mean what he composed, or was he just trying to limit what could have been growing resentment against him at Clairvaux? We cannot know, but the brethren of the monastery remembered him as telling a novice that during his absences from Clairvaux, he regularly returned to the brothers in the spirit: "It has been granted me by the Lord's grace to do in the spirit what physically I could not do. I have returned in spirit, going through each of the workshops, diligently exploring how the brothers are behaving themselves." Bernard is said to have visited Clairvaux in the spirit three times during his stays in Italy. These stories, contained in the *Exordium Magnum Cisterciense*, from the end of the twelfth century, are not part of the materials used for the *Vita Prima*. But they reflect how Bernard was remembered at Clairvaux decades after his death: as an abbot and a father who was available to his monks for their needs, even when he was not physically present at the monastery. On this spiritual visit Bernard is said to have especially encouraged a novice who was grieving: "The holy father put to flight the sorrow gripping him and recalled him who had just been nearly overwhelmed by sadness to the freedom of spiritual joy." Bernard is seen here as being concerned with the spiritual well-being of his monks, and novices. It is possible that this novice persevered and became a monk and years later told his story to his brethren.

Beginnings of the Schism

In 1059 Pope Nicholas II had tried to create uniformity in papal elections by decreeing that only cardinal bishops could participate in such a choice. In the course of time, however, cardinal priests and clerks also cast their votes, and by the time Pope Honorius II died on 13 February 1130 the elective process was still in flux. There were two parties in Rome, each with its own candidate for the succession: Pietro Leone and Gregorio Papareschi. Pietro was elected pope as Anacletus II, while Gregorio chose the name of Innocent II. Peter's family had converted fifty years earlier from Judaism, while Gregorio belonged to the ancient family of the Guidoni. Both men were consecrated pope on 23 February: Innocent in the church of Santa Maria Novella and Anacletus in St. Peter's. Anacletus had more supporters within Rome, so it soon became necessary for Innocent to leave the city and concede its possession to Anacletus. Innocent went to Cluny and then to Clermont, where he held a synod. From here he journeyed to the great Benedictine abbey of Saint-Benoît-sur-Loire and then to Chartres. He had made contact with the German king Lothair, with Louis VI of France and Henry I of England, but Innocent's relationship to the French bishops was not clarified until the Council of Étampes at the end of August or early September 1130.

It is often claimed, as in the biography of Bernard by Watkin Williams, that the abbot's intervention here was decisive for the acceptance of Innocent by the French bishops. Williams based his assertion on Arnold of Bonneval, who described Bernard as "speaking for all": "He named Innocent the supreme pontiff, to be accepted by all, and they all at once acclaimed this judgment and ratified it." The abbot of Saint Denis and adviser of the French king, Suger, provided another version of the event, and here Bernard is not even mentioned: "The king gave his assent to Innocent's election on the recommendation of his men."

The omission of Bernard's name cannot, of course, be used to say that he had no influence. Suger emphasized that the election of Innocent was accepted by the king because of Innocent's personal character, and so the form of the election itself was not decisive. He pointed out that the Roman mob was often a factor in the papal choice, and its choice was rightly to be ignored. Suger implied in a fairly subtle manner that he himself was central in the king's acceptance of Innocent, but his account warns against exaggerating Bernard's influence. Arnold does, however, reveal something else that sheds light on Bernard's presence at Étampes: he is said to have come there in fear and trembling. It was only because he had a vision at night of the united Church that he gained courage. Here as at other crucial moments in his life, as in the early days of Clairvaux, Bernard received some kind of inner light that enabled him to overcome his hesitations. We can at least be certain that it took some courage to accept the rigors of travel. Today the distance by road from Clairvaux to Étampes is about 153 miles. In the twelfth century with inadequate roads, trackless forests, and the danger of robbers, the journey would have been much longer. But Bernard came.

Was he summoned by the king of France, as Arnold claims? Or was it actually a question of the king asking all bishops and abbots to attend? Our sources do not reveal how Bernard's attendance was arranged. But it is clear that once he had been to Étampes, he became one of the champions of Innocent II. The council was a turning point in his life.

Arnold indicates that Bernard accompanied Pope Innocent after Étampes, first to Orléans, and then to Chartres, where they met King Henry I of England. The king was apparently wary about recognizing Innocent, and here Bernard is said to have intervened: "What are you afraid of? . . . Incurring a sin if you obey Innocent?" Bernard asked Henry to think of his many other sins "for which you are answerable to God. Leave this one to me; let this sin be mine." This remarkable assertion, in which Bernard took responsibility for another man's conscience, is found elsewhere in accounts of Bernard. The *Exordium Magnum* tells how Bernard dealt with a brother who was afraid of taking communion. He told the man to go ahead, and any fault or problem the brother thereby incurred with the Lord would be Bernard's problem and not his: "If you have no faith of your own, I order you by virtue of your obedience to receive communion on my faith."

Such anecdotes might perhaps seem late and thus not credible, but the Cistercian storytelling tradition about Bernard is more than hagiographical filling. At Clairvaux stories circulated about Bernard that were not written down until well after his death. But these vignettes point to Bernard's supreme confidence that he was in harmony with God's will and could rightly take other people into his paternal and maternal care.

We cannot take for granted the French king's support of Innocent. Louis VI had only recently, in 1129, backed the canons of Notre Dame in Paris in their opposition to their bishop's reform program. The matter had reached Rome, and Pope Honorius II had tried to reconcile all parties, but without any success. Thus in 1130 the French church was in disarray, and Louis could have chosen to stay out of the disputed papal election. Bernard's intervention may have been significant, although I suspect that it was the powerful Suger in particular, abbot of Saint Denis, the king's closest adviser, who made the difference in the end. As sober an account as the entry for Innocent II in the Catholic Enyclopedia claims that it was "the eloquence of Suger" that swayed the king. Bernard's presence at the Council of Étampes can be looked upon more as a turning point in his own life than as a decisive moment for the Western Church. When he left Étampes, he was on the way to becoming a central contributor not only in the papal schism but also in the governance of the Western Church.

Liège and Clairvaux: Making a Difference

Meanwhile, Innocent remained north of the Alps and met with the German king Lothair at Liège. He tried to use the weak position of the pope to regain the royal right of investiture of newly elected bishops, a matter that for decades had been controversial, but had just been settled in 1122 at a council in Worms. Apparently the Romans, as Arnold calls the papal party, were afraid to make too strong a stand on the matter, but Bernard "put up a strong bulwark against the proposal." Bernard is said to have blocked the king's demand "with astonishing authority."

Once again we are faced with the problem that we have only the *Vita Prima*'s assurance that Bernard made a decisive difference. But here at least we have a letter from Bernard touching on the matter. Bernard expressed his opposition to Lothair's demand: "An angry and avenging king at Liège could not enforce, by means of his barbarous and threatening sword, acceptance of what he claimed, something shocking and irresponsible." This statement belongs to a letter from 1133, thus more than two years after the meeting at Liège in March of 1131. It does not provide proof that Bernard's intervention decided the issue. What matters is that the abbot of Clairvaux, instead of returning to his monastery, had remained with the papal party and was defending its policies. The first medieval reformation of the Church, better known as the Gregorian Reform of the eleventh century, had established that secular authorities no longer could make or unmake bishops and popes. Bernard defended this vital change in the way kings and popes administered their power.

After Liège, Innocent II came to Clairvaux. Arnold could not have been present but perhaps heard of the event from monks who were eyewitnesses. His account emphasizes the poverty of the place, where the pope was greeted by "the poor men of Christ" who carried not "gold-plated gospel books" but "a rugged cross." The church had only "bare walls." The food served for the papal party was "plain bread in place of fine wheaten loaves, herbal tea for sweet wine." I find here an implicit comparison with the sumptuousness of Cluny, where rich food and copious decorations characterized monastic life.

There was an incident, however, when one of the brothers claimed to be Christ himself. Bernard's reaction was to ask everyone to pray for the disturbed man. Arnold called him a "wicked man" who wanted to upset the brothers but did not succeed. In such a situation it was often thought that mental illness was the result of the devil's intervention, but Arnold used the incident to conclude that the brothers henceforth "guarded themselves with greater care." Their numbers increased and so did Clairvaux's possessions:

"so that the monastic way of life in that place spread very nearly throughout the whole of the Western Church." This is quite an assertion, but it shows how Arnold saw the person and initiatives of Bernard as providing a point of departure for the growth not only of Clairvaux but of Cistercian monasticism in general. This claim gains more credibility because Arnold was not a Cistercian.

Can we dismiss Arnold's description of Innocent at Clairvaux as pure exaggeration? Surely the brothers there would have tried to offer their best food to the papal party, even if it was not sumptuous. And clearly the outburst of the mentally ill brother must have embarrassed all who were present. Arnold was a dedicated follower of Bernard, and so there were to be no difficult moments for Clairvaux's abbot. But behind the idealized facade, there was an abbot who influenced his surroundings and made a difference. To this extent Arnold told the truth, even if he was cloaking it in the genre of hagiography.

Taming Aquitaine

Innocent remained in France for the remainder of 1131, and we know that Bernard was with him in Paris on 11 November, the feast of Saint Martin. By the end of March in 1132 Innocent was back in Italy, but in the meantime he apparently had assigned Bernard to deal with the area north of the Alps where allegiance to Anacletus remained steadfast. This was the rich duchy of Aquitaine, which we today call the south of France, but in the twelfth century it was a separate region with its own politics and culture. Apparently Bishop Gerard of Angoulême had been displeased with Innocent's making Bishop Geoffrey of Chartres his legate over France, Burgundy, and Aquitaine. So Gerard went over to Anacletus and succeeded in convincing William X, Count of Poitiers and Duke of Aquitaine, to back Anacletus.

Arnold has a long and careful account of how Bernard, probably at the end of 1134, came to dialogue with Count William. There was a theological discussion about the unity of the Church, ending with Willam's assertion that he would accept Innocent as pope. But he would not reinstate the bishops whom he had forced out of their sees, for he looked upon their behavior as an insult. The debate continued, and then Bernard began to say Mass. The duke remained outside the church, but after the consecration and the kiss of peace had taken place, Bernard took the host and went out to the duke. He lashed out against him for his behavior, and claimed the man was persecuting not only the Church but Christ himself: "Behold the Son of the Virgin comes now before you, he who is the Head and Lord of the Church that you have persecuted." According to Arnold the count collapsed on the spot, "nor could he speak or understand anything." His reaction is described as something like an epileptic seizure: "His saliva dribbled over his beard."

Bernard ordered the count to rise and to speak to the bishop of Poitiers, who was present: "With a kiss of peace join with him in a treaty and restore him to his see." The count obeyed Bernard, approached the bishop, and gave him the kiss of peace. The bishop and his colleagues were given back their sees. Afterwards Bernard "spoke familiarly and kindly with the count and admonished him in a fatherly way." We have seen Bernard acting as both father and mother for his monks, and here he took on a fatherly role toward one of the most powerful lay authorities in Western Europe. He was able to dramatize a situation and use the Mass and the Eucharist as a means to convince a powerful man to drop his resistance to bishops who had defied him and whom he had cast out of his dominions.

If we look at these events from a distance, Bernard was merely asserting what popes and bishops had claimed since the middle years of the eleventh century: no secular power could give them office or take their spiritual power away from them. The first medieval reformation of the Western Church had made it clear that counts, dukes, and kings could not invest bishops with their spiritual functions, nor could they divest them of these functions. Bernard followed a clear pattern, but he did so in a dramatic manner that may have put the fear of God into the count. We can ask whence Bernard received this ability to tackle a difficult political situation and resolve it by means of a striking performance. We simply do not know enough about Bernard's youth and early years, but surely at that time he mastered scholarly discourse with a knightly display of prowess. The result was stunning, and here the account of Arnold seems credible, a reflection on how a charismatic figure could function.

At the same time, however, there remains the pedestrian fact that the performer was not a bishop or a pope. He was the abbot of a monastery that until recently had been quite obscure. Once again we find a contemplative monk taking on the world and becoming very much a part of it. The question remains how Bernard did so and remained faithful to a way of life that emphasized separation from the world.

The confrontation over Aquitaine spanned several years. Bernard wrote, probably in the summer of 1131, to the bishops of Aquitaine and attacked Gerard of Angoulême. This is one of the longest letters in the collection and amounts to a minor treatise on the papacy and the government of the Church. What began as an exposure of Gerard's motives became a much larger consideration on the wiles of ambition, "the mother of hypocrisy," which "prefers to skulk in corners and dark places." Ambition became a kind of greed, and here Bernard returned to Gerard and accused him of consecrating new bishops. Bernard lamented that the scandals "foretold in the Scriptures must come to pass. But woe to the man through whom they come." He made use of canon law: once a bishop was elected, a second one could not be chosen. This is "no election at all." In other words, Gerard had no right to appoint new bishops. Bernard did not directly attack the count himself, who after all was the central person in the redistribution of bishoprics in his domain. Gerard of Angoulême was made into the scoundrel, not the count.

The final sections of the letter assert the legitimacy of Innocent as pope. Bernard named the various monastic orders, including his own Cistercians, which had recognized Innocent, and then asked, "What about the kings and princes of the world?" These too had acclaimed Innocent. Toward the end of the letter Bernard even reviewed the process of election and asserted it was "valid according to the decrees of the Fathers." Innocent had been chosen by "cardinal bishops and priests and deacons," and so Bernard skipped the sore point that the decree of 1059 mentioned only cardinal bishops. The letter as a whole appealed to the bishops of the one area in northern Europe where there still was support for Anacletus. Bernard's tactic was to undermine the legitimacy of Gerard of Angoulême and to emphasize the election of Innocent as being in accord with tradition. He may have been right: it had become traditional for all types of cardinals to participate in papal elections, not just cardinal bishops.

Bernard's drama with Count William did not solve problems concerning William's tendency to regulate the affairs of the Church according to his own wishes. At some point after their meeting Bernard sent off a rather brief communication reminding the count of what they had settled there: "I lately left your presence . . . and determined to do all in my power to help you." Bernard claimed that he had gained from William "an assurance of your peaceful intentions towards the Church." But now William had broken his promises by expelling priests, and so Bernard asked: "Who can have beguiled you to leave so soon the path of salvation and truth?" He warned William that if he did not alter his decisions, he would have to face the wrath of God.

The letter shows that Bernard could continue his policies insisting that William's behavior was harming the Church. It is noteworthy that the abbot did not claim that the count had no right to influence the Church, simply that he was violating his promise to bring peace to it. Bernard can seldom be seen as making bold statements about canon law and the relationship between secular and religious authority, but he was determined to guard the freedom of the Church from lay power. He dedicated himself to seeing that Count William no longer was under the sway of Gerard of Angoulême. But at least according to Arnold of Bonneval, it was only Bernard's personal confrontation with the count that seems to have convinced the man.

In the meantime Clairvaux was sending out monks to establish new monasteries. The year 1132 saw the foundation of four new houses from Clairvaux: Longpont, Vaucelles, Moreruela, and Rievaulx. Longpont is outside of Reims in northeastern France. Vaucelles is in the north of France, while Moreruela is located on the southern side of the Pyrenees in what today is Spain. Bernard had intitially been hesitant about founding monasteries far from Clairvaux, but he seems to have given up his resistance. Also he accepted sending monks to Yorkshire in England. The abbey of Rievaulx was headed by Bernard's former secretary William, so the abbot of Clairvaux, however much he was involved in the politics of the schism, must have been aware of the new foundation. It is likely, however, that Bernard had little to do with the practical matters involved in sending at least twelve monks and an abbot to the new sites and preparing them for habitation. Here as in so much else his function as abbot must have been assumed by others, including the brothers in his biological family who had made Clairvaux their abiding home.

Descent into Italy

Bernard knew that the key to the acceptance of Innocent as pope lay in Italy. Rome itself was partly controlled by the adherents of Anacletus, and they had the support of Count Roger of Sicily. Anacletus in 1130 crowned Roger as king and thus assured his loyalty. Bernard rightly considered Roger to be the main secular impediment to the universal acceptance of Innocent. But first he had to make sure that the powerful cities of the north of Italy backed Innocent. Probably in early 1133, Bernard crossed the Alps and paid a visit to Genoa. We lack a firsthand account of his visit there, but about a year later, he wrote to the people of Genoa and thanked them for their warm reception. What remained, he wrote, was for the people of the city "to continue as you have begun." The letter seems very general and does not make much sense until the final section, where Bernard wrote that the Genoese had received messengers "from Count Roger of Sicily." It is notable that he calls the man count and not king!

Bernard warned the Genoese of "Greeks when they come with gifts," echoing the familiar phrase from Vergil's *Aeneid* (2.49). He asked them to overcome "the Church's enemies and preserve your honor against the

Sicilians." Bernard was clearly preparing for a confrontation with Roger and trying to wean the northern Italian cities away from the count whom Anacletus had made king.

Bernard was encouraging an Italian city to make war against the most powerful political entity in the region, Sicily. He did the same with the people of Pisa. He told them that God had chosen them for a special favor. Pisa had been selected as the papal stronghold. In this situation Bernard saw God's providence, for the Lord had said to Innocent, "Let my home be here and I shall bless it." He asked the Pisans to revere the one "who is your father and the whole world's father." Once again the resident of a monastery based on peace and tranquility was asking the population of a bustling Italian city to prepare themselves for conflict. Innocent had already spent much time in Pisa and considered the city his base in Italy, as long as Rome was too dangerous for him, but Bernard seems to have been encouraging the Pisans to show their support by going to war against Roger of Sicily after making peace with the Genoese.

In late March 1133 peace was concluded between the Genoese and the Pisans. Pope Innocent was joined by the German king Lothair, and the two made for Rome, where on 30 April they were met by Roman nobles. But Anacletus was still safely lodged in Rome's Vatican quarter. Innocent had to accept the fact that Lothair had his own challenges in Germany, to which he wanted to return. On 4 June Innocent crowned Lothair as Roman emperor, thus confirming the agreement made by his predecessor at Worms in 1122 and accepted by Lothair in 1131. The new emperor, dependent on the pope, would respect the limitations on lay investiture of bishops that were the foundation of the first medieval reformation of the Church.

It is likely that during these months Bernard was in Italy with Pope Innocent, but it is impossible to establish a chronology on the basis of Arnold's narrative. His main concern was the miraculous cures now being ascribed to Bernard, but behind these events is the fact that Innocent soon had to leave Rome for a safer place. In the mid-1130s the outcome of the schism was by no means a foregone conclusion, and yet Bernard felt he had to return to his monastery.

Arnold reflected on Bernard's behavior in this period by asserting that he had no ambition for worldly power. He listed the churches that elected him bishop, including the prestigious church of Milan. In a very Cistercian assertion, Arnold claimed that Bernard did not want "the tiara and the ring over the hoe and the mattock." We are reminded here of the Cistercian devotion to cultivating the land. What Arnold does not say is that by refusing to be made bishop, Bernard could maintain his freedom as a kind of roving ambassador of the pope, influencing those who would listen to his pleas and his letters.

I do not think Bernard was cynical. To a large extent he went where he wanted, in the knowledge that his brothers at Clairvaux would take care of the daily running of their monastery. This was a privileged situation, only possible for a man with charism, self-confidence, and the conviction that he was carrying out God's will. Behind this belief was the solid support of his brothers, both the biological ones and those who had come from other families. Bernard could leave his charge to others because he trusted that in his absence the monastery would continue in a manner in harmony with the Rule of Saint Benedict and the Cistercian constitutions.

During these years Bernard was apparently becoming well known in circles far outside monastic ones. Arnold described how when he crossed the Alps, "shepherds and herdsmen and country folk" came to ask for his blessing. When they received it, they returned to their duties "rejoicing that they had seen the holy one of the Lord." As in other references to Bernard as a kind of spiritual star, we can ask if our narrator exaggerated what he had heard. There is no way to check Arnold's information, but it should be seen in the context of an oral society, where stories about Bernard could have been circulating. He was known as a man of God, and so it was worthwhile for anyone, including shepherds and herdsmen, to go out of their way to acquire his blessing.

Back at Clairvaux: The Challenge of Growth

On one of his returns to Clairvaux from Italy, Bernard met some of the brothers outside the monastery. Arnold emphasized that the reception took place in a dignified manner. The brothers "moderated their show of affection so that they might not decrease the maturity of their religious attitude with a semblance of disorder." It was important for Arnold to show that there was no room at Clairvaux for jealousy, envy, or any other kind of evil that he would have ascribed to the devil. His description of how the brothers lived together is evocative of the familiar expression in the Acts of the Apostles (4:32) concerning how the first Christians coexisted in peace and harmony: "They all lived together in free rapport, a harmonious society."

But there were problems, and it was up to the prior of Clairvaux, Geoffrey, and other officers of the monastery to inform Bernard "that the domestic requirements demanded his attention." They told him that Clairvaux had become too crowded. The buildings could not house all the new recruits, and the whole community could hardly fit any longer in the church. The brothers in charge suggested moving the entire monastery to a site farther down the valley, where there would be space not only for the monastic buildings but also "for fields, for farms, for shrubberies, for vineyards."

Bernard's response is given in great detail. He pointed to the fact that the brothers had already expended much labor in constructing their buildings and an aqueduct to bring water to them. If they left these behind, the monks risked that "men of the world" would think of the monks as "fickle and changeable." It was necessary to be sure about the cost of such changes and whether the monastery could shoulder them. Otherwise, the brothers would be like the foolish man who "began to build and was not able to finish" (Lk 14:30).

This is a remarkable passage, for it reveals a fear in Bernard that the monks would be ridiculed for not completing their building project. The abbot was thus concerned with the way the world would look at his monastery, and this worry overcame the need for expansion. The brothers apparently replied by pointing out that God had chosen to continue sending new recruits to the monastery. It was the duty of the brothers to give them a place where they could be housed: "God forbid that on account of our lack of confidence in him about the expenses we should incur his displeasure."

Monasteries in modern times have experienced the kind of expansion that was current at Clairvaux in the 1130s. In the 1940s the Trappist-Cistercian monastery of Gethsemani in Kentucky, partly thanks to its renown from the writings of Thomas Merton, had so many men seeking entrance that they had to be put up in tents in the cloister. Since then, the populations of most contemporary Cistercian monasteries in Europe and the North America have declined in numbers. Some monasteries have even closed, but medieval and modern generations that remembered "the good old days" could see the influx as a sign of God's blessing. This was certainly the case for the twelfth-century brothers of Clairvaux, who did not have Bernard's hesitations about a building program. According to the Vita Prima, Bernard gave way not so much because of material need but because he was impressed by the "faith and charity" of his brothers.

This is not the only time Bernard is said to have respected criticism and concerns expressed by his monastic community. We have the incident he himself narrated in a letter mentioned above, where he had dismissed a monk named Bartholomew, who then took refuge on one of Clairvaux's granges. In the meantime the brothers back at Clairvaux told their abbot that he had acted in a vindictive manner and had failed to give the brother an opportunity to account for his actions. Bernard came to realize that the brothers were right, just as he came to accept that it was necessary to follow the community's consensus and engage in an expensive building program at Clairvaux.

Arnold not surprisingly demonstrated that Bernard's decision was the right one. The news of Clairvaux's expansion brought immediate support from individuals such as Count Theobald of Champagne, as well as bishops. The brothers themselves took on tasks such as cutting down trees, building walls, and constructing canals: "The walls were soon built with incredible speed." The description rings true in relation to the Cistercian love of place and of the land. What was missing was the consent of the abbot, but once this was obtained, then anything was possible, in harmonious agreement between monastery and benefactors. Arnold must have been dependent once again on the information provided by the brothers of Clairvaux themselves. His account reflects the challenge Bernard faced in spending so much time away from his monastery and having to count on its members to tell him what they needed.

A Double Election and Two Murders

Bernard, meanwhile, had to deal with a situation in France that was directly linked to the papal schism and which indicates how the papal controversy affected a church far from Rome. The rich see of Tours became vacant in 1133 upon the death of its bishop, Hildebert. Two men were elected in his place; one, Philip, was a highly respected monk and a relative of a former bishop. He was not yet ordained as a priest, but Anacletus took care of his ordination and consecrated Philip bishop. Anacletus thus gained a foothold in a central French diocese. When Bernard got the news, he wrote Philip what appears to be an intensely personal letter, but one that also was a declaration to the world that the man had gained his position without a canonical election: "You are the cause of much sorrow to me, dear Philip." Bernard spoke of the hope that not only he but all of France had invested in the young man, but now this had been disappointed. The letter, not surprisingly, did not change the bishop-elect's mind.

Subsequently Bernard wrote to Pope Innocent and described the situation. He reviewed the arguments for and against the election of the other candidate, Hugh. Bernard referred to a letter from Innocent giving the abbot the prerogative to settle the matter, and so nullified Philip's election "on papal authority." There were still canonical problems with Hugh's status, but Bernard left them to the care of Innocent. The abbot of Clairvaux described the case in terms of the Church's "ordeal" and said he refused to accept "the delays of persons whose concern was only for their own interests and not for the situation of the Church." The language here does not make it clear whether Bernard was referring to the Church as a whole or the church of Tours. In any case Bernard functioned as a papal envoy to whom the matter had been entrusted. He had presided at least one meeting, and again we have to imagine how it was for the abbot of a contemplative monastery to take on a function that had nothing to do with the office to which he had been elected.

The matter dragged on, but Anacletus rewarded Philip for his loyalty by making him bishop of Taranto in Apulia, a post from which he was degraded after the victory of Innocent. Surprisingly, Philip eventually came to Clairvaux and was accepted there as a simple monk and deacon. In a remarkable letter Pope Eugenius, probably written in 1150, Bernard asked the pope to extend forgiveness to the man: "Our Philip has raised himself up and now been cast down." Bernard wrote that his request was not his alone: all the brothers of Clairvaux joined him: "Our petition is not for the individual but for our Order." Some kind of dispensation must have been given, for we know that when Bernard died a few years later, Philip was his prior.

Bernard could thus not limit himself to dealing with the repercussions of the papal schism. He had become a papal envoy, and he had to act as such in dealing with the murder of Thomas, the prior of Saint Victor in Paris. The canons had been reformed a few years earlier, in connection with a major controversy at Notre Dame. On a journey with the bishop of Paris, Stephen of Senlis, Thomas was murdered and died in the bishop's arms. The perpetrator was Theobald, nephew of the archdeacon of Paris, whose main interest seems to have been to accrue as much wealth as possible. Thomas had been his enemy. Bernard, probably in August 1133, wrote about the incident to Pope Innocent. He explained the deed solely on the basis of the archdeacon's greed and "illegal exactions." To Bernard, Theobald represented the worst elements in the Church: "Could any abuse be worse or anything more unfitting for the Church than someone's claim to church offices on the basis of pure force and not because of holy life?"

The bishop of Paris had to take refuge at Clairvaux, and from there he wrote to the apostolic legate, Geoffrey, bishop of Chartres, giving a full account of the events. If Bernard was at Clairvaux at this time, he must have gotten a graphic impression of the murder. His letter to Innocent is a passionate appeal against those who use violence to obtain their goals. He had to deal with a second murder, that of Archibald, subdean of Orléans. The office of archdeacon at Orléans had been taken over by a certain John, who was opposed by Archibald, who was subsequently killed. This happened in 1133, but it seems to have been some months before the pope got news of the act. Bernard called upon him to punish the offenders: "This blood makes its cry . . . so powerful that it can shake heaven's own palace." Bernard saw the two murders as one heinous act and demanded that the two perpetrators, John and Theobald, be punished. If such men were allowed to go free, then other criminals would find refuge with their "friends bearing weapons."

The matter dragged on, and it looked as if nothing would be done, in spite of the holding of a council at the Benedictine abbey of Jouarre. But Bernard would not let the pope forget the matter. In 1134 he wrote to Pope Innocent for the church of Orléans, speaking of its wretched state: "How long will it take for you to take care of the children and their mother, who weep in your wake and ask for mercy?" Bernard implicitly criticized the pope's tardiness in dealing with the question. Thus "they who so patiently have endured, because they trusted in you, in the end will have no reason to regret the patience they have shown."

In these cases a number of interests were involved: local churches, the French king, the bishop of Paris, the abbot of Cluny Peter the Venerable, and Bernard himself. Bernard's strongly worded statements of right and wrong, his claim that he was defending the integrity of the Church and the churches, and his very personal appeals to Innocent all indicate that the ecclesiastical world of the 1130s was a complex one, where no one authority could be decisive. It is not at all clear what happened to John and the murderers of Archibald of Orléans, only that Bernard found it necessary to take up the matter and to use his network to influence the outcome. But the silence in the sources may indicate that Bernard did not achieve his goal.

Peace in Bamberg and Riots in Milan

Bernard's unofficial position as Pope Innocent's champion summoned him to new duties. On 17 March 1135 he participated in the Diet of Bamberg. Our information is provided not by Arnold but by Geoffrey of Auxerre in the fourth book of the *Vita Prima*, perhaps because events in Germany did not interest Arnold. Geoffrey explained that Bernard's purpose was to restore peace between King Lothair and the nephews of the former emperor, Henry. Bernard is said to have greeted the representative of the archbishop of Mainz by telling him that "another lord" (Our Lord) had sent him. In the ensuing conversation, it emerged that the man would become a monk. Geoffrey seems to have included the anecdote not because of interest in Bernard's political mission in Germany but to frame a spectacular conversion to the Cistercian Order. The next chapter concerns the brother of the French king, Henry, who became a monk of Clairvaux. Geoffrey remembered such conversions with greater interest than the complicated political events surrounding the schism, which he mainly left to Arnold.

Bernard may have gone directly from Germany to Italy for his second sojourn there. In November 1134 Pope Innocent had issued a bull convoking the Council of Pisa, which would take place 30 May–6 June 1135. The king of France refused to allow his bishops to attend and claimed that they would not be able to stand the heat! Bernard naturally saw through this pretext but instead of challenging the king's motives tried to take the high ground and wrote diplomatically, claiming that kingdoms would only endure if they were governed in accord with "God's ordinances and decisions." He insisted that nothing the council would do would endanger royal interests. Indeed, the council was bound to acknowledge the fact that Louis was the first monarch to recognize Innocent as the true pope. In Bernard's words, "There the gratitude owed you will be shown by all who have gathered together." He added that the council fathers would be offering prayers for the king.

The first part of the letter is unusual for Bernard, for he did his best to flatter. In the second section he came close to jesting with Louis: "You claim that the heat will be too great. But we are not made of ice!" Bernard went on to promise, however, that if the king considered some of the pope's decrees too harsh, then his representatives at the council would do their utmost to have them altered or removed "in accord with your honor." Bernard promised he himself would contribute to this effort.

As so often, Bernard was full of surprises. Even though he was a champion of ecclesiastical independence, he was offering the French king a special position in his relation with the Church. We might consider such an exchange the beginning of the Gallican Church, which in coming centuries distanced itself from the Roman Church. Bernard was at a crossroads, and he accepted the need to give the king influence, in return for his allowing the bishops to travel to Pisa and support Innocent.

The king apparently relented, and the Council of Pisa went ahead. According to Arnold, Bernard was a central figure: "Everyone showed him great reverence." There was apparently a surge of popular interest in seeing Bernard, so the doors of the council chamber had to be guarded. Unfortunately Arnold did not concern himself with describing what the council actually agreed on, only "the excommunciation of Peter Leonis and the definitive rejection of his actions." Once again we are reminded that we are dealing with hagiography, whose purpose was to elevate Bernard to sainthood, not to tell the complex story of his involvement in the papal schism.

This purpose is apparent in Arnold's florid description of how Bernard was received after the council, when he was sent to Milan. His arrival was apparently anticipated with great enthusiasm. People left their homes "and went out from the city. . . . They received the man of God with incredible reverence. . . . The whole world kissed his feet. . . . They plucked bits from his clothing when they could." Bernard had become a living relic, a source of spiritual power for miraculous cures. Such figures were not uncommon in medieval Europe. Once again we find that a man who had dedicated himself to separation from the world had become a center of the world's attention and even devotion.

Arnold's description of Bernard's entrance into Milan is more than a celebration of his appeal. He saw in Bernard "a new form of legate" who did not follow "the law of the Roman court" but instead "the divine law of God." For Arnold, Bernard wrote letters "in the blood of Christ." A number of chapters describe the healings Bernard is said to have performed, and in this way we almost completely lose sight of his papal mission in Milan.

Fortunately we have letters Bernard sent to the people of Milan. In the first he rejoiced in the devotion of the city, which had rejected schism and returned to the Church. Bernard wrote that he was hurrying to the council but would visit Milan on his way back. This must be the Council of Pisa, and so Arnold must have reversed the chronology in putting the council before Bernard's first visit to Milan. In any case the archbishop of Milan, Anselm, had been a firm supporter of Anacletus. The canon Landulf of Saint Paul wrote in his "History of Milan" how the archbishop was expelled and the populace accepted Lothair as emperor: "For this the pope had a suitable angel, as Bernard abbot of Clairvaux was." Here we have a rare reference to Bernard outside of standard twelfth-century Cistercian literature. Landulf had apparently been won over to the abbot and was willing to consider Bernard a papal messenger with the legitimacy of an angel!

Milan was the jewel in the crown of northern Italian cities, probably the largest and politically the most influential. Thus it was an absolute necessity for Innocent to have its allegiance, but the question of the papacy had been complicated by rivalry between Conrad and Lothair over the kingship of Germany. The archbishop had sided with Conrad, but now the population had gone over to Lothair. With Archbishop Anselm out of the picture, Bernard could inspire a surge of reform that led to a cleanup of the city's wealth. As Landulf wrote, "Not only the men but also the women had their hair cut as tonsures, and they were dressed in hair cloth and the poorest woolens." The transformation of the wealthy Milanese to what sounds like Cistercians in the cheapest clothes can remind us of what happened much later in Florence under Savanarola. Bernard seems to have mesmerized the population and initiated not only sympathy for Innocent but at least a temporary transformation of everyday life for the privileged.

Bernard's reception at Milan resulted in the appearance of a group of men who wanted to enter the Cistercian Order. In April or May 1135 he wrote them a brief letter of encouragement: "If heaven rejoices when one sinner repents, all the greater will the joy be when so many men are converted from a city that is as great as yours is." He promised to visit the brothers on his way back from Pisa. We know that on 22 July 1135 the monastery of Chiaravalle-Milanese was founded, probably with these brothers. Bernard was not present, but he had certainly inspired what came to pass that summer outside of Milan.

The great city continued to occupy Bernard's thoughts, for probably in the summer or early autumn of 1135 he wrote to its people and warned them that the Roman Church was long suffering but also able to punish: "I provide necessary advice to you, worth noting, that you should not tax her patience or you will come to experience her power." Bernard was rarely so direct in threatening the exercise of ecclesiastical sanctions. Surely he must have been thinking about the possibility of an interdict to force the Milanese to return to their allegiance to Innocent as pope. For those who claimed that it was sufficient to show reverence to Innocent, Bernard required "reverence without any reserve." The pope was endowed, he insisted, with fullness of authority over all the world's churches. The Latin term here is *plenitudo potestatis*, which in the coming centuries would form the basis of what has been called "the papal monarchy." Bernard made it clear that the pope could establish new bishops where there were none. He could remove existing bishops or raise them to the status of archbishops. The pope could summon the clergy from anywhere on earth, "not once or twice but just as often" as he chose. Bernard asked the Milanese what benefit they gained from their recent opposition to Innocent. The pope could cut off the church of Milan's many privileges and prerogatives. He did not, but now "if you again fail to comply, then there is no one who could keep you from far greater punishments." Bernard warned against listening to those who might encourage the Milanese to obey the Roman Church in some respects but not others. They should know better, for they had already once felt the duress of the Church. So the Milanese must do their best to be in harmony with their "mistress and mother" and do what they could to please her.

I find this letter unusual for Bernard because it was rare for him to appeal to the naked exercise of power. For him papal power was spiritual, but time and again in these lines he was referring to the canonical authority that subjected everyone to the decisions of the pope. It should be remembered that papal plenitude of power was not a given fact in the twelfth century. Certainly popes since Gregory VII (1073–85) had done their best to assert an unrestricted power given by Christ to Peter and his successors to rule the Church. But for many bishops and theologians, there were clear limitations, and Bernard's claim that the pope could do what he wanted in making or unmaking bishops was not universally accepted. It was only with the papacy of Innocent III at the end of this century that this assertion became more fact than claim.

Bernard must have found that in spite of his arguments about papal power, the northern Italian cities persisted in their own policies. Probably in September 1135 he wrote to Pope Innocent that there was opposition to him in the city of Cremona, while at the same time the Milanese were going their own way. Thus it was a consolation to Bernard to have received a letter from Innocent that told of the success Innocent was having in furthering his cause. The letter's conclusion, however, gave reason for concern. Bernard mentioned the bishop who had been transferred to the see of Milan. Innocent apparently was dissatisfied with him and perhaps even was threatening to remove him. Bernard saw such a move as uncalled-for. The new bishop's situation should be considered: "He has problems everywhere." The man was loyal to the pope, and now Bernard asked Innocent "to show consideration for your very loyal servant." He encouraged Innocent to remember the Gospel story of the fig tree that for three years did not bear any fruit (Lk 13:6–9). The Lord then waited three years, while Innocent apparently would not wait three months for the bishop of Milan. The pope was already getting the axe ready to cut down the tree. But Bernard encouraged the pope to let the bishop have the rest of the year to cultivate Milan's "sterile ground," to fertilize it with his tears, and to make his church bring forth fruit.

The apparent impatience of Pope Innocent and his threat to remove the new bishop provide another dimension in Bernard's understanding of the fullness of papal power. Later when the schism was over and Innocent in full control, he called a council, held at the Lateran basilica and thus known as the Second Lateran Council (1139). Here the pope made it clear that there would be no forgiveness for those who had opposed him. Their punishments would be permanent, and hardly any of the clergy would be reinstated in their former positions. The final canon of the council (30) stated: "All ordinations made by Peter Leone and other schismatics and heretics we withdraw and consider to be null and void." Bernard did not favor such intransigence. This letter to Innocent is a harbinger of the distance that would develop between the two figures: Bernard did not consider his enemies as permanent, while

Innocent did. Bernard advocated patience, while Innocent could not wait, as it were, for the fig tree to bear fruit.

Bernard chose not to be vindictive, as can be seen from a letter to Lothair's wife, Richenza, addressed as the empress of Rome and probably from the summer of 1135. As in several other letters from this period, Bernard dealt with the Milanese. In accord with the emperor's instructions, they were not to be received back into the pope's favor until they had disowned Lothair's rival, Conrad. Bernard thanked God, who had overcome Lothair's and Richenza's enemies without there being a war. But now he asked that the people who had opposed Lothair be treated with leniency "so that they do not come to regret that they accepted good advice." Bernard warned the empress (and thus her husband) that it would be problematic if those who had worked for their interests were shamed. This would be the case if the victors turned out to be unforgiving and thus disappointed the Milanese.

This letter can be looked upon as a parallel statement to the one sent to Innocent. In both cases Bernard recommended clemency, and it is clear he feared rigorism and vindictiveness. He did not seem to object to the fact that the fate of the Roman Empire (Germany) and that of the papacy (Rome) had become intertwined. He looked upon Lothair as a necessary ally for Innocent, especially in the forthcoming struggle with Roger of Sicily. Thus Bernard had become a political schemer, but at least on the surface of his writings, there remained a quality of humility and even gentleness. However much he was willing to assert papal plenitude of power, he could still remind the pope to forgive and forget those who had rebelled against him. Bernard was by no means a simple human being, but the message of the Gospel about loving one's enemies may well have influenced the way he looked upon the world and expressed himself.

An Expanding Order: Yorkshire and Poitou

Bernard was so occupied with the papal schism that he seems not always to have participated in the founding of new daughters of Clairvaux. But he did so in 1132 in connection with the establishment of a new monastery in England's Yorkshire, Rievaulx. In order to show his support for the foundation, Bernard wrote to King Henry I and told him he was sending him men "from my army" who would reclaim land as "the Lord's booty." The Latin word is *praeda*, which can mean "property taken in war," and so the new monastery was looked upon as a conquest for God. The letter's opening sentence is thus an indication of how Bernard could convert the language of feudal society into a celebration of the Cistercian Order in expanding

God's realm. Bernard may have used military language because he believed it would impress the king (or those around Henry who could read Latin). He called the founders the Lord's vassals and assured Henry that in helping them he would secure his own life and make possible "a good and peaceful end."

In the Latin edition of Bernard's letters, this letter takes up only eight lines, but it expresses a world of meaning in conveying the Cistercian way of life in feudal terms. Bernard was preparing the way for a new foundation whose immediate founder was the Norman lord Walter Espec. His castle lay a few miles from the site of the new abbey. The first abbot was William, who had been one of Bernard's secretaries, and so Bernard was parting with a trusted helper. A later abbot became much better known, Aelred (1147–67), the exponent of spiritual friendship in the monastic life. Today the visitor can lose herself in the elegant ruins of the early Gothic church, the heritage of Aelred and his friends.

Bernard did not have to expend too much energy in making Rievaulx happen. The case was quite different for another Yorkshire Cistercian foundation from this period, Fountains. A group of monks at the Benedictine house of Saint Mary's in York decided that they wanted to live the Rule of Saint Benedict more strictly. They asked their abbot, Geoffrey, for reforms, but they did not get a clear answer. Eventually the reform party asked if its adherents could live elsewhere, in accord with their ideals. The abbot refused to give permission. The prior, Richard, appealed to the archbishop of York, Thurstan, who called for a meeting with the parties involved. The abbot said he could not act on the matter without the consent of the Chapter. When the archbishop appeared at the monastery and asked to confer with the Chapter, he was refused entrance. There was a fracas, and the archbishop placed an interdict on the abbey. Richard and his allies had to seek the protection of the archbishop, in order to avoid being put into the monastery's prison.

At this point Archbishop Thurstan took the reforming party into his care. It was October 1132, and now Abbot Geoffrey appealed to Bernard for his advice. Bernard answered that it was not on account of his own encouragement or advice that the monks had left their monastery in York. He admitted that it was difficult for him to avoid offending the abbot, but he had to turn to the maxim of Gregory the Great in his *Pastoral Care*, that the second-best choice is not lawful for the one who has chosen what is best. In other words, the brothers in question had chosen the best way of life, for it was stricter than their original one. Once they did so, they were obliged to maintain it, and it would be wrong for them to return to what was easier. Bernard claimed that the result was not his decision, for it was up to the brothers themselves to decide. He warned the abbot against trying to stop the brothers from making their choice. "Instead," he said, "you ought to be proud about what your sons have achieved, for as it is written, a father takes pride in a wise son."

This was a kind but firm response to the question of how to deal with a breakaway group of brothers who by Christmas of 1132 were established on the archbishop's own land outside of York. Richard became the first abbot, and soon the monks were seeking affiliation with the Cistercian Order. Bernard's response to the abbot of Saint Mary's at York was diplomatic but left no room for doubt: he did not give the abbot what he wanted, an assurance that he would not support the renegade brothers' establishment of their own monastery. Abbot Geoffrey was not satisfied with the response, for the following year, 1133, Bernard felt obliged to compose a much longer letter. In its opening he expressed an inability to respond to all of the York abbot's concerns. But in the letter's second section he made clear his stand: it should not be a problem if someone atttempts "to keep the Creator's laws in a stricter manner." Bernard encouraged the abbot not only to let go of the brothers who had broken away but also to ensure that those who remained would observe the Rule more strictly! He mentioned specifically some monks who had left the York community but then returned to it. For Bernard there were different types of scandalous behavior, but brothers who returned to their original communities should not be called apostates. Here as in much else in his life Bernard showed a surprising flexibility and acceptance of human weakness: "It is not up to me to condemn these brothers." God knows who belongs to him. What mattered was to move from what is good to something better, as the original group had done.

Abbot Geoffrey had apparently written to Bernard asking him to assent to an excommunication of the renegade brothers, but the abbot of Clairvaux flatly declined cooperation with any such procedure. The last sentence of the letter points out that "the law cannot judge a man unless he is giving a hearing," and one cannot excommunicate a person who is absent. Bernard refused to cooperate with Geoffrey, but his refusal is politely worded and gentle in tone, even though he apparently in no manner gave way to Geoffrey's request that the brothers be disciplined.

Probably at about the same time, Bernard wrote a much shorter letter to Thurstan, archbishop of York. Here his gratefulness and enthusiasm knew no bounds. He did not specifically mention Thurstan's support for the new monastery, but this was clearly in his mind toward the end of the missive, where he praised Thurstan for "taking care of our temporal needs." As in the letter to Abbot Geoffrey, Bernard was diplomatic and did not criticize the original monastery at York nor extol the virtues of the new foundation. But his intentions are much clearer in the following letter, where he addressed the abbot of the new monastery, Fountains, and its brothers. Bernard wrote that he had heard "great things" about their success in moving "from what was good to what is better." As so often in Bernard's writings on the monastic life, he made the point that it is acceptable for a monk or a monastery to leave behind a good way of life for one that is better, meaning stricter. Bernard congratulated the brothers in what they so far had achieved, for in their observance of the Rule they had decided not "to stay at a level below that which it requires." Here he made clear what he only implied in his letters to Abbot Geoffrey, that the brothers who had broken away from Saint Mary's York were looking for a stricter and better way of life. They were doing precisely what the first brothers of Cîteaux had done in leaving Molesme. The Cistercians had begun with a rebellion, and Bernard was justifying such behavior.

Bernard ended this letter by apologizing for not writing more. He appealed to "the demands of my daily duties," as well as to the fact that the messenger was waiting for his reply. We have no way of knowing if there was in fact an impatient messenger, but it does seem more than possible that Bernard did not have the time he wished to address the brothers of Fountains. He was, after all, in the midst of his campaign for Pope Innocent and may have written from outside of Clairvaux. But he did not leave matters as they were. Probably in 1134 he wrote to King David of Scotland on behalf of the monastery of Fountains. He spoke of David's fame and expressed a desire one day to see him in the flesh. The monks of Rievaulx had been the first to benefit from the king's attention: "I am as grateful to you as if you personally had bestowed your favors on me." Now King David was helping out the brothers of Fountains, who had come to "a place of isolation" from York, where "the monastic way of life was limited." Here Bernard allowed himself to criticize the monastery of Saint Mary's York openly. The brothers of Fountains had to live through many trials and attacks. If they had belonged to the world, then the world would have favored them. But since they were not in the world, the world persecuted them. Bernard ended the letter by asking the good king "to give them comfort because they are poor."

This letter was an appeal for material support, while at the same time it praised the spiritual status of the brothers of Fountains. If we look at the correspondence from Bernard concerning Fountains as a whole, we find different types of letters: diplomatic missives to the abbot of York, letters of encouragement to the brothers of Fountains, and requests for material aid to the Scottish king. Such letters make it clear that in the first half of the 1130s Bernard was doing more than dealing with the papal schism. He was shepherding the flocks of new foundations and benefiting from the fact that Cistercian monasticism was generally looked upon as stricter and thus superior to the conventional Benedictine way of life. In the case of Fountains, there was a reform group prior to the monastery's associating itself with the Cistercian Order. Bernard seems to have done his best to make it appear that he was not on the lookout to grab wayward monks and expand his Order with them. But his cautious inspiration was much more effective than outright criticism of the old monasticism.

Sometimes Clairvaux itself would send out a colony of monks to establish a new foundation. This was necessary in order to keep numbers down in the mother house, which, as we have seen, was barely able to house all those who came to her. In 1135 a monastery known as La Grâce-Dieu was founded from Clairvaux in the Poitou. Not long after its establishment, Bernard wrote a letter of just a few lines that confirmed his bonds with the brothers. He wanted to see them in their new home and to hear them singing the office. He had already been with them in his imagination, but later he would come to them in the flesh, "if the Lord ever gives me back the strength I once had." Meanwhile he encouraged the brothers to continue the life they were leading.

There is nothing original in these phrases, but for brothers facing the challenges of a new place and probably missing their home monastery, Bernard's words would be read again and again as his guarantee that they were on the right track. So far as I can tell, he was never able to come to them, but the brothers had his letter and its words of consolation. Presumably there were many other letters from Bernard that have not been preserved and which expressed similar affection: the desire to be physically present with brothers who had been sent out and the spiritual union that came instead. As Bernard moved across Europe he must have carried with him concerns about all the new foundations either coming from Clairvaux or handing themselves over to Clairvaux. He was part of much more than Clairvaux, but it was here he had his home, also in the years when he must have slept under many different roofs.

Preaching with the Milk of Love

Bernard returned for a time to Clairvaux from Italy in the autumn of 1135, and at the beginning of Advent, he gave the first of what turned into a series of eighty-six sermons based on the Song of Songs, the book of the Jewish Bible that celebrates passionate love. Like other readers since the time of Origen, Bernard interpreted the Song's language in spiritual terms, but his sermons show that he was keenly aware of its sensual vocabulary, and not afraid to make use of it. In what follows here I will try to summarize the first Sermon as indicative of how he proceeded. It is clear that the text as we have it is not what Bernard said to his monks. The written language is so sophisticated that it would have been impossible for the brothers to follow the thread of his thought. It is likely that Bernard first gave a sermon in chapter and then at a later point wrote it up. Eventually the sermons were copied and transmitted to other monasteries, and they quickly became celebrated as outstanding statements of Christian spiritual life. Bernard must have worked hard on them, and his purpose was not to provide a full commentary on the text of all the chapters of the Song but to use its language as a point of departure for a discourse about love, yearning, and the desire of the soul for God. There could also be reflections on the Church as the bride of Christ, as well as praise of the union and harmony that could lead the monk through this life to the next one.

Bernard began the first Sermon by telling the brothers that he was addressing them in a different manner than he would "people in the world." He would follow Saint Paul in giving such people milk to drink "rather than solid food." The monks, however, would get something more substantial. The bread that Bernard gave his monks was that of the Song of Songs: "Let us bring it forth then if you please, and break it." The brothers had received two loaves: first, the book of Ecclesiastes, warning against "the false promises of this world," and then the book of Proverbs, giving them maxims for their conduct. Now they could receive the third loaf, which must be the Song of Songs. This required consumption of the first two loaves, which guarded against "misguided love of the world and an excessive love of self."

Once the attractions of the world have been put aside, it is possible "to study spiritual doctrines." Here it is necessary to divide the loaf, but this is something that Bernard could not do. He described himself as "one of the seekers, one who begs along with you for the food of my soul." It is God alone who can break the bread. And it is God he asked in the next paragraph to explain the first line of the Song, "Let him kiss me with the kiss of his mouth." Bernard wondered why the speaker used the intimate term "with the kiss of his mouth." The reader was thus inspired to seek "what lies hidden."

At this point Bernard considered the meaning of the book's title, the Song of Songs, a title that he found to be unique. He was certain that God himself "inspired these songs of his," which celebrate Christ and his Church, holy love and "the sacrament of endless union with God." Bernard calls the text a "nuptial song," but there is no doubt from the very beginning that he is describing a spiritual marriage.

Bernard then addressed the brothers and asked them to consider their own experience (*experientiam tuam*), which had shown them how their faith wins out over the world. In celebrating this victory, they can sing a new song for God's "gracious renewal of your life." When a brother finds that a dark and difficult passage in Scripture "becomes bright with meaning for you," then he can make a song of joy and praise. In the brothers' daily conflicts with the world, the flesh, and the devil, they can learn that our lives on earth consist in endless warfare. For the victories to be won, songs need be sung.

But beyond these songs is the Song of Songs. Only "the touch of the Spirit can inspire a song like this," and only experience can learn what it is. The English translation interprets the word *addisco* as "unfold its meaning." But the main point here is that personal experience is essential in order to fathom the visitation of the Spirit that can come, for example, from the text's inspiration. This sentence is perhaps the key to all eighty-six sermons: "The touch of the Spirit teaches" and "personal experience informs." The term *experientia* appears fairly often in Bernard's writings. Sermon 3 opens with the declaration "Today we read in the book of experience." Each brother was asked to be personally aware of what Bernard told him. Experience in Bernard has nothing to do with the romantic idea of the individual's unique-ness. He appealed instead to the person's ability to penetrate the depths of his own being in order to discover the imprint of God. We are close here to the world of Augustine of Hippo's "If I know myself, I will know you [God]." In Bernard's context the individual soul is united to those of his brothers in making use of the Song of Songs as a way of reaching out for the divine touch or its anointing.

Bernard ended the first Sermon on the Song of Songs by reminding his monks once again that what he offered was not for novices or anyone else who recently had left the world. He was addressing those who through study and discipline were ready "for nuptial union with the divine partner." He would promise to describe such matters in what was to come, but for the time being the tasks of the day called upon the monks. This may well be a rhetorical flourish, but I think Bernard wanted to remind his audience, both at Clairvaux and at other monasteries, that such spiritual conferences had to be put into the context of the monastic day. It was the abbot's duty to spare his monks endless sermons, just as it was the monks' obligation to listen to what their abbot could tell them. When the first Sermon on the Song of Songs actually was given during Advent 1135, Bernard may indeed have ended it in this manner, so the day's work could be done. Afterwards he kept this ending, to remind his audience that monks do not just sit and listen. They also attend to the practical side of their vocations.

I could continue this review and summary of these Sermons on the Song of Songs, but this introduction is sufficient to provide a sense of how Bernard sought to convey to his monks the meaning of the mystical life. Bernard revealed his identity in such sermons. [For such sermons as sources for Bernard as a person, see question 13 in the Fifteen Questions about Bernard: The Background for My Portrait section.] He was confident that his monks would be able to digest the solid food he was giving them and use their personal experience to open themselves to the inspiration of the Holy Spirit. His expectations were high, and he trusted the impulses and yearnings he found within himself and within his monks.

Toward the end of his life, in Sermon 83.1, Bernard opened up the perspective he provided in these sermons and claimed that every human person could benefit from his insights: "Every soul, I say, standing thus under condemnation and without hope, has the power to turn and find it can not only breathe the fresh air of the hope of pardon and mercy, but also dare to aspire to the nuptials of the Word." Bernard thus departed from his early assertion that his sermons were suitable only for a monastic audience, and the response he gained after his death confirmed the relevance of these sermons, for they were soon translated into French. However much Bernard lived in what seems like an exclusively monastic world, he was able on occasion to emerge and to convey his thoughts to a much larger audience. This ability is most apparent in his crusade preaching, but here, on the threshold of eternity, Bernard invited every Christian "to the nuptials of the Word."

These sermons, continuing right up to the time of Bernard's death in 1153, indicate that the abbot of Clairvaux was able, amid his political involvements, to formulate ongoing contemplative experience. He was, of course, a writer and needed to express himself. During the first half of the 1130s, however, he apparently only wrote letters. But now he put aside time to read in the book of his own experience and use the Song of Songs as a way of addressing divine love and its embrace of the human person.

Bernard was no Pelagian and did not imagine that God comes to the individual because he conjures him by fasting and prayers. In the sermons he spoke of the divine presence as coming unexpectedly. But Bernard was confident that a loving God would embrace the human person as the groom does the bride in the Song. He never lost sight of this hope, and this hope may surprise a modern observer, for whom disillusionment and even cynicism seem to be the end of many human commitments. Bernard continued to go where he was called, but always returned to his community at Clairvaux. He certainly got tired, and his perennial stomach problems continued. At the same time his reputation meant that in Milan and other Italian cities he was besieged by sick people more or less demanding miraculous cures.

What was it like to be Bernard? The question defies answering, even though we know so much about his movements and can follow his train of thought in his writings. It would be correct to categorize him as mystic, church politician, founder of monasteries. But all these titles fail to capture the phenomenon of Bernard, and the word "saint" hardly begins to match his complicated life. Perhaps the best that could be said is that Bernard in these sermons and in consciousness waited for the coming of the Word of God into his mind and heart. Time and again he experienced this advent, and so he could continue his restless existence. As he wrote for his monks in Sermon 74.5,

> I admit that the Word has also come to me . . . and has come many times. But although he has come to me, I have never been conscious of the moment of his coming. I perceived his presence. I remembered afterwards that he had been with me.

Bernard here allowed his monks to peer into his inner life. The abbot who so often was absent now in his presence in his monastery gave himself the opportunity to speak of what he perceived in his inmost being. By so doing he handed over to his monks in his Sermons on the Song of Songs one of the most transformative expressions of Christian spirituality. But soon after preaching his first Sermon on the Song of Songs, Bernard left his monks at Clairvaux and returned to the highways and byways of Europe in his attempt to resolve the papal schism.

CHAPTER 7

Victory and Defeat: A Conflicted Church, 1136–1140

A Third Mission in Italy (1136–1137)

The autumn and early winter of 1135–36 provided sufficient time for Bernard to give his first sermons on the Song of Songs at Clairvaux and also to familiarize himself and come to terms with the brothers' ambitious building program. But just when he may have felt he had returned to the routine of monastic life, he was called back to Italy. In February he probably crossed the Alps, though it is possible he sailed on the Mediterranean. His companion now as previously was his brother Gerard, Clairvaux's capable cellarer whom Bernard felt he needed at his side rather than leaving him behind to deal with the material affairs of the monastery.

In April an imperial army was marching toward Rome. The German king Lothair had been crowned Holy Roman Emperor in Rome in 1133 and now was demonstrating his support for Pope Innocent II against his rival, Anacletus. Sometime before the middle of 1136 Bernard wrote to Lothair and reminded him of what he owed the Church, from whose support Lothair was benefiting. Thanks to God's help, Lothair was experiencing an increase in power. Therefore his enemies should be terrified at the prospect of Lothair opposing them.

Bernard admitted that it was not his duty to encourage a worldly sovereign to go into battle, "but I tell you, with no hesitation, that it is the duty of someone who is the Church's friend to preserve her from the madness of those in schism." Lothair in Bernard's eyes thus had two enemies to defeat: first, the king of Sicily, Roger, whom Bernard called a usurper; and, second, Anacletus, the "person of Jewish race who has taken for himself the papacy." The fact that Anacletus's grandfather had converted to Christianity from Judaism gave Bernard and other advocates of Innocent a point in their propaganda against the antipope. Later in life, as we shall see, Bernard did his best to defend the Jewish people of the Rhineland against the fanaticism that came with the Second Crusade. But in opposing Anacletus, he unfairly suggested that someone of Jewish ancestry could not possibly occupy the see of Saint Peter without doing injury to it.

This remarkable letter has two themes in its first section: it was the duty of the emperor to remove the antipope, and it was in the emperor's interest to defeat anyone who elevated himself to king of Sicily. On this second theme Bernard more or less told Lothair how he should act as a secular ruler. Sicily had previously had a count, but now Roger had made himself king, and Bernard pointed out that such a title threatened the position of the German king and Holy Roman Emperor. Bernard allowed himself to define right and wrong in the lay world. His perspective is evidenced in the last section of the letter, which specifies his view of secular power. He began with the classic words of Christ to give God what is God's and Caesar what is Caesar's (Mt 22:21). If that is the case, Bernard argued, how could Caesar allow the possessions of the church at Toul to be minimized, "with no gain to Caesar"? The church here was being mistreated, but Lothair had apparently kept the pope from involving himself in the matter. Bernard asked the emperor to act in a "more prudent" manner. Lothair was to give way and allow justice for the church of Toul in order to save it.

Bernard closed the letter by asserting, "I am faithful to you." "If I seem overeager, perhaps that is the reason." Bernard's declaration of humility is also a statement of loyalty. Because he was faithful to his friend, then the friend should listen to him and do what he showed to be best. We find here a number of seemingly simple statements that express how Bernard saw the relation between the Church and secular rulers. They were obliged to listen to the good advice churchmen such as Bernard gave them. As a faithful friend, Bernard demanded a hearing.

Once again it is relevant to ask: How could he? How could the abbot of a monastery in Champagne allow himself to tell the Roman emperor how he should act in his own dominions? Bernard would naturally have been aware of historical precedents, going back to the time when Bishop Ambrose of Milan excoriated the Roman emperor for harsh behavior. There was always a fine line between showing respect for Caesar and telling Caesar to show respect for what was God's. By this time in his life Bernard seems to have had no difficulty defining this relationship, but it is significant that his lofty presentation of imperial foreign policy should end with a down-to-earth defense of the rights of a single church.

Bernard sent a second letter to the emperor at about the same time or perhaps slightly earlier. He wrote defending the Pisans, who he said were the first in Italy to defend the Roman Empire and thus Lothair. They had done their utmost to "support the imperial crown and its concerns." It was Pisan troops that overcame one Italian city after another, places previously thought to be impregnable. But instead of supporting those who had defended the emperor, Lothair had turned against them: "You have favored those who were your enemies and those who have showed loyalty have met with your anger." Bernard demanded that the emperor revise his attitude and actions toward the Pisans. Once again he was intervening in a purely secular matter and making himself the arbiter of good princely behavior.

There is no question here of church politics, except for the fact that the Pisans were known to have given a home to Innocent II after he had been forced to leave Rome. But otherwise Bernard was dealing with the delicate matter of the bond between the emperor, who after all was mainly a German king, and the Italian cities that were supposed to recognize him. This relationship was generally a tense one, and Bernard's intervention may have been quite unwelcome. But the letter indicates no hesitation at all. He claimed to know what was best for Pisa, for the emperor, and for society in general. If we assume that Bernard's international career began either at the Council of Étampes in 1130 or soon afterwards, it is no surprise that six years later he could take it for granted that he had a right to speak out concerning the governance not only of the Church but also of lay society.

In February 1137 Lothair's ally Duke Henry of Bavaria succeeded in capturing the city of Lucca. According to the annalist Saxo, "Once some bishops and the abbot of Clairvaux mediated, and a great amount of money was given, they [the Luccans] placated the duke." This description of the consequences of the conquest is rendered by Elphège Vacandard in the following manner in his 1895 biography of Bernard: "Thanks to the clergy and particularly the abbot of Clairvaux . . . they [the Luccans] were treated with indulgence." In the 1953 volume marking the eight hundredth anniversary of Bernard's death, it is baldly asserted: "Thanks to the intervention of Bernard, the city was spared."

This is the classic tale that the Danes call "The Feather That Became Five Hens." When one goes back to the original source, it does not say what was claimed later. Vacandard's assertion that it was Bernard's intervention in particular that made the difference is not supported by the contemporary annalist Saxo. The 1953 chronology of Bernard's life exaggerated Vacandard's statement. It might seem irritating to the reader who wants a bread-and-butter biography to pause here for a classic discussion about historical sources and their use or misuse. But in order to know Bernard as he functioned in his own time, it is essential to identify later attempts to credit him with an importance that he did not actually have. Lucca was saved from total destruction because a number of prelates, including Bernard, appealed for mercy. And the Luccans paid a hefty price to avoid the sack of their homes. Neither Vacandard nor the editor of the 1953 biography deemed it necessary to include this detail. Their central focus on Bernard, of course, explains this. But here as often elsewhere, Bernard was not at the center of events and occupied only the periphery.

In March or April 1137 at Viterbo, Bernard's brother Gerard became severely ill. Bernard and Gerard were together with Innocent II. Bernard stormed heaven with his prayers to make certain that the two of them could get back to Clairvaux before Gerard died. The situation is described in some detail by Bernard at the end of his Sermon 26 on the Song of Songs. Most of that sermon deals with Bernard's sorrow on the death of Gerard, but the final section provides information about the situation in Viterbo:

> I felt it unthinkable that my companion on my journeys, and so wonderful a companion, should be left behind in a foreign land. I had to restore him to those who had entrusted him to me. All of them loved him because he was so utterly lovable.

Bernard then appealed to God: "Wait O Lord till we return home." He wanted to return Gerard "to his friends," and then God could take him. This is precisely what happened: "I lost sight of my agreement with you [Lord], but you did not forget." Gerard had been handed over to the brethren, but now, Bernard said, "you have claimed him back; you have but taken what was yours."

Bernard's description of events emphasizes how important it was for him to restore Gerard to his monastic community so that he could die there. But behind this concern was the love of one man for another, brother for brother: biological and spiritual brother. Later in this chapter I will return to this remarkable sermon, and its expression of human love. For the moment it is enough to point out that during the last year of Gerard's life Bernard must have lived in fear that he soon would lose the man whose company and guidance had shepherded him since childhood. Just as the papal schism was coming to a seemingly happy end, Bernard was facing the end of the world that had made him.

The Last Months of the Schism (May 1137–January 1138)

In May 1137 the troops of the impressive warrior Henry of Bavaria had moved south of Rome to the area of Monte Cassino, the great abbey founded by Benedict himself in the sixth century and since then destroyed and rebuilt. Its abbot, Reginald, was known as a partisan of Anacletus, so it remained to be seen if the abbey could be made to go over to Innocent. On 23 May the city of Benevento submitted to Innocent, and then a week later, Pope Innocent and the emperor Lothair met at Bari. It was probably at this time that Bernard wrote the monks of Clairvaux about his bad health: "I have had to give way to the emperor's insistence, the order of the pope, the Church's prayers and those of secular lords, and so I have let myself be dragged to Apulia."

Bernard was still with his brother Gerard, but otherwise he seems to have felt quite alone. Lothair was preparing to return home from Italy without having defeated the one secular prince still defending Anacletus: Roger of Sicily. Roger had attacked Campagna, and now it was up to Bernard to oppose him. Arnold of Bonneval describes how Bernard went to Roger and "implored him that if he began the conflict he would be defeated and depart in disorder." In Arnold's account we find Bernard encouraging the army and during the battle going to a village and praying. Bernard is thus portrayed as a Moses figure, inspiring the army and praying for victory. Here as elsewhere it is apparent that in the twelfth century a mixture of secular and religious power was not a problem. Bernard was seen as carrying out the will of God to save the Church from the advocates of the antipope.

Roger was defeated by Innocent's forces. He had to withdraw from the field, but he was by no means completely defeated. On 13 September, the German army was encamped at the foot of Monte Cassino, where Pope Innocent, accompanied by Bernard, had rejoined the emperor. Once again it was a question of how far the authority of the papal Church extended. Who governed Apulia? Was it under papal or imperial rule? For once Bernard was quite clear in passing the matter on to the emperor: "It is Caesar's prerogative to win the crown from the Sicilian usurper." Bernard thus handed the territory over to the emperor, once he had eliminated King Roger. Vacandard provides a rare criticism of Bernard for ignoring the special rights of the papacy over the South of Italy.

The situation in southern Italy underlines the fact that the dispute between Innocent and Anacletus was more than rivalry over church power.

It was a question of who ruled Italy. Was Italy to be a territory attached to the German kingdom, or could another prince take over its southern half? Italy would of course continue to be a focus of territorial disputes, with the pope insisting that he had special rights, given to his predecessor long ago by the emperor Constantine. Bernard generally supported the papal point of view, but not without reserve, as in conceding the Roman emperor hegemony in southern Italy.

In mid-September Innocent II named a commission to deal with the office of Abbot Reginald of Monte Cassino. A contemporary source mentions that Bernard was present at these discussions. Bernard gave a sermon, which we do not have. It may have concerned the question of what to do with a monastery whose abbot could not remain in his office. But we really do not know the subject of Bernard's discourse. According to Vacandard, he spoke "on the religious and political disorder of the monastery." Vacandard even provides a summary of what he thinks Bernard must have said. On this basis the 1953 review of Bernard's life claims that the sermon concerned "the religious and political disorder of the monastery."

Once again, we are faced with the fact that Bernard was present at a decisive event, but his actual contribution to events is not at all clear. Putting him at center stage would be doing him a disservice. He was at Monte Cassino and certainly must have contributed to the decision to compel the monks to elect a new abbot, Vibald. These deliberations are described in detail in a contemporary Monte Cassino chronicle, but Bernard's contribution of a sermon is described succinctly: "After a sermon was held by the abbot of Clairvaux, the cardinals by papal authority placed an interdict over the abbacy of Reginald of Cassino." Bernard was a participant, not a prime mover.

Sometime in late August or early September 1137 Bernard wrote to the Cistercian abbots gathered together at the General Chapter in Cîteaux and described his situation: "Frail in my body and heavy in heart, as God knows, I write you." This opening might be looked upon as formulaic, but Bernard certainly was not in good health. He continued in the same vein, describing himself as "melancholy and down on my knees in front of you." He asked for his fellow abbots' pity, so that their tears would storm heaven on his behalf. Then God would tell him to return to his brothers, so that he would not die "among strangers."

The next sentence comes across as a genuine statement from a person who really was exhausted: "I am worn down by so many tasks and anxieties that my very life has for me become a burden." Bernard avoided any reference to God's will that he do his work. He told the abbots that he was addressing them in a human manner because of his weakness. There are no apologies here, only the desire to return to Clairvaux and Cîteaux "so that I will not die until I can be with you."

In his superb translation of Bernard's letters, Bruno Scott James has inserted a note after Bernard's declaration of his weakness and fear of dying abroad: "We do know he lived an active life for many years" after he wrote this letter. James was quite correct: Bernard had sixteen more years of life ahead of him. But the meaning of this letter does not have to do with whether or not it describes a dying man. Perhaps Bernard was dealing with what we would today call depression. He was burning out and wanted his fellow abbots to know that he could not continue for much longer in this peripatetic way of life.

At the same time Bernard left his fellow abbots with a message of peace and unity. His exhortation that they "keep to the good, the honest and the wholesome" might seem generic. But he was appealing to the Cistercian sense of unity "in peace's bonds," thus handing them over to a God who brings peace. The last sentence is taken from Paul to the Philippians (4:9). Almost everything Bernard wrote is derivative of biblical language, but it is worth noting that his reference to his humanity is his own. Thus the letter, brief as it is, can be an expression of exhaustion, stress, and discouragement, even though Bernard was on the verge of experiencing the fulfillment of his long-standing project of gaining recognition for Innocent as the true pope. But it is quite human for a person so close to a long-sought goal to lose heart.

On 30 October 1137, Roger of Sicily was again defeated in battle. Bernard offered him terms of peace, requiring that he recognize Innocent, but he refused. At the end of November or early December, Bernard met with Roger, but he persisted in his support for Anacletus as true pope. On 4 December 1137 the emperor Lothair died while crossing the Alps. The political situation thus became quite unstable. Bernard accompanied Innocent to Rome at the end of December. In the meantime he had convinced one of Anacletus's most important supporters, Cardinal Peter of Pisa, to embrace Innocent. Arnold of Bonneval summarized a speech Bernard is supposed to have given to Peter to convince him to abandon Anacletus. He apologized for the fact that Cistercians were "more accustomed to using mattocks than fine speech."

Bernard's central argument was that there could only be one faith, not two. If the division between allegiances to two popes became permanent, then the world as it was known would collapse: "The whole of the West will perish, France will perish, Germany will perish . . ., Spain . . ., England." Bernard is said to have provided a terrifying picture of Christian society torn to bits, with all the religious orders in disarray, including the Cistercians.

Then Arnold described how Bernard took Peter by the hand: "If you now believe my advice, let us enter together into the safer ark." Bernard did not only make use of words. He used his body to connect with the body of his enemy, who by joining his hand became his friend.

We are, nevertheless, given little insight into what it was that convinced Peter of Pisa, only that he "was at once persuaded." He had gone through an exhausting process of hope and defeat and probably could see that Bernard's side was winning. But what matters here is the weight given to persuasion: Bernard did his best to convert Peter to the side of Innocent on the basis of rational arguments, and not through an appeal to military might or the fact that by now most of the Western Church had accepted Innocent as true pope. For Bernard the unity of the Church was the major issue, and this conviction could have made a difference for Cardinal Peter.

On 25 January 1138, Pietro Pierleoni—Pope Anacletus II—died. Like many of his antipapal successors in the coming centuries, Pierleoni represented a distinguished Roman family that challenged another such family. For almost eight years he and his adherents had held onto the greater part of the city of Rome, as well as to southern Italy. But once France and other kingdoms of northern Europe had recognized Innocent, Anacletus had only a small chance of winning out over the other pope. His adherents still elected a successor, Gregorio Conti, who took the name Victor IV, but he soon accepted the hopelessness of his situation and was reconciled with Innocent. Bernard's response to the new situation is reflected in a celebratory letter he sent to the powerful and respected abbot of Cluny, Peter the Venerable. He thanked Peter for his letter, which provided consolation to him "where I have been in exile." Bernard claimed that he was proud "to have your affection's privilege." But what mattered most to him was the victory of the Church: "If we have shared the task she gave us, then also we can share the comfort she now has."

Bernard's language is eminently precise. The two nouns, *labor* (task) and *consolatio* (comfort), are perfectly balanced. The hard work of the first provided the basis for the consolation of the second. In the second section of the letter Bernard rejoiced over the fact that winter was over and spring had come. Anacletus had died, and another enemy of the Church, probably Gerard of Angoulême, had disappeared. Now the time was approaching for Bernard to return to his brothers. He promised, if he was still alive, to visit Peter on his way back.

The precise nature of Bernard's relation with Peter the Venerable has long been a subject of controversy and speculation. But if we take the letter at face value, it is a declaration of Bernard's joy that the long cold schism was over. Soon he would get back to Clairvaux. He wanted Peter to know how happy and relieved he was. But in telling Peter, he was making known to the whole world that he had put the schism behind them.

One Pope in a Divided Church

At the end of May 1138 Bernard celebrated the fact that the Church once more was unified and there was "peace for the city of Rome." Thus he wrote to Geoffrey, the prior at Clairvaux, and in this way he addressed not only the brethren of his home monastery but all Cistercian monks. Bernard described how on 29 May, all the former supporters of Anacletus gave up their allegiance to his successor and prostrated themselves at the feet of Pope Innocent "to take the oath of fealty." This was a demonstration of loyalty, converting a feudal practice into an ecclesiastical one.

Now, Bernard rejoiced, had come the peace that he had known would come, but not when. Here surely is an admission of Bernard's state of mind during the schism. He had trusted in God's help, but he had had no idea when that assistance would manifest itself: "I felt certain [peace] would come, but not when!" This statement reveals a dimension of Bernard's interior life. God was there for him, but not a God who could be ordered in a given situation to provide a remedy. Throughout history God has been used as a gimmick, a fixer to take care of human needs. Bernard's God was available, but on his own terms, and in his own time.

With the Church united under one pope, Bernard could tell his prior Geoffrey that "there is nothing that can keep me back any longer." He added a reference to one of the Psalms (126:6) to express his declaration of victory: "I will return rejoicing, for I bear sheaves of peace."

It was rare for Bernard to be so unreservedly positive in celebrating a task brought to a happy conclusion. But it is significant that he admitted he had been in doubt about the outcome of the schism. The peace of the Church would come, even though he could not tell when this would be. The historian who prefers to look upon the writing of letters as manipulation of facts and attempts to fudge the truth has to consider what Bernard was doing here, telling the world that he did not take the disappearance of Anacletus as a foregone conclusion. It would have been easier for Bernard to claim that he had never hesitated and had always known the will of God. But the abbot of Clairvaux admitted that he had felt insecure about the outcome of the schism.

On 3 June 1138 Bernard left Rome behind. Before he did, he was probably informed that an episcopal election had taken place in Langres, the bishopric where Clairvaux was located. This news apparently came as a shock to him, since it had been decided in Rome that the election would not be held immediately. Bernard decided to return home by way of Lyon, where he could speak with the archbishop about the result of the election. But, in the meantime, events overcame Bernard. A monk of Cluny who had been elected to the post at Langres received the investiture of regalia, the secular symbols of office, from the French king. The episcopal consecration took place. Bernard was furious, and in the autumn of 1138, in spite of being ill, he dictated a number of letters, and the pope annulled the election.

We have a detailed report of the events in a long letter from Bernard to Pope Innocent II, dating from sometime between June and October 1138. Bernard described how after crossing the Alps he was informed that the man chosen as bishop of Langres was one "concerning whom I might have wished to have heard better reports." We are never told the name of this candidate, but there is no doubt he was a monk of Cluny. Bernard then approached the archbishop of Lyon, who was responsible for the bishop of Langres as one of his suffragans. Bernard reminded him of the agreement made in Rome, but the archbishop blamed the son of the Duke of Burgundy for failing to honor what had been accepted.

According to Bernard the entire procedure was incorrect, for the man whose qualifications were in question had gone directly to the king and obtained investiture of his bishopric's regalia, "but on what basis only he could tell." Bernard was convinced that what was done was dubious. In another letter, sent to the dean and treasurer of the church of Lyon, he described how "our church suffers from a great malady." He allowed himself the hyperbolic language that at times could flow from his pen: "Know that the church of Lyon, which is our loving mother, has selected for her daughter not a bridegroom but a monster." Now it only remained for such men "to complete the praiseworthy task you have begun and bring it to a rightful ending."

Another letter to Pope Innocent expresses the same concerns, making use of emotional language: "I cry out to you once again, knock on your door once again, and my sighs are full of tears." Bernard was outraged that in spite of the pope's decision, the bishops of Autun and Mâcon had consecrated the man that they had elected. These bishops were known as "friends of Cluny," and here Bernard revealed that his rival was the abbot of Cluny, Peter the Venerable. Bernard tried in this letter to remind the pope that he had the final say in the matter, but his decision was not being respected. It was a question of payments being made: "When gold decides and silver sits in the judgment seat, church law and its canons have nothing to say."

In the second part of this letter Bernard referred to his own state of being. He had returned safely to his monastery from Rome, "with my health broken" but yearning for peace. He had hoped to restore himself to the spiritual way of life he had left behind, but instead he felt "sorrow and pain." He described how he now lay on his bed and his pain was more mental than physical. Bernard claimed he would have preferred to give up the fight, but then he would be endangering his own salvation for not following what was right. So he asked the pope for his pity, but he also reminded Innocent that God had done wonderful things for him. In return he should cancel or undo what had been wrongly done.

Occasionally in his writings Bernard appealed to his own weakness and illness. This letter can be read in two ways. Either it is a rhetorical demonstration to convince the pope to act. Or it is a genuine description of Bernard's state of mind after his return to Clairvaux in the summer of 1138. Perhaps the letter is to be read in both ways: a call to action and a description of a man who was physically and spiritually drained. The contents of the letter may reveal how Bernard experienced coming back to his home and feeling that he could not resume his former way of life. At the same time his brother Gerard was either dying or else already dead. The extreme language of the letter may be an indication that Gerard had died and that Bernard felt lost without him. But he was not yet ready to tell the world that he had experienced this loss. In any case, it must have been upsetting to return to Clairvaux believing that once he got back, life would be easier and more harmonious, since on his return Bernard had to face one matter after another that demanded his attention. He could not let go of his role as arbiter of right and wrong in the Church and settle down to life at Clairvaux.

A further letter to Innocent claims that Bernard wanted to review the entire case, but he was too upset to do so: "Sorrow has paralyzed my hand and my mind is overcast with grief." To the bishops and cardinals of the Roman Curia, probably at about the same time in the summer of 1138, Bernard repeated his complaint: "They have placed a man above our heads whom good people cannot stand." He reminded these prelates of their position in the Church, and thus that they had an obligation to do what was right. He begged for help from a cardinal named Umbald: "At Langres we find that Christ again suffers and is persecuted." How strongly Bernard expressed himself! A man whose life was unworthy to be bishop had been elected in a manner that was not canonical. Finally, Bernard described to Pope Innocent how it had been agreed that there would be another election.

Bernard's massive letter-writing campaign seemed to be working, but now he turned to the king of France, Louis VII, to tell him that in a new election the prior of Clairvaux, Geoffrey, had been chosen as bishop. This was "against everything I had expected." Apparently the electors had first chosen Bernard himself, but he had refused. It was then that Geoffrey came into consideration. Now Bernard had to convince the king to accept someone other than the Cluniac monk who previously had received the symbols of secular authority from him. Bernard warned the king not to contradict what he was convinced was the will of God. The abbot of Clairvaux did his best to convince the king to accept the new bishop and to invest him with the symbols of his authority in the lay sphere, such as the lands he would hold from the king.

Bernard does not emerge from this dispute in an attractive manner. He clearly resented the fact that the bishop of Langres was elected without his knowledge and participation. He naturally could refer to what had been decided in Rome, but bishops at this time were made not by popes but usually by the canons or other clerks who were their electors. Bernard did not like the fact that it was a monk of Cluny who was elected, and he showed his disdain for the man by never mentioning him by name. Instead Bernard did his best to smear his reputation, and this tactic is hard to accept in view of the fact that Peter the Venerable apparently approved of the man. We have a fairly long letter from Peter to Bernard in which the former defended the man and gave a much more sympathetic description of the initial election than what Bernard had provided.

At Reims Bernard was offered the archbishopric. He wrote the pope that "the church of Reims has collapsed." He referred to fighting that had been taking place, and this must have been in connection with the fact that the city had established a commune, headed by the mayor. The episcopal chapter and the city were in opposition to each other, and at this point Bernard told the pope that the "madness" of the people of Reims had to be dealt with, and so the chapter should go ahead with the election.

It was at this point that Bernard was elected. He wrote the king that he could not accept the office, for he was ill and "for me only the grave is left." Bernard claimed that those who had elected him should have taken his fragility into consideration. At the same time, he insisted that he knew himself well enough to realize that he could not shoulder such an office: "I know myself better than anyone else, and no one can know me as I know myself." Bernard indicated that only he could see himself from within, while others saw what was on the surface. After this introduction, Bernard described to the king the state of the church of Reims.

At some point in the discussions concerning the new archbishop, Bernard entered the city. Unfortunately for us, the description of Bernard's arrival at

Reims by William of Saint-Thierry concentrates on the miracles he is said to have performed there. James claims that Bernard preached to the townspeople in the marketplace, but I find no such reference in the *Vita Prima* or in his letters. Vacandard is more restrained and simply indicates that Bernard was present at Reims: "But it seems that his eloquence failed in the face of the responses of the commune and the demands of the popular factions." What seems to have made a difference was probably the intervention of the king. Bernard showed his awareness of this fact in his letter to the king. The abbot of Clairvaux was caught between the traditional feudal world and a newly emerging urban one. He did not want to get too involved, and so passed up the opportunity to leave Clairvaux behind and accept the archbishopric of Reims.

In any case the reunited Church that Bernard thought he left behind in Rome was now plagued by one dispute after another. Instead of having a pope whose decisions were respected by all churchmen, the post-schism Church was dominated by local and regional concerns. The pope could not decide an episcopal election, and the abbot of Clairvaux could not enforce the pope's decision. It was a matter of local interests, something for which Bernard had little or no respect. At the same time, he was probably in pain, both physical because of his chronic ailments and mental because he had lost his brother Gerard, half his life and his staunch supporter and helper. Without Gerard, Bernard was unsure how he would continue. Gerard had always been nearby to take care of Bernard's everyday needs.

Seeking Consolation for a Dead Brother

When Vacandard reached this point in Bernard's life, he merely provided a medley of quotations from the twenty-sixth Sermon on the Songs of Songs, Bernard's lament on the loss of his brother Gerard. It is tempting to use Bernard's own language, because he expressed so eloquently his pain and grief. But Bernard's words need to be put into context, and instead of reducing his sermon to its stylistic elements, I interpret it as a human statement whose sentiment marks a turning point in the Western expression of human affection.

The text as we have it is not necessarily what Bernard said to his brothers at Clairvaux. He began the sermon with his usual exposition of the Song text and then broke off, thus providing a dramatic effect that does not have to reflect what happened in real life. We are dealing with literature, but literature reflecting lived experience. What Bernard composed can indicate what he had lived. Bernard's lament is all about consolation, the comfort that his brother Gerard once gave him, the consolation that Bernard now sought in telling others what he had lost.

Consolatio is good classical Latin. Our Roman ancestors knew what it was like to seek comfort following the deaths of those they loved. Cicero, the great classical humanist, was especially fond of the word and could use it to speak of consolations offered. Bernard had been brought up with this kind of Latin, but here he could only use the word to express his lack of consolation after the loss of his brother: "As for me, already so miserable, what consolation remains to me, and you, my only comfort, gone?"

Bernard dramatized his reactions to Gerard's death not only by breaking off in the midst of his sermon but also by describing how his first reaction to the loss was not to show emotion. He had "stood with dry eyes at the graveside till the last solemn funeral rite was performed." He did his best not to react by weeping. His self-control was, however, in vain: "Growing all the more bitter I realized because it found no outlet, I confess, I am beaten. All that I endure within must needs issue forth."

After explaining why it was necessary for him at this point to express his loss, Bernard defined the roles that Gerard had played in his life: "My brother (*germanus*) by blood, but bound to me more intimately by religious profession." A *germanus* is a close relative, a brother, and Gerard became all the closer because he shared the monastic vocation (*religione*) with Bernard. But instead of adding the usual nostrum that we must accept God's judgment when we lose a loved one, Bernard burst out: "Why has he been torn from me? . . . We loved each other in life: how can it be that death separates us?" The lament turns into an accusation against death itself: "death indeed so aptly named, whose rage has destroyed two lives in the spoliation of one." Gerard's death also became Bernard's. Such sentiments hardly fit the idea of a monk's accepting God's will, and it is probably not by accident that the *Exordium Magnum Cisterciense*, the later collection of Cistercian stories that dedicated twenty chapters to Bernard, left out this passage from its citation of the sermon. One can only guess why, but perhaps Bernard's complaint was too human for a man who had to be made into something more.

Bernard here addressed his dead brother and reminded him how his practical assistance made it possible for him to pursue his spiritual pursuits. Now Gerard could find consolation with others, but for Bernard there could be no consolation at all. He could only look back on what they had shared with each other. He described himself as sinking "beneath the weight of cares and afflictions, deprived of the support you lent to my feebleness." Bernard assured Gerard that his brother's love would persist: "Since love never comes to an end, you will not forget me forever." There are clear references here to Paul in First Corinthians (13:8) and to the Psalms (13:1).

Bernard's language is seeped as ever in biblical quotations, but there is an element of protest against what had happened to him: "In every emergency I look to Gerard for help, as I always did, and he is not there." The section beginning at this point was again included in the *Exordium Magnum*: grief was more acceptable than anger in remembering what Bernard had lost. He seems almost to have been resentful that Gerard had abandoned him. Gerard had been his helper in everyday life, so that Bernard could distance himself from practical affairs. Bernard's honesty about making use of Gerard in this capacity is quite disarming and hardly edifying when one thinks of the portrait of the responsible abbot in the Rule of Saint Benedict: "How often did you not free me from worldly conversations by the adroitness of your gifted words, and return me to the silence that I loved?" The result was that whoever spoke to Gerard "had rarely need to see me." Gerard had been a buffer between visitors and the abbot, but he did so in a manner that satisfied people, while Bernard could devote himself to "prayerful absorption in divine contemplation," something necessary for teaching his monks.

Gerard thus made it possible not only for Bernard to read, think, and meditate, but also to formulate the sermons and other works that were the fruit of his meditation. This assertion seems surprising in view of what Bernard was doing in the years between 1130 and 1138, and he provides little sense of how Gerard had functioned when he and Bernard were traveling, as on the three voyages within Italy. But Bernard's brother must have been a shield between the abbot and all the people who would have wanted access to him. Bernard could be stormed by people begging him for cures for their ills. Bernard does not mention this, but Arnold certainly does.

Almost as a second thought, Bernard added that Gerard was a model monk "in the maintenance of discipline." Bernard did not limit this remark to the ascetic dimension, quickly adding that Gerard had a wonderful sense of what was going on in the monastery, "in the buildings, in the fields, in gardens, in the water systems, in all the arts and crafts of the people of the countryside." He could associate with all types of skilled workmen and knew their trades, while at the same time he did not realize how wise he was. Bernard here was repeating himself, in emphasizing how Gerard's contribution made it possible for the abbot to function better: "My preaching was more effective, my prayer more fruitful, my study more regular, my love more fervent."

Bernard continued in his lament and complained about the burden that he had to shoulder now that Gerard was gone: "To survive you can only mean drudgery and pain." Gerard was not the one who had died, for he had come to a new life: "It is I who died, not he." And so the tears that Bernard previously held back could now come: "Let my tears gush forth like fountains." He blamed himself for his sins and hoped that in seeking forgiveness, "I shall find the grace of consolation, but without ceasing to mourn, for they who mourn shall be comforted" (cf. Mt 5:5). This is what Bernard sought, to be comforted in his distress, and he was expressing his pain in every way he could find in biblical language and in lived experience.

At this point Bernard questioned the cause of his sorrow and asked if his weeping was the result of selfishness. Could it be, he asked, that he was like the people who wept for such a reason? "My emotional outburst is certainly like theirs, but the cause, the intention, differs." The key word in this discussion is *affectus*, a term that means more than affection. It cannot be translated into modern languages but indicates the attachment of the individual to a beloved object or person. Bernard insisted that he was not lamenting for himself but for Gerard, "my brother in the flesh, but next to me in the spirit, the companion of my devotion."

The next paragraph repeats what Bernard had already indicated about the closeness he had experienced with Gerard. But in this demonstration of affectivity Bernard made a statement that I find to be a turning point in Western culture. He stated that it was human to love in such a manner, even carnal. "Yes I am carnal, sold under sin" (Rom 7:14). Gerard was everything to him: "mine, so utterly mine." The pain Bernard felt at his loss was something he accepted, and from this awareness he generalized about human affection in general: "It is but human and necessary that we respond to our friends with feeling, that we be happy in their company, disappointed in their absence. Social contacts, especially between friends, cannot be purposeless." The term is *socialis conversatio*, and *conversatio* is normally used for the monastic discipline and way of life, but Bernard expanded the term by adding *socialis* to capture the pleasant exchanges that take place between friends. He added that such friends are reluctant to be separated from each other and long for each other's company when they are apart. Such feelings "indicate how meaningful their mutual love must be when they are together."

There is nothing completely original in such statements, for Cicero had already expressed something similar in his essay on friendship. But Bernard was transforming the monastic ideal of separation from the world and allowing the tenderness and intimacy of human bonds into the cloister. He must have conveyed this awareness when the young monk of Rievaulx, Aelred, in the early 1140s visited him and Bernard asked him to write a work showing how monastic asceticism and human affectivity could coexist and strengthen each other in the cloister. Bernard dared to allow himself and his monks to show their feelings in seeking and living out friendships. He was saying that what he had experienced with Gerard was something other monks could experience. For human bonds, especially those between friends, could not be dismissed as distractions. They are essential: "It is but human and necessary that we respond to our friends with feeling."

When we think of friendship in the Christian tradition, the first name that comes to mind is Augustine. Certainly he could not live without his friends, and his description of their being together as a community at Hippo is attractive. But with Augustine as with other Church Fathers there was an element of hesitation, a questioning of the value of bonds of friendship. With Bernard, however, there were no second thoughts. In expressing what he had experienced with Gerard, he was willing to generalize and concede that it is "human and necessary to express affection toward those who are dear to us."

The twelfth century was fascinated by human bonds. But as I pointed out in chapter 3, this awareness is usually seen in terms of the ethos of courtly life found in the troubadours. Their celebration of human attachments is only part of a much larger development, which rightly can be called the first wave of romanticism in the West. It dreamed of attaining a spiritual or physical goal, whether it was found in a beloved woman or a cherished male friend. For Bernard there could be no doubt. In losing Gerard he left behind someone beloved: "All by myself I experience the sufferings that are shared equally by lovers when compelled to remain apart." There was no virtue in remaining separated and pining for the beloved: Bernard wanted to be with Gerard again, and thus he would conquer death. Gerard had gone to the fatherland and had defied death. Bernard would follow him.

Once again Bernard considered how he mourned his loss: "I bewail my own wounds and the loss this house has suffered." He also lamented what the poor suffered, for Gerard had looked after them. Bernard wept for "the state of our whole Order." Here he reviewed some biblical examples of mourning, concluding with Christ at the tomb of Lazarus: "Christ neither rebuked those who wept nor forbade them to weep, rather he wept with those who wept." The tears of Christ were witnesses of his nature (as a human person) and not of lack of faith. Tears thus became for Bernard a necessary way of expressing human emotion, a recognition of the validity of human feeling, and a bond with the Jesus who had wept over his dead friend.

Bernard repeated this point in the next section: "Our weeping is not a sign of a lack of faith, it indicates the human condition." But it was necessary for him to accept God's will: "I do not forget that he was given to me and offer thanks for my good fortune in having had him." In the final section of the sermon, Bernard provided the facts already mentioned: how Gerard became ill at Viterbo and Bernard had prayed that he could return home with him before he died: "Wait O Lord, till we return home. Let me give him back to his friends, then take him if you wish and I shall not complain." Bernard called the agreement he made with the Lord a covenant. It can be asked, of course, if anyone rightly can hold God to a covenant. It is the Lord who makes the covenant, not the human person. Bernard took a passage from Ezekiel 16:60: "Yet I will remember the covenant I made with you in the days of your youth, and I will establish an everlasting covenant with you." This is God speaking, while Bernard made it sound as if the covenant was as much his as God's.

Theologically Bernard was innovative, but the most remarkable aspect of this unique expression of human loss and suffering is that consolation came to mean expressing the rightful need of one person for another. Bernard had no apologies for his feelings for Gerard. His pain might be seen as the result of his frustration at losing his right-hand man, who was always there when he needed him. But Cistercian *affectus* as Bernard configured it meant that friends and brothers need each other and can mourn when those whom they love are lost.

Loving God and Losing Yourself: *De deo diligendo*

The question of love was very much on Bernard's mind during these years, and so it is not surprising that his treatise *On Loving God* (*De deo diligendo*) was composed sometime between 1136 and 1140. It is dedicated to Cardinal Haimeric, the figure at the papal curia who had shepherded Bernard through the long schism and worked together with him. It perhaps reflects conversations the two churchmen had had with each other, but Bernard was rather cagey in his Prologue about how he came about his material, and merely made use of traditional clichés about an author's claim not to be competent to treat the subject at hand.

As with Bernard's other writings, I do not intend to provide a summary of the contents of this treatise but to draw attention to some passages that cast light on the way Bernard understood himself and the world around him. He asked "which generation finds consolation in remembering God." The Latin term here is *solamen*, not *consolatio* (4.11), but immediately afterwards Bernard used the latter term, borrowed from Psalm 76: "My soul refused to be consoled." Bernard discussed in these opening passages how it is for the individual to make a commitment to God and discover how light a burden he bears: "The faithful soul sighs deeply for his presence, rests peacefully when thinking of him." In loving God there are to be no limits. Every rational being wants what gives fulfillment to mind and will. There is endless desire for more possessions and high honors. The restless mind, "running to and fro among the pleasures of this life, is tired out but never satisfied." Such a person desires what he does not have.

Bernard's portrayal of human anxiety and nonfulfillment can reflect what he found not only among churchmen he frequented on his travels but also in his own monastery. But Bernard can also have been looking into his own life and detecting the same kind of unrest in his members that Paul and Augustine long ago had described. The search for the love of God meant depriving oneself of the goods of the world.

After this introduction to the wayward human heart, Bernard structured his exposition according to the stages in loving God. In the first degree of love, a person loves himself for his own sake. In the second, a person loves God for his own benefit. In the third, one loves God for God's sake. In the fourth, a person loves himself for the sake of God. This final stage is rare in this life, for it means "to love yourself, as if you no longer existed, to cease completely, to experience yourself, to reduce yourself to nothing." Bernard claimed that such an awareness could take place but once in a lifetime, if at all, "and for the space of a moment." He was describing what we would call mystical experience, a term that was not available for him, but the very fact of his leading the reader to this climax indicates that Bernard considered the possibility that one could reach this peak sensation. But more often, he added, he could feel weighed down by sin, in which "the evil of the day disturbs him."

Bernard saw the possibility that the individual comes to a point where his life is in conformity with God's will: "The satisfaction of our wants, chance happiness, delights us less than to see his will done in us and for us." God's presence is perceived everywhere, as in Psalm 27:8, "Lord I will seek your face." As always Bernard was guided by biblical language, and especially that of the Psalms. *On Loving God* is a statement of the individual's progression from self-love to the love of God but also a declaration of what Bernard was experiencing in his monastic vocation and mission for the Church.

In moving through the stages of life, he looked forward to the time when God would be all in all, when "all human feelings melt in a mysterious way and flow into the will of God." One can ask what remains of the human when God takes over completely, and there is just a hint of pantheism in Bernard's image of how a drop of water disappears in wine. But the image is not meant as a definitive theological statement. It is a suggestion of what Bernard perceived in his own experience. His language in its prayerful harmony and endless confidence helps us understand what was happening to him in these years: he was confident that he could embrace the coming of divine grace and thus was able to cope with endless demands. Only the death of Gerard could dissolve this sense of unity and shake Bernard's life to its very foundations.

Facing a Vindictive Pope and Coping with Roger of Sicily (1139–1140)

In the spring of 1139 the archbishop of Armagh in Ireland, Malachy, stopped at Clairvaux on his way to the Second Lateran Council. According to the account later written about Malachy by Bernard himself, it was an overwhelming experience for the archbishop to be at Clairvaux, and he later arranged for monks from that monastery to come to Ireland: "Once he had seen the brethren he was deeply impressed and they were greatly edified by his presence and his conversation." At Rome Malachy asked Pope Innocent II for permission to return to Clairvaux on his way home and to remain there as a monk. In his portrait of Malachy, Bernard was diplomatic in describing the pope's refusal: "He did not obtain what he asked for, for the pope judged that he ought to be occupied in more fruitful endeavors."

In a note to the English translation it is claimed that the pope saw that Malachy would do more good as archbishop than as monk, but this interpretation of Innocent's decision may be too generous. Bernard had not accompanied Malachy from Clairvaux to Rome. He remained behind in his monastery, and Innocent may have been angry with him for staying away. There is no proof that Bernard did not attend the Second Lateran Council, but his presence would have been noted in contemporary chronicles. Strangely, Vacandard and other modern biographers do not mention his probable absence, but it would have been a deliberate act, a demonstration to Innocent that he was going too far in his reprisals against those who once had held with Anacletus.

Innocent opened the council with a condemnation of his former enemies, and the final decree of the council declared that all the ordinations of clergy made by Anacletus (here called Pietro Leone) were null and void. Innocent did not have to act in this manner. He was leading a victorious Church that was continuing what I have called the first medieval reformation, the reform of the clergy, the removal of the practice of simony, and the separation of the spiritual sphere from the temporal one so that kings and other lay rulers could no longer have a decisive say in the affairs of the Church. But Innocent allowed himself to be vindictive, and Bernard's response, even if it did not involve open protest, was probably to stay away and not add his own prestige to papal policy.

Sometime after the Second Lateran Council Bernard wrote to Innocent and asked the pope how he could have accused him of being "a traitor." Bernard pleaded that he had only done what the pope had asked, making it possible for Cardinal Peter of Pisa to be brought back into the Church from the side of Anacletus. "If you deny this, I can prove it by as many witnesses as there were men in the Curia at the time." Peter was returned to his former position, according to the pope's word. But now, Bernard asked, who was it who had given him such bad advice as to revoke his pardon of Cardinal Peter, for "it is clear that the punishment ought to fit the crime"? Bernard's message seems to be that Peter's sin deserved lesser punishment because he abandoned Anacletus at an earlier point in time. But Innocent was apparently making no distinction between those who stayed with the antipope to the bitter end and those who like Peter went over to Innocent at an earlier date.

For Bernard, Innocent was showing unacceptable harshness, first granting forgiveness, and then punishing: "By reinstalling him whom you have once installed, honor your first wise and unbiased decision." He ended the letter by pointing out that he had previously written the pope on the subject but had not gotten an answer: "I suppose my letter did not reach you," he concluded, thereby indicating that he well knew the letter had gotten to the pope, who did not want to deal with the matter.

Bernard's frustration with Innocent II's treatment of a distinguished prelate is obvious. The abbot of Clairvaux even involved Christ himself in his plea for mercy: "For the sake of him who, that he might spare sinners, did not spare himself, remove this reproach against me." The reproach was the fact that Bernard had seemingly obtained pardon for a repentant Peter, and this pardon was now being revoked, implicating both Peter and Bernard. But his plea did not work. Innocent remained adamant, and it was only his successor, Celestine II, who four years later reinstated Peter of Pisa as cardinal.

In describing the Second Lateran Council, Vacandard, who was a staunch supporter of the modern papacy, allowed himself the comment "It cannot be doubted that Innocent in this situation made use of excessive severity." Peter had actually been present at the opening of the council, for he signed a bull of Innocent II, but afterwards his name disappeared from papal acts for the next four years. He became a nonperson, outside the ken of the Roman Church, and even the pleadings of the papal ally Bernard failed to make it possible for him to return to favor.

The last active enemy of Innocent was King Roger of Sicily. The Lateran Council had issued a solemn excommunication against him, but he ignored it and launched a new campaign in southern Italy. A few weeks after the closing of the council, Roger debarked at Salerno with an army. His goal was to attach the duchy of Apulia and all of southern Italy to Sicily, making it one kingdom, a rival to the kingdoms of northern Europe and a threat to papal hegemony in central Italy. Innocent responded by raising an army and heading south, to San Germano, near Monte Cassino, which had been so central during the schism. Roger announced that he would accept papal suzerainty on the condition that all of southern Italy be attached to Sicily. Innocent refused, and the Roman army advanced but was soon surrounded by Roger's troops. The papal commander, Robert of Capua, escaped Roger's grasp, but the papal party that unwisely had been accompanying the army was captured on 22 July. Innocent had no choice but to lift the excommunication of Roger. The pope confirmed his disputed title as king of Sicily and invested his two sons with the duchies of Apulia and Capua, in return for an annual payment of homage for these territories.

These provisions were enshrined in the treaty of Miniano, signed on 25 July 1139. They were a real blow for the activist papacy that Innocent favored and a severe limitation on papal power in southern Italy. Vacandard asked what Bernard must have thought when he heard "this distressing news." Sometime after Miniano he wrote to Conrad, king of the Romans (called thus because he never managed to be crowned as emperor). The letter's language is indirect and unclear, but Bernard seems to have been responding to Conrad's concern that his own power had been challenged: "I have never wanted the king to suffer dishonor nor the empire to be undermined." Bernard asked Conrad to show devotion to the pope, "just as you wish reverence to be shown to you by the empire." In other words, pope and king should show mutual respect. He concluded by saying there was much else he would like to say, but it was preferable that these matters not be written down: "It would be better that you be told in person."

In an indirect manner Bernard was trying to balance secular and ecclesiastical power. Both were to be respected. The king was to be honored. The empire was to be maintained. He made no direct comment here on the victory of King Roger, but he implied that the pope was not to decide in secular affairs. The Innocent who traveled with his men to the scene of a battle was not a pope that Bernard could celebrate. The abbot of Clairvaux had temporarily withdrawn from the affairs of church and empire and preferred to communicate with rulers orally and not through detailed written statements.

The treaty of Miniano changed the status of Roger of Sicily. He now was accepted as the equal of the kings of Western Europe, and as a sign of his acceptance, monks were sent from Clairvaux to Sicily to make a foundation. Bernard wrote Roger, probably from Clairvaux in 1140, and said that the king would be able to perceive his presence not in his weak body but in that of his "children, for who can see to it that I be separated from them?" In the Cistercian brothers Roger possessed Bernard's "heart and soul." His body did not matter: it was his soul in his monks that was the best part of him. The king therefore had a responsibility to take care of the monks: "It would not be right that they be brought from far away without any purpose." Bernard envisaged problems, and they do seem to have emerged.

In another letter to Roger, Bernard asked him to receive the bearer and to show understanding, for surely it was "need and not greed that brought him into your presence." The "need of the brethren" is not specified, but the indication is that the new community was experiencing difficulties. In a third letter Bernard recommended Master Bruno, who had been one of his close friends at Clairvaux and now was leading the colony in the south: "May he benefit from the king's generosity. . . . Whatever you do for him, you also do for me." Such letters are completely different from Bernard's earlier epistles against Roger, who during the schism was made into almost an Antichrist figure. From this time onwards, the development of the Cistercian Order in southern Italy and Sicily was linked to Roger. Bernard had gone full circle in accepting a man who once had been the main supporter of the antipope. But in the post-schism world, Roger was a key figure in expanding the Cistercian Order. At the same time he was more approachable than the pope who refused to forgive his former adversaries.

We have a final witness to the division between Bernard and Innocent in the story of how the pope blocked an attempt to found a new monastery and directed it according to his own interest. The abbot of the Benedictine house of Farfa in central Italy approached Clairvaux and asked for it to send brothers for a monastery. But according to Geoffrey of Auxerre in the third book of the *Vita Prima*, the pope stopped the plans, "taking them for himself and choosing another place for them."

The abbot of Farfa was furious, for he had collected a large amount of silver to finance the new foundation. He offered it to Bernard when he saw him and was willing that the new house be on the northern side of the Alps, "since he had not been given the happiness of having one in his own domain." In the meantime, however, the silver mysteriously disappeared. Bernard considered it to be a blessing, for there was too much money: "He gave thanks for the gift but thought that the amount fraudulently and violently taken away was enough to build about ten monasteries."

Bernard's biographer, Geoffrey of Auxerre, was mainly interested in how Bernard refused to pursue a legal case and instead accepted that a huge sum of money was missing. The anecdote is included because it was meant to illustrate Bernard's character, but for our purpose it reveals how Pope Innocent was carrying out his own policies and ignoring what Bernard wanted. Apparently the pope was interested in converting the monastery of Saint Anastasius in the Campagna outside Rome into a Cistercian house. The pope therefore thwarted the plans of the abbot of Farfa and redirected them. Bernard's response is not made clear, but surely these events are one more reflection of the fact that in Italy he had little say even in establishing new daughter houses of Clairvaux. The pope had taken over not only the administration of the Church but also the foundation plans of Bernard's monastery. With Innocent as with his successors Bernard was to experience a gap between his expectations and the treatment he received from Rome. Even when the pope was one of his own monks, as we shall see in the case of Eugenius III, Bernard found that Clairvaux and Rome often did not speak the same language.

Seeking the Lord's Protection: Sermons in the Shelter of the Most High

It cannot be by accident that during Lent of 1139 Bernard preached sermons for his monks based on Psalm 91 (in the Latin Vulgate, 90). This remarkable Psalm, which I translate directly from the Latin, expresses joy and gratefulness for the protection provided by God from all that can threaten and undermine a human life. Nothing can take away the shelter, for the Lord is "my hope. . . . No evil shall befall you." In the last verses it is the Lord himself who speaks to the human person, offering deliverance "because he hoped in me. . . . He will call to me and I shall answer him. . . . I shall rescue him."

These lines are part of the Cistercian liturgy and were repeated regularly in every monastery, and they are included today in Cistercian monasteries in connection with the last service of the day, Compline. Bernard may have chosen this Psalm for Lenten sermons because he had experienced what it was like to escape danger and feel the Lord's protection. He prefaced his sermons with an address to the brethen and said that he wanted to give them comfort. He knew they needed encouragement because they were "being killed all the day long by much fasting and frequent labors." This was as it needed to be, in sharing the sufferings of Christ, but this state meant the brothers would be able to share the comfort he could give them. In this way "this great tribulation will discover sure consolation." Once again the theme of consolation is central for Bernard. He offered his monks the comfort they needed in the midst of their trials.

Further on in his Preface, he asked his monks if they were "enduring something beyond human strength." It is only because Christ assisted them that they could continue. They would find "consolation in God's word." The word *consolatio* appears yet again, and for Bernard as abbot it was essential to provide comfort to his monks, especially in the Lenten fast when "your fatigue is somewhat greater." But the comfort given was not for monks alone. The abbot himself in preaching these sermons was seeking the consolation that the Psalm could provide. The sermons can thus be looked upon as Bernard's reflection on the evils through which he had lived and the consolation given him in returning to Clairvaux and reestablishing his monastic vocation. He did not express regret at what he had experienced, but he clearly felt that he had been assaulted by the wicked.

In the first Sermon Bernard described the type of brothers who begin the process of conversion but then lose track of it. At first, they are "fairly God-fearing and careful," but once they have begun their new life, they start acting as if they were saying, "Why should we go on doing our service when we have now received all that is to be given?" There are also some who have lost hope, but they will need to turn to the Lord as protector and refuge, the subject of Sermon 2. The theme returns time and again to the help that the Lord provides, but the brothers have to accept that, in order to get this protection, they must "lie hidden. . . . This is why we hide bodily in cloisters and in forests." Bernard says it is necessary to "be hidden not only from other people's eyes but from your own as well." In view of his own life, exposed to the world, there seems to be a gap between what he recommended and the public sphere that Bernard had come to occupy.

In Sermon 6, he considered the state of the Church and made some comments that show he had not at all left behind the world outside the monastery. He excoriated clerics who pursued "positions of ecclesiastical dignity and in this they sought not the salvation of souls but the extravagance of riches." He criticized those who "scrap shamelessly to get archbishoprics and archdeaconries" so that they can milk the incomes of churches "in wanton waste and vain pursuits." This language is close to the kind of statements Bernard made in his letters, but we can ask why he was confronting his own monks with the state of the Church outside the monastery. The answer lies in Bernard's own refusal to separate monastic life from the larger world. He was telling his monks about something that concerned him deeply, even after he had left behind papal controversies. He had recently had to deal with the bishoprics of Langres and Reims, and there would be many more such cases to absorb him.

These sermons are thus more than commentaries on a Psalm. Bernard brought into them his immediate concerns and at one point described how a brother "only a few days ago" woke up after having had terrifying nightly visions, and "could scarcely keep control of himself." The brother scared the others when he "yelled in a terrible voice." For Bernard this incident was a reminder of how the devil assaults the brothers because he "is racked bitterly by your devotion." He assured his listeners that they need not be afraid, for the Paraclete would be present to comfort them. Bernard was, as so often in his writings, not only speaking of what his audience experienced but was reflecting on his own situation, his need for a consoling God. Thus it is appropriate that his sermon here turned into a prayer: "O good Jesus, if only you would always be at my right hand. If only you would always hold my right hand." He continued in this vein with all the hope he had of finding a Jesus, "as long as you are my protection on my right side."

Bernard did not leave behind a collection of prayers in the tradition, for example, of Anselm of Canterbury. But the abbot of Clairvaux time and again broke into prayer in the course of his sermons, especially those on the Song of Songs. It is as if the intensity of Bernard's language required the genre of prayer, but these addresses to God or Christ can be swallowed up in the sermon literature. Here, however, is a physically aware Bernard, asking Jesus to hold his right hand and protect him from adversity. Bernard contrasted this with his left side, which could be taunted and insulted, but this exposure he could handle "as long as you are my protection on my right side." The purpose of these sermons is precisely to show that the monk could depend on the care provided by a loving Jesus. Bernard was consoling his monks and in so doing providing consolation for himself.

Sermon 9 covers the verse "Because you, O Lord, are my hope. You have made the most high your refuge." Bernard asked what is the high refuge, and describes "an open city of refuge for us, a mother's open bosom." Hope must spring eternal, amid tribulations, for "his consolations are going to cheer your soul" (Ps 94:19). So once again Bernard offered his monks comfort and support in the hope their lives gave them.

Sermon 10 quotes from Psalm 91: "No evil shall befall you. No scourge come near your tent." Bernard brought together verses from other Psalms showing how the soul rejoices in the deliverance it receives. He concluded that "these words show clearly that he considers he has received great rest and benefit from the Lord in being freed from trials and dangers." This may be a description of Bernard's own experience. In his journeys back and forth across the Alps, confrontations with difficult lay rulers, controversies with churchmen over bishoprics and the papacy, and the loss of his brother

Gerard, there had been one matter of concern after another. But Bernard felt he had been delivered and now was offering similar deliverance to his monks.

At this point Bernard considered the fact that the time he spent preaching for his monks might be keeping them away from the manual labor to which they were obliged. He admitted that his sermon could sometimes be "contrary to the usage of our Order," but he reminded the brothers that he had been given special permission to be exempted from manual labor, something William of Saint-Thierry had made clear. Bernard seems to have seen preaching as his manual labor.

Sermons 12 and 13 deal with how the monk can cope with temptation, and Bernard devoted much space to the need to resist demons: "What other psalm so wonderfully encourages the weak-willed, warns the careless and instructs the ignorant?" Opposed to demons are the angels who are our companions, for they instill "confidence because of their guardianship." In Sermon 15 Bernard characterized his monks and sought assurance "that no one murmurs or disparages in secret, behaves hypocritically or negligently." The sermons have become more pastoral and less an exposition of Bernard's inner state of mind. Naturally any author's writings reflect his or her interior world, but Bernard began these sermons in expressing the consolation he himself had experienced, while now he was concentrating on what he thought would encourage his monks.

The seventeenth Sermon is based on the final verse of Psalm 91: "With length of days shall I satisfy him and show him my salvation." Bernard encouraged his monks to accept tribulation. "It is good for me to be troubled, Lord, as long as you are with me. . . . It is good for me to embrace you in tribulation." This sentiment can be an echo of Bernard's response to the cares he had experienced, for now he could trust a God saying, "I will show him my Jesus, so that for all eternity he may see him in whom he has believed, whom he has loved, whom he has longed for."

The sermons are basically about how to overcome fear. Shadows, monsters, and interior conflicts disappear in the salvation that is offered. Bernard was confident that the monastic life makes this change possible. The sermons are his response after the loss of his brother Gerard. In his twenty-sixth Sermon on the Song of Songs he told the brothers and thus the world how he had been close to Gerard and how he had reacted to his death. Now, he insisted, there was nothing more to fear. The Lenten season and preparation for Easter brought hope of the resurrection and its renewal of life.

Converting Clerics and Attacking the Clergy

Sometime between Lent 1139 and the beginning of 1140, Bernard visited Paris and gave a sermon that he later wrote down as "On Conversion to Clerics." Geoffrey of Auxerre provided the background for the sermon in the fourth book of the *Vita Prima*, for it had been a turning point in his life. Bernard was traveling with the bishop of Paris, Stephen of Senlis, who asked him together with their companions to visit the city, presumably so that Bernard could preach. But according to Geoffrey, "He declined to attend public meetings." The next morning, however, Bernard accepted going to Paris, and here there was a large gathering of clerics to hear him: "At once three of them were struck with compunction and turned away from their inane studies to engage in true wisdom."

Geoffrey did not name himself as one of the three clerics, but it is likely that he was present and chose this opportunity to leave behind his studies and follow Bernard back to Clairvaux. The sermon as Bernard later formulated it concerns the interior life: conversion is after all a turning away from one way of life for another, from a superficial, unexamined life to a fruitful meeting with a divine voice. No one can be converted to the Lord unless he conforms himself to the Lord's will "and unless his voice cries out interiorly." The conversion of souls that takes place is the working of the divine, not the human voice. The process of conversion requires application, and one that trusts in the experience of the individual: "Apply our hearing within, roll back the eyes of your heart, and you will learn by your own experience what is going on." As so often in his life and writings Bernard called upon himself and his listeners or readers to be aware of what they themselves experienced and to have confidence in what they learned.

After these introductory passages Bernard added some reflections on what happens to the soul that does not find salvation. He described the pain of body and soul after death and the state of the body in being kept in the state of its sin. The body will be in constant torment without being consumed by torments. This type of classical hellfire-and-damnation sermonizing was clearly meant to terrify indifferent university students and make them leave behind their "empty studies."

As signs of conversion Bernard presented parts of the body and the drama of their transformation. Thus the tongue speaks out: "It is just as you have heard tell. I too have been ordered to restrain myself from story-telling and lies." From now on, the tongue says, "I may say nothing but serious things." This type of moralizing literature resembles what would become popular in the later Middle Ages, with such dialogues as are found in *Piers Plowman*. Bernard's goal was to show the state of confusion the soul experiences when its reasoning powers have been limited. In contrast comes the gentle breeze of consolation, when one hears of the blessedness of heaven.

Bernard described graphically the man ruled by his senses: "The belly swells up as though pregnant, not alas with healthy fruit but burdened with corruption." Unrestricted sensuality and "frivolous images" are useless for body and soul. Curiosity provides but "vain, fleeting consolation." The abjection of the human person is the result of an unreflected life, in contrast to what we have been given, "endowed with faith, adopted in the Spirit." For those who seek conversion, experience shows that they have to deal more immediately with the lust of the flesh. While we struggle we weep, after the struggle we have comfort, for blessed are they who weep. Once again as so often in his work Bernard considered the need for comfort or consolation. He admitted the rigors of monastic life, it asceticism and temptations, but he also saw in it an element of human warmth, tears, and mutual concern. Here he was translating what he himself had experienced to what he thought possible for the novices who came from the academic world to that of the cloister.

After mourning and consolation comes a desire for heavenly contemplation. In this contemplation rest is found, and in savoring the Lord are delight and learning. This is an alternative to the mindless learning of the student. It has been said, "Taste and see that the Lord is good" (Ps 34:8). There is here a hidden manna, something only the one who receives knows. It is not learning but anointing that teaches here, and it is not knowledge but conscience that grasps this experience. I include the Latin phrases because Bernard's meaning can hardly be directly translated into a modern language. Every term is charged with meaning. Learning (*eruditio*) is not in itself a negative term, but it is inadequate as a teacher in comparison to the anointing (*unctio*) provided by God. Knowledge (*scientia*) is again a positive fact, the knowledge a person can gather, but it does not give the insight that conscience delivers.

This is perhaps one of the central passages in Bernard's view of what happens to the person who leaves behind secular learning and pursuits and hands himself over to the insight given by God. Bernard assured his audience that this process was necessary as an alternative to the ways of the world. He described how he had known men "sated with this world and sick at the very thought of it." They had money, honors, and pleasures but were repelled by these "to the point of repugnance." Bernard challenged his listeners, "If some of you perhaps do not believe me, let him believe experience, either his own or that of many others." Once again *experientia* as lived by the individual person could for Bernard be a criterion of how to live life and improve it. One can almost see him in harmony with the gurus of the 1970s saying that we should trust our experience, but for Bernard such an awareness did not stop with the individual's identity. This awakening was the point of departure for embracing God's grace.

In this section Bernard was reviewing the beatitudes as signposts on the way to God. "Blessed are the merciful," for they will obtain mercy. Being reconciled to God, they may have peace. Reaching the peacemakers, Bernard expressed astonishment that "certain men usurp the supreme dignity of peacemakers." Regretting the Church's present state, Bernard bemoaned "seeing a petty prince" who was "looking for money, not justice." Also he saw the impure "not ashamed impudently to defile sacred orders." Clerics had multiplied in the Church "beyond number." They entered into holy orders "without stopping to think" and took to themselves "the ministry which awes angelic spirits." Bernard's sermon turns into a harsh condemnation of church and society, where "avarice reigns, ambition commands, pride dominates, and iniquity has its seat."

As far as Bernard was concerned it would have been better for such clergy "to marry than to burn," in the Pauline sense, "to be saved in the humble ranks of the faithful than to live less worthily in the lofty ranks of the clergy." Instead they used the freedom they had in their state "as an opportunity for the flesh." They kept themselves "from the remedy afforded by marriage and give themselves up to all forms of vice."

This is a remarkable passage, for Bernard was on the verge of questioning the practice of clerical celibacy, which he saw was not working. The Lateran Councils, including the one from which he was absent, continued to insist on clerical celibacy, and their repetition of the demand through the twelfth century shows that in this respect the first medieval reformation of the Church was a fiasco. Bernard saw marriage as a "remedy," much as Paul had done, but he also sensed that clerical status made it easier for men to solicit sexual favors. In the contemporary situation of the Roman Catholic Church, dealing with decades of abuse, Bernard's complaint can seem timely: celibacy of the clergy is for the few and not for the many. He ended this section with the exhortation "Let there not be an empty appearance of the celibate life which is void of truth."

Bernard thus concluded his sermon with an attack on the lifestyle of the secular clergy. He may have done so because he wanted to remind clerics considering conversion to the Cistercian way of life to be aware of what they would leave behind. Just as Bernard challenged false celibacy, he also warned against learning for its own sake and insisted on the anointing that comes from above. This is certainly not an edificatory discourse. It is hellfire and damnation, telling especially the many young men who had flocked into the ranks of the secular clergy that they were in danger of losing their souls to the pleasures and allurements of their station. In the face of these dilemmas, it was necessary to leave the world behind and enter the monastery. Bernard looked into his own experience, but he also considered the Church as a whole. He did not like what he saw: his years abroad had left him with a bad taste in his mouth, and he spat it all out.

A Champion of Reform Returns to the Cloister—and Yet . . .

If we look at Bernard's sermons on conversion as indicative of his state of mind in 1139–40, he then felt repelled by what we can call the clerical Church. He wanted to leave it behind and to get back into his monastic community at Clairvaux. He was probably also fed up with a pope whose harshness did not correspond with Bernard's own sense that forgiveness is possible. Bernard's eagerness to fulfill the desire of King Roger of Sicily to found a Cistercian monastery on his lands shows that he was willing to forgive and forget after all the name-calling in which the abbot had engaged.

Bernard for much of his life did his best to live up to the Pauline description of becoming *all things to all* so that by all possible means he might save some (1 Cor 9:22). He wanted to be present for his monks, but he allowed himself time and again to leave the monastery for shorter or longer periods. His goal in doing so was sometimes to lure more men into the monastery. But other concerns could make him absent himself from Clairvaux. His next external involvement would be in the condemnation of Peter Abelard's theology. At first he tried to keep a distance and refused to attend the meeting that would confront Abelard. But as we shall see in the next chapter, Bernard let himself get deeply involved. However much he claimed to desire to be only at Clairvaux, Bernard kept confronting the world and going out into it to face its moral and theological dilemmas. So long as he lived and breathed, he could not let go and leave the great questions to other churchmen.

✎ CHAPTER 8

The World after the Schism: One Thing after Another, 1140–1145

The Abelard Controversy

If Bernard thought that in returning to Clairvaux, he would find peace and solitude in monastic company, he was greatly mistaken. In the years that followed his final departure from Italy, he encountered what might be called "one damn thing after another," the chaos that makes up the very stuff of history and human life. Probably during Lent of 1139, he faced his first challenge. His friend and later biographer, William of Saint-Thierry, sent him a brief treatise attacking the theology of Peter Abelard. Bernard wrote back that he had not had time to read the text but he had given it a quick look. He suggested they meet and discuss the matter, but it could not be before Easter, for it would be wrong to neglect the prayers that were appropriate in the Lenten season. In the meantime, he asked William to be patient, "for at this time I have little or no knowledge of these affairs."

Bernard was too modest here in describing his theological background. But at least in the coming months he acquired the knowledge he claimed he lacked. Sometime between May 1139 and June 1140 he composed a fairly lengthy treatise attacking what he considered to be the heresies of Abelard, concerning the doctrines of the Trinity and the Redemption. He addressed it to no less a person than Pope Innocent II, the very man from whom he temporarily had broken off contact because of Innocent's refusal to reinstate

Cardinal Peter of Pisa. The Abelard affair thus forced Bernard to get back in touch with Rome and abandon the solitude he must have sought at Clairvaux after the death of his brother Gerard.

Peter Abelard can be known through his own autobiographical text, *Historia calamitatum* (The Story of My Calamities), where he describes his tumultuous academic career and his affair with Heloise. The son of a knight in Brittany, young Peter decided, in his own words, to give up a military career for the sake of academic jousting. Here he was phenomenally successful: he found he had a talent for moving in on the recognized teachers of his own day, showing their inadequacy, and attracting their students. In the first half of the twelfth century, a teacher would set up shop in the shadow of a cathedral and hope to acquire pupils who would sit at his feet and pay for the privilege. The more pupils, the greater the teacher's income. Abelard did extremely well and became one of the most celebrated teachers of his day. But as he admitted in his account, he grew bored with success and became interested in a beautiful and intelligent young woman, Heloise, the niece of a canon of Paris cathedral, Fulbert. Abelard arranged that he would be Heloise's tutor, and in this way could spend time alone with her. The result was first lovemaking and later pregnancy. When Fulbert discovered that he had been deceived, he arranged to have Peter Abelard castrated. Peter describes the shame and mortification he felt, but what is remarkable is that he remained in contact with Heloise. He convinced her to become a nun, even though she claimed to have no desire but to be his whore, as she put it in a letter she wrote her former lover.

This remarkable story continues with Heloise and her fellow nuns being thrown out of their monastery by one of the most powerful clerics of the time, the abbot of Saint Denis. At this point, Abelard rescued the nuns by handing over to them the place where he had taught, the Paraclete, named after the third person of the Trinity, the Comforter. For the rest of his life Abelard showed what looks like genuine devotion to Heloise, while at the same time Bernard was in contact with her and her monastery. Both Abelard and Bernard thus showed common recognition of Heloise's intelligence and spiritual insight.

This overview of the career of Abelard and Heloise is necessary to understand how Bernard, in getting involved with Abelard, was challenging one of the best-known and most controversial figures of his time. So far as I can tell, he would have preferred to leave Abelard alone. But for his friend William of Saint-Thierry, Abelard had to be stopped, and, after a while, Bernard came to agree with him. We have his response in a long memorandum that leaves no doubt that Abelard was a heretic. In presenting this work, I want to emphasize that I find Abelard's theology to be brilliant and insightful; but he expressed himself at times in an untraditional manner and so called down upon himself the wrath of the monastic establishment. Abelard was pointing the way to the scholastic theology of question and answer that would reign at the University of Paris, and can therefore be rightly called one of the founders of the first great university of northern Europe.

Bernard's work is included in his Latin letter collection, but it needs rightly to be called a letter-treatise. It was too long for Bruno Scott James to include it in his translation of Bernard's letters, but there is a translation from 1904 by Samuel Eales that I use here. Bernard opened by telling the pope that it was his duty to use his authority to "crush the corrupters of the faith." He presented Abelard as "a new theologian who in his early days amused himself with dialectics" but now indulged in "wild imaginations upon the Holy Scriptures." This is Bernard at his polemical best, complaining that Abelard was "prepared to give a reason for everything, even of those things which are above reason." Thus he had gone "against reason and against faith."

Bernard was considering the meaning of faith and reason and how they contribute to each other. Faith does not exist if its content is proven. Mary is praised "because she anticipated reason by faith" (Lk 1:20). Abelard had confused faith with reason. He used reason "to attempt to transcend reason." From here Bernard turned to the doctrine of the Trinity. Abelard had claimed that God the Father "is full power, the Son a certain kind of power, the Holy Spirit no power." Bernard objected to the distinction of the persons of the Trinity: "Who does not shudder at such novel profanities of words and ideas?"

Bernard claimed that Abelard was joining with the heretic of old, Arius, in denying the consubstantiality of the persons: "He says, if the Son is of the substance of the Father, the Holy Spirit is not; they must differ from each other." Abelard would have it that the Holy Spirit "does not proceed from the substance of the Father and the Son," with the result that "no Trinity remains, but a duality." Bernard's point is that there can be "no inequality, no dissimilarity." The doctrine of the Trinity had long demanded distinctions and explanations that preserved unity but expressed difference. Abelard's categories were mistaken in Bernard's view: "He says that Power properly and specially belongs to the Father, Wisdom to the Son, which indeed is false." Bernard taunted Abelard as a "second Aristotle." As far as the abbot of Clairvaux was concerned, the definition of the Trinity was "long ago settled"; it was "ill-fitted for debate." In other words, the Church Fathers had laid forth the principles and definitions that Abelard was now manipulating.

My intention here is not to review Bernard's text in its nuances but to provide an impression of how he had read and understood Abelard. At our distance he can seem to exaggerate and distort what Abelard had written; at the same time, Bernard was troubled that Abelard was providing a new language for describing the interrelationship of the persons of the Trinity. For Bernard, Abelard was defining faith as private judgment. The abbot of Clairvaux insisted that "faith is not an opinion, but a certitude."

I think Abelard would to a large extent have agreed with Bernard on this point, but the two of them differed in the way they presented not only the Trinity but also the Redemption. In the second half of the letter-treatise Bernard attacked Abelard for his teaching that the devil had no power over man "except by the permission of God, as a jailer might, nor was it to free man that the Son of God assumed flesh." Bernard insisted on the interpretation of the Redemption that had been standard until Anselm in his *Cur Deus Homo* had challenged it: that the devil had assumed a rightful power over humanity until he abrogated that power by asserting it over Christ. Thus the devil was tricked into overextending himself, a conception that Abelard rejected, just as Anselm had done.

It is not clear from Bernard's exposition whether he was aware that Anselm already had taken the step that Abelard did in rejecting the view that the devil had lost a legitimate power over humankind. But elsewhere in this section, Bernard probably did borrow from Anselm's view that the Redemption had to take place through an act of satisfaction by which the God-man Christ gave something to the Father that was not already owed to him. Anselm had developed Paul's concept of justification gained through the sacrifice of Christ, and Bernard may have been inspired by Anselm's interpretation, where justification becomes linked to the idea of satisfaction. In any case, Bernard could not allow what he considered to be Abelard's view: that Christ's death took place "merely so that he might give many by his life and teaching a rule of life."

Bernard's representation of Abelard's teaching is not quite correct. For Abelard what took place in the act of Redemption was a demonstration of God's overwhelming love for us by sending his Son. This interpretation is quite scriptural (Jn 3:16), but Bernard insisted that it left out the act of justification that was necessary for humankind's redemption. It is the question of necessity that for Bernard made Abelard's demonstration of love inadequate: "The necessity was ours, the hard necessity of those sitting in darkness and the shadow of death." He could not accept that Christ's death was a kind of "instruction." "There come from Christ, as he deigns to confess, merely illumination and enkindling to love. Whence come redemption and liberation?"

Toward the end of the treatise Bernard repeated his main theme, that the Redemption must be more than a demonstration of love: "Neither the examples of humility nor the proofs of charity are anything without the sacrament of our redemption." Christ came in order to restore us by grace. The Redemption works through humankind's justification and not solely through the expression of God's love. Bernard understood the content and meaning of Abelard's approach to redemption, and his careful arguments, often quoting Abelard verbatim, went deeper than polemics. He took his opponent seriously and wanted the pope and learned members of the Church to be aware of how Abelard's teaching contrasted with what was to be found in the Epistles of Paul and the writings of the Fathers. For Bernard the Redemption had to involve more than exemplary action: "But what profits it that he should instruct us if he did not first restore us by his grace?"

This letter-treatise is relatively unknown in Bernard studies, except in the work of Anthony Lane, perhaps because it is hidden away in his letters and only available in the elderly English translation to be found on the internet. But its contents reveal how Bernard did his utmost to understand the meaning of Abelard's theology of the Redemption and of the Trinity. Here he devoted more attention to the Redemption. Bernard started out in caricaturing the way his rival "played with Holy Scripture," but he ended by taking a close look at Abelard's meaning.

We have no indication of how Pope Innocent II responded to Bernard's review of Abelard's theology. But we know that a hearing of Abelard was arranged for 2 June at Sens, the archiepiscopal seat of northern France. It used to be thought that this hearing took place in 1140, but careful source criticism by Constant Mews and others has redated the synod to 1141. This dating makes better sense in terms of the time it must have taken for Bernard's letter-treatise to be written, read, and reviewed. In one letter, now redated to before 2 June 1141, we find him summoning the bishops of the archdiocese of Sens so that they would show themselves as "friends in adversity." To the bishops and cardinals at the Curia in Rome, Bernard similarly wrote that it was their responsibility to act: "The beliefs of simple people are being scoffed at; God's secrets are being torn open, matters that are most sacred are being talked about in an irresponsible manner." Bernard made a list of Abelard's teachings that he considered to be dubious: "Let the one who has reviewed the heavens now descend into hell, and let darkness and its actions that have trespassed the light be revealed by the light."

Shortly after 2 June 1141 Bernard wrote to Pope Innocent and expressed his regret that he now was unable to find the tranquility he had imagined would come after the end of the schism: "I am weary of life and do not know if it would be best for me now to die." The synod had met, but there had been no discussion of the dubious aspects of Abelard's theological teaching. He had simply appealed to Rome, and the church meeting was thereby over. It may be for this reason that Bernard wrote: "Now the Church has peace, but I do not!"

Bernard here indulged in polemical language that is much sharper and more drastic than what is found in his letter-treatise. He wrote of how Abelard's writings had spread from one country to another: "A new gospel is being preached. . . . A new faith is being expounded. . . . Virtues and vices are being wrongly discussed, the Church's sacraments also. . . . Everything is expressed perversely." Bernard linked Abelard with the social revolutionary Arnold of Brescia and claimed that Abelard preferred pagan philosophers to church doctors.

The archbishop of Sens had written to Bernard to fix a day for the meeting. "I refused because I am only a youth in this type of conflict, while he has been used to it from youth. Also I considered it inappropriate to deal with our faith in the place of controversy." Bernard protested that Abelard's writings "made up sufficient material against him," and at the same time claimed that it was up to the bishops "to pass judgment on the teachings of which they were the ministers." His claim that the judgment of Abelard's teachings belonged to others belies the fact that he already had written his treatise to the pope and asked him and those associated with the Curia to condemn Abelard. There is something disingenuous here: Bernard claimed that he had nothing to do with the judgment of Abelard, and yet he had long since involved himself and passed sentence!

He also claimed that he had come to Sens "unready, without protection." Surely Bernard was very much prepared when he arrived at the council. This was to be a performance for him, in the face of "masters of the schools . . . and many clerics of education." The French king was present, and so Bernard described to Innocent how he read out the chapter headings for Abelard's works, but that his rival would not listen and walked out of the meeting. Abelard appealed to Rome, something Bernard thought he had no right to do.

Once again Bernard was stretching the truth. If anyone was prepared to meet Abelard, it was he, after his careful review of Abelard's teaching on the Trinity and the Redemption. But he clearly wanted the pope to take notice that Bernard's rival had refused to debate with him. The purpose of the letter was to get the pope to take action: "God has brought forth mad heretics in your time so that they can be defeated by your hand."

Why was Bernard so caught up in the matter? Even though he had great theological insight, he did not need to pursue Abelard in this way. He could have left the matter to the bishops of northern France. He began his letter to the pope in telling him how tired he was and how he even wanted to die. He claimed to be disappointed that he could not rest, even though "peace has been brought back to the Church." It is as if Abelard had become an obsession. Probably at about this time he wrote to Cardinal Guy of Castello, a former disciple of Abelard. Bernard warned him against supporting Abelard: "Master Peter has in his books made use of expressions that are new and profane. This he does both in their formulations and in their meanings." Bernard associated Abelard with the heretics of old: "When he deals with the Trinity, he is close to Arius; with grace, he is near Pelagius; concerning the person of Christ, he smacks of Nestorius." Arius had denied the equality of the persons of the Trinity. Pelagius had guaranteed that grace would be given to all to be saved. Nestorius provided a wayward definition of the union of two natures, God and man, in Christ. Bernard was thus accusing Abelard of harboring some of the most problematic teachings that Christian orthodoxy had to overcome.

To another cardinal, Ivo, Bernard warned against "Master Peter Abelard, a monk without a rule, a prelate without care, who does not keep to his order and is not held by order . . ., having nothing of the monk except the name and the habit." This is pure slander, expressed in a language that is impressive for its malicious eloquence. Bernard revealed concern that Abelard could feel secure "because he has cardinals and clerics in the Curia as his followers." They would defend him, Bernard feared. Pope Innocent was sent yet another missive on the same subject, reminding him that "we have escaped the roaring of Peter the Lion" (Pietro Pierleoni, who became Pope Anacletus) but now had to deal with "Peter the Dragon," who was attacking the faith of Simon Peter. Once again Bernard went through his trinity of heretics: Arius, Pelagius, and Nestorius. He expressed the desire to see with his own eyes the pope defending the Church against Abelard: "If only the care of the brethren did not detain me! If only the weakness of my body did not hold me back!" Here as in the previous letter Bernard reminded the pope of his frail health, while he at the same time demanded that Innocent act.

The Bernard who had kept a distance from Pope Innocent was now in regular contact with him. He did not return to Rome, but he made his presence felt with both the pope and the cardinals. There are further letters, such as to Stephen, bishop of Palestrina, and to an unnamed cardinal, accusing Abelard of "arguing with boys and being in collusion with women." Bernard repeated what he had written elsewhere about how the Church had escaped "Peter the Lion's roar" while now it faced "Peter the Dragon." The members of the Curia must have felt by the summer of 1141 that they more or less knew in advance what Bernard would write to them. But his missives did have an effect. On 16 July 1141 Pope Innocent condemned the teachings of Abelard, equating him with the heretics of old: Arius, the Manicheans, and Nestorius. Perhaps at about the same time Bernard wrote to his old friend and ally Cardinal Haimeric, the papal chancellor, accusing Abelard of "throwing what is holy before dogs." Bernard indicated that Abelard's learning was undermining the faith: "The faith of the pious has belief and does not discuss. But he . . . does not want to believe unless he first discusses through reason." Bernard lacked here the formula that had been so important for Anselm—"faith seeking understanding" (*fides quaerens intellectum*)—but this was his point of departure. He found in Abelard an attempt to seek faith through reason, putting, as it were, the cart before the horse.

At the end of the letter to Haimeric, Bernard referred to "my Nicholas," who could better orally deliver his message. This is Nicholas of Montiéramey, also mentioned in the last letter to Pope Innocent. Thus the two letters were probably delivered at the same time, and Nicholas was given the opportunity to tell both the pope and the cardinal what Bernard did not want to convey in writing. Bernard was doing everything he could to get the pope and Curia to condemn Abelard's teaching, and he was entrusting the task to a clever secretary who later would betray him.

We do not have Bernard's letters or the text from Pope Innocent on this matter, but it would appear that the abbot of Clairvaux succeeded in getting the condemnation of Abelard's teaching that he sought. Fortunately, we do have a letter from the abbot of Cluny, Peter the Venerable. Peter also wrote Pope Innocent and told a different story than Bernard had. After leaving the meeting at Sens, Abelard had headed for Rome, where he certainly would not have been well treated, thanks to Bernard's missives. But he stopped on the way at the abbey of Cluny, and here Peter convinced the sick and broken-down man to stay for the time being. But then the abbot of Cîteaux came to Cluny. This was Rainald of Bar, a former monk of Clairvaux who was abbot of Cîteaux from 1134 to 1150. He is known today for his contribution to the early Cistercian documents concerning the founding of the Order and its governance. There are also stories about him in the great collection of tales about the first years of Cistercian life, the *Exordium Magnum*. He was clearly a man of deep spirituality, and this quality seems to have drawn him to Cluny and Abelard.

According to Peter the Venerable, Rainald spoke to Peter and to Abelard about some kind of settlement with Bernard. Peter urged Abelard to go with Rainald to make peace with Bernard. Peter wrote Innocent that he had encouraged Abelard, if he had written anything unacceptable for "Christian ears," to accept the abbot of Cîteaux's advice and delete such expressions from his writings. Abelard complied and probably accompanied Rainald to Clairvaux, apparently resolving his issues with Bernard. Peter was absolutely clear about this outcome: "He [Abelard] obtained his peace with the abbot of Clairvaux, with the intervention of the abbot of Cîteaux, so that previous elements of discord were resolved."

Peter the Venerable described how the mediation by the abbot of Cîteaux made a decisive difference. Since Rainald was father abbot of Clairvaux and thus responsible for the daughter house and its abbot, this arrangement was in conformity with standard practice in the Cistercian world. But there is not a hint of this reconciliation in the letters of Bernard that have been preserved. Perhaps there was no need for a written statement, and the meeting of Cîteaux's abbot with the abbot of his daughter house and the wayward monk Peter Abelard was sufficient. In any case, the role of the abbot of Cluny cannot be overestimated. Here was the scion of established monasticism opening his abbey not only to a troubled theologian but also to a representative of the rival monastic order. In the end, all parties obtained peace, for Peter Abelard "made the decision to give up the confusion of the schools and teaching and to stay for good . . . at Cluny."

Peter the Venerable concluded his letter in asking Pope Innocent to accept Abelard's decision to spend the rest of his days at Cluny. He closed by mentioning the love that Innocent had for him, and asked that Abelard be protected by the shield the pope could provide. In other words, no one would in the future be able to accuse Abelard of unorthodoxy. Abbot Peter also indicated that Abelard probably did not have long to live. He was apparently a broken man when he got to Cluny and died there in communion with the Church. It was thanks to a Cistercian abbot, but not Bernard, that Abelard was able to avoid the papal condemnation that had been unleashed on him.

We can only speculate about how it was for Abelard, probably sick and possibly already dying, to come to Clairvaux and there ask for Bernard's forgiveness for what Abelard must have considered to be his rightful theological views. Somehow a compromise was reached and words were exchanged that satisfied Bernard and exonerated Abelard. It was Rainald, the abbot of Cîteaux, otherwise hardly mentioned in accounts of the twelfth-century Church, who proved to be the hero of the hour, convincing his brother abbot to stop his attacks on Abelard and making Abelard understand that he had to give way on some of his theological assertions.

Through these events it becomes clear that Bernard was not alone in magisterial grandeur, able to make decisions involving all the Western Church. He was very much part of the first well-organized monastic order. As a Cistercian he had to listen to his father abbot, even if the man was a former monk of Clairvaux. Rainald was responsible for Clairvaux and its abbot. He exercised his authority in making possible a meeting between Abelard and Bernard. Perhaps Peter the Venerable is the one who engineered the entire arrangement, but it was Rainald who followed his inspiration and came to Cluny. For once Bernard seems to have chosen a gentle resolution for a harsh dilemma. Instead of pursuing Abelard beyond the grave, he relented and accepted what Abelard offered.

Bernard does not emerge admirably from his pursuit and even persecution of Peter Abelard. The entire course of events leaves a bad taste, except for the final resolution, in which Bernard was by no means the prime mover. But it would be wrong to embrace the traditional clichés and view Abelard as the representative of modernity and Bernard as the Dark Ages. Both Bernard and Abelard were seeking novel ways of expressing and interpreting old truths. Their interpretations clashed, but in the end they did reach some kind of understanding.

Appealing to Pope Innocent

However much the Abelard affair seems to have filled Bernard's time and concerns in the first years of the 1140s, there were other matters that captured his attention and brought about his involvement. Here time and again he turned to Pope Innocent II, as if their disagreement about punishing schismatics was all but forgotten. Probably in 1141, he wrote to the pope on behalf of Arnulf, bishop-elect of Lisieux. Apparently the Count of Anjou had opposed the election and appealed to the pope. Arnulf had probably backed Stephen in the English civil war, and so the Count of Anjou, who was on the other side, had tried to prevent him from taking up his bishopric.

Bernard emphasized what Innocent had accomplished in his papacy, how schismatics had been defeated, heretics brought to silence, and "Sicily's tyrant" (Roger) also had been overcome. One enemy remained, however, and this was the Count of Anjou, who was destroying the Church's freedom. In persecuting the church of Lisieux, the count was hindering the bishop-elect from entering the sheepfold. Why was Bernard entering into this controversy? Most likely because he was asked to do so by Arnulf or Arnulf's friends. And with the dating of this matter in 1141, it took place at the same time that Bernard was turning to Pope Innocent for his support in condemning the theology of Abelard. Bernard had by now taken on a European role as arbiter of orthodoxy and supporter of churchmen whose positions were endangered by lay interests.

At times it is much easier to understand why Bernard intervened in a dispute. Also presumably in 1141 he wrote to Peter, the dean of the church of Besançon, and reproached him for his treatment of Guy, abbot of Cherlieu. This monastery was a daughter of Clairvaux, founded in 1131, and Peter's behavior meant that Abbot Guy had gone to Rome to put his case before the pope. Bernard appealed to the dean: "Do not persecute God's servants. . . . Avoid plucking from my heart any good opinion I harbor towards you."

Bernard not only wrote to Peter the dean. He also sent a letter to Pope Innocent to support "my cherished friend Guy, the abbot of Cherlieu." Because of the harsh treatment Guy had received from his enemies, he had risked the hardship and expense of traveling to Rome. Bernard wrote also of how dangerous it was to set out for Rome at this time. He is not specific, but his reference reminds us of his own travels in the 1130s and the difficulties he must have faced.

Rhetorically Bernard asked why he was involved in the matter. He explained that he had tried to solve the conflict in other ways but had failed. Therefore, it was necessary to go to the pope. He was a last resort for the oppressed. He promised that the abbot who bore the letter would explain what was happening not only at Cherlieu but at a nearby monastery, "likewise oppressed by the harsh assaults of evil men." There is a further letter to Pope Innocent on the same subject, but it does not provide more detail. What is noticeable here is the way Bernard had come to accept that the only solution for controversies in the Church was to go to the successor of Peter, even if that man had shown himself to be vindictive toward his former enemies.

Papal power grew in these years because bishops, abbots, and others turned to the pope to solve problems. It was not a question of popes reaching out to grasp more power. They were being sought out as the one source of hope and help when everything else had failed. In this way popes became the real heads of the Western Church, for the Curia became the court of last resort for difficult cases.

Yet another indication of this development concerns a bishop of Angers, Ulger, and the abbess of Fontevrault. Bernard wrote to the bishop concerning a dispute concerning a bridge over the Loire owned by Fontevrault. Ulger, in 1140, had built a second bridge and thus jeopardized the income the nuns had been receiving from their crossing. The abbess went to Pope Innocent, who supported her complaint and removed the bishop from office.

The bishop in turn went to Rome, and shortly before his death in September 1143, Pope Innocent reinstated him on the condition that he give the abbess satisfaction. The matter dragged on with the next popes, but our concern is Bernard's involvement. In the spring of 1142 he wrote to Bishop Ulger and then in mid-1143 to Pope Innocent, asking him to show mildness to Ulger. Bernard stated that he was not aware of what had happened between the bishop and the abbey, but if Ulger had done for the nuns what he had promised, then he should be given back his office.

There is one more letter to Ulger in which Bernard expressed his sympathy after a terrible deed whose nature is not described. It was up to Ulger to establish peace between the warring parties. Bernard wanted the bishop to write to the pope so that the matter could be resolved. The letter is not sufficiently detailed to indicate whether it was connected to the dispute with Fontevrault. In any case we see once again how Bernard involved himself in an affair that was far from Clairvaux and looked to the papacy to provide a satisfactory solution for all parties. The content of these letters indicates that it was Bishop Ulger who had turned to Bernard for guidance and access to the pope. To some extent Bernard could help him. If we try to visualize the abbot of Clairvaux's reception of daily letters from churchmen in need, it is hard to imagine that he ever had time to clear his mind and meditate or pray. His life in these years was indeed one thing after another.

Intervening in the Affairs of Bishoprics

On 10 January 1142 Bishop Henry of Sens died, and Bernard involved himself in the choice of a successor. He wrote to the clergy of the province of Sens and instructed them in seeking a new bishop "not to do so with haste, confusion or lack of consideration." He warned against repeating the bad experience of the neighboring bishopric (which is not named). The church of Sens could be plagued by troubles if its clergy acted in an irresponsible manner: "Let a fast be declared, bishops be summoned, religious men be brought in, and may God prevent you from failing to secure so sublime a cleric's election of the solemnity due to it." Bernard had been at Sens in June 1141 for the synod where he sought a condemnation of Abelard's theology. He thus would have known Bishop Henry and perhaps felt concern about the succession to the most important bishopric in the north of France. The letter demonstrates how he had taken it upon himself to be the arbiter of good behavior in the clergy. He was telling its members how to behave in an election where he had no vote. His attitude is remarkable, but this role of informal judge is what Bernard had taken on, in warning the clergy of Sens to avoid "the bad experiences" that their neighboring diocese had suffered.

With the bishop and clergy of Troyes, Bernard was on home ground, for Clairvaux was located in its diocese. Around 1140, Bernard lay down for them the canon law that said clergymen were not to bear arms and not to shed blood, nor were subdeacons to be married. In a letter that can only be dated sometime between 1138 and 1146, Bernard criticized Bishop Atto of Troyes for conferring the archdeaconate on a child, instead of someone else whom Bernard thought much better qualified for the office. He accused Atto of trying to please men, observing, "But it would be better if you obeyed God."

Sometime between 1138 and 1143, Bernard wrote to Pope Innocent on behalf of Bishop Atto, who apparently was experiencing disagreements with his clergy. There was one "unimportant young man" among them whose insolence the bishop would have to master. Bernard promised that the bearer of the letter would tell the pope who the troublemaker was. There is a series of letters to Innocent defending Atto, "a revered old man who is our friend." These letters indirectly reveal that Atto had tried to reform his clergy and had met with resistance. Bernard used various formulae of friendship in order to emphasize his attachment to Atto: "He is my friend and thus yours."

Bernard encouraged Innocent not to listen to stories told about Bishop Atto but instead to help his cause. The confidence with which he expressed himself to the pope hints that he was writing in the aftermath of the schism and before he became aware of how harsh Innocent could be with his former enemies. The other possibility is that these letters were sent during the Abelard controversy, when Bernard once again turned to Innocent for help. Whatever the exact dating, Bernard demonstrated willingness to go to bat for a friend, to defend his interests, and so to write not just one but several letters.

It was not always the case that Bernard wrote to Pope Innocent only for the sake of others. Occasionally he wrote for himself, as in a letter probably from 1143. He complained that once he had counted for something with Innocent: "My lord's eyes were fastened on me, and his ears heard my prayers." Now, Bernard felt he had lost his position with the pope, "for my lord has turned his face away from me." He had been accused of handing over Cardinal Ivo's funds according to his own preference and not in accord with the man's instructions. Bernard protested that he very well knew that a churchman's income reverted to the Church if no testament was left behind and there was no indication of how the money should be distributed.

In the letter, Bernard provided his own account of what had happened. Bernard was not present when the cardinal died, but he was told that Ivo had made a will, dividing his funds between the two abbots who were with him, while also leaving something to Bernard, to be given to poor religious houses. When the abbots arrived at Clairvaux and did not find Bernard (he was elsewhere negotiating peace between the French king and the Count of Champagne), they handed over the money to the impoverished institutions as they thought best. This took place without Bernard's knowledge or advice. He therefore entreated Innocent to "turn away your anger in the face of the truth and stop looking on me any longer with displeasure and indignation."

Bernard wrote in the same letter that he had heard Innocent was displeased with him because of his many letters, but this situation the abbot claimed he could "easily remedy." He had written not for his own sake but for that of his friends. There could, however, be too much of a good thing. He promised to be more prudent in the future and to seal his lips. He would therefore not write Innocent about the dangers threatening the Church, but he had written the bishops who were with the pope, and they would tell him of Bernard's concerns!

This letter reveals a great deal about Bernard's situation in 1143. There were clerics in Rome who accused him abusing funds from a dead cardinal and putting them to his own use. At the same time the pope apparently had had enough of his many missives and refused to take Bernard seriously. He thus did what he had tried before in his career: if the pope would not listen, then he would turn to those who were close to the pope in the Curia. Bernard insisted on conveying his message, whether or not Pope Innocent liked its content. He had come to believe that he knew what the Church needed, and, no matter who the pope was, it was essential that Bernard get his message to him. In the last fifteen years of his life, Bernard came to accept a role as defender of the Christian faith. His contemporaries were sometimes in awe of him, but they could also doubt the unselfishness of his motives. This must have been the case with Pope Innocent.

Confronting the French King

Bernard chose at this time to address three bishops in the Curia instead of the pope. Before considering this pivotal letter, it is necessary to provide some background. When the bishopric of Bourges fell vacant in 1142, King Louis VII promised the cathedral chapter a free election, in accord with the reformed Church's attempt to separate its functions from secular power. But Louis made one exception: he would not accept Peter de la Châtre, a nephew of Cardinal Haimeric. The king took an oath that he would never accept him as archbishop of Bourges. The chapter nevertheless went ahead and elected

Peter, who then went to Innocent to consecrate him. But on his return to France, Peter was prohibited from entering Bourges by the king's men. He fled to Count Theobald of Champagne, and the pope declared an interdict on any place where King Louis set foot. It was this awkward situation for monarchy and papacy into which Bernard now stepped.

Bernard started with a historical sketch about the evil that schism had created in the Church. The recent wound of the Church had hardly had a chance to heal before it was about to be torn open anew. Therefore he asked the three bishops to do everything they could in order to avoid a new schism. He blamed the king for taking an unlawful oath (against Peter as bishop) and for maintaining it contrary to justice. Bernard asked for the king to be pardoned, but not excused: "He should be spared if this can take place without damaging the liberties of the Church." Bernard had been calling for this solution for a year and had allowed himself in his eagerness to express himself in ways that he now regretted. In other words, Bernard had failed to act discreetly and diplomatically, probably also because he was being accused of misuse of the inheritance from Cardinal Ivo. At this point he was hoping that the king's goodwill and the pope's desire to heal the French Church would be sufficient to avoid a break between monarchy and papacy, the schism that Bernard saw coming.

In a letter from about the same time, Bernard assured King Louis that he was doing all he could to maintain the king's honor and the good of the kingdom. Louis had complained about a papal anathema unleashed against Count Ralph of Vermandois. Ralph was the royal seneschal, thus one of the most important figures in the kingdom, and he had been married to Leonora, the niece of Count Theobald of Champagne. Subsequently he had turned to Petronilla, the sister of Queen Eleanor of France, a relationship that had King Louis's blessing. In order to get his marriage to Leonora annulled, Ralph claimed consanguinity with her. The matter was submitted to a group of bishops who, in order to follow the king's will, accepted Ralph's plea that his marriage to Leonora was invalid. The pope, however, ordered the question to be submitted to a council. This was held near Paris, at Lagny, in 1142, under the papal legate Cardinal Ivo. The council declared Ralph's first marriage valid and the second one, to Petronilla, void, and threatened an interdict against Ralph.

King Louis was furious that his seneschal—and his wife's sister—were being treated in such a manner by the papal Church. He took his revenge on Count Theobald and invaded his territory. When threatened with interdict, Louis promised to evacuate Theobald's lands if the pope would lift his interdict on Ralph. At this point Bernard wrote the king and said that he could do nothing to remove the sentence on Ralph: "I cannot help you unless I oppose what the pope has commanded." Bernard asked Louis what Count Theobald had done in order to incur such anger from the French king.

We thus have two issues entangled in each other: the king's opposition to the new archbishop of Bourges and his fury that his sister-in-law was being separated from the official he trusted, Ralph of Vermandois. The situation now worsened. King Louis invaded Champagne and marched to the town of Vitry, which was besieged, captured, and razed to the ground. Hundreds of innocent people are said to have died. Meanwhile bishops of Châlons-sur-Marne and Paris died, and King Louis would not allow successors to be chosen. By the treaty of Vitry in late 1142, Theobald obliged himself to obtain the removal of the excommunication of Ralph, and Louis was to withdraw from the territories he had occupied. But the treaty did not specify that Ralph had to give up his second wife. The pope revoked Ralph's excommunication but later renewed it because the seneschal failed to separate from Queen Eleanor's sister.

Sometime in 1143, Bernard wrote to Pope Innocent and complained about the situation: "Nowhere is there faith; nowhere is innocence safe." Bernard lamented that Count Theobald, a great lover of innocence and piety, was exposed to his enemies' mercy. Theobald had sought to lift the sentences of excommunication and interdict, but Bernard worried that they might be imposed again. He did not mention the perennial question of Ralph's marriage to Petronilla, and so ignored the matter that had brought about the interdict. Thus the matter of marriage was allowed to remain unresolved and ruined any attempt to bring peace between king and count and reconciliation between the French monarchy and the papacy.

Soon after the treaty of Vitry, Bernard wrote to King Louis and told him that he had asked the pope to accept the peace conditions that Louis demanded, but on the condition of recognizing the divorce of Ralph of Vermandois. By this time, however, Bernard must have known that the pope would not accept the second marriage and that a second excommunication was on its way. Bernard pleaded that he was doing what he could to save the king's honor and to promote the good of his kingdom. As for the excommunication of Count Ralph, Bernard could do nothing to remove it "and even if I were able to do so, I do not think it would be reasonable for me to do so." In other words, Bernard agreed with the pope that Ralph's liaison with Petronilla was illegitimate.

Bernard added that he grieved that the king had written him that the anathema of Ralph would hinder the peace Louis had made with Count Theobald. The count had been forced, in order to make peace with Louis, to promise to obtain absolution from the interdict on Count Ralph. Thus the marital situation of the French seneschal continued to haunt high politics between France and Champagne and threatened the fragile peace that had been established between them. Bernard refused to accept this state of affairs: "How is it that you wish to add sin on sin and bring down God's wrath against you? Let it not be so!"

Bernard concluded the letter by telling Louis that he had spoken so harshly to him because he feared harder things for the king. He would not have addressed the king in such a manner "if I did not so intensely love you." Such statements belong to letters of friendship, but this is hardly one. Bernard was daring to speak to the king almost as a subordinate, who had to be corrected and reminded of God's wrath. Bernard, the son of a relatively minor knight, was daring to address the most powerful sovereign of his day in Europe. We take it almost as a matter of course that he was willing and able to write to anyone and tell them what to do, but his boldness and directness indicate that he was totally convinced that he knew what was right and how to express it. In such a case kings and popes simply had to listen to him!

A second letter to King Louis is even more direct. Bernard emphasized how fond he was of the king and with what trouble he had tried in the past year to obtain peace. But the king had failed to listen to him, "while the scars of your past evil actions are still fresh and which you recently rightly regretted." Bernard was probably alluding to the attack on and burning of Vitry in Champagne, something that he claimed must have delighted the devil himself. The king was not to make the excuse of Count Theobald as the reason for his actions, for the count was willing to keep to the terms settled with the king (presumably the treaty of Vitry). But for Bernard the king was immune to good advice: "You want to reverse everything so perversely that you consider disgrace as honor and honor as disgrace." The king could do as he wished with his kingdom, but "we the sons of the Church" could not ignore its mistreatment. Bernard and his fellow churchmen were willing to "stand up, and if it is required, to fight all the way to death for the sake of our mother [the Church]." Bernard wrote that he daily prayed for peace and had written to the pope on the king's behalf, "practically, I have to admit, in opposition to my conscience." Here he hinted about his failure to deal with the wrongful marriage of Ralph, and the reaction he had to experience from the pope: "even to the extent that I provoked against myself the Supreme Pontiff's rightful anger."

Bernard expressed anger in a manner that is relatively rare in his letters but shows how he at times dropped diplomacy, possibly as an expression of frustration with a hopeless situation. He told Louis that because of his bad behavior, "I am starting to regret that I have foolishly favored your youthful-ness more than I should have done." He accused the king of associating with persons who had been excommunicated and who were "robbers and thieves in killing men, burning their homes, destroying churches and scattering the poor."

One wonders how such a tirade affected the young king if and when it was translated for him by one of his clerics. He had assumed the throne at seventeen, in 1137, after the death of his older brother Philip in 1131. Later his queen Eleanor would call him a monk, and Louis does seem to have been attached to the Church, for he spent time at Saint Denis and there befriended Abbot Suger. In 1143 Louis was twenty-three and certainly wanted to be on good terms with the abbot of Clairvaux. But Bernard reminded him at the end of this letter that Louis had not withdrawn the oath he had made against the church of Bourges, concerning the election of its archbishop. At the same time Louis was violating church property by having soldiers and others occupy the houses of bishops. "I am telling you that it will not be long before you will be punished if you insist on this behavior. . . . Desist now from your evil practices."

Bernard ended the letter with a few conciliatory words, but the tone was still harsh. Louis apparently felt he had been tricked into making peace with Count Theobald, even though the matter of Ralph's marriage had not been solved. So he renewed his attack on the count. Bernard now turned to Lou-is's advisers, Jocelin, bishop of Soissons, and Suger, abbot of Saint Denis. According to Bernard, the king had told Ralph that Bernard had promised to take Ralph's sins on himself if the king would support Count Theobald. Bernard denied vehemently that he had made any such statement and said that the count also had no knowledge of such a promise. And yet we know that Bernard on occasions promised to take responsibility for the inadequa-cies of someone else. There is in fact a story in the *Exordium Magnum Cister-ciense* where Bernard was to have promised a doubting brother that he would supply his faith for him, and the *Vita Prima* has a similar assurance Bernard is supposed to have given in taking responsibility for King Henry I of England. Thus Bernard could have made a statement that he had taken on Ralph's sins, but he could have remembered the matter differently. But now he was insist-ing "if there is anyone to whom I gave such a message, then he can come forward and accuse me."

The main statement of the letter, however, is that Count Theobald was ready and willing to serve the king as his lord. And even if Theobald deserved harsh treatment, what about the Church and its suffering? The king was delaying episcopal elections and was laying waste to the Church's lands. At the end of the letter Bernard asked Suger and Jocelin how they could possibly support the king in such actions. The wrong being committed was the fault not of "the youthful king, but of his aged advisors." Bernard was once again leaving diplomacy behind for fierce language, but in the next letter in the collection, he pulled back from the brink and insisted that it was not his desire to lay a curse on anyone. He was addressing only Bishop Jocelin but said he thought he previously had answered both him and the abbot of Saint Denis: "I did not say nor did I write or thought of you as a schismatic or someone who created scandal. I assert this with total composure." But Bernard did wish that Jocelin and Suger would pay more attention to the liberty of the Church: "I might have wanted . . . that you demonstrated your eagerness towards that boy the king." For the king was abrogating the agreement he had made and disregarding the advice he was given: "He upsets for no reason his entire kingdom, makes war everywhere, destroys churches, desecrates what is holy . . ., persecutes the good and murders the innocent."

The purpose of this and the previous letter was clearly to make it clear that responsibility for the king's actions lay with his advisers. Bernard dismissed Louis as "a boy," a term that could have made the young king furious with the abbot. But the questions of an episcopal election and a seneschal's predilection for a second wife had been allowed to unsettle the entire kingdom and cast part of it into the tumult of war.

After the death of Innocent II on 24 September 1143, and with the election of his successor, Celestine II, perhaps in early October, Bernard tried to summarize his involvement in this complicated and painful situation by writing to a former monk of Clairvaux, Stephen, who was now cardinal bishop of Palestrina and thus a central person in the Roman Curia. Bernard claimed that he had loyally represented the French king before the former pope. The king had made many a promise but now he was "giving back evil for good." The Church in his kingdom was suffering from his refusal to accept the election of bishops, as in the diocese of Paris. At Châlons the king had handed over to his brother Robert the administration of the diocese, even though a new bishop had been chosen. Louis had furthermore begun to look for excuses to abrogate the peace he had made with Count Theobald and "what we had thought was a solid pact of friendship." Finally, he had brought back into his household a man who was an adulterer and who had been excommunicated.

Bernard was here almost certainly referring to Ralph of Vermandois. The question of his alliance with Queen Eleanor's sister was thus still unresolved, but now Bernard added a further incendiary element by asking how the king could legislate on matters of consanguinity "when it is apparent that he is living with a cousin related to him within the third degree." Bernard thus challenged the marriage of King Louis and Queen Eleanor, and this may have been the parting shot of a breakup that would eventually make it possible for Eleanor to marry Henry of Anjou. Bernard only mentioned this situation in passing and then went on to defend other marriages where the question of consanguinity had been brought up for the son and the daughter of Count Theobald.

The purpose of Bernard's letter becomes apparent at its ending, where he stated that he himself could not correct the errors that he had described, but he could warn the one who was able to do so. He was referring to Cardinal Stephen and using his Cistercian network to get into contact with the new pope. But hope came from another quarter, as can be seen from a letter to Jocelin, bishop of Soissons. Bernard expressed the desire to see Jocelin at a meeting to be held at Saint Denis. This took place in April 1144, after an earlier meeting at Corbeil. Bernard was present on both occasions. Geoffrey of Auxerre in his rough drafts for the *Vita Prima* has a remarkable story about how Queen Eleanor had an interview with Bernard and expressed concern that after the miscarriage of her first child she had become sterile. Bernard is to have answered her that if she worked for peace, then God would reward her with children. Geoffrey ends: "About the same time when peace was made, she is known to have conceived."

The story cannot be substantiated by anything in Bernard's own writings, but it would not be surprising if he had told it to Geoffrey. What is surprising is the fact that Bernard had just challenged the very legitimacy of Eleanor's marriage to Louis. Now he was listening to her lament about losing a child and perhaps being unable to have another. But the narrative is very much in character with Bernard: once he set out on a cause, he followed it all the way to the end. Just as he recruited a Cistercian cardinal for his purposes, so too he made use of the French queen. At the same time he accepted once again being absent from Clairvaux and his daily functions in his monastery. He had become a European figure, perhaps the first European, concerned with matters of war and peace and dynastic succession, making use of his own international Cistercian network and trying to reconcile royal with clerical power.

Sometime in 1144 Bernard wrote to King Louis and lamented that it had been a long time since he had put aside his own everyday life at Clairvaux in order to make peace possible "in your kingdom." Bernard claimed to be sad that there was so little to show for his efforts. The poor wept when they met him, and the countryside was devastated. Wicked people looked to the king as their inspiration. Bernard had hoped that God's grace would move the king toward peace, but this had not happened. He mentioned the recent conference at Corbeil from which Louis "unreasonably" had backed out. If he had shown more patience, Louis would have realized that nothing was said that the king could not have accepted. "We still hope that you look into your heart and complete with success that which you began so prudently."

Bernard's phrase at the start of the letter about having left his home sets the tone for perhaps the most critical of all his letters to the king. He wrote it in his own name and that of Hugh, the bishop of Auxerre. Hugh had been one of Bernard's first disciples, mentioned in the *Vita Prima*. After being Bernard's monk at Clairvaux, he was sent to become abbot of Pontigny and from 1136 was bishop. Bernard once again was taking up his own Cistercian-Clarevallian network and making it apparent to King Louis that it was not just the abbot of Clairvaux who was dealing with him. There was also a distinguished bishop. Bernard added that he was sending "our very dear brother Andrew of Baudimont" to negotiate further. Andrew was Count Theobald's procurator. If the king refused the good advice being offered him, then Bernard would disown him, for "God will not permit that his Church be oppressed much longer."

This type of language recalls Pope Gregory VII's challenge to the authority of the German king and Roman emperor Henry IV's position in the 1070s. Bernard was not a subject of the French king, except indirectly because his secular lord, Count Theobald of Champagne, owed allegiance to Louis. But the abbot of Clairvaux had taken on a role that shows how openly and directly a churchman in the twelfth century could address a king. Freedom of expression is supposed to be a practice that did not come until the eighteenth-century Enlightenment, but here is an instance where a churchman allowed himself a direct and even insulting mode of expression toward a king. Bernard's letter shows how the first medieval reformation of the Church, often called the Gregorian Reform, had succeeded in making it possible and even necessary for priests and abbots to correct and even challenge powerful men in the secular domain.

Somewhere in the midst of these negotiations and probably in 1143, Bernard wrote to Bishop Jocelin of Soissons and appealed to him as a friend. The abbot of Clairvaux claimed that he was provoked by his conscience and weighed down by God's hand. He now was kept in a bleak prison where he had to pass judgment on himself. Bruno Scott James interprets this phrase as Bernard's description of "the seclusion of his monastery," but this reading does not agree with the way Bernard usually referred to Clairvaux as a paradise. He may have been indicating that he felt himself mentally isolated and in need of a friend like Jocelin. After the stern words of previous letters to the bishop, it is surprising that he now would turn to him in such a manner. The letter is not specific enough in its language to reveal precisely what Bernard was asking for, but he certainly was appealing to the man: "If you still are my father, as I find you once were, then let me as your son feel it, for I am the son who still harbors a warm affection for you."

After so many harsh words to the king, it is remarkable to see how Bernard could turn on an old warmth toward someone from whom he earlier had kept a distance. Apparently the meeting at Saint Denis in April 1144 had made a difference, even if the dilemma of Ralph of Vermandois and his marriages remained unresolved (it would drag on until a council at Reims in 1148). But the stream of letters dries up, and we are left guessing what happened. There is one letter to the new pope, Celestine, recommending Count Theobald as a "son of peace." Bernard asked the pope to provide the necessary reconciliation: "Perhaps we do not deserve peace, but you owe it to the Church." This desire was for Bernard a command. In his own way he was telling the pope what to do! The controversy between King Louis and Count Theobald thus ended on the highest possible level, with conferences, messages, and assurances. Once again Bernard had given up his solitary life in the monastery in order to write and speak with everyone involved in an affair that had nothing to do with the Cistercian Order. But here as so often in his life Bernard involved himself in what concerned a friend. With Abelard he had followed the request of his friend William of Saint-Thierry. With King Louis he defended his friend Count Theobald. He could not leave well enough alone, ostensibly because of friendships and the loyalty they engendered. At the same time, of course, Bernard could not remain passive when the king invaded Champagne and devastated a town.

Trying to Stay at Home but Getting Involved Anyway

In the midst of Bernard's political involvements, probably in January 1143, he wrote Peter the Venerable, abbot of Cluny. He complained that Peter had failed to answer his recent letters, including one from Rome. This reference is confusing, because so far as I can determine, Bernard had not been in Rome since 1138. On the surface the letter is about friendship and what it requires, even though some modern interpreters of the relationship between Bernard and Peter have failed to see their relationship as anything more than a polite and suspicious distance between two powerful abbots. Certainly both Peter and Bernard were aware of how they addressed each other, for they knew their correspondence would be noticed in the learned Latin world. Bernard may have been reaching out in this letter and telling Peter that he forgave him for not answering his letters: "Perhaps I have cooled off toward you, something you criticize me for having done. But I am certain that warmed by your love, I shall once again grow warm."

Bernard chose to emphasize friendship, even if we can have our doubts whether two such powerful churchmen with such different interests could afford a close relationship. But Bernard indulged in the kind of effusive language that reflected his talent for putting together his thoughts: "Your letter I welcomed with my hands open. Greedily and happily I have read and reread it; the more I read it, the more pleased I am with it." Bernard obliged Peter by telling the abbot of Cluny about how he intended his future life to be: "I have made the decision to remain in my monastery. I will not go out." The only exception Bernard would make, he promised, was the General Chapter at Cîteaux. So with the help of Peter's prayers and goodwill, he would stay at Clairvaux for the brief time left to him: "I am broken in my body and have a valid reason for not getting about in the way I used to do."

Bernard in his letters occasionally referred to his bad health and proximity to death. Yet Bernard did go out, for we know that in the spring of 1144 he was at both Corbeil and Saint Denis. He did not change his ways, and he was sufficiently strong to encounter the French king and queen and tell them what God's will was for them. It is always difficult to relate what Bernard wrote to what he actually did and felt. "I will sit still and maintain peace," he promised Abbot Peter, but this is precisely what he did not do.

Perhaps at about the same time as Bernard wrote Peter, he contacted three bishops in the Curia on behalf of the abbot of Lagny. This was a wealthy abbey on the Marne in the diocese of Paris. Apparently the abbot here had refused to receive a messenger from the pope, but Bernard claimed the abbot had only been trying to deal with some difficult monks, whom he wanted to send away. Apparently they had complained to Rome, and now Bernard insisted that the pope had been deceived in the matter. Bernard dramatized events in his usual way and claimed that Benedict, the founder of Western monastic observance, would have wept, for he was being opposed, "even so that monastic observance in all its strength is being destroyed by monks who can contradict their abbot." Once again we find Bernard dealing with affairs that had nothing to do with Clairvaux or the Cistercian Order. The dating of the letter between June 1142 and September 1143 does not allow us to determine if it was written after his promise to Peter the Venerable to remain home at Clairvaux and not get involved in other matters. But in appealing to "our master Benedict," Bernard demonstrated his commitment to monastic observance and continued to involve himself in one dispute after another.

On a more personal note is a letter of consolation to Abbot John, who had abandoned his monastery. His abbey was Buzay near Nantes in Brittany, founded in 1135 by Bernard on land given by the Duchess Irmengard and her son Conan. The place must have been dear to Bernard's heart, for according to tradition its first prior was Bernard's youngest brother, Nivard. Now Bernard complained that he had written twice to the abbot and received no answer. He tried a third time, shedding "bitter tears": "Who will make it possible that you, my brother, will return again the embrace of our mother?" Bernard wanted a return to "peace of soul, the community way of life, spiritual brotherhood and peace of mind in which I once held you." He assured John that the rumors were false that said the abbot of Clairvaux as father abbot was thinking of removing him from office. John had only to come to his senses, by looking into his heart. Then he could return to his monastery and his office as abbot. It was understandable that John was a man like everyone else, "sailing over life's immense ocean. . . . Who can claim that he never has been cast about by strong winds and thrown by huge waves?"

Bernard asked that John realize that his doubts and hesitations were only human. He begged him to return "before I die, so that I who have loved you in this life will not be driven apart from you in death." There were meekness and gentleness in Bernard's appeal, but also a threat. If John persisted in his absence from his monastery, then Bernard's undying affection would be useless. Bernard would no longer have any responsibility for him. He balanced his appeal to solidarity with a warning that charity might disappear. In the heading for this letter it is claimed that John had sought solitude. I find nothing in the body of the letter to indicate John's whereabouts, only that he had left his community. There is also no further indication of John's behavior. We do not know whether he returned to his abbey or not. But such a letter must have been included in the collection because it demonstrated Bernard's concern for his monks. In spite of all his travels and commitments outside the Cistercian Order, he still kept in touch with the abbots of his daughter houses. Or at least some of them. In the case of John, he seemed to have tried to smother the man with his love.

The York Election

At the same time as Bernard was trying to resolve the dispute between Louis VII and Theobald of Champagne, he spent some of his energy on the election of an archbishop that in principle had only peripheral relevance for the Cistercian world. On the death of Archbishop Thurstan of York in 1140, King Stephen brought forth his candidate, William Fitzherbert, who was the son of the king's sister, Emma, and thus Stephen's nephew. The Cistercian abbots of Rievaulx and Fountains and the Augustinian priors of Kirkham and Gisburn objected to the choice, and so the papal legate, Henry of Blois, encouraged William Fitzherbert to take his case to Rome. At this point the Yorkshire abbots in turn decided to send a delegation to Rome (1142). It is almost certain that they stopped at Clairvaux and conferred with Bernard. Rome decided to send the litigants home and ordered all those involved to return the following year. On 7 March 1143 the case was heard again, and once again there was no settlement. William Fitzherbert appealed to the testimony of the dean of York, William of Saint Barbe, and Pope Innocent stipulated that William would have to swear that no pressure had been exerted on him and his chapter by King Stephen's men.

An initial candidate for archbishop, Waldef of Kirkham, was eliminated because King Stephen considered him to be too close to his rival for the monarchy, Matilda. King Stephen wanted a man he could trust. The dean of the York chapter, William of Saint Barbe, avoided taking an oath to declare he had not been subjected to political pressure and tried to substitute other witnesses willing to guarantee the fact of a free election. These men did as they were told, and on 26 September 1143, William Fitzherbert was consecrated archbishop of York.

Bernard by now was deeply involved in the matter and claimed he wanted to come to England. Instead he sent the abbot of Vauclair, Henry Murdac, an Englishman who had been Bernard's monk at Clairvaux. When Murdac arrived at Fountains Abbey in Yorkshire in 1144, he was elected abbot, and it was in this position that he carried out Bernard's designs for removing William Fitzherbert. The first indication of Bernard's intentions is a letter to Pope Innocent, probably from 1142, warning him against William Fitzherbert: "He places his trust not in God as his helper but in the amount of his riches." Bernard accused Fitzherbert of having purchased his office and asked the pope to treat him as Saint Peter had done with the one "who thought he could buy with money God's gifts." He was referring to the case of Simon Magus (Acts 8), at a time when the reformed Church of the twelfth century was doing its utmost to be freed of simony.

When Aelred, monk of Cistercian Rievaulx, and Walter of London, archdeacon of York, stopped at Clairvaux in 1142, Bernard provided them with a letter of introduction to Pope Innocent. These men, Bernard assured the pope, had no personal interest in the matter. They were selfless. Their sole purpose was to obtain justice, and so they had come from a great distance and did not fear "the perils of the sea, the heights of the Alps and . . . the expense of such a trip." For once we get a sense of how Bernard visualized the dangers of travel. He had braved the Alps and the Mediterranean in the 1130s, and now in the 1140s was encouraging Aelred, a fellow Cistercian, to do the same. Medieval literature seldom provides a sense of how people experienced nature, and Bernard's brief description of the perils of travel may well be a set of clichés in order to impress the pope. But it was difficult, dangerous, and expensive to travel from Yorkshire to Rome, and Bernard dramatized this fact.

A similar letter of recommendation was addressed to Cardinal Gerard and is dated to the first months of 1142. In 1144 he would be elected pope as Lucius II, but at this point he was papal chancellor and thus a central figure for the Yorkshire delegation. Another letter was composed to Guy of Castello, who on 25 September 1142 would succeed Innocent as Celestine II. We thus have a succession of three popes, from Innocent II through Lucius II, but the one who was decisive would be Eugenius III (1145–53). It is remarkable how many letters Bernard composed on this concern, which in itself was peripheral to Cistercian interests. But here as in the Abelard affair, Bernard probably thought of himself as responding to the needs and concerns of friends: in sending Henry Murdac to England, Bernard was making a lasting commitment. It is not by accident that the York chapter ended by electing Murdac as its archbishop.

Bernard composed a number of letters on this matter in the first months of 1142, but one of them, to the Cistercian cardinal Stephen of Palestrina, stands out. Bernard reminded Stephen that he "often had helped others in many situations, and so I think that you in this affair cannot fail to help your own people." The Latin is much more compressed than any translation can provide, for Bernard was writing to someone who knew him and would understand his meaning. The next year he wrote the papal legate, Henry, bishop of Winchester, after the case had been referred back to England. He encouraged him to deal with the question "in a manner so that there be no hint of unpleasant suspicion to question the recognition you should receive." What mattered was to make it possible for the canons of York freely to elect whomever they chose. In other words, the first election had not been free, and therefore not legal.

In a letter to Robert, bishop of Hereford, Bernard asked that he make the right decision for the honor of God and the Church's liberty so that "the evil situation not be any further extended." In another letter, in mid-1143, Bernard both begged and threatened King Stephen. With "his whole heart" he beseeched the king to change his mind on the matter and not to block the outcome of the affair, in accord with the pope's decision. The canons should be allowed to elect another archbishop, as all canons in all churches should be free to elect their bishops. If Stephen acted in this way, then God would be on his side.

Bernard was telling the king, in the midst of civil war, that if he followed Bernard's recommendation and removed William Fitzherbert, then he would prosper. God would make him "glorious and raise up your throne." Bernard also wrote to Stephen's queen, Matilda, saying that if she had the fear of God, then she should keep "that man" (Fitzherbert) from continuing as archbishop of York. Bernard assured the queen that "religious men whom I find to be completely trustworthy" had informed him about Fitzherbert's dubious way of life.

In a letter from mid-1143 to the abbots of Rievaulx and Fountains, Bernard described his own situation. He had to carry out his duty as a Cistercian abbot "to leave my house and make visitations." But he was obliged to see the brothers in Yorkshire who were suffering because of ill treatment for their resistance to Fitzherbert. Because of his own "weakness," Bernard was sending Henry Murdac, the abbot of Vauclair: "Listen to him, I implore you, as if he were myself." He was a good man "who has taken on something of my own concerns and burdens and has a part in my functions in correcting faults and maintaining the state of the Order."

Bernard was handing over his function as father abbot and visitor of Rievaulx and Fountains to Henry Murdac. The Cistercian constitutions did not formally give a father abbot the right to do so, but Bernard with all his activities could hardly have avoided delegating some of his functions to other abbots. He ended this letter with a request for prayers: "Throw me a rope of prayer." He described himself as being out at sea while the brothers he addressed were safely in harbor. Such a passage is conventional, but the use of conventional language does not have to mean it was not meant sincerely. Bernard needed help and could not function without a network of trustworthy abbots and friends.

After the death of Innocent II and the election of Celestine II in September 1143, Bernard wrote the new pope and used harsh language to describe how Fitzherbert had been chosen. He called him a "vile and evil person" and asked how he could have been made bishop. William the dean of York's avoidance of taking an oath was seen by Bernard as more or less an admission of guilt, and so Fitzherbert was "judged and convicted." At this time Bernard wrote an even more polemical letter to all the Curia, saying that the matter had made him weary of life, for "in God's house we see horrible things." He may have been referring to the fact that Walter of London, who had accompanied Aelred on the first visit to Rome, had been captured and mishandled. Also at about this time marauders attacked and plundered Fountains Abbey. Bernard saw the installation of Fitzherbert as archbishop as a "sacrilege," a "great scandal," and added he was afraid that the authority of the papacy itself was being undermined by such an illegal election. At the end of the letter he asked that the Curia "hold back from consenting to such a heinous action." His language is even harsher here than in his polemics against Abelard.

Sometime between March 1144 and February 1145, Bernard wrote the next pope, Lucius II, that he had returned home to his own affairs after "a superb meeting, with much gratitude to the Lord and in rejoicing." The word *curia* was seen by Bruno Scott James as indicating that Bernard had been in Rome, but this was not the case. Bernard was probably referring to the court held on 22 April 1144 at Saint Denis in order to solve the conflict between Louis VII and Theobald of Champagne. It is here that Bernard had met with both the king and the queen. Now Bernard was waiting for the pope's decision about the archbishop of York, in view of the fact that William of Saint Barbe had refused to take the oath required of him. Bernard attacked the papal legate, Henry of Blois, and of course William Fitzherbert. Henry of Blois is described as "the old whore of Winchester," language that thankfully is rare in Bernard's vocabulary.

Why did Bernard involve himself in a distant archbishopric at a time when he was caught up in trying to establish peace between the French king and the Count of Champagne? His initial involvement in the last years of Pope Innocent II is understandable, the result of what he was told by the English envoys and especially the young Aelred of Rievaulx. But Bernard then had to face two popes who only headed the Church for a year each, and he must have realized that his campaign against William Fitzherbert was being complicated by the civil war raging in England. Bernard's decision to transfer Henry Murdac to Yorkshire was a brilliant move that placed a native Yorkshireman on the side of those who opposed Fitzherbert. And perhaps Bernard was not at all surprised when the monks of Fountains elected Murdac as their abbot, or when later the chapter of York chose him as their archbishop. Thus the affair ended as Bernard wanted, but the energy required to achieve this goal was enormous.

Here as in so much else, Bernard was relentless. He probably got involved in the affair after he heard rumors about the election of Fitzherbert, and he became convinced that it was his duty to intervene. It is difficult to understand, however, how he could have persisted with such vehemence.

Sometime in the first years of the 1140s Bernard completed a small treatise that shows a gentler side. Known as *On Precept and Dispensation*, the treatise was ostensibly a response to a query from two Benedictine monks from a monastery near Chartres. They were apparently having difficulty following monastic obedience, and they wanted to hear from Bernard about the limitations on their obligations to carry out what the abbot imposed on them. Bernard's response can at first seem conventional in emphasizing the Rule of Saint Benedict's strictures about the importance of unquestioning obedience. But then come reservations that show how Bernard as abbot knew that there had to be limitations on his authority: "Nor is the abbot above the Rule, for he himself once freely placed himself beneath it." There is one rule above the Rule of Benedict, and that is the rule of charity.

The treatise surprisingly turns into a series of warnings to abbots not to go too far in their treatment of their monks: "Let superiors then hold their subjects to what they themselves have promised rather than to their own whims." Bernard added, however, that what religious superiors ordered was normally to be obeyed "as the commands of God." The Rule of Benedict does not require anything that is impossible, but we are to obey as we would God. The Rule consists in what is normal and natural for a religious community, but the abbot is not to imagine that his desires are always in agreement with the Rule. Bernard admitted that "nobody can always obey his superiors perfectly," but "disobedience is only a light fault" so long as the monk was willing to accept "the discipline of regular penance."

It was during these years that Bernard was formulating his claim that a monk could leave one community and join another one without the permission of his abbot, so long as he was going from a less rigorous to a more rigorous way of life. The Benedictines and Cluniacs were naturally not keen on such a practice, for they would only lose monks and the Cistercians only gain. The Cistercians took it for granted that their way of life was more ascetic than traditional monastic observance. But instead of writing a treatise on this topic, Bernard chose to take a greater perspective and considered the entire question of obedience and stability of life for a monk. In doing so he went beyond a Cistercian agenda and looked at the monastic *conversatio* or way of life as a whole. His treatise would have a rich afterlife and was even of use for the chancellor of the University of Paris and theologian, Jean Gerson (1363–1429), in his own deliberations about the meaning and limitations of obedience. Gerson was no Cistercian: he was a secular priest and a university theologian, but he found Bernard's thinking enlightening.

Bernard could sometimes reach out beyond parochial concerns and make a statement that embraced all of Christianity. This he did with *On Precept and Dispensation*. In the last ten years of his life he would appeal time and again beyond the Cistercians to a European audience.

A Cistercian Pope and Great Expectations

On 15 February 1145 Bernardo Paganelli was elected pope and took the name Eugenius III. He was abbot of the Cistercian house of Tre Fontane outside of

Rome. He had been canon of the cathedral of Pisa but in 1135 had followed Bernard from Italy to Clairvaux, where he became a monk. He had been sent out to refound the abbey of Farfa, but Innocent II had diverted Bernardo and his brothers to Tre Fontane. The circumstances of Bernardo's election were dramatic: he was chosen by the cardinals on the very day that Pope Lucius II died. Lucius had been seriously injured leading an army opposing the Roman republicans. He died soon after his attempt to storm the Capitoline Hill. The cardinals were afraid that any delay in choosing a successor would mean the Roman mob would influence the election and force the new pope to accept the newly established "Senate and Roman Republic." Rome was too dangerous for the new pope, who had to receive episcopal consecration in the very monastery of Farfa that he was supposed to refound as a Cistercian. From here he came to Viterbo, the refuge of many a medieval pope.

When Bernard heard about events in Italy he was delighted that one of his own monks had been chosen pope. As far as we know, he had no influence on the election of Bernardo, who was removed from his abbacy because the cardinals needed a worthy candidate who could quickly fill the post. Shortly after receiving news of the election, Bernard wrote Bernardo, now Eugenius III. Bernard said that he had been waiting for a reliable messenger to come and tell him "everything precisely as it had happened." His friends asked Bernard to convey "whatever small portion remains with me of my life." Two manuscripts add the sentence "I have only a few days left to me now, for only the grave remains." This assertion, however, is not included in the Latin critical edition of the letters. But the tone is already established: Bernard did not expect to live long. The expression of self-pity is not a common theme in his writings, but he could make his physical frailty into a concern.

After this hardly celebratory beginning Bernard played with the fact that Bernardo, once a son to Bernard, had now become his father: "I was your father, but now I have been made into your son." Bernard reminded Bernardo that it was he who had begotten him, in the sense of making him a monk and being his spiritual father. Thus Bernardo would always be fundamentally dependent on Bernard, something to which Bernard in the coming years would return. Bernard was confident that the Church rejoiced in the new pope, especially because it did not have time to enjoy his predecessors. Three popes had reigned in rapid succession. The new pope should be aware of his position: "How terrible, how awful is the place you hold," for the pope occupied the holy ground in the place of Peter, the prince of the apostles.

As Bernardo, now Eugenius III, read carefully through Bernard's magisterial sentences, he may well have been thinking to himself, "I wonder what he wants." This concern becomes immediately apparent after the references to the primacy of Saint Peter. "I am writing to you prior to the time when I had intended to do so," said Bernard. The bishop of Winchester and archbishop of York were in disagreement with the archbishop of Canterbury. Henry of Winchester was being challenged as papal legate, and now it was up to Eugenius III to resolve the matter. Bernard envisioned how the Church had been in the time of the apostles and hoped before his death to be able to see it again in such a state. He recalled the time "when the Apostles cast their nets not in order to catch gold and silver but mens' souls." The final section of the letter asked Eugenius to have courage and to remember that he was human: "How many Roman popes have died, as you have seen with your own eyes, in a brief time." Bernard considered the deaths of Eugenius's predecessors a warning. The pope should always be thinking of his coming end.

These lines suggest that Bernard was already planning his *De consideratione*, the treatise on the interior life that he would compose for Eugenius. As he wrote earlier in this letter, he had put aside the name of father but still had a father's concerns as well as a father's affection. He felt that Eugenius and with him the entire Church were his responsibility.

At about the same time Bernard wrote to the members of the Curia. He claimed that they had recalled a dead man from his grave and given him back to his fellow men. In other words, they had taken Bernardo Paganelli from the grave of the cloister into the life of society. Bernard saw the new pope as a Cistercian, who had lived apart from the world—an ironic description in view of what had happened to Bernard himself, who according to his biographers drew crowds whenever he went out into the public. Bernard described the new pope as a rustic; the cardinals had removed "his axe, mattock or hoe" and enthroned him. He asked if there was no other suitable candidate for such a post. It was "ridiculous" to lay hold of a man dressed in rags and have him take on the papal functions. But such a choice, being so absurd, could only be an expression of the will of God!

Bernard claimed to be worried that a man who was so used to contemplation and solitude would find himself cast into a confusion of affairs, like "a child that was taken suddenly from his mother's arms." The new pope, he was afraid, would be crushed by the burdens placed upon him, and so it must be the concern of everyone, but especially the Curia, to support the man in his work. Bernard here made use of his literary talent to characterize and even poke fun at Eugenius, who was more used to manual labor than to palatial surroundings. Bernard himself was struggling to comprehend what had happened; the election of Eugenius seems to have taken him by surprise.

The abbot of Clairvaux revealed his concern that the new pope would pass him by. He wrote to Eugenius about how two brothers had come from the pope to provide Bernard with consolation. When the letter with the papal seal was opened, it had the apostolic benediction that Bernard wanted and needed. Bernard said these words brought his spirit to life, so much so that he threw himself on the ground to thank God and the pope's brethren. Then everyone else did the same. Are we to imagine the brothers of Clairvaux falling over each other and casting themselves to the ground because their abbot did so? Or was Bernard exaggerating, as he often did, in trying to describe his relief that he had the pope's attention and good graces?

A further indication of Bernard's state of mind is a letter to Cardinal Robert Pullen, papal chancellor. He rejoiced in Eugenius's election, even though this monk now had been taken away from Bernard. He asked the cardinal to give him comfort and good advice, containing the simplicity of the dove and the wisdom of the serpent "against the old serpent's cunning." There were many things Bernard wanted to say, but he could confide in the "living voice" of the brothers who brought the letter. Here Bernard was more restrained than in what he wrote to Eugenius. Perhaps he had matters on his mind that were not to be made public in a letter.

Another letter to the new pope, from March 1145, expressed Bernard's dismay that the election had imposed new burdens on him. He claimed that it was being said "that you are not the pope. It is I, and from all places people hasten to me with their cases." Bernard admitted that among these petitioners were those whom he could not refuse to help. But his reason for writing Eugenius now was due to "the idol of York." He reminded Eugenius of his responsibility as pope. Because of the office's fullness of power he alone had the right and prerogative to depose bishops. "It is reserved to you, that which should be done. God's Church, over which its Founder has placed you, must see your dedication's fervor." Here Bernard was telling the pope what to do, at the same time as he was reserving to the pope an authority that no other bishop had. Bernard may seem to contradict himself in conceding power and qualifying it. But in his view papal authority had to be responsive to the good advice he could give. He asked Eugenius "not to be deaf to our sobs and cries, so that your brothers' sighs can penetrate your heart."

This language was more emotionally charged than the language Bernard had used to address previous pontiffs. He pointed out how Cardinal Hincmar had been to York with the pallium, the piece of clothing that signified papal recognition of an archbishop. But the cardinal had been scandalized by what he had heard and seen, and so returned to Rome without conferring this sign of office. As papal legate the cardinal could demote the archbishop. Bernard appealed on behalf of the archbishop of Canterbury (who clearly was the rival of the archbishop of York). Bernard insisted that the pope should consider his request, presumably to remove William Fitzher-bert. Canterbury's archbishop is described as "a friend of our brethren." Here Bernard was openly encouraging the Cistercian pope to consider his Cistercian brothers.

Bernard made no attempt to be diplomatic. He was asking the pope to resolve the situation at York by removing the archbishop. How much lon-ger, he asked, would he have to wait "in suspense"? He was listening for the pope's messenger to arrive, but he did not come. So he could only beg the pope not to delay: "Let me know what you are doing about the question and what you would like me to do." Bernard could not accept the delay after his former monk and abbot of a Clairvaux daughter house had become pope. Eugenius, however, was trapped by the mechanisms of the Curia and unable to act with the speed that Bernard required. Bernard's impatience was natural for a churchman who had been able to depend on the efficiency of the Cistercian network, providing ready communication and relatively swift decisions made at the General Chapter. The Western Church did not function like the Cistercian Order. It was a top-heavy mechanism, obliged to take into consideration endless local interests. Whatever Eugenius III wanted to do about the situation at York, he had to proceed with caution, aware of the English civil war and other bishops who were wary about their own positions.

Sometime between March and November 1145, Bernard again wrote Pope Eugenius. He praised him for various actions and encouraged him to assist the "hapless Church on the other side of the sea," the first indication we have of Bernard's coming involvement in what we call the Second Cru-sade. The main topic, however, was the archbishop of York: "How can you allow such a man to remain when you have a number of excellent reasons for removing him?" Bernard claimed that he knew the pope wanted to do so but "it is not my place to tell you what to do."

This, however, is precisely what Bernard was doing! The following year Bernard again wrote Eugenius. William Fitzherbert had been suspended but had not yet been deposed. In the meantime there had been an attack on Fountains Abbey, presumably by supporters of William Fitzherbert. William was close to King Stephen, and it may well have been the king's men who carried out the raid on Fountains. Bernard spoke of the monks as his chil-dren "who have been scattered." In this situation, he said, "words provide no consolation." Bernard grieved, and yet he was himself partly responsible for contributing to what had become an overheated situation, with insinuation, name-calling, and demands that the wrath of God be visited upon William Fitzherbert and his supporters.

At this point the letters cease. We know, however, that Eugenius did depose William Fitzherbert. A new archiepiscopal election took place in 1147, and the choice of the canons of York was none other than the abbot of Fountains, Henry Murdac. Once again Bernard's intervention in an episcopal election ended up securing the office for a Cistercian. There is no doubt that Murdac was a good choice, but after his death, William Fitzherbert was again elected archbishop. He came to be widely admired as a holy man and worthy archbishop. Bernard's taunts sound slightly hollow in view of later developments, and his only excuse is that he probably sincerely believed that Fitzherbert had been elected because of outside pressure. But Bernard had exhausted all his political and personal resources in sullying the reputation of a man who later came to be considered a saint.

This unpleasant controversy left behind one genuinely beautiful letter that is a masterpiece of Cistercian spirituality. After the young monk Aelred of Rievaulx visited Clairvaux on his way to Rome in the Fitzherbert controversy, Bernard wrote Aelred and encouraged him to write a work on the way charity can coexist with the ascetic life of a monk. Apparently Bernard and Aelred had discussed the possibility while the latter was at Clairvaux, but the young monk had pleaded lack of learning: "You have claimed that you have no grammar, that you are practically illiterate." Aelred insisted that he had been trained in "the kitchen" and not "the schools." Such claims only inflamed Bernard's desire to make use of Aelred's talents: "I am thankful to accept your excuses . . . for learning that comes from the Holy Spirit's school rather than those of rhetoric." This would be all the better for Bernard. He would thus accept no prevarication: "In the name of Christ I command . . . that you now write down what you have considered in your long meditations, on charity's excellence." Bernard even gave the work a title, "The Mirror of Charity," and this became an outstanding expression of Cistercian spirituality in the twelfth century, a statement of how the ascetic life and affectivity can join in gentle harmony. Bernard saw that Aelred was his man, for he had indeed spent more time in kitchens (at the court of King David of Scotland) than in the schools. Aelred knew what it meant to meditate while being absorbed in practical affairs, and in this way his early life had been an ideal preparation for his Cistercian vocation.

Bernard himself experienced that the practical life was a suitable point of departure for the monastic one, and now he ordered Aelred to write about what he had learned in combining the two. So he should tell "what charity is, what sweetness it had . . . and that outside difficulties, instead of diminishing charity . . . can only help to increase it."

Bernard referred to Aelred's earlier life, when he apparently had been trapped in sensuality and living in "the house of death." The exact content of Aelred's youthful sins has long been a subject of controversy among scholars, but what mattered for Bernard was that Aelred had profited from what he had learned and now had integrated his insights into the Cistercian way of life. Since the time of Bernard and Aelred generations of men and women have followed the same path in combining what they learned "under a tree's shade in the noonday heat" with the meditations that arise during a monastic way of life. Bernard's genius was being able to see that Aelred could write "The Mirror of Charity," which Bernard himself could not complete. Aelred became the mouthpiece of affective Cistercian spirituality.

And what about Pope Eugenius III? His pontificate was marred by the fact that he was hardly ever able to reside in Rome. He had to leave in February 1145 for the city for Farfa, about twenty-five miles to the north, in order to be consecrated there. The citizens of Rome had been influenced by Arnold of Brescia, one of the heretics that Bernard was pursuing, and now there was a commune at Rome under a patrician—with no room for a pope.

Eugenius's troubles were complicated by the news of the fall of Edessa in 1144, prompting him to summon what we call the Second Crusade. He worked heartily for the reform of the Church and held synods in Paris, Reims, and Trier, spending more time in northern Europe than in Italy. He died in July 1153, just a few weeks before Bernard, and he had to acknowledge the failure of many of his programs: the crusade, a papacy resident in Rome, and maintenance of the failed marriage of Eleanor of Aquitaine and Louis VII of France. The only Cistercian aspect of his papacy is the claim that he wore under his papal robes the habit of a Cistercian monk. Otherwise he was the victim of the politics that characterized the papacy in the twelfth century.

Neither his Cistercian background nor his bond with Bernard provided him with the solutions he needed in order to guide the Church. Bernard's legacy to Eugenius, however, is apparent in the first books of *On Consideration*, in which he warned Eugenius and all future popes that they would lose their souls if they got completely lost in papal politics. Thus, Bernard's contribution to the papacy of Eugenius was not to gain influence but to warn that his former monk might lose his position. He alerted Eugenius to the prospect that his attention to church business might mean the loss of his eternal soul. Bernard gained no great influence in experiencing the election of a Cistercian pope, a fact he seems to have acknowledged in his later letters to Eugenius.

Perhaps the immediate aftermath of the election of Eugenius, however, brought some hope to Bernard that he would now have a direct link with the papal bureaucracy, but he soon came to realize that Eugenius made his own decisions. Bernard had to reconcile himself with a former monk who in every way made clear that he was following his own agenda, not that of his former abbot.

In Pursuit of Heretics: One More Tired Voyage

The first half of the 1140s was a crowded time for Bernard, with his pursuit of Abelard and involvement in the quarrel of the French king and the Count of Champagne. Abelard was by no means the only major figure whom Bernard looked upon as threatening the unity of the Church. Another was Arnold of Brescia, a fascinating and disturbing figure, a former student of Abelard, and an advocate of removing all property from the Church and handing it over to the secular authorities. He was condemned already in 1138 and banished from Italy, but in 1142 he was threatening to return. At this point Bernard wrote the bishop of Constance and spoke of Arnold as a thief who had forced his entry into the Church. Bernard associated him with Abelard, but now "he is doing ill among you and consuming our people as if they were bread; his mouth is filled with cursing and harshness. . . . Destruction and suffering are what he offers and he has no knowledge of the way of peace." Bernard was even more eloquent here than usual in presenting a danger to the Church. The letter dates to 1142, before Arnold returned to Italy.

To Cardinal Guy, the papal legate in Bohemia, Bernard wrote that he had heard Guy was befriending Arnold. Bernard described Arnold as a "man whose life has the sweetness of honey and whose teaching the bitterness of poison." He had been expelled from Brescia, Rome, France, Germany, and Italy. Anyone who supported Arnold was guilty of acting against the pope and even God. So Bernard was confident that Guy, having ascertained the danger that Arnold posed, would act accordingly. The letter is probably from 1143, after Arnold's return to Italy. He would incite the Roman population and give them hope of restoring the republic of old. Because of Arnold, Eugenius III would not be able to reside in Rome, and it was not until the time of Hadrian IV in 1155, two years after Bernard's death, that Arnold was caught and put to death.

From May to August 1145 Bernard traveled through what is now the South of France with Cardinal Alberic of Ostia and Bishop Geoffrey of Chartres. Their aim was to deal with the errors of the monk Henry, who claimed that infants are not saved by baptism, that all churches should be destroyed as useless, that the crucifix should not be venerated, and that prayers and alms are a waste of time. Bernard seemed to understand the essence of Henry's anticlerical teaching, for in a letter to the Count of Toulouse, Alphonsus, he said that Henry wanted "churches that have no people; people that have no priests; priests without the reverence that they are owed." Bernard told the count that it was count's responsibility that Henry was present in his territory: "Only with your protection is he able to maraud the sheep of Christ." Bernard called Henry an apostate who had abandoned his monastic garb and now in his worldly ways was found to frequent prostitutes. He brought his filth to wherever he went, and for this reason Bernard said he had come to Toulouse with his companions.

After Bernard left the area in August 1145, he wrote to the people of Toulouse and said that he was pleased to hear from his brother Abbot Bertrand of Grandselve that they had genuine faith in God. Thanking God "that it was not in vain that we came to you," he promised to return "to work for your instruction and salvation, even though I am weak and sick, but I shall not bother about the cost." Bernard warned the people not to allow any unknown preacher to come to them. He commended the letter's bearer, the abbot of Grandselve. His monastery had lately been affiliated with the Cistercian Order and was now a daughter of Clairvaux. This had just happened in 1145 and shows the success of Clairvaux's lineage, not necessarily in founding new houses but in converting established ones to its allegiance.

Bernard clearly thought he had been successful in his mission, and he had no idea that Toulouse and its region hid a much greater threat than Henry. This was the Cathars, the "good men" who totally rejected Christianity in their dualism but whose leaders came across to the people as "good Christians" because they seemed to imitate the apostles in their poverty and simplicity of life. Bernard had been warned about the Cathars in a letter from Eberwin of Steinfeld, the prior of a Premonstratensian house near Cologne. Bernard preached two of his Sermons on the Song of Songs concerning the danger of the "little foxes," whom he accused of maintaining illicit relationships with women. Such people, he said, cannot avoid having sex: "To be always in a woman's company without having carnal knowledge of her—is this not a greater miracle than raising the dead?" Bernard did not think highly of male-female companionship, but he believed in the sanctity of marriage, in opposition to the Cathars, who condemned it.

The fullest account of Bernard's preaching and mission of conversion in the South of France is provided in a letter to the brothers of Clairvaux by Bernard's secretary, Geoffrey of Auxerre. At Poitiers, before the beginning of the mission, Bernard was unwell, but he recovered sufficiently to visit Bordeaux, Bergerac, Cahors, and Toulouse. For Geoffrey it was the heresy of Henry that was the object of Bernard's preaching: "The abbot spoke in the villages which he [Henry] had led astray." Geoffrey promised the brothers of Clairvaux that they would see Bernard again, soon after August 22. The purpose of his narrative seems to have been to show the monks that Bernard's absence from their monastery was for a good reason and was having a worthwhile result. But neither Geoffrey nor Bernard seems to have realized that it was the Cathars and not the Henricians who were the most dangerous opponents of orthodoxy. Bernard, however, in promising to work for the instruction and salvation of the entire population of Toulouse, had redefined his function as a Cistercian abbot. He showed no hesitation in making such a commitment, and so he abandoned the Cistercian impulse to seek isolation from the world and accepted a pastoral role for himself in the Church. [For Bernard's understanding of his commitment as monk and abbot, see question 6 in the Fifteen Questions about Bernard: The Background for My Portrait section.]

Endless Involvements

It seems almost impossible to keep up with Bernard's involvements during these years, and any biography of him is in danger of turning into a list of people met and places visited. But there is a general pattern that is worth noticing: Bernard worked to define orthodox belief and at the same time responded for the most part generously to the churchmen and others who turned to him for counsel and assistance. In concluding this chapter I will present two examples of Bernard's defense of the faith and assistance to various causes. For the first case I have to reach back to 1139 when he wrote to the canons of the church of Lyon. His purpose was to criticize their holding a special observance to celebrate the immaculate conception of the Virgin Mary. For Bernard such a feast was without precedent: "The Church knows not of it, reason cannot recognize it, and in tradition there is no form of authority."

Bernard was not right. The feast of the Immaculate Conception existed in England and a few places on the Continent. But he was right that it had not become established in the universal Church. He accepted that Mary was holy before she was born, but he refused to accept that her conception was totally free from sin, in the same way as that of Jesus had been. For Bernard the conception of a child always, except for Jesus, took place together with "carnal lust," and here there was always some sin. "Would it not be truer to claim that because her conception was not holy, then after she had been conceived, she was sanctified? Therefore, her birth was holy." Thus "the privilege of a holy conception was to be kept for him alone who brought us all to sanctification." In that case there was no reason to celebrate the conception of Mary, and to do so was "superstition."

Some of the modern interpreters of this letter claim that Bernard was not opposed to what became the Roman Catholic teaching on the doctrine of the Immaculate Conception. But I fail to see the difference between the view of Mary that Bernard attacked and the understanding of her identity found today in Catholic orthodoxy. Bernard rejected this teaching because of his understanding of the Church's tradition. He overstated his case in claiming that the Church knew nothing of this observance, but he was right that it by no means had become universal. He was here, as in so much else, a traditional theologian, looking carefully at what he found in biblical texts and the teachings of the Church Fathers. For him the observances of the English Church did not count!

The second instance of Bernard's involvement is from late in 1145, when he wrote Pope Eugenius. He praised the pope for having refused the French king's petition on behalf of the bishop of Orléans, who was accused of crimes and would resign his see the following year. Bernard assured the pope that it gave him "joy to hear similar reports of your actions." But for himself, Bernard said he was not able to handle the burdens imposed on him. Eugenius should know that insofar as he spared Bernard, he would be sparing himself. The implication seems to be that any further tasks would crush Bernard and thus hand over the burden to Eugenius.

In the Latin text there is a further significant sentence which for some reason Bruno Scott James did not translate: "My resolution not to go outside my monastery I believe is not hidden from you." In other words, Bernard had, after his exhausting trip to the South of France, decided not to leave Clairvaux, and he assumed that Eugenius knew about this decision. He had promised the citizens of Toulouse to return to them to preach and teach, but now he was pulling back. And yet at the same time he had a list of concerns for the pope. First of all, he was sending a new abbot to the monastery from which Eugenius had come, St. Anastasius, also known as Tre Fontane. Concerning this measure, Bernard promised that his envoys would inform the pope "in a clearer and fuller matter."

Bernard asked Eugenius that the action taken by Baldwin, the archbishop of Pisa, concerning the excommunication of a judge (corresponding to the rank of prince) in Avora, Sardinia, be confirmed by papal authority. Baldwin had been a monk of Clairvaux, and Bernard was maintaining contacts with him. We find him mentioned in the later *Exordium Magnum Cisterciense*. Finally, Bernard asked that the judge of La Torre be welcomed by the pope, for he was a good prince. This is probably Gunnar or Gonario of Sardinia, also found in the *Exordium*, which described how he eventually became a monk at Clairvaux. Bernard is said to have prophesied that Gunnar would return to Clairvaux from Sardinia.

This relatively brief letter reveals a number of concerns of which Bernard wanted to make the pope aware. It is as if he had almost forgotten that Bernardo was no longer a Cistercian abbot. Bernard wanted to involve him in Cistercian affairs in Italy and Sardinia. But the key indication of Bernard's state of mind is his claim that he had chosen no longer to leave his monastery. That he certainly did: we will find him in the next chapter outside the great pilgrim church of Vezelay preaching the Second Crusade. It was 31 March 1146, shortly after Bernard had written the people of Rome and excoriated them for driving out Pope Eugenius. Bernard would have liked to have been at the side of his former monk and to have protected him from the political pressures of his time. Eugenius, however, seems to have distanced himself from Bernard and chose to be an independent agent. It was a difficult, dangerous world for both abbot and pope. Bernard had succeeded in preaching and teaching, but what had happened to his own vocation as a Cistercian monk and contemplative?

CHAPTER 9

Preaching a Crusade and Leaving Miracles Behind, 1146–1150

The Bernard who had decided in late 1145 not to leave his monastery nevertheless journeyed in March 1146 to Vézelay and its Benedictine abbey church of Saint Mary Magdalene, which was perched high on a rock above the surrounding plain and for centuries had been a place of pilgrimage for those seeking the saint's relics. Bernard had accepted an invitation to preach what in his age was called a pilgrimage (*peregrinatio*), while we use the term "crusade." The idea was that the knights of France, Burgundy, Champagne, and elsewhere should band together and embark on an armed pilgrimage to make Jerusalem and other holy places safe from the encroachment of the Saracens.

Bernard's decision to support the crusade cannot be explained in terms of his Cistercian background. [For background, see question 7 in the Fifteen Questions about Bernard: The Background for My Portrait section.] Monks were after all expected to remain in their monasteries and pray, and not to send off crusaders to the Holy Land. But in supporting the creation of a "new militia," as he called it, the Knights Templar, Bernard had already more than fifteen years earlier thrown his support behind a unique kind of soldier monasticism. Now after the fall of Edessa in 1144 Bernard decided to support not only monk-knights but also knights of all kinds and to inspire them by his preaching to take the cross and go to the Holy Land, now in danger of being taken again by non-Christians.

Bernard was not static in his personality or view of the world. He developed as a person and as a leading figure in the Church, and he came to accept a need to leave the monastery and to traverse the roads of northern Europe, just as he had done in Italy and Aquitaine in the 1130s in dealing with the papal schism. Thus the cloistered monk had become the peripatetic, not because the pope now was a Cistercian but because the knighthood of France was asking him to be its spiritual leader. It is a beautiful idea, so long as one does not consider the outcome. Bernard committed himself to the cause because he was asked to do so, just as in his confrontation with Peter Abelard. He had become too well-known not to be asked to call for a new "armed pilgrimage," as the crusade then was called. Of course, he could have said no and certainly he must have considered the price he was going to pay in saying yes.

We do not have the text of what Bernard preached on 31 March 1146, but we can imagine the situation. There were so many knights and their lords that there was insufficient room in the abbey church, so a platform was made below the east end of the church. Today the level area behind the church is set aside for picnics, but then it was used to accommodate hundreds, perhaps thousands, of listeners. They could look out over the plain below and feel that they were somewhere between earth and heaven, about to take up a great cause for the Lord.

A brief account of the meeting at Vézelay is given by the chronicler Otto of Freising, who in his *Deeds of Frederick Barbarossa* provided background in quoting a letter of Eugenius III calling for a crusade. Otto deemed Bernard to have been papal representative at Vézelay. "There Louis the king of the Franks, with great eagerness of spirit received the cross from the aforesaid abbot and volunteered for military service," together with counts and barons and other nobles.

An account of the entire crusade was made by the chaplain of King Louis VII, Odo of Deuil, and begins with the grand scene at Vézelay. He explained that Pope Eugenius wanted to be present to bless the effort but was unable to do so because of his problems with Roman citizens, so he handed over the task to Bernard, "Clairvaux's holy abbot": "Since there was no place within the town which could accommodate such a large crowd, a wooden platform was erected outside in a field, so that the abbot could speak from an elevation to the people standing round about."

Bernard is said to have spoken with "heaven's instrument" in issuing "God's word." The supply of crosses that had been previously prepared to be handed out to those who took up the cross was soon exhausted. The abbot of Clairvaux had to rip his own monastic garb into pieces so that crosses could be made of it. It was agreed that the knights should head for the Holy Land at year's end. Bernard subjected "his frail and almost lifeless body" to the cause and continued preaching the crusade, so that the number of those who took the cross was greatly increased.

What is noticeable here is how Bernard had come to the forefront of his age in Western European history. He was looked upon by contemporaries as a central actor, regardless of his complaints about health and his claim that he only wished to remain in his monastery. His willingness to act in harmony with kings and princes is remarkable in view of the fact that he previously had been criticizing and even taunting the French king, calling him a "boy," and threatening the wrath of God on him. Perhaps it was the invitation of Eugenius that made the difference; it should be clear by now that Bernard acted not so much in response to a papal summons but more in accord with his own inner conviction. Eugenius alone could not have made his former abbot leave his monastery and travel across Burgundy to what must have been a boisterous assembly of men not necessarily interested in listening to a sick old abbot. Bernard somehow found the will and energy to take up a task that involved much more than one brilliant sermon.

In the months that followed, Bernard accepted the task of preaching the crusade. First, he traveled through Flanders, stopping at Villers in Brabant, a daughter house of Clairvaux, on 18 October. From here he went to Liège and Worms, and then to Mainz. We can follow his movements almost daily thanks to the collection of information largely compiled by Bernard's secretary and biographer, Geoffrey of Auxerre. The account of Bernard's peregrinations and miracles appears in the *Patrologia Latina*, volume 185, as the sixth book of the *Vita Prima*, but its content has not usually been included in modern biographies of Bernard. Watkin Williams in his work did try to summarize this book of travels and wonders, but the recent standard Latin version of the *Vita Prima* does not include this book, nor is it translated into English by Hilary Costello. I will do what I can with this neglected source, for it provides a sense of Bernard's impact on his surroundings outside of monastic circles. At the same time, I include the letters Bernard wrote that show how he looked upon his commitment to crusade.

Bernard's Language of Crusade

In August or September 1146 Bernard wrote to the archbishops of the East Franks and Bavaria, as well as their bishops and clergy and all the people. The term *orientalis Francia* was probably meant to indicate the eastern part of what had been Charlemagne's empire, now making up the Holy Roman

Empire. Bernard encouraged the Franks and Bavarians to take up arms to defend the Eastern Church, but in this effort the Jews were not to be persecuted. The Jews were to be protected in the expectation that at the Second Coming of Christ, they would all be converted. [For tolerance toward Jews in Bernard, see question 8.] Because of the sins of Christians, the enemies of the cross had committed sacrilege. They had emptied the Holy Land of its people and polluted its holy places. He encouraged the "servants of the cross" to take up arms. Instead of destroying each other, they should unite against a common foe.

This was the logic already present in Pope Urban's appeal of 1095. The new theme in Bernard was his insistence on protecting Jews. He quoted the Psalms and said that the Jews had been scattered to all regions of the earth, but one day at the end of time, "all of Israel shall be saved": "If the Jews are obliterated, what hope of salvation will they have? As it has been promised in the end, their conversion will take place."

I will return shortly to Bernard's defense of the Jewish people, an aspect of his teaching that I find important and sympathetic at a time when a fanatic element in the Crusades was unleashing a wave of anti-Semitism. But he ended this letter with a warning, that the participants of a new crusade avoid the fate of Peter the Hermit on the First Crusade. Then people died of hunger or by the sword. Bernard's point seems to be that the coming crusade must not end in confusion and slaughter. The crusading army would have to be properly organized and led. He did not go into detail, but he pleaded that the crusaders learn from the mistakes of their predecessors.

Probably in August or September 1146 Bernard wrote the archbishop of Mainz warning him against the attacks made on the Jews by a former Cistercian monk, Raoul. Bernard found three elements in the man's activities that were unacceptable: first, he had no right to preach; second, he had no respect for episcopal authority; third, he was inciting people to murder. "Is it not far better that the Church persuade and convert the Jews rather than having them put to the sword?" Bernard referred to a prayer made for the Jews, based on 2 Corinthians 3:16, that the veil be lifted from their hearts when they turned to the Lord. They were to be brought by persuasion from the darkness of error. Bernard considered Raoul's teaching to be "opposed to the prophets, in contradiction with the apostles, and undermining piety and grace."

At about the same time (August–September 1146) Bernard wrote a more general letter to the English people, whose content is close to that found in his letter to Eastern France and Bavaria. He lamented the fact that "the enemy of the Cross" was ruining the Holy Land and threatened to invade

Jerusalem. Now was the time to serve God and seek one's salvation: "I call it blessed when a people can take advantage of the possibility to gain so rich an indulgence as you are being offered." Bernard added that the land of the English was known to contain many powerful men whom the world praised. Instead of fighting with each other, they should fight the infidel. He was indirectly referring to the English civil war, which was dragging on. And he was using every possible argument for going to the East, even appealing to merchants to consider the possibility of profits, which were not to be missed!

Bernard ended this letter by repeating his appeal for respecting the Jews. They were "not to be persecuted, killed or driven into exile." He saw them as "Scripture's living words, for they bring to mind the sufferings of Our Lord. They are spread all over the world so that by making amends for their crime, they may provide in all places living witnesses in the redemption we have received." According to Saint Paul, in the fullness of time, all of Israel will be saved. The Jews thus would be given the opportunity of salvation. In the meantime, Bernard condemned Christian moneylenders whose usury was worse than that practiced by any Jew. Bernard harbored the prejudices of his age against Jews, but he at the same time believed in their right to exist and the duty of Christians to protect them. In the face of the outbreaks of anti-Semitism that came with the crusade and especially the fanatic preaching of Raoul, Bernard spoke out for a necessary tolerance.

Another worry that concerned Bernard at this time was the fact that many monks tried to leave their monasteries and join the crusade. At some time in 1146 or 1147 Bernard dealt with this situation in a letter to his brother abbots. The letter has been given the heading that it was addressed to Cistercian abbots, but its context does not make it clear whether it was also intended for all abbots in the Benedictine tradition. In any case Bernard lamented that brothers "have looked down on our holy life and are doing what they can to get involved in the world's confusion." He regretted the fact that such monks spent their time in wandering about the countryside, even though their profession was to lead lives of solitude. They had chosen to wear the sign of the cross outside their clothing instead of having it on their hearts in their religious lives.

For Bernard any monk or lay brother who left the monastery to go on crusade was under sentence of excommunication. He thus registered the social and institutional upheavals that the crusading movement helped bring about. What began in a great wave of enthusiasm on the high plateau behind the great pilgrimage church of Mary Magdalen at Vézelay could turn into Jew-baiting and the abandonment of monastic vocation. Bernard faced the consequences and insisted on the integrity of the Jewish people in Christian

Europe. And he ordered his brothers back to their monasteries. Crusade was for knights who would fight abroad and not for Rhineland merchants to slaughter Jews and profit from their wealth.

We probably have only a fraction of the letters Bernard dictated for the crusade, but in March 1147 in Frankfurt he issued an exhortation to all Christians to join in a crusade against the Wendish people in the north of Europe. Thus Bernard had come to accept that the idea of crusade was not limited to the Holy Land but included any area where Christianity was in danger. Bernard described how there had been a meeting of kings, bishops, and princes at Frankfurt "for the total destruction, or at least, the conversion of these people." Any Christians who had not yet taken the cross to go to Jerusalem should know that they would gain similar spiritual privileges by joining the expedition against the Wends.

Not since Charlemagne's conquest and conversion of the Saxons in the last decades of the eighth century had Christian Europe accepted the idea that it was right and just to force pagan peoples to accept baptism. But Bernard had no qualms about what was required: "We forbid absolutely that any kind of truce be made with these peoples, whether for money or for tribute, until the time comes, with God's help, that they shall either be converted or be destroyed." Bernard announced it had been agreed that the crusading army was to meet at Magdeburg on the feast of the apostles Peter and Paul (29 June). Already in the time of Otto the Great in the ninth century, Magdeburg had been a center for the conversion of Eastern Europe, and now it would be the staging place for a crusade.

Frankfurt-Constance-Speyer

From October 1146 until February 1147 Bernard was constantly on the move, preaching the crusade. He indeed became like the monks he condemned for wandering about the countryside and abandoning the solitude of their lives. Certainly at other times in his life, he had left his monastery; but his commitment to the crusade was combined with a willingness to meet the flocks of people who came to him in the hope of relief from pain and suffering. The contemporary account of Bernard's movements as made by his companions is mainly focused on the miracles of healing he is said to have performed. For this reason, most modern accounts of his life either leave out or minimize the sources dealing with the miracles.

The first part of the journey began at Frankfurt, where Bernard apparently negotiated with the German king Conrad about the latter's participation in the crusade. The account was authored mainly by Bernard's loyal secretary, Geoffrey of Auxerre, but there are others who contributed their observations and experiences, including Bishop Herman of Constance. Each of these men claimed to describe only what they had seen, and so the brethren were careful to limit themselves to eyewitness accounts. At the same time we know that one of the main purposes of Bernard's journey was to discourage people from attacking Jews and to insist that they belonged to Christian society. Our account makes no mention of this theme: what mattered for Geoffrey and his companions was the way Bernard preached to the people and performed miracles.

At Frankfurt the bishop of Constance asked Bernard to visit his diocese, but the abbot at first refused, saying that his concern was for his own monks at Clairvaux, "for a mother cannot forget the sons to whom she has given birth." Bernard is said to have complained that it was nearly a year since he had been separated from his loved ones. And yet he did not return to Clairvaux for the time being. Here we find a list of the men who accompanied Bernard. Besides Herman, bishop of Constance, there were his chaplain Eberhard, abbots Baldwin and Frowin, the monks Gerard and Geoffrey (of Auxerre), Philip, archdeacon in Liège, and the priests Otto and Franco. During the journey they were joined by the priest Alexander from Cologne. He was on his way to Rome, but his encounter with Bernard's power and speech won him over to the monastic life.

The narrative of the trip to Constance starts with Bishop Herman's description of how a man who had been blind for ten years was blessed on the Sunday before Advent with the sign of the cross by Bernard. As soon as he arrived home, he regained his vision. Herman admitted, however, that he had only secondary knowledge of this miracle: "This I have heard from someone else, but the whole district is convinced of its truth." There are more accounts of cures for the blind, and Abbot Frowin contributed his evidence: "Brother Geoffrey with me saw the man who gained his vision." The record of Bernard's healings makes up a narrative with comments by each of the accompanying brothers. But the purpose of preaching the crusade was not forgotten. On leaving Freiburg, Bernard ordered a prayer to be said for rich people, "that God would take away the covering from their hearts," since they were hesitating to take up the cross.

The journey continued to Basel, where Bernard preached his usual sermon and handed out crosses for those willing to commit themselves to the crusade. He loosened the tongue of a woman who could not speak. The bishop of Constance witnessed the healing. The other companions described their presence at similar cures that day: "Many things were done on that day, which we could not know about because of the crowd." The narrative frequently emphasizes the number of people who frequented the scene, making it impossible for Bernard's followers themselves to witness all that happened. But sometimes they could offer firsthand witness: "I was in the hospice on that day and saw a blind boy given sight," reported Gerard. Philip added: "I saw a blind girl who was given sight near the village and many of our group and the people saw it." Geoffrey of Auxerre contributed: "We saw many things on that day which we cannot remember. But one thing happened, which I saw, for it is of great joy and to be remembered. I speak of a woman who for a long time had been lame. She was in a certain village through which we passed. Now everyone saw her standing up." Another of the party, Eberhard, here tried to count the number of miracles. Here thirty-six miracles took place on the same day. Eleven blind persons gained their sight. Ten lame persons and eight who were paralyzed came to walk. Eleven with withered hands were restored, and one deaf man came to hear. "But if the sum comes to more than thirty-six, it is that first I counted the number of persons, and afterwards the signs that took place."

The main narrator, however, is Geoffrey of Auxerre, who played a central role in the group following Bernard and clearly already looked upon these miracles as signs of Bernard's holiness to be used in getting him recognized as a saint. As hagiographer he wanted to be precise in recording exactly what happened. Thus the miracle count could be according to individuals or according to the number of healings, as with one girl for whom "many things were done, for she was blind, lame on each foot, and she was deaf and had each hand shriveled." Apparently all these ills were remedied, so her case counted for many miracles. But Geoffrey admitted that much took place that was impossible to account for: "We heard many other matters from the people singing behind us, but since we could not return we did not see these things."

When the company reached Schafhausen, a town along the Rhine and today in Switzerland, the crowd had become so overwhelming that Bernard had to abstain from blessing the sick and to flee, for people were pressing in on him. The brethren had to beg Bernard not to place his healing hands on anyone, for they had no idea how they would be able to extricate him from the place. He turned to accompanying knights to protect him from the crush of the crowd. The description resembles that of pop stars in our time who engender such unbridled enthusiasm that they can be in danger of being crushed by their fans.

Afterwards the company crossed the Rhine and heard singing on the other side. The people got hold of boats and came in celebration of a lame boy who again could walk. This description is by an Abbot Baldwin, who added that he had seen the boy himself: *quem ego vidi*. The Latin is awkward and may reflect a vulgar Latin spoken among monks and clerics. The narrative gains vividness precisely because the language is not polished. It expresses what was seen and experienced, in the midst of noise and confusion and at the same time in demonstrations of fervor.

It was not only the villagers who benefited from Bernard's miraculous powers. There were also knights who came to him. The son of a certain knight who was suffering from a withered hand was brought to Bernard. The bishop who was present and witnessed the event described the reaction: "Immediately I heard singing and asked what had happened. A certain knight answered that the hand of his lord's son had been healed."

The reader can easily forget the purpose of Bernard's travels: he was preaching the crusade and trying to get as many people as possible to make a commitment. Instead he had become a celebrated maker of miracles, with so much success that the crowds made it almost impossible for his companions to see what was going on. Geoffrey of Auxerre complained: "We are ignorant of some of what was done at Constance. Because none of us dared to mix in with the crowds, and we had decided to speak of the things we saw." In other words the brothers limited themselves to eyewitness accounts. This was the case with brother Philip, who recounted how the diseased hand of a woman was cured while Bernard was on the shore of the lake, ready to leave: "This I saw."

Later in the same week Bernard is described as first giving a sermon and then lifting up a lame boy in the midst of the church. Everyone shouted, for the boy began walking, while those around him were acclaiming the miracle. This procedure—first a sermon, then a cure—seems to have been almost standard. If only we had the text of the sermon, but the purpose of the narrative is to present Bernard as maker of miracles, not as preacher.

On Christmas Eve 1146, Bernard and his companions arrived at Speyer, where he joined a meeting of King Conrad of Germany with his princes and bishops. Bernard's purpose is said to have been to make peace among the princes, who because of enmities were being held back from joining the crusading army. "Truly it was proven that the king's heart was in God's hand." Apparently Bernard had previously met "in secret" with Conrad, at Frankfurt, and had been told that he was not planning to join the crusade: "The most gentle man was silent and said that it was not for his humility to press royal majesty." Now, however, Conrad changed his mind, thanks to what is called Bernard's careful coaxing: "At the end of his sermon he freely addressed the king not as king but as a man. He was speaking of the coming judgment, how man stands before the tribunal of Christ." Bernard's sermon apparently brought tears to the king's eyes, who is to have said, "I recognize fully the divine gifts of grace and am not ungrateful for them. I am ready to serve him since I am being encouraged so strongly to do so." King Conrad took the cross and received a banner from Bernard at the altar so that he could carry it himself in his army. His grandson Duke Frederick joined in, as did other princes, "whose number had no limit."

Bernard had a sense of drama and could take advantage of a situation. But the conversion of Conrad to crusading was not just a public event. It came in the wake of intimate conversations. Bernard had reached a position in Christian Europe where he could speak freely with kings and remind them of Judgment Day and what it required of them. He could balance persuasion with threats, and in Conrad's case the strategy worked. In the meetings of Conrad and Bernard it is possible to gain some sense of what Bernard's life had become: he was a respected instrument of persuasion in both religious and secular society. Because of Bernard, King Conrad could say: "I recognize fully divine gifts of grace and am not ungrateful for them: I am ready to serve him [God] since I am being so strongly encouraged to do so." Did he utter precisely these words? Or is this what Bernard's men wanted to hear? Clearly, however, something took place that fulfilled their hopes.

When the king spoke thus in public, he apparently got an immediate response from those around him: "They cried out in praise of God and the earth resounded with their voices." If this account had been written down some years later, it would be possible to question its accuracy, but we are dealing with multiple authors who were constantly questioning each other's information and who jotted down their account very soon after the events described. This procedure, of course, does not mean that its contents are completely dependable, but it was essential for Bernard's companions to describe to the world his presence and impact in the most reliable manner possible.

That Saturday morning, the feast of the Holy Innocents (28 December 1146), Eberhard, the secretary of Bishop Herman of Constance, encountered Bernard leaving the hospice where he was staying. Eberhard brought a knight who wanted to take the cross. In the crowd there was a blind boy, but Eberhard could not understand what he said "because he was speaking in the romance language." Bernard asked that the boy be brought to him, and as soon as he blessed the youth, he gained his vision. The narrative indicates the confusion of tongues that could have manifested itself. Bernard's voyage along the course of the Rhine brought him into German-speaking and French-speaking areas.

The same day there was an assembly where Conrad summoned all the princes and knights who had taken the cross. Bernard preached a sermon "not with human speech but with divine." When Bernard was leaving and was accompanied by the king and the princes "so that the crowds not crush him," a lame boy was brought to him. Bernard made the sign of the cross and told the youth to walk. He then turned to the king: "Because of you, this has been done, so that you will know that God is truly with you and what you have begun has been received." Once again Bernard conveyed himself in terms of high drama: sermon, exit from the church with the crowd, lame youth, and declaration to the king.

On the Road from Speyer to Cologne and Liège

A copy of a letter written by the monks of Clairvaux to the clerics of the church of Cologne is included at the beginning of a new section of the miracle narrative as a kind of preface. The letter indicates that the monks assumed that the clerics had read a copy of a book that was given to Henry, the brother of King Louis VII, who had entered Clairvaux as a monk. This book contained the miracles that took place from the first Sunday of Advent until the time when Bernard and his companions left the court at Speyer. The Clairvaux brothers were certain that many more miracles took place on the journey than they could have known or could be recorded, "but we have written down what was certain and proven."

In the continuation of the miracle narrative, it is said that Bishop Herman of Constance was absent, and his place was taken by "our brother Wolkemar," presumably a Cistercian monk. Once the court at Speyer was dissolved, Bernard indicated that he was eager to preach elsewhere. He had passed through Worms two months previously and had recruited a number of people for the crusade, and so now he continued his journey. Continuing to follow the path of the Rhine, he came to Koblenz. Outside the town, a well-known person who was lame was brought to Bernard on a horse. Bernard blessed him and ordered him to dismount and walk. But the man did not understand what Bernard said. Here again we are reminded that Bernard's travels took him to areas where Romance languages were almost unknown. The cripple probably spoke a version of German. Bernard kept silent, but the man was freed from his ailment: "He was walking freely and magnifying God."

Wolkemar's narrative is superseded by a contribution from Geoffrey of Auxerre, the central witness to Bernard's life and miracles: "It will always be remembered how this city of Cologne deserved to receive the holy man, whom it always had desired." Already in the morning on Friday, before Bernard and his companions entered the church, a blind woman came to the hospice and was cured. She went to the altar to thank God. Meanwhile Bernard said Mass at the altar dedicated to Mary, in the eastern part of the church. When he finished, more miracles took place. Going to the pulpit to preach a sermon, Bernard cured a blind old man. The next day, Saturday, his companions witnessed many more wonders while they were in the hospice, "but we neglected to note them down." Because so many happened, "we have wholly lost track of them." The phrase is telling: the memory of precise events disappeared in the chaos of that day and those that followed.

At this point, however, Geoffrey added an incident that is almost unique in the narrative: Bernard excoriated the clergy, for he apparently had no desire to go outside that day to the people waiting for him. Instead he used the Scriptures to warn against the lax lives of the clergy. He referred to the Psalms and to Isaiah, for the example of the wicked man who fails to learn to do what is just. He has done evil things, and so will not see the glory of the Lord (Is 26:10). This is one of the few times in these accounts that we are given a somewhat detailed report of one of Bernard's sermons.

That Sunday Bernard performed a great number of miracles. He said Mass at the altar of Saint Peter, in the western part of the church. This was presumably in Cologne cathedral, and the number of people who came to hear Bernard's sermon was supposed to be greater than what the priests there had ever seen before. Once again, our narrative takes on the character of a list of miracles attested by different witnesses, in this case Hervin, abbot of Steinfeld, and the abbot of Kamp or Altenkamp, a Cistercian house founded in 1123. The latter described how after Bernard finished his sermon and the party returned to the house where they were staying, "before he touched the threshold of the hospice, in my presence, he lifted up a boy who was crippled." An insane woman regained her senses. A lame person came to walk, and a woman who was blind in one eye was cured. As the monk Gerard commented, one of the brothers was amazed that it seemed so easy for Bernard to provide all these cures: "Truly his speed was worthy of all admiration."

According to Eberhard, secretary to Bishop Herman, who seems to have stayed with the group after his lord was called away, Bernard stood in a window of the hospice, and sick persons were handed over to him. The brethren did not dare to open the hospice door, for fear of being overwhelmed by the crowds. The daughter of a certain wealthy citizen, well known in the town, got back her hearing after being deaf for many years. Her parents had sent her to a nunnery, but she was sent home because she had become completely deaf. But now she could resume her vocation.

Sometimes it took time for a cure to work. The abbot of Cistercian Altenkamp described how after the imposition of hands, a woman remained blind for two or three hours. Finally she wanted to leave, "and not having what she sought, she was weeping and sobbing miserably." The brothers felt sorry for her, but then she suddenly announced that she could see: "Hastening to her we determined this by many indications to be the case." In this situation as in so many others, the companions of Bernard felt obliged to test the result of his cures. They had to see and feel, as doubting Thomases, for they assumed the world would claim that they were making it all up.

Brother Gerard added his description of what he experienced while the cures happened inside the hospice: "I was standing outside but could not in any way enter." From morning to evening he remained in this way with some of the brothers: "I could not get to the door or to a ladder, for there was a great multitude everywhere." The description was probably influenced by the scenes of tumult described in the Gospels, when the crowd pressed in to see what Jesus was doing. But the Cistercians may well have been describing what they in fact experienced: "When we dined, because of the multitude of the sick who assembled, we asked the Father that he bless them so they would go."

On the Monday morning there were more cures, but also great confusion and crowding, so it was hardly possible to bring Bernard back into the hospice. This situation provoked the following remark by brother Philip: "I do not know whether it was the greater miracle, that he could escape unharmed." Bernard was in danger of being crushed, and so it may have seemed a wonder that he escaped without injury.

By the third hour of the day, which must have been about 9 a.m., the multitude of the sick insisted that Bernard come out to them. He went into the square, presumably in front of the hospice, and blessed those lying down. Before the eyes of all present, fourteen were cured. Seven cripples, five deaf persons, a maimed boy, and a blind woman. Each time a miracle was witnessed the people would cry out and sing in praising God: *Christ, uns genade. Kyrie Eleison. Die heiligen alle helffen uns.* (Christ have mercy on us. . . . All the saints assist us.) These words were recorded by brother Gerard. It was important for him to jot down exactly what was said and thus to add German language to a Latin narrative. Once again it seems to have been important for Bernard's companions to provide authenticity to their description, in this case by telling their readers exactly what the Cologne crowd sang.

The abbot of Altenkamp added a comment here that from this time onwards the crowd was so overwhelming that no one could enter or leave the house. The company decided that Bernard should be brought into the archbishop's house so he could move about more freely. Here more cures took place. There is a defensive tone, not because of Bernard's avoidance of the crowds, but in pointing to the fact that the cures normally happened "not in a corner but in public." Anyone who doubted should accept these "proofs. . ., especially what was done not for obscure or unknown persons." In other words Bernard's healing powers worked for individuals well known in society, who could be questioned about what had happened to them.

On a Tuesday the brothers left Cologne and stopped at the monastery of Brunweiler, whose church was dedicated to Saint Nicholas. A blind boy standing in front of the altar was given his sight. Many more miracles are said to have taken place that day, and Eberhard described how the crowd each time roared: *Christ uns genade*, "Christ have mercy on us." Bernard ended up in a chapel where the space was narrow, and the crowd pressed in: "Because of this many things were done which are unknown to us." Once again it is apparent how frustrating it could be to accompany a religious figure who was so sought-after. Attempts to record Bernard's actions accurately were hindered by the noise and crowds that accompanied him.

The narrative is interrupted at this point with a copy of a letter written by Geoffrey of Auxerre to Herman, the bishop of Constance, who at an earlier point had accompanied the group. Geoffrey wrote that he had prepared a "little book" containing a record of Bernard's miracles, but it was impossible to account for all the things that had happened. When they left the German-speaking region, they no longer heard *Christ uns genade*, but they found that those who spoke the Romance tongue had their own songs when they thanked God for miracles. Geoffrey added that he had on purpose omitted some of the events, for he was afraid that the great number of miracles would overwhelm the reader. But he assured Bishop Herman that he had written nothing that he had not seen "with my eyes" or that had not come from the trustworthy relation of "our brothers who were present."

From here Bernard and his companions came to a monastery at Laon where they lodged, and then traveled on to Reims, where the miracles continued. The Rhineland journey had thus turned into a tour of the north of the French kingdom. On 2 February 1147, the feast of the Purification of Mary, Bernard met King Louis VII at Châlons-en-Champagne, about thirty miles southeast of Reims. Also present were a number of princes from France and Germany, as well as the legate of the "king of the Romans, King Conrad, "so that they might establish a common plan for the journey to Jerusalem."

Bernard engaged in discussions with the secular lords for two days and in the meantime refused to meet the people who sought him out for his healing powers: "They sought him with great insistence."

Bernard continued toward Clairvaux, more than sixty-two miles distant, with more miracles on the road. But the narrative at last focuses on the purpose of his journey: the preaching of the crusade and its planning. The last stop before Clairvaux was the town of Bar-sur-Aube, where Bernard said Mass in the church of Saint Nicholas. The author of this segment of the account, Geoffrey of Auxerre, lists a great number of cures that took place here. The same day Bernard returned to Clairvaux and is said to have brought thirty men with him, presumably candidates for the monastic life. He is described as "a happy man, whose touch was so saving, whose speech was so lively and efficacious."

It might be expected that Bernard after a journey of many months would have wanted to remain at his monastery. But it seems he only spent a few days there. During this time, he forbade any of the sick to be brought to him, for he wanted "to provide for quiet for the brothers." But when Bernard went out of the monastery gate, he found a multitude of the sick waiting: blind, lame, and crippled. He was followed by what is called a "tumult" of people, and the next day in the main church of Troyes, the capital of the county of Champagne, there gathered a huge crowd, which listened to Bernard's preaching. He healed many, and the account emphasizes the personal danger he faced in coping with large crowds, which made "an intolerable tumult." That evening Bernard ordered the sick who were waiting for him to be placed next to the chancel of the church. He went out and blessed them, one by one. The bishop of Langres, Geoffrey, was present. He was a cousin of Bernard who had first been monk of Clairvaux and then abbot of its daughter house Fontenay. Bernard had fought for his election to the see of Langres, and now the man could see his cousin surrounded by the desperate and hopeful.

The next morning Bernard left Troyes. The narrative indicates that he rarely stayed more than a day or two at one place, and this practice seems to underline that his purpose was to engender support for the crusade. The healings were secondary, while for Bernard's companions they had become a primary concern. At Étampes, directly south of Paris, there was a meeting dealing with preparations for the crusade, but Geoffrey does not indicate who was present besides Bernard. From here he continued to Sens, the ecclesiastical capital of the region, and to Joigny, about twenty-two miles to the south. Farther south he arrived at Auxerre, where a monastery contained the relics of Saint Germanus, bishop of the town in the fifth century. There were more cures, and then Bernard headed for Molesme. Geoffrey gives this monastery special acknowledgment because it was from here "our fathers once left, from where the Cistercian Order had its beginning." There were no hard feelings toward the brethren who around 1100 had returned from Cîteaux to Molesme with their abbot Robert. Geoffrey only noted that a book of Cistercian Usages existed where "the careful reader will find this written down." He was probably referring to the foundation account known as the *Exordium Parvum*. It is not really clear why Bernard went to Molesme, unless it was to show his solidarity with the place his monastic order had originated.

From here Bernard and his company returned to Clairvaux, a little under forty miles northeast of Molesme. Geoffrey described how here "one of our people met him." He brought a deaf and mute boy who for fifteen days had been awaiting the coming of the saint. As soon as Bernard blessed him, the youth is said to have gained his hearing and speech. At first, he could scarcely utter the name of God, but then he called out the Virgin's name, and finally "his speech was loosened so he could say all things." He burst forth in "tears of joy." The brothers of Clairvaux seem to have known the youth well and spoke with him. They "heard him fully forming every word." So much for monastic silence when it was a question of looking after a person in need!

It would be repetitive to narrate in further detail the last stages of Bernard's journey. On 27 March he went to Trier, and the account of numerous healings leaves out any mention of crusade preparations. At Frankfurt the sick were brought in to him through a window, and "there was an innumerable multitude." At Toul, where he was on the Sunday before Pentecost in early June, Bernard had to leave the city at night to avoid the crowds, but he was seen and could not get away without further healings. Here Geoffrey ended his account, adding that many other miracles took place, but he had only recorded what he could "faithfully write." Geoffrey and his companions recorded a long, exhausting journey through the Rhineland and northern France. Bernard seems to have been tireless.

The Meaning of Miracles

For modern people this record of one miracle after another is of only limited interest. It reflects the reaction to Bernard more than it provides insights that reveal his inner life. But Bernard did wonder about the meaning of what seemed to take place in this symbiosis combining belief in God with attention to people in need. Bernard's disciple Geoffrey of Auxerre, in accompanying him on these travels and recording Bernard's actions, was well placed to characterize Bernard's understanding of his charism. At one point in the

Vita Prima Bernard is said to have spoken to some of the brothers and told them that he was "amazed that anyone should want these miracles to be ascribed to oneself," for they were due to God. When Bernard read of miracles in the past, he found them to be due to men who were perfect or frauds: "But I am not conscious of being perfect or of being a fraud." He could only conclude that these signs came about only "so that I may show others how to live. They come about less to commend me than to admonish others."

It would be tempting to dismiss such self-understanding as false humility or to conclude that Geoffrey here as elsewhere was doing what he could to promote Bernard as a saint. Geoffrey did his utmost to further Bernard's name and commitments in the Church, but eyewitness accounts cannot be dismissed out of hand. Though we might attribute a number of the miracles to self-suggestion, hysteria, or imagination, something remains that defies rational explanation. It should be recalled that Bernard began his cures as a relatively young abbot of Clairvaux. At one point his brother Gerard and his Uncle Gaudry went after him for promising the nobleman Josbert that he would recover from illness. Bernard's answer was something like "It is easy for God to do what you can only believe with difficulty." But his relatives refused to accept Bernard's gifts: "They did not spare him, even abusing him with harsh words to shake up his tender diffidence," with the result that they drove him to tears.

Miracles were never taken for granted in medieval Christian Europe. In an age when medicine for the most part had limited effect, the direct intervention of God was considered necessary for most human ills. Sometimes holy men or women were thought to be conveyers of divine power. Since nothing succeeds like success, a figure like Bernard could attract crowds of admirers and be called upon to remedy the ills of the blind, the deaf, the mute, and the lame. Clearly there are parallels between such miracles and the cures described in the Gospels. But our narrator, presumably Geoffrey, made it clear that Bernard was not just duplicating the role of Christ. In describing how Bernard once came to Clairvaux, Geoffrey described him as "more than a prophet, and the honor of a prophet was not lacking." In other words, Bernard did not share with Jesus the attribute of failing to be recognized as a prophet in his own country (Lk 4:24). In his own homeland around Clairvaux, Bernard apparently did gain recognition.

Not everyone agreed with Geoffrey, and perhaps the best-known exposé of Bernard's miracles is that provided by Walter Map, in his scurrilous *Courtiers' Trifles*, probably written in the 1180s and early 1190s, thus some decades after Bernard's death. Walter was a ubiquitous church figure who served successfully under King Henry II and became canon at Lincoln cathedral. He ended his career in 1196–97 as archdeacon at Oxford, thanks to Hugh, bishop of Lincoln, a saintly figure who recognized Walter's abilities. Walter recalled being present during a meal at the table of Thomas Becket when he was archbishop of Canterbury, so this would have been in the 1160s. Next to Walter were two Cistercian abbots who were going on about the "wonders done by that man, I mean Bernard." There was a discussion about Bernard's opposition to Abelard, and the two abbots praised Bernard "and extolled him to the stars." Then John Planeta, one of Becket's clerics, described how Bernard had ordered a demon to leave a madman. But the poor fellow began throwing stones at Bernard and chased him through the streets.

Archbishop Becket was not happy with this story and challenged his cleric, who answered that the madman was known for being gentle and was mean only to hypocrites. On another occasion two Cistercian abbots were discussing Bernard in the presence of Gilbert Foliot, London's bishop. One abbot conceded that even though the stories they told about Bernard were true, he on one occasion failed to show his powers. A man living on the border of Burgundy asked Bernard to come and heal his son, but by the time the abbot got there, the boy was dead. Bernard asked that the body be carried to a private room and told everyone to leave. He threw himself down over the boy, who remained lifeless. Gerald's comment was "I have heard before now of a monk throwing himself upon a boy, but always, when the monk got up, the boy promptly got up too."

The anecdote is full of sexual innuendo, and Walter added to the snub by claiming that this "failure of grace" was followed by a second one. Walter, Count of Nevers, was buried at the Chartreuse, and Bernard hurried there. He refused to come to dinner "until my brother Walter speaks to me." He cried out in a loud voice ordering the count to come out of the tomb. "But Walter, not hearing the voice of Jesus, had not the ears of Lazarus, and did not come." The lesson, of course, was that Bernard could not imitate Jesus in raising people from the dead.

Walter Map knew well that there was meant to be a parallel between the miracles of Jesus and those of Bernard as expressions of what we might call the Cistercian propaganda machine. He enjoyed poking fun at the monks and especially at Bernard, even though he wrote his chronicle well after Bernard's canonization in 1174. But Walter's satire underlines the fact that saints can be controversial figures, and the pious actions of one figure can be questioned. Bernard no doubt had his failures and would probably have been the first to admit them. The key to his inner life is not what he achieved in his exterior existence. What seems genuine are his admissions of incompetence and even failure. And here the debacle of the crusade gave him rich opportunity to consider the meaning of his life and vocation.

Reacting to the Crusade's Failure

What we call the Second Crusade had begun in the most auspicious manner, and Bernard was associated with it from the start. The chronicler Otto of Freising, who ended his life as a Cistercian, described in his *Deeds of Frederick Barbarossa* how Bernard was "endowed with wisdom and a knowledge of letters, renowned for signs and wonders." He was summoned by the French lords and asked, "as from a divine oracle," what was to be done, but Bernard referred the matter to Pope Eugenius. He should be asked first.

Otto's chronology may be incorrect, but in connecting Bernard with the origin of the idea of a crusade, he provided a symbolic truth: Bernard had become the spiritual leader of the church and society in the West. His knowledge, insight, and power were sought when important decisions were being made, especially in committing the Christian knighthood to their "pilgrimage" to the Eastern Church, as the crusade was called. When Bernard took up such a cause, virtually no one questioned its necessity or likelihood of success. And so it was a shock when the Christian warriors came home (or failed to come home) having to admit that they had failed in their mission.

Already on 25 October 1147 the Seljuk Turks in Anatolia had wiped out the army of King Conrad of Germany, the man whom Bernard less than a year earlier had pleaded with to join the crusade. In January 1148 the army of King Louis of France was defeated by the Turks. The crusaders then decided that it would be wiser to concentrate on Damascus than Edessa. Strategically they were correct: the city of Damascus was the lynchpin of the Muslim states, but in July the crusaders were at the mercy of the Muslim armies. King Conrad and his army retreated on July 28 to Jerusalem. Both King Conrad and King Louis felt betrayed by the other side. Meanwhile Louis's marriage was falling apart, and had become a matter of public comment.

How did the bad news, especially Conrad's defeat in Anatolia and the whole army's fiasco before Damascus, reach Bernard? We do not know precisely, but surely returning crusaders would have brought the dire tidings and have described the scene of men and horses lying dead in the desert. Bernard must have thought he knew about fighting from his upbringing, but he had never himself experienced anything of the kind. For him Jerusalem was a vision of heaven, and now he was confronted with a scene worthy of hell.

Bernard's response to the fiasco seems to have been to foster a new expedition. In writing to Peter the Venerable in March or April 1150, he admitted how bad the news was. He assumed that Peter was aware of the plight of the Church in the East: "A man with your lofty rank must demonstrate compassion for your mother and all the faithful's mother." In Bernard's view, the Church of Jerusalem had given birth to all the churches of the West. He conceded that it would be wrong to ignore what had happened: "If . . . we have little compassion in this sorrow, then how can we harbor love for God and for neighbor?"

Bernard announced that the French bishops, together with the king and princes, had agreed to assemble at Chartres on the third Sunday after Easter to consider the situation. Easter in 1150 was on 16 April, so this meeting would have been in early May. Bernard asked Abbot Peter to attend. A similar letter was addressed to Suger, abbot of Saint Denis and regent of the kingdom in Louis's absence on crusade in 1147–49. In the face of the failure of the crusade, a new one was to be planned.

In May or June 1150, Bernard wrote to Pope Eugenius and made use of a quote from Seneca in a letter to his friend Lucilius: "The man is not brave when his courage does not come forward when difficulty faces him." Bernard included one of his favorite images: that of two swords, spiritual and temporal. It was up to the pope now in this second passion of Christ to draw both swords in defending the Eastern Church. Bernard had no qualms about comparing his own times to those that preceded the death of Christ. It is as if he was seeking a second crucifixion: "Was it not a wonderful and unique gift of our salvation that was preceded by our Savior's death?"

For Bernard it was Eugenius's responsibility to help organize a new crusade, for "it is as if the very foundations of the Church . . . have been shaken." The pope by now had probably heard that the assembly at Chartres "in a very surprising decision" had chosen Bernard as the head of the new expedition. Bernard responded: "This has never been and is not now what I advise or desire, and it is beyond my powers . . . to carry out such an assignment. How can I set forth armies in order of battle and lead armed men?" He added that he could conceive of nothing that was more in conflict with his vocation: "But you know this already and I cannot instruct you." Even so, he asked the pope to keep him from becoming the victim of what might be decided without proper attention to Bernard's proper vocation.

It is not really surprising that Bernard was asked to lead a new crusade. He had, after all, been the main source of inspiration for the previous effort, while at the same time he was not compromised by having participated in the catastrophe in the Holy Land. The assembly at Chartres may have thought in terms of how God had favored Bernard with all the miracles that came from his presence. Now he might work a military miracle in Jerusalem.

But Bernard pulled back from the temptation to become such a leader. His Cistercian identity did not allow him to take on such a task, however much he might be tempted. By writing to Pope Eugenius with his refusal, Bernard was announcing to the Christian world that he would not lead a new army to the Holy Land.

Bernard was, however, still willing to contribute to the effort to plan a new crusade. In May or June 1150, at about the same time as he wrote the pope, he sent another letter to Peter the Venerable. In the wake of the assembly at Chartres on 7 May, he asked the abbot of Cluny to attend a second assembly, to be held at Compiègne, in order to organize a new crusade. The Holy Sepulchre had been mistreated, to the shame of Christendom. Christ was suffering again, and yet the meeting at Chartres had not been fruitful. He gently chided Abbot Peter: "We needed your presence there and waited longingly for it." But Peter the Venerable had stayed away. Now Bernard begged him to come to Compiègne.

The letter ends with a greeting from Bernard's secretary Nicholas of Montiéramey: "Nicholas, who is mine, sends his greeting as if he belonged to you as much as he does to me, for he is certainly [yours]." This is the Nicholas who a few years later would run away from Clairvaux and take one of Bernard's seals with him. But for the time being he was a great favorite and provided a bond with Peter the Venerable in the uneasy relationship Bernard maintained with the powerful abbot of Cluny. Bernard knew that the crusading movement needed a figure like Peter to rally support, and it seems as if he was counting on Nicholas to create or strengthen his relationship with the abbot of Cluny.

At about this time Bernard included his thoughts and reactions to the failure of the crusade in his new work, *On Consideration*. I will look at the whole of this important treatise in a separate section, but Bernard's summation of what had happened to the Christian armies can be reviewed here. He began by describing the sad spectacle of Christian men lying "prostrate in the desert." The princes had handed themselves over to strife and had wandered in the desert. Bernard asked how God could have allowed such a disaster: "Why did we fast and he fails to notice; why did we humble our souls and he ignores us?" The answer was to remember that God's judgments are incomprehensible. The human heart forgets: "What we know when it is not necessary, we forget in time of need." Bernard referred to the Old Testament and the trials of the Israelites. They perished because of their sins, and so "are we astonished that today those who do the same thing suffer the same fate?"

Bernard found hope in the experience of the Israelites, who "did not think back over their first and second failures, but made preparation for a third time and triumphed." He hoped that a new crusade would be a success, and if not, then a third one! Bernard closed this section with the desire that his words would provide some consolation both for himself and for Eugenius, "so your conscience may gain some explanation from me with which it can excuse me and yourself also." He knew that the failure of the crusade was being discussed and blame was being handed out. The only valid explanation he could provide was that both he and Eugenius had followed their consciences: "A completely valid excuse for anyone is the testimony of his own conscience." Bernard had done what he thought was right, but he also subsequently excused himself from leading a new crusading army. Although he had become the conscience of Christian Europe, he could not be its military leader.

There would be no more crusading until what we call the Third Crusade (1187–89). This crusade would again be led by kings and would also turn into a terrible fiasco. The crusade was called because of the fall of Jerusalem in 1187, realizing the fears that had engendered the Second Crusade. By the time of the Third Crusade Bernard had been in the grave for thirty-five years, and few contemporaries would remember that he had offered himself as a leader of this new crusade. It was hard for knights and even for monks to accept that taking the cross did not necessarily bring success or help to shore up the Latin kingdom of Jerusalem. In fact, the Second Crusade weakened the political and military structure of Jerusalem, contributing to its collapse in the Third Crusade. Like the Second, the Third Crusade devolved into mutual recriminations, as well as a falling out with the Byzantines, which led in 1204 to the Latin Christian conquest of Constantinople. One more failed crusade. The noble vision of taking the cross that emerged in the enthusiasm of Vézelay had been replaced by a tale of woe. For Bernard it was the sins of the crusaders that undermined their mission. For us what took place was a fatal breach of understanding between the Muslim and the Christian worlds—a gap that remains to this day and continues in a game of blame and guilt. Remarkably, however, the Crusades attract more attention than ever in the academic world and popular culture, and new generations invest them with an element of heroism, in spite of the betrayals and deaths that accompanied them. This romanticization aside, it is clear that the Crusades were an early manifestation of Western imperialism, not a demonstration of selfless idealism.

Arnold of Brescia and Gilbert de la Porrée: Two Enemies

Early in the 1140s Bernard had condemned the preaching of Arnold of Brescia, the cleric who encouraged the citizens of Rome to create a republic.

Arnold had been in exile for some years but had returned to Italy, and in 1146 Pope Eugenius was forced from Rome, thanks to Arnold's agitation. Surprisingly we have no letters from Bernard that take up this situation, perhaps because he was otherwise caught up in the crusade and trying to get the Trinitarian theology of Gilbert de la Porrée condemned. In order to get a sense of what Arnold was doing in Italy, we must turn to one of the great humanistic writers of the period, John of Salisbury, who was close to Eugenius during these years and whose *Memoirs of the Papal Court* offer a superb portrait of events and personalities.

John did not include many dates in his account, but he did describe how in 1149–50 Eugenius negotiated with the Roman people to make peace. The greatest problem, according to John, was the Romans' refusal to rid themselves of Arnold of Brescia, "who was said to have bound himself by oath to uphold the honor of the city and Roman republic." John found Arnold to be an intelligent man, eloquent, and "a vehement preacher against the vanities of the world." But wherever he went, he "prevented the citizens from being at peace with the clergy." Arnold attacked Bernard, who John said was "renowned above all others for his many virtues," but in Arnold's view was "a seeker of vainglory, envious of all who won distinction in learning or religion unless they were his own disciples."

Some comparison can be rightly made between Arnold and Bernard. They were both firebrand preachers who could engender sympathy and enthusiasm in an audience. John also pointed out that Arnold "had disciples who imitated his austerities and won favor with the populace through outward decency and austerity of life." This description brings to mind the early Cistercians and their asceticism. Bernard and Arnold also resemble each other in not tolerating those who went against their understanding of the Gospel and its teachings. Bernard attacked Abelard for his Trinitarian theology, while Arnold attacked the pope for failing to live like Christ in humility and poverty. In this matter Bernard was not far behind Arnold. Bernard's *On Consideration*, as we shall see, was an extended warning to Pope Eugenius about the dangers that surrounded him in his position, in a court where money mattered more than ideals.

As mentioned above, besides fostering the crusade during these years Bernard spent a great deal of time attacking an influential theologian for his teaching on the Trinity. Once again our most judicious witness to events is John of Salisbury, who tried in his *Memoirs* to be fair to all interests. He described how Gilbert, bishop of Poitiers, was summoned to respond to the abbot of Clairvaux, "a man of the greatest eloquence and highest repute." John was in doubt whether those who attacked Gilbert "acted out of zeal for the faith or jealousy of his fame and merit, or a desire to propitiate the abbot," as Bernard was then at the summit of his "influence . . . and [his] counsel was most weighty in the affairs of church and state alike." John admitted that there were different views of Bernard "because he attacked the two men most famous for their learning," Peter Abelard and Gilbert. For John, however, it was impossible to "believe that a man of such sanctity was not guided by the love of God." At the same time John respected Gilbert's learning "after spending almost sixty years in reading and close study." John did his best to reconcile the two men by assuring his readers that "now [in the afterlife Gilbert] . . . no longer disagrees with the abbot . . . for they both see face to face the truth they spent their lives in seeking."

While John must have been writing after the deaths of both Bernard and Gilbert, he clearly wanted to understand these two opponents and the differences in their theological orientation. He described how Bernard asked the important churchmen gathered at the Council of Reims in 1148 to meet him first in his residence, where "the abbot, the most pious and learned among them, then delivered a short and eloquent discourse." Bernard told his distinguished listeners that they were obliged to "remove all scandals from the Church of God." They were asked to correct Bernard if they believed he had wrongly brought a case against Gilbert. If he was mistaken, then it could be because "he had been carried away by charity and zeal for the faith."

Even though John was recalling a situation from some years earlier, his description of Bernard's attitude rings true. The abbot was not a fanatic, but he was allergic to formulae describing the interactions of the persons of the Trinity when they seemed to be at variance with what already had been agreed upon in the Church Fathers and in the early councils. John's narrative reveals some of the backstairs discussions that took place once Bernard set in motion an attempt to censure Gilbert. Bernard turned to Pope Eugenius "as a friend" and "urged him to put on zeal and manly courage in the Lord's cause." In the end, however, Bernard could not muster sufficient support to get a condemnation of Gilbert. John noted that Bernard nevertheless "often spoke openly against the bishop . . . both in letters and in his book, *On Consideration*, to Pope Eugenius," as well as in one of his Sermons on the Song of Songs, "but he at least seems to have been inspired by zeal for the faith and ardent charity in all he wrote."

I wonder whether this last characterization of Bernard was sincerely meant or indicates that John had his reservations about the abbot of Clairvaux. John functioned as a go-between for Bernard with Gilbert. Bernard suggested that Gilbert meet him to discuss questions regarding the Trinity. Gilbert answered that the matter had already been sufficiently discussed between them. If Bernard "wished to reach a full understanding . . . he should first seek further instruction in the liberal arts," Gilbert suggested. Gilbert here seems to have been quite patronizing, but John tried to reconcile the differences between the two men by saying that both were "learned and eloquent" but "excelled in different branches of learning." John considered Bernard to be an outstanding preacher whose talents exceeded those of any other figure since Gregory the Great. Bernard excelled in his ability to absorb the formulations of Scripture. Using the language of the prophets and apostles, "he had made their speech his own and could hardly converse or preach or write a letter except in the language of Scripture."

This observation corresponds to what Bernard himself admitted, as recorded by Geoffrey of Auxerre: that during meditation and prayer he could see the whole of Scripture, "as if it were placed open before him." Bernard lacked, according to John of Salisbury, "knowledge of secular learning," while Gilbert was outstanding in this area. John saw both figures as "gifted interpreters of Scripture, but the abbot was more experienced and effective in transacting business." This attribution defies the common characterization of Bernard as an impractical, otherworldly figure. His relative success in condemning Abelard's teaching and in almost condemning Gilbert's theology can be attributed to his ability to organize an opposition and get a result. Gradually in the course of comparing Bernard and Gilbert, John revealed a preference for the latter. Bernard was the master of the Bible, while Gilbert had at his fingertips the doctors of the Church such as Hilary, Jerome, and Augustine: "He made use of every branch of learning as occasion demanded." Thus he had a breadth of knowledge that Bernard did not possess. "In his lectures," according to John, "he [Gilbert] took every opportunity to fight heresies." John spent many pages of his *Memoir* reviewing the Trinitarian teaching of Gilbert, ostensibly to show that it was quite orthodox and profound. Disputes about the Trinity characterized the early scholasticism of the twelfth century, and John's purpose in going into such detail was surely to show that Gilbert's theology was in harmony with that of the doctors of the Church. Indirectly John refuted Bernard's attack on the man.

Another, but quite different matter also brought Bernard to the Council of Reims in 1148: the question of the marriage of Ralph, Count of Vermandois, to Queen Eleanor's sister, after he had repudiated his first wife. Several popes had refused to recognize the new marriage, and the question had soured relations between King Louis VII and Count Theobald of Champagne, whose niece had been Ralph's first wife. Now Ralph received absolution from Pope Eugenius. The first marriage was declared invalid because of consanguinity.

As John of Salisbury pointed out, Eugenius "was rescinding the sentence of his predecessors Innocent, Celestine and Lucius."

Bernard was present at these proceedings, and John describes him as "fervently attached to Count Theobald because of his pursuit of justice and reputation for uprightness." Bernard could of course not contradict the decision of Pope Eugenius, but he did declare that any descendants of the now legitimized marriage would not be blessed. John noted the offspring of the marriage: a son who became a leper and daughters who were unable to have children: "So it seems . . . that we should believe the words of the man of God." The case of Ralph of Vermandois became a lesson of God's wrath against those who misused the sacrament of marriage, and here Bernard emerged as the righteous man who refused to compromise because of political concerns.

Yet Bernard did not bring his project to realization either in preaching the crusade or in organizing the censure of Gilbert de la Porrée. That a sensitive observer such as John of Salisbury expressed admiration for Bernard's insight and intentions is an indication that he was generally respected. Nevertheless, even in occupying center stage of church and society Bernard could not make events conform to his own views. If history is the record of one problematic event after another, then Bernard's life was an account of one commitment after another, and some of these ended in defeat.

A Semblance of Business as Usual

At times Bernard did reside at Clairvaux and write letters that had nothing to do with heresy or crusade. In August or September 1148, he wrote Suger of Saint Denis and praised him for restoring the Parisian abbey of Sainte Geneviève to order and discipline. He asked him to continue in this work, which "you have begun so magnificently." Bernard felt it was not necessary for him to trouble Suger on behalf of the abbey of Saint Victor, "for I know that the care of all religious houses has been handed over to you." While the king was away on crusade, Suger had been made regent and had been given a special prerogative to supervise monasteries. Bernard, who earlier had criticized the way Suger administered his own abbey north of Paris, had become convinced that Suger's reform of Saint Denis was a model for monastic and religious life elsewhere in the kingdom.

Most likely a few months later Bernard wrote another and similar letter to Suger, perhaps after a report that the regent was not attending to the duties the king had left to him. It was up to Suger to restore the observances of the abbey of Sainte Geneviève, and Bernard wrote "to ask you [Suger] to conclude in a satisfactory manner the task you began so well." Bernard looked to the abbot of Saint Denis as one of the central figures in the administration of the French kingdom but especially in maintaining standards in religious life. Shortly before 8 May 1149, he wrote again to the abbot of Saint Denis, to make sure that he attended a forthcoming council at Chartres. If he came, then "everyone will know that the king and his realm have a good friend, a wise counsellor and a powerful helper."

Bernard was not always positive in his contacts with Suger. In a letter to Suger in the first months of 1149 Bernard expressed concern about men who had returned from crusade and planned to engage after Easter in "those cursed tournaments." Some of the greatest lords, including the king's brother and a count's son, had agreed to attack and even kill each other on the field. After so many dangers in the East, while there was peace in the kingdom and the king still absent, these two would return and plague the land with their warfare. Bernard pleaded with Suger to make use of his position "to oppose such practices with all your strength," by using either persuasion or outright force. Bernard's letter reveals how the practice of holding tournaments, already forbidden by the Church, continued to attract magnates. One would think that after living through the carnage of crusade these men would have had no desire for further warfare, but apparently this was not the case.

Besides writing to Suger, Bernard also contacted the bishops of Reims, Sens, Soissons, and Auxerre, as well as Counts Theobald and Rudolph, on this matter. In this letter, and another that cannot be more precisely dated than to sometime in 1149 Bernard told the regent of France what to do. He wrote on behalf of the brothers in the Maison-Dieu, a hospital in the diocese of Bourges. The king had rich crops in this area, which were being sold cheaply. In Bernard's view, the brothers should be given as much of this produce as possible, for the king traditionally helped them when he was in the area.

Also sometime in 1149 Bernard wrote that he was sending an abbot who was poor to Suger, who was rich, so that the needs of the one could be taken care of by the wealth of the other. This unnamed abbot apparently had experienced a failed harvest, and Bernard considered it to be Suger's responsibility, thanks to his wealth, to provide assistance.

In such missives Bernard acted as if it were his right to regulate the affairs of the French kingdom, even though Clairvaux was not in France at all. His own secular lord, Theobald of Champagne, had had his traumas with the French king, but by the end of the 1140s these were in the past. An understanding seems to have arisen among King Louis, Count Theobald, and Suger that made it possible for Bernard regularly to express his concerns and appeal to them. Once again it is difficult to see Bernard as the abbot of a monastic order that had chosen to be far from the madding crowd in order to seek God in solitude. Bernard inserted himself into the very midst of social and political concerns, even though he himself would probably have justified his behavior in terms of moral imperatives.

During this period of what seems like endless travels, we know that in October 1148 Bernard was at Clairvaux, where he received the archbishop of Armagh, Malachy, who had decided to live out his life as a Cistercian. In the next chapter I will consider Bernard's only hagiographical work, on Malachy's life and death. Here it is fitting to consider his *Sermon on the Passing of Saint Malachy*, for this must have been preached at Clairvaux shortly after Malachy's death on 2 November 1148.

Bernard saw it as "a gift from heaven" that Malachy had come to die at Clairvaux: "He came from the ends of the earth to be buried here in our earth." The language of the sermon emphasizes joy in the fact of Malachy's life: "Therefore brothers, let us be glad, let us rejoice, as is fitting with our father." Bernard expressed joy that Malachy had died on the same day that the bones of the first Clairvaux brothers were being reburied after having been moved from the original cemetery. The day of his death, 2 November, was also the day of general commemoration of all the faithful departed. Malachy's life and death were a gift to Clairvaux.

For Bernard, Malachy's loving presence and peaceful death manifested the meaning of Clairvaux as home not only for young men leaving their families behind, but also for old men, who had pursued careers in the Church and now wanted to end their lives in peace and harmony. Bernard had succeeded in making Clairvaux attractive as a place of fervent devotion. Although he was frequently absent from his monastery in the years after 1130, he could still attract churchmen such as Malachy to his monastery. Also, in the aftermath of the failure of the Second Crusade, and probably also as a result of his own physical ailments, in his last years Bernard did spend more time at Clairvaux.

Bernard's Testament: *On Consideration*

The work *On Consideration* is usually dated to 1147–53 and thus occupies the last years of Bernard's life. Its title is misleading to modern eyes, for the term "consideration" now means something like "looking over a problem." A better title might be something like "On the Interior Life," although in this treatise Bernard also wrote about exterior life. He addressed the work to Pope Eugenius III, in order to warn him of the dangers and temptations of public life and provide some recommendations for living a more "considered" life.

At the same time, however, Bernard was writing about himself and how he experienced the Church's situation. He was leaving behind a testament that through the centuries proved useful and even inspiring for church reformers, including Martin Luther.

In his Preface Bernard wrote that he no longer had any maternal obligation toward Eugenius, who had once been his monk, "but I am not stripped of affection for you." A monk under Bernard remained always in his charge. He would not let Eugenius go: "I will instruct you not as a teacher but as a mother, indeed as a lover." This is genuine Cistercian language, the affectivity that Bernard fostered and for example asked Aelred of Rievaulx to describe in his *Mirror of Charity*. Bernard clearly felt that Eugenius, no matter what his position in the Church, remained his responsibility and thus should be given special affection and attention.

The first part of the work was sent already in 1149 to Peter the Venerable at Cluny. The first book of *On Consideration* looks at the demands of papal office. The problem is that there is no end to these demands, so Bernard was afraid that Eugenius would devote himself completely to business, "leaving no time or energy for yourself." "What is the point of wrangling and listening to litigants from morning to night?" His "poor body" never gets the rest it requires. At the papal court Eugenius had to deal with all kinds of dubious persons: the ambitious, the avaricious, the sacrilegious, and so on. Criminal types were coming from everywhere in order to gain ecclesiastical privileges or office. Because of this endless flow of petitions, there is no time for anything else: "When are we to pray or to teach the people?" It is a great danger to "apply your experiences and knowledge to activity and have nothing for consideration." The pope had received the keys of heaven to have power over sin, not over property, but instead he spent time and effort in a military campaign invading someone else's territory. He must give himself to consideration, following Psalm 46:11: "Be still and know that I am God."

Bernard provided a historical precedent for a pope who devoted himself to such consideration, offering the case of Gregory the Great (590–604), who, while Rome was being besieged, went ahead in writing a commentary on an obscure final section of Ezekiel's prophecy: "He did so carefully and elegantly." The times were now different. Everywhere the powerful oppressed the poor, and it was wrong to abandon them to their fate: "We cannot refuse judgment for those who suffer injustice." The pope should try cases, but in a "suitable manner." Bernard wrote that he was amazed that "you a man of piety can bear to listen to how lawyers dispute and argue in a way that tends more to subvert the truth than to reveal it." The Church was filled with ambitious men, who were to be avoided. The pope must "refuse to deal with some business and assign some to others." He must decide which cases deserved to be heard.

This presentation of the demands of papal life provides an excellent illustration of how successful the popes of the twelfth century had been in attracting the attention of many churchmen and laypersons who felt that they could not find justice in their own legal systems. The papacy could be a last, best resort, and so the causes and concerns of all Western Europe were ending up at the papal court. For Bernard the excessive ambition of those who sought out the pope distracted Eugenius from the spiritual life he needed to have. But the same phenomenon can be looked upon as a sign of the success of the reformed papacy in functioning as a kind of high court for church and society. For Bernard this was no blessing, for it deprived the pope of an opportunity to be teacher and preacher.

The second book of the treatise begins with Bernard's lament over the situation of Jerusalem after the failed crusade, and thus places its composition in 1149 or 1150. This is followed by his division of the types of consideration: looking at what is below the pope, what is around him, and what is above him. The plight of humankind is to be ashamed because one is naked, to weep because one was born, to complain because one exists. Bernard here was describing his own perception of life as much as that of the pope's situation: "If you consider how great you are, also ponder what sort of man you are."

The third book turns to what is below the pope: he must correct heretics, convert pagans, check the ambitious, for today it is ambition "that wears down the doorsteps of the Apostles." Bernard saw a special dilemma in "Italian greed." He had spent time in Rome in the 1130s and had seen how papal government functioned, so his characterization cannot be dismissed out of hand. For him it was necessary to help the oppressed and restrain the ambitious. But the pope had to deal with appeals "made to you from the whole world." Bernard recognized this situation as the result of papal primacy, but appeals could become an obsession: "How long will you fail to keep watch over the confusion and abuse of appeals? . . . If you love justice, you do not encourage appeals but tolerate them." It was best with most appeals to hand them over "to men who are acquainted with them."

The pope should not seek litigation but do his best to avoid it. "Yours is not the only power from God; there are intermediate and lesser ones." Bernard lamented the failure of the statutes drawn up at the Council of Reims in 1148 to be observed. It was forbidden there for clerics to wear clothes of many colors or to do up their hair. Luxury in dress was condemned but not hindered. Punishment was prescribed but not enforced. It was now more than four years since the decrees had been issued (thus placing this segment of the work in 1152), but no cleric had been deprived of his benefice, and no bishop had been suspended from office.

The fourth book considers what was around the pope. Here Bernard warned against the behavior of the clergy and the Roman people, their arrogance and obstinacy: "They are a people unaccustomed to peace." It was hardly necessary to say these words to a pope who spent most of his reign outside of Rome because of the restlessness of its population. "Everything is given to honor, little or nothing to sanctity," Bernard continued. The pope in his finery was more the successor of the emperor Constantine than of the apostle Peter. Bernard formulated his conception of the two swords, with the spiritual drawn by the priest and the material by the knight, but at the priest's bidding. He provided two examples of churchmen who were not corrupted by the times. The first was Martin, a Cistercian who became cardinal and died in 1144. As papal legate he returned from his mission without having acquired any material gain: "What do you say, my Eugene. Is it not an event from another century?" Then there was Bishop Geoffrey of Chartres, papal legate to Aquitaine. Bernard himself saw how the man refused the gift of a fish because he considered it bribery. But he knew how Eugenius might have reacted: "You are hesitating and with a deep sigh are saying to yourself: 'Do you think what is said can happen? . . . Who can make us live so we can see it?'"

Bernard lamented how popes "each day . . . carefully review the expenses of the day but are unaware of the continual losses of the Lord's flock." Every day they had to dispute with their servants about the price of food and the number of loaves of bread purchased, instead of meeting with priests about the sins of the people. The pope should be aware of the character of each person who served in his house: "Let your fellow bishops learn from you not to have boys with luxuriously curled hair and foppish young men in their retinue." This concern with lavish attire for clerics can be found in the canons of the Second Lateran Council of 1139, so Bernard's warning was not unique. Bernard's main point was "in all things moderation is best." In the palace Eugenius was to be pope, but in his home he was to be "father of your household." The pope was not "lord of bishops but one of them and the brother of those who love God and the companion of those who fear him."

Bernard elsewhere showed understanding of the papacy in terms of its endowment of plenitude of power in the Church, but here he was limiting papal authority to headship in collegiality. Certainly Boniface VIII in his declarations of papal power a century and a half later would not look to Bernard. It seems likely nevertheless that future occupants of the papacy might have learned something from *On Consideration* in terms of leaving time for the interior life and avoiding an obsession with legal matters.

The work culminates in the fifth book, where Bernard looks at the things above the pope. Here he was touching on theological matters and returned to the subject of Gilbert de la Porrée's Trinitarian theology. Bernard clearly had difficulty accepting his failure to have Gilbert condemned for his teaching in this area: "I do not know how he could say that he worships the Trinity, after having overendowed it with such a multiplicity of elements." A large part of this book, however, consists in anticipation of the vision of God to come: "A blessed vision for which he rightly sighed who said 'My face has sought you, your face, Lord, do I seek' (Ps 27:8)."

The treatise ends with the assertion that God "must still be sought who has not yet sufficiently been found." The best way to him is not discussion but prayer, and thus Bernard ended by asserting the power of prayer in seeking God. And yet the entire treatise is an assertion of the value of discussion, for Bernard in his "consideration" discussed the meaning of papal power and the life of the papacy and the role of the priesthood in general in the Church. In calling to mind the limitations of papal power, Bernard was to a large extent defining his own limitations as the conscience of Christian Europe. Ever since the 1130s, the entire world had been coming to him for advice and assistance. Now he was summing up the possibilities and limits of what he was doing. More than anything, Bernard wanted to meet the presence of God: "He must still be sought who has not yet sufficiently been found and who cannot be sought too much." In such paradoxes was embedded the meaning of Bernard's life.

Saying Goodbye to Suger

In December 1150 Bernard wrote to Suger of Saint Denis, who was dying. The first part of his letter is rather conventional: good advice to someone on his deathbed. Why should he be bothered with the clothing of the flesh when he was about to don the clothes of immortality in heaven? The man who belongs to God and the man who belongs to the earth will be in conflict with each other, and there would be no peace for Suger until the two were separated.

In the second part of the letter Bernard allowed himself to be more personal. He strongly wanted to see Suger "so that I might be able to receive the blessing of a dying man." But Bernard could not promise something that he was not sure he would be able to deliver, "yet I will do my best to carry out what I so far cannot see that I can do." Bernard did not refer to his own health, but it is possible that at this point he felt too weak to travel to Paris: "Maybe I will come, maybe not." Whatever came about, he felt his love for Suger: "I cannot lose someone whom I have been able to love until the very end, one to whom my soul is so attached that it cannot be separated."

This is the language of monastic friendship and affectivity, even though we have to remember that for much of their relationship, Suger and Bernard were rivals more than friends. But in later years Bernard seems to have come to accept Suger as an ally, and now deliberately forgot their differences and emphasized only his attachment to the great man.

Bernard expected that he would soon follow Suger in dying: "May I be allowed to come soon after you and to reach you." He would not forget the Suger he cherished in his memory, although the loss of his presence gave him sorrow. These sentiments may have touched Suger, for he responded with a brief letter thanking Bernard for the consolation extended to him.

The contents of such a letter contrast sharply with a brief communication sent in the spring of 1148 to Ida, Countess of Nevers. Bernard told her how the abbot of Vézelay (where he had preached his crusade sermon) had complained that Ida and her vassals prevented merchants from coming to Vézelay at will. Count William and his son completely disavowed such a practice in the presence of the bishop of Auxerre and Bernard himself. Bernard advised and warned Countess Ida from doing this kind of thing in the future: "If you start acting in this manner, you will come to damage yourself in this world and your husband where he now is." Bernard threatened that the wife's actions might affect the count in the afterlife. Theologically this is a dubious assertion, but it shows the force of will that Bernard could display.

I consider Bernard's relations with women elsewhere. I include this letter here not only because it belongs in this chapter chronologically, but also because it provides a necessary contrast to the attachment expressed to Abbot Suger. Bernard knew how to use the language of affectivity and friendship, and to Suger on his deathbed he may have been expressing true sentiment. But he could also be tough and uncompromising, and it would be wrong to reduce Bernard to anything like a gentle soul. When he believed in his own cause, he was relentless, as in returning to Gilbert's theology when the matter had been shelved for good. With Abelard, however, there was a surprising reconciliation, even though we hear of it only indirectly, from Peter the Venerable.

Bernard can puzzle the observer, with his sensational contacts with ordinary people and his frequent assertions of what he saw as God's will. He is in many ways a difficult saint, not easy to love and yet hard to ignore in an attempt to grasp the meaning of medieval Christianity. Bernard came to occupy its very center.

🦋 CHAPTER 10

Business as Usual in Preparing for Death

Defining His Identity

Bernard's last years, from 1150 until his death on 20 August 1153, were spent in a flurry of activities that provide little indication that he was a dying man. A few times in his letters he described his physical condition. Probably in early 1151 he wrote Pope Eugenius, as his Cistercian father: "Your young man is more ill than usual. Life flows out of me drop by drop, perhaps because I am unworthy of an easy death and a quick entrance to life." The term *puer vester* (your young man, your boy) is one of jest but also of familiarity. This remark, however, comes at the end of a description of problems at the Grande Chartreuse, where Bernard was convinced the pope had been deceived. He was still involving himself in matters outside the Cistercian Order, so his commitment hardly reflects the situation of someone in the process of dying.

Bernard's descriptions of his illness are too vague to allow any conclusions about his condition. His hagiographer Geoffrey of Auxerre was similarly unwilling to provide any detail: "Lying on his bed, Bernard's body was beset with many ailments." Geoffrey's concern was to record the healings that Bernard could still manage to offer those who sought him out, or the manner in which he could revive from his weakness in order to get involved in new controversies. A letter that Bernard is said to have dictated to Arnold, Benedictine abbot of Bonneval and later author of the second book of the

Vita Prima, provides some detail, however, describing, for instance, how even in taking a small drink of liquid, it "causes me great discomfort, but it is even more severe if it is altogether removed." The authenticity of this letter has been challenged, and the text was supposed to have been made up by Geoffrey of Auxerre after Bernard's death. Leaving aside the issue of whether the letter is Bernard's own work, we can still make use of it as a description of his last illness.

If we consider the *Vita Prima* as a whole, especially in view of what it tells about Bernard's illness already a few years after he became abbot of Clairvaux, he seems to have suffered from some kind of gastric disturbance, perhaps a result of his ascetic way of life. In this respect William of Saint-Thierry was far more specific and detailed than Geoffrey of Auxerre. William described how Bernard could not keep what he ate inside and would "vomit it raw and undigested." When he ate, it was not so much to "sustain his life as to defer his death." This could be a description of an illness that lasted the rest of Bernard's life and perhaps developed into stomach or intestinal cancer. Geoffrey does not provide many details, but the letter to Arnold, whether written by Bernard or by Geoffrey, indicates that Bernard's inability to eat and drink had become chronic.

It is something of a wonder that a man who for years had experienced stomach cramps and could hardly consume food or drink could continue to be active for such a long time. In preparing to write about Bernard's final years I have been surprised by how he still managed to involve himself not only in the affairs of Clairvaux and the Cistercian Order but also in many other matters of church and society. Bernard refused to make any concessions to his own weakness and went ahead with his concerns, dictating one letter after another. We can assume that for the most part he had to remain at Clairvaux during these years, except for a final excursion that brought him to the city of Metz in what today is the north of France. Bernard was tireless, willing, perhaps obsessed with responding to requests for help from other churchman.

Bernard made one attempt to define himself and his life. The self-description is often quoted as if it seemingly provides a key to his personality and self-understanding. I will make use of it here, but with the reservation that everything he wrote was the result of a brilliant mind that loved to play with words. Just when we think Bernard has revealed himself, he escapes our grasp. There can be no final statement of who Bernard was, but here is one of his own contributions. He was writing, probably in 1150, to the Carthusian prior of Portes, who was also called Bernard:

The time has come to remember who I am. My monstrous life cries out to you, my conscience that is plagued. For I am a chimera of my age. I live as neither cleric nor lay person. I have long since abandoned the way of life of a monk, but not the habit. I do not want to write about myself: what I think you have heard through others, what I do, what I intend, what I desire, and the dangers I confront in the world, indeed the cliffs over which I am cast. But if you have not heard of these matters, I ask that you enquire and according to what you have heard, that you provide advice and the strength of your prayers.

The passage is usually noticed for the term "chimera," in mythology a monster breathing fire and having the head of a lion, the body of a goat, and the tail of a serpent. Bernard thus acknowledged the duplicity—or triplicity—of his life as contemplative monk, active church reformer, and political figure in the society of his day. [For Bernard as contributing to a persecuting society, see question 14 in the Fifteen Questions about Bernard: The Background for My Portrait section.] But it would be wrong if this elegant description were to suffice as the last word in describing Bernard. He was playing with words, making fun of himself and his way of life, and by no means giving a complete admission of his own self-understanding. Precisely when Bernard seems to tell all, he remains elusive.

What emerges from this description, however, is Bernard's understanding of himself as some kind of monster, made up of disparate parts in opposition to one another. [For Bernard as a monster, see question 10.] He knew precisely what it meant to be a Cistercian monk and abbot, and admitted that his many pursuits were taking him away from this life. He did not apologize or ask for understanding. He told the world that he had become something other than a good Cistercian. Bernard was aware of his vocation and its obligations while he ventured into a way of life that constantly pulled him away from the monastery and contemplative life. At the same time, he was leaving behind the brothers in Clairvaux for whom he cared but whose lives became distant from his own.

Defending His Record with Carthusians and Premonstratensians

Bernard's self-description comes at the end of a letter to Bernard of Portes, and it needs to be seen in the context of his attempt to reconcile himself with this Carthusian prior. He admitted to being upset with the man. He was concerned about the monastery of Portes. Seemingly, there was a problem with a brother Noel, who had been elected to office but had been challenged. The pope himself refused to confirm the election. Eugenius seems to have been afraid that detractors would say that brother Noel had gone to the desert (the Carthusian way of life) in order to gain high office in the Church. Bernard insisted that he had nothing to do with the pope's refusal to recognize Noel's election, and no one had any right to assert that the pope was acting as a result of Bernard's urging. He claimed to be interested only in promoting good men as pastors in the Church. But then he added that brother Noel was known for an indiscretion in his youth.

The letter is classic Bernard, implying a great deal, asserting pure motives, but also indicating that he had been involved where he claimed to have kept a distance. The description of brother Noel is followed by Bernard's expression of regret that two abbots had written harsh letters to Bernard of Portes. This section of the letter seems to be intended to tell his correspondent that Bernard had not shown ill will to his namesake. Bernard had not made public the letters that Bernard of Portes had written to him against these abbots. In other words, Bernard was innocent of making trouble: "You can be certain that they did not learn about [these letters] because of any intention or effort of mine."

The bulk of the letter concerns rivalry between the monasteries of La Grande Chartreuse and Portes. Brother Noel was chosen to be bishop of Grenoble, but the monks of the Grande Chartreuse opposed the election. The pope annulled it, and the purpose of this letter seems to have been for Bernard to make it clear that he had not involved himself in the matter and did not try to influence the pope's decision. But by pointing out that Noel had a troubled past, Bernard was adding fuel to the fire. He could not keep himself from being a party to events, or from becoming involved in the affairs of other monastic orders. At the same time he revealed a sense of who he was, this triple-bodied monster that had long since left the monk's way of life but had kept the habit.

A much longer letter can be dated to September 1150 and was sent to Abbot Hugh of Prémontré, the sister order to the Cistercians that had been allied to them by a pact dating from 1142. Bernard started by asking Hugh why he had written so harshly to him. In return for Hugh's abuse, Bernard wrote that he would tell how he had treated him and his Order. He pointed out that he had himself provided the land on which Prémontré was founded. He added a number of other places where the Premonstratensians had established themselves and where he had been helpful, often in making it possible for land to be given to the brothers.

Bernard asked Hugh whether he was giving back evil for good when he threatened to sever relations with the Cistercians. He admitted that he had received a Premonstratensian, Robert, into the Cistercians. Bernard, however, had explained the circumstances not once but several times. He had done nothing to get Robert to leave his Order and had in fact for years tried to dissuade him from such a step. There had been many brothers in the Premonstratensian Order who wanted to come to the Cistercians, but Bernard claimed to have encouraged them to stay where they were. He did, however, receive Robert, and in fact the pope had ordered him to admit the brother. Robert told Bernard that Abbot Hugh had given his consent, which was extended not as a result of any papal command. "If you deny that this happened, then it is not my responsibility but his," wrote Bernard. Hugh might want to claim that the pope was showing duplicity, but Bernard could only trust and obey the pope. He had sent an Abbot Gottschalk to look into these matters, and he obtained from Abbot Hugh the release of the brother and his acceptance of the fact.

Another brother's transfer to the Cistercians is also mentioned, as well as the Cistercian takeover of a Premonstratensian house: "I wish that before you accused me, you had made the effort of asking the persons involved both who overtook the house but also why it was removed from you." Bernard had asked the Premonstratensian brothers to avoid future disputes by giving up the house.

The letter continues to list one controversy after another, and it is apparent how easily misunderstandings and rivalries could arise. The bishop had done his best to prevent the Premonstratensians from building their new house. Bernard claimed to fail to understand Premonstratensian resentment. Lately there had been a chapter of the Order at Bar-sur-Aube, and from here came Hugh's letters "complaining and indeed abusing" Bernard.

One protest led to another. Abbot Hugh had been after Bernard because a lay brother from the Cistercian monastery of Igny had burned down a hut belonging to the Premonstratensians. Bernard insisted that it was not even a hut, just a shelter of branches where the brothers could find shade. It was burned because it was in a field belonging to the brothers of Igny and took up land they cultivated. The Premonstratensian abbot of Braine was supposed already to have received satisfaction for the deed, and so was not complaining. But if this was not the case, then Bernard wrote that he was ready to provide compensation.

Another issue was the fact that the Cistercian abbot of Villers had gotten the church of St. Follian placed under an interdict. This was due to the misbehavior of the abbot of St. Follian. It was he who deserved Abbot Hugh's anger. The matter is complex but ended with the abbot of Cîteaux's asking Bernard to find some solution. In the absence of the abbot of Villers, it was agreed by the bishop of Cambrai that if the abbot of St. Follian kept to what had been accepted, then the bishop would not issue an interdict, forbidding all church functions. But Bernard claimed that the abbot broke the agreement as soon as the bishop had left the scene.

Bernard claimed that he had arranged for the sentence of interdict to be delayed until after Epiphany, in the hope that there would be some kind of resolution, and he still prayed this would happen. He told Abbot Hugh that he had no justification for complaining against Bernard: "Rather I am the one who has reason to make complaint against you." He referred to the pact of unity, peace, and love arranged some years earlier between the two Orders and said the bond was just as useful to Hugh as to Bernard. And then Bernard added an assertion that expresses how he understood himself in his dealings with others: "I, however, whatever you should do, have decided always to love you, even if I am not loved. Let him seek reasons who wants to leave a friend. It is my desire not to give a friend any reason for leaving me." Bernard insisted that he would remain loyal to the friend, no matter how difficult and demanding the relationship might be: "I will cling to you, even if you do not wish me to do so; I will do so, even if I have no desire to do so."

Bernard asserted that in response to Hugh's anger he would return peace: "I will not allow the anger of those who want to quarrel with me." This would be to allow the devil to enter. His assertion is, of course, pure Christianity in giving good for evil, and these last lines of a long letter are full of biblical references: "My soul is sorrowful [Mt 26:38] that I have offended you in one way or another." Bernard sought Hugh's forgiveness: he would knock on his door.

This letter has two distinct parts: first, a review of the case together with Bernard's defense of his actions; second, an assertion of love and friendship, in spite of discord and misunderstandings, and an insistence that Bernard would hang onto this bond, come what may. It would be interesting to note how Abbot Hugh reacted, but on the basis of this letter alone it is apparent that the two monastic orders, however close they were in terms of their foundations, easily could become each other's rivals. Bernard attracted men to his monastery and his Order, and this fact caused resentment. The Cistercians could appear in their surroundings as agricultural imperialists who were taking land away from others. But for Bernard it was a question of maintaining not only good relations but also bonds of brotherhood: "Whatever you do, I have decided always to love you, even if I am not loved. The one who wants to leave behind a friend searches for reasons to do so, but it is my desire not to give you any reason for leaving me." In the heat of controversy Bernard used the language of friendship. He defended his own behavior and insisted that he would cling to Abbot Hugh.

Pleading with the Pope: One Appeal after Another

The above letter to a Premonstratensian abbot reveals that in the last years of his life Bernard was still willing and able to involve himself in complex affairs of property and personnel. At the same time he could appeal to the affective spirituality that had characterized his earlier years. We see his tenacity in the many letters he wrote to Pope Eugenius. Bernard maintained a certain distance and no longer tried to make use of the fact that the pope had once been his monk. But one can imagine that when a messenger showed up at the papal court with a missive from Bernard, the pope may have asked himself, "What now?"

Probably in 1150 Bernard wrote on behalf of Philip, who had been bishop of Taranto but had lost his position because he had supported Anacletus in the schism. Afterwards he became a monk at Clairvaux, but he was not allowed to exercise priestly powers. Bernard now pleaded for a dispensation, saying that he represented all the brethren of Clairvaux: "Brother Philip does not make the plea for himself and he has not asked others to do so for him." Bernard claimed not to know whether Philip wished such a move: "We ask not for Philip but for our Order." Great benefit would accrue if Philip's situation were regularized. It is hard to believe that Philip was unaware of his abbot's appeal, but the very fact of it shows how repercussions of the papal schism continued to affect lives, more than a decade later. Bernard was turning to Eugenius for a matter that directly involved him as abbot of Clairvaux.

Another Clairvaux matter concerned a brother Rualene, who had been sent from his monastery to that of St. Anastasius to take the place of the abbot who became Pope Eugenius. These letters are slightly earlier than 1150, possibly from 1145–48, but I include them here because they cast light on Bernard's relationship with Eugenius. Rualene apparently did not like his new position and wanted to return to Clairvaux. Bernard appealed to Eugenius for a "remedy that not only he needs but also I!" Bernard played with the parental roles to which he regularly returned in his writings: he said he had handed over the position of father to Eugenius, and so he was not Rualene's father. But he still felt affection for him: "A mother is unable to forget the child to which she gave birth." Rualene was Bernard's son, for in assuming his care, Bernard had taken on the role of mother. Such language is more than rhetoric. It is an expression of the relationship Bernard conceived with his monks. He had to take care of Rualene's needs. Bernard and Eugenius had forced him to assume the office of abbot, but if he continued to do so against his will, then it would be difficult for him and do no good for anyone: "The office will suffer, and it is you and I who will be worthy of blame." So only one thing could be done. Eugenius had to show a father's heart and "give back this child to his mother." It would be better to let him live than to divide him up, Bernard suggested, referring to the story of Solomon. At the end Bernard added that Rualene's letters worried him because they indicated he was considering running away.

A second letter to Eugenius also concerns Rualene. Bernard wrote that it had formerly been his wish for the man to take over the monastery of St. Anastasius, but now that Rualene was unwilling, Bernard no longer wanted him in the post. Bernard had obeyed the papal command, but the letter indicates that he felt torn between obedience to the pope and concern for his former monk. In a letter to Rualene himself Bernard expressed his sympathy for the man's predicament. He grieved at Rualene's situation, "for I sense your burden to be much more than my own and consider it to be much harder to bear than my own loss." Bernard claimed that he had risked the pope's anger in his attempts to get Rualene freed of his obligations, but to no avail. So he had to "yield in exhaustion to heaven's decision and to the weight of an authority that is greater than my own." The outcome was a defeat for Bernard: "Spare yourself and spare me, for I in my love for you have not spared myself." This relatively brief letter indicates that Bernard may have felt he was trapped in the very system in which he believed. He had to obey Eugenius, who insisted on Rualene's continuing as abbot. At the same time he felt responsible for the man, who remained his monk and thus his personal concern.

Another case where Bernard took responsibility and appealed to the pope concerned a Benedictine abbot. A Knight of the Temple wanted to become a Cistercian monk but could not transfer in this manner from the one Order to the other. So instead he took on the Benedictine habit so that from there he could be received into the Cistercians. They had accepted not receiving any Templars into their fold, but they were not prevented from taking in Benedictines. Bernard seems to imply here that such a transfer was legal because the man would be going from a less strict to a more strict monastic order. When Bernard became aware of the situation, he submitted it to the Cistercian General Chapter, a rare indication of how Bernard could make use of this body. But the assembled abbots did not comply with his wishes. They suspended the former Knight from the Order, but even so the Templars were not satisfied. They asked that the pope issue letters ordering the bishop of Châlons to suspend the abbot of St. Urban. It was he who had clothed the Knight Templar in the black habit of the Benedictines.

Bernard insisted that the abbot of St. Urban had acted in good faith, and now he asked that the pope release the abbot of St. Urban from any charge of misconduct. This is a brief missive, about twenty lines, but it indicates how wide-ranging Bernard's monastic involvements could be. It shows that his plans and ambitions could fail at the level of the Cistercian General Chapter. At the same time he had to take other Orders into consideration, such as the Templars, who clearly had obtained a great deal of influence in the Church and refused to accept losing a member to the Cistercians.

Even briefer is an appeal to Eugenius for the monks of a Benedictine monastery at Saint Mary of Mouzon. Bernard complained about wrongful treatment they were receiving and about harm done by "persons who seek evil." He added that the messenger would tell the pope in detail about these unfortunate men who "call on you for help." Also involved was the archbishop of Reims, Samson. It is noteworthy that Samson, instead of appealing directly to the pope, went to Bernard, who in these letters appears to have been powerless to alter the course of events.

Bernard was willing to involve himself in the affairs of other monastic orders that had no influence on the Cistercians. This was the case in a letter to Eugenius dated to early 1151. The Carthusians had been at odds with each other because the prior of La Grande Chartreuse had created dissension as a result of doing his best to remove certain relaxations of the Order's strict practices. The brothers who had objected were sent away from the monastery, and some of them went to the pope, who gave them absolution and reinstated them in their monastery. Bernard now stepped in and told Eugenius that it was the devil himself who was making trouble in the monastery. Their departure from La Grande Chartreuse was something bad, but their return was even worse: "Can you not realize, dear father, how seriously you have been deceived?" Eugenius had been fooled by appearances.

Bernard wrote to the pope as if Eugenius had been naive and unaware of the situation. He warned him that if the prior was not reinstated, then the Carthusian Order would be endangered. He more or less ordered the pope to act: "May God give you inspiration to deal with this matter in a fatherly way and to give a favorable answer that will provide consolation for all of us, for we are sad and weighed down by this matter, almost beyond what we can bear." At the end of the letter Bernard provided the news that the abbot of Cîteaux, who was Rainald of Bar, had recently died. We know this took place on 13 December 1150. Bernard asked Eugenius to support his successor, Goswin, abbot of Bonneval. He finally turned to the subject of his health, as

mentioned above. Bernard was here indicating to Eugenius that he still considered the pope to act as a Cistercian, attentive to the affairs of the Order.
His appeal for the prior of Grande Chartreuse can be seen as an indication
of how he involved himself in matters that had nothing to do with the Cistercian Order. Presumably Bernard responded to whomever came to him in
their need. This is the positive view. The negative one would be that Bernard
could not keep himself from getting entangled in the affairs of others.

Bernard's dealings with Eugenius as pope could be positive. In September 1152 he wrote and thanked the pope for his concern for the Order. Eugenius had issued a bull, *Sacrosancta Romana,* confirming Cistercian statutes.
Then on 5 August he had written the abbot of Cîteaux and the General
Chapter to remind them of the principles of the Order's founders. He was
perhaps concerned about the phenomenal growth of the Cistercian Order,
"that you not degenerate from the virtues of these [founders], but what you
were in the seed, you may also be in the tree." Bernard stated in flowery
language that the papal text was read out at the following General Chapter:
"The turtle dove's voice has made itself heard in our chapter." He did not
state whether he himself attended, but if so, it was his last appearance.

For once it seems as if Bernard was writing to the pope merely to praise his
concern for the Cistercian Order. But the second half of the letter includes a
lament on the loss of Hugh, who had been abbot of the important Cistercian
house of Trois Fontaines, founded in 1118 as the first daughter of Clairvaux.
Its abbot, Hugh, had been summoned in 1150 by the pope to be attached to
the Curia as cardinal bishop of Ostia. Since the monastery was a daughter
of Clairvaux, Bernard as father abbot was responsible for finding a successor
for Hugh. This was proving impossible, and now Bernard asked the pope to
allow Hugh to return to his monastery: "You will deeply wound my heart if
you do not have him sent back, for he and I share one mind and one heart."
The reference is to the Acts of the Apostles (4:32) and their description of
solidarity in the first Christian community. Bernard was making a bold
statement in comparing his union with Hugh to the apostolic world, but he
seemed determined to avoid what he considered to be potential damage to
the entire Order. But he added that if Eugenius was adamant about keeping
Hugh, then he asked the pope to value the man and to ask God to provide a
fit candidate for the abbacy of Trois Fontaines.

The letter ends with a request for a quick reply to various matters that
Bernard had entrusted to the abbot who brought the letter to the pope. As so
often in letters from Bernard and in medieval letters in general, the body of
the letter hardly contains all that was to be communicated. Information by
word of mouth concerned matters not found in the letter itself. Bernard did,

however, indicate that he was contacting the pope "on behalf of the whole Order." He was writing in the interest of the Order, but his main concern seems to have been to get the abbot of Trois Fontaines back to his post. However much Bernard praised the pope, he also expected him to listen to his concerns.

Bernard's letter collection includes one to Hugh in Rome. He admitted to having made a mistake in writing on behalf of a young man, perhaps a letter of recommendation. Bernard had backed the youth in gaining an office in the Church, and now he conceded that he did so because of his attachment to the youth's uncle. This man had recently died, and Bernard's sorrow apparently moved him to do what he could for the nephew. Bernard only indirectly indicated that it was Hugh of Macon, bishop of Auxerre, who was behind the youth's preferment. Now it was apparent that the young man could not take up the office, and it remained to clear the bishop of the taint of any wrongdoing and to see to it that the young man could find an alternative position. Such a letter may seem trivial, but it reveals the way Bernard involved himself in one sensitive affair after another. First, he tried to get Hugh back as abbot of Trois Fontaines; second, he tried to benefit from Hugh's residence at the papal court in order to look after the career of an unnamed youth. The letters indicate that the abbot of Clairvaux could not keep himself from continuing involvement in church affairs. Even though Bernard's health apparently forced him in these last years mainly to remain in his monastery, he was still looking outside Clairvaux and involving himself in matters that had nothing to do with Clairvaux. But the Cistercian family as such required his attention.

For Bernard, once a Cistercian, always a Cistercian. He felt free to turn to Hugh for business at the papal court, but he would have greatly preferred to get the man back to his monastery at Trois Fontaines. The world for Bernard was made up of Cistercian men and their monasteries, and even though he accepted that the pope had to look beyond the Cistercian world, he still expected him to take special care of Cistercian affairs.

Contested Episcopal Elections and Conflicted Bishops

The matter of a youth's preferment is put in a larger context in a letter from Bernard to Pope Eugenius, probably from 1152. Bernard described how the bishop of Auxerre had died almost intestate and had left little or nothing to the poor and to the churches of the diocese. This bishop was Hugh of Macon, one of Bernard's earliest friends, who had entered Cîteaux with him and in 1136 became bishop of Auxerre. At his death it became apparent that he had left all his property to a nephew, presumably the young man whom Bernard at an earlier point had tried to help. Now he wrote to the pope asking him not to confirm Hugh's testament. In general, the matter seems to have been a painful one for Bernard, in coming to the realization that his friend of youth had lost his good judgment and handed over his worldly goods to a youth who apparently was not trustworthy.

An episcopal election took place for Hugh's successor, and a candidate was chosen by the priests of the diocese. The outcome, however, displeased William, Count of Nevers, who tried to arrange that his own candidate was chosen at a second election. Now Bernard asked Eugenius to appoint someone of papal choice to the bishopric, thus ignoring both the initial election and the count's machinations. Eugenius instead appointed a commission of three, including Bernard, to look into the matter. Bernard submitted the name of Alan of Regny, abbot of the Cistercian house of L'Arrivour, but the other members of the commission would not agree to his choice.

In a further letter to Eugenius Bernard claimed that when he first had written to the pope concerning the matter, he had heard of the first election but not the second. The planning of the second election was a trick, with the intention (presumably by the count) that after the second candidate had been chosen, a third would be brought in. Bernard insisted that it would be wrong to let evil triumph. Wisdom should not be manipulated, nor was it right that the outcome should be delayed any longer. Here as so often in his career Bernard was involving himself in an episcopal election that basically was none of his business. But at Auxerre as at York and elsewhere, he found a suitable candidate among his own Cistercian abbots and thus contributed to a growing network of Cistercian bishops.

In yet another letter to the pope, Bernard defended his actions. He said that the course of events exhausted him, but he had to go ahead with the matter. "Have I ever asked on my own behalf that churches be ordered or that bishops be deposed or created?" This plea of innocence is hard to accept in view of the fact that Bernard involved himself in the creation of a new bishop of Auxerre. He described how he had been part of a commission whose two members could not accept Bernard's candidate for bishop. Now he asked the pope to do the right thing and confirm Bernard's man, the abbot of L'Arrivour: "In my view nothing can better confirm your good name than such a choice." The opposing party, according to Bernard, simply wanted a candidate who would be easy to control. As for the Count of Nevers, Bernard accused him of failing to imitate the virtues of his father. His concern was to get hold of the goods and property of churches. If Eugenius wanted to avoid seeing monasteries in the diocese of Auxerre reduced to poverty, and religion despised, then it was up to the pope to make certain that Bernard's candidate, Alan of Regny, was consecrated bishop.

"Where is the spirit you demonstrated in the matter of York?" Bernard asked, thus making an exact parallel between what happened in England and what was going on in France. In spite of all the reforms of church and society that had taken place in the last century, secular powers were still able to interfere in episcopal elections. Bernard resisted such practices, but his response was to place one of his own abbots in the episcopal chair. He concluded the letter: "An appointment that is a mistake will always be noticed, but when it takes place after long deliberation, it is something disgraceful." He was practically saying that if Eugenius did not remedy the situation, he would create a scandal.

Toward the end of the letter Bernard reminded the pope of the situation of the bishop of Lund in Denmark. I will look at Eskil's situation below, but its mention here seems to indicate that Bernard wanted the pope to look upon conditions at Auxerre and in Scandinavia as parallel: bishops needed to be chosen on a just basis and their dioceses protected from selfish secular interests.

A final letter in the matter was sent by Bernard to King Louis. Apparently the king had opposed the episcopal election because his prerogative had not been observed. Now Bernard asked, "Have I at any time attempted to subtract from the king's honor or the renown of his kingdom?" Such a statement is pure Bernard: he did not concede that Louis had the right to choose a bishop, merely that he, Bernard, was sympathetic toward the king's position. Bernard insisted that the electors of Auxerre were acting against the king's interests, for their concern was to get hold of income from the churches. Bernard stated that he was present at the Auxerre election, a valuable indication that at this late date in his life, 1152, he could still leave Clairvaux on church business. The distance was more than eighty miles. At the election the king's consent was thought to have been given in a letter, and Bernard could not understand why it had to be acquired a second time. And so he addressed the king boldly: "You have no reason to abrogate the elections that have been held, for you had previously given your consent." He asked the king to provide new instructions, "so that the church which for a long time has been plagued and troubled will no longer continue in this deplorable state."

In the end it appears that the pope did intervene, as Bernard required. According to Bruno Scott James, whose translation of the letters to this day remains useful, Eugenius's decision brought about the charge that "the pope was a tool in the hands of St. Bernard." The abbot of Clairvaux quite naturally denied the assertion, but as we have seen from his letters to Eugenius, he more or less ordered the pope to act in confirming Bernard's own choice of bishop. I have reviewed this disputed election with some care because it shows how Bernard even late in life could involve himself in a dispute that initially had nothing to do with Cistercian life and spirituality. But once Bernard had forwarded a Cistercian candidate for the bishopric, the election became his concern.

Another affair with a bishop was, if possible, even more sensitive. Shortly after Easter in 1150 Bernard wrote to Pope Eugenius on behalf of Henry, the bishop of Beauvais. Henry was the brother of King Louis. Eugenius had summoned the bishop to his presence, but Bernard had intervened, "especially because it was not clear to me why you [the pope] wanted him to come." Bernard objected that Henry and his brother the king were at odds, and so it would not be safe for him to be away from his diocese for a long period. Henry had shown respect and deference to his brother, "but they have had no effect." Once Henry knew why the pope was summoning him, he would come immediately. Bishop Henry of Beauvais had apparently stopped at Clairvaux when he was summoned to Rome, and now Bernard had taken responsibility for what he saw as the bishop's sensitive situation.

In the next letter Bernard wrote not to the pope but to Hugh, cardinal bishop and a Cistercian. He explained that the bishop of Beauvais had come to Clairvaux during Lent "and he would have continued if I had not convinced him to wait." The bishop intended to set out as soon as he could. Apparently Cardinal Hugh had complained about the bishop's behavior, and Bernard replied that the man was no longer his responsibility: "His actions are a concern for his own bishopric. If he sometimes acts in a manner he should not . . . then I can regret what he does, but it is beyond my powers, whatever I may desire, to correct him." Hugh had apparently claimed that the bishop of Beauvais was spending too much time traveling outside his diocese. Bernard replied that he was not aware of this practice. Also there was a charge that the bishop's brother, Robert, had acted in an inappropriate manner. Bernard claimed that he was unaware of any such behavior. He only conceded that he would do what he could to get the bishop to return "when I have an opportunity to do so without offending him."

Bernard was here both taking responsibility and refusing to take it. His message seems to be that so long as Bishop Henry was staying at Clairvaux, then Bernard was obliged to look after his interests. But now he was gone, and Bernard refused to believe rumors about the bishop's bad behavior. It is interesting that he was writing here not to Eugenius but to Cardinal Hugh, who once had been abbot of the Cistercian house Trois Fontaines. Bernard used the Cistercian network and would not let papal politics dominate his own.

He added here a sentence about his state of health, which by this time must have been a concern throughout the Church. He wrote that he was indeed dying: "I am sick and in the process of dying, but for the time being I have been recalled from death and I do not think that I will last long." A remarkable statement and quite true, for Bernard was ill and dying but still had some time left. The letter ends with a description of how the archbishop of Lyon had set out on a journey with money and a retinue. He had been ambushed by his enemies. He had just enough money to continue his journey, but with only a few men. He had three or four servants and disguised himself as one of them. It is not clear why Bernard wanted to add this information to a letter that concerned other matters. Perhaps he was replying to a query in Hugh's letter about what had happened to the archbishop. In any case Bernard was showing how well informed he was. As always, he wanted to know what was happening around him and to control events, at least by being aware of what took place. For a dying man, he was still holding onto his old habit of trying to influence the world around him.

Cluny and the Monks of Miroir

In June 1152 Bernard wrote to the pope on behalf of the monks of Miroir, a Cistercian house in Burgundy. The monks of the nearby Cluniac priory of Gigny had attacked Miroir and caused serious damage. The issue was the fact that the Cistercians since the time of Innocent II had been exempted from paying tithes, with the result that the Cluniacs lost about a tenth of their revenues. The attack on Miroir was a Cluniac priory's revenge for this status, and now Bernard intervened on behalf of a Cistercian monastery. In the letter to the pope he described how he had met with the monks of Gigny at Cluny: "We did our best to make peace, but nothing resulted from our efforts except the collapse of our hopes." Bernard referred to a letter from the pope about the payment of compensation, but what the Cluniacs offered as reparations was trivial in comparison with the cost of the damage done to Miroir. Bernard mentioned the abbot of Cluny, Peter the Venerable, and praised him faintly by saying that his assistance in obtaining a settlement was fairly useless. In a brilliant phrase he damned Peter for being "affective rather than effective." Bernard's relationship with Peter the Venerable remains a matter of controversy even in our day, but here he was accusing Peter of being better at showing emotion than offering a solution. [For their relationship, see question 11.]

No agreement was reached. The Cluniacs claimed that the damage had been done by some evil persons and not by themselves, so it was not their concern. Bernard labeled this excuse "ridiculous." It was known in the entire neighborhood that the crime was carried out by men belonging to the monastery, that some of the monks were there, and that everyone gave their consent. Bernard concluded the letter by insisting that the matter could only be settled by someone who had a strong hand, and this "hand is awaited from you," he wrote Eugenius.

Perhaps the most remarkable aspect of this controversy is the fact that Bernard was able and willing just a little more than a year before his death to travel from Clairvaux to Cluny in order to get compensation for the monks of Miroir. It was at least 150 miles from Bernard's monastery to Peter's, and the road led through the capital of Burgundy, Dijon, with all the hazards and distractions that such a journey might offer. Bernard's letter is quite businesslike. He did not lament the difficulties of travel or emphasize his shaky physical condition. He simply told the pope what he thought he should do, and, in this sense, Bernard continued in his last years to keep the pope informed about how the Church should be run. Having made certain that he could not be elected to papal or episcopal office, Bernard involved himself in the affairs of popes and bishops and expected them to listen to his recommendations (or commands) about how to act. But Bernard's commitment was not always sufficient to make a difference. The question of compensation for Miroir remained unresolved at his death.

Bernard's criticism of Peter the Venerable was not always harsh. At the end of 1151 he wrote to Pope Eugenius on behalf of Peter. Bernard stated that Peter did not need his letter to recommend him to the pope, but the abbot of Clairvaux wanted to express his affection for the man. Bernard thus used more or less the same term he had employed in his dissatisfaction with Peter, but now it was meant in a positive manner. He called him his friend who was on pilgrimage. "Who will keep us apart, not the heights of the Alps not their freezing snows, nor the length of the journey? And now I am present, giving assistance to him in my letters," wrote Bernard. It is an open question why Bernard was writing for Peter, for his request to the pope on behalf of the abbot of Cluny is quite general: "Send him back with joy." Peter was praised for helping out poor Cistercians: "He supports our brothers from what his monastery owns." Bernard expressed concern that Peter might have asked to be released from his monastery's rule. But Bernard found that he had improved the Cluniac Order in terms of maintaining fasting and silence, as well as limiting expensive clothing. There is clearly an element missing in Bernard's letter, a statement of what it was Peter the Venerable was asking from the pope and why Bernard had chosen to support his cause. But these two letters need to be placed alongside each other, the one expressing Bernard's frustration that Peter was unable or unwilling at Cluny to reconcile the wronged monks of Miroir, and the other giving Bernard's wholehearted support to the concern that brought Peter to the papal court.

Telling Off Lay Lords, Protecting Pigs, and Advising Women

Bernard accepted that lay lords often had power and influence that church officials did not. Probably in 1152 he wrote to the Count of Champagne, Henry, later known as the Liberal and the son of the Theobald who had been Bernard's close ally and even friend. Bernard explained that the abbot of Châtillon had entrusted his property to Bernard when he had set out for Rome. In the meantime, the servants of a certain Simon had rustled the abbot's pigs. Bernard felt personally responsible: "I tell you I would have preferred that my own pigs had been stolen." For Bernard this mundane affair set in motion divine justice: "The king of kings has placed you as a lord on this earth. By his power and on his behalf you are meant to strengthen those who are good, check those who are evil, look after the poor and provide justice when anyone is harmed." Bernard warned that if Henry failed to carry out his just functions, then his right to rule would be lost. The possession of pigs might seem like a minor matter, but they were of course a major product in the agriculture of the twelfth century. Bernard involved himself in their care. Just as he took responsibility for other human beings, he did the same for the pigs that were a source of sustenance for persons for whom he felt concern.

Sometimes Bernard could express himself in so direct a manner that he came close to being insulting. He wrote, perhaps in 1150, to the Count of Angoulême on behalf of the brothers of Boix. This monastery had been founded in 1143 from Clairvaux. The problem was that the count was charging an excessive rent for a property that the brothers were using, and Bernard explained, "It has not been customary for us to pay anything of the kind." Here Bernard took on direct responsibility: "We have founded many abbeys and none of them has been subject to such exactions." Under the circumstances, however, Bernard promised he would respect the agreement the brothers had made with the count, at least "until God shall move you to provide something better, which I do not doubt he will do." In other words, the count one day would see the light and follow God's guidance. This last statement was practically an insult, for Bernard was telling the count that he was in the wrong but hopefully would eventually have to change his ways for the better!

Bernard seems to have been especially close to the family of the Counts of Champagne, as can be seen in a letter from about 1152 to the Countess of Blois, the wife of Count Theobald. He expressed regret that her son had behaved badly toward her. This was presumably the same Henry that he wrote the same year concerning the problem of pigs. Henry was born in 1127, and so would have been in his midtwenties at the time. Instead of reproaching Henry for whatever he had done to his mother, Bernard asked her to be understanding toward her son: "Youth is always likely to faults of this kind, and the fact of youth in itself provides an excuse for the young." As far as Bernard was concerned, the qualities found in the father would lead to an improvement in the young man. Meanwhile, "a mother should not and cannot give up the maternal affection she feels for her children." Bernard found in Henry "many outstanding qualities," and so he encouraged the countess to shed tears and offer prayers so that her son would come to imitate the virtues of his father.

At this point Bernard formulated a general principle that might seem surprising in view of the strictness of the disciplined life according to which he lived: "He [Henry] must be shown a spirit of gentleness and kind understanding, for in this way he will be brought to do good, rather than if he were tired out by reproaches and blame." Bernard was applying the gentle side of the Rule of Saint Benedict, where there are passages that call for leniency, as in chapter 27: "For the abbot must show the greatest care, and to exercise every form of prudence and diligence, so that he can avoid losing any of the sheep entrusted to him." Bernard was certain that if the countess followed this gentle treatment, then she soon would find improvement in her son. But Bernard at this point perhaps revealed his own limitation, for he said that he had always experienced young Henry's behavior as beyond reproach. He thus was not really able to understand the mother's concern. He nevertheless promised to continue doing whatever the countess asked Bernard to do: "I am always reproaching him for his conduct towards you."

A recent biography of Henry has dated this letter to 1149 in connection with the return of troublemakers from crusade. I find this letter to be so personal in character, however, that it reflects not so much a reaction to a rowdy group of young men as the strained relationship of the countess with her son, thus bringing about Bernard's intervention on her behalf. What is surprising is that Bernard suggested gentle treatment. We do not know what Henry was doing that upset his mother, but Bernard was more or less telling her not to worry and just to pray and trust that her son would become like his father. In a way he was right: Henry the Liberal did become a count who used power effectively and graciously. At the same time Bernard recommended the same gentleness that he at times could demonstrate toward one of his wayward monks. We do not know, however, how the countess reacted to this letter or whether she found it at all helpful.

A much more down-to-earth letter was sent to Sancia, the sister of Alphonsus, king of Castile and Leon. The monastery of Toldanos had tried to affiliate itself with Clairvaux in order to avoid being subject to another abbey, Carrezeda. This monastery had appealed against the attempt and won its case. Bernard explained that he had been absent at the time and had not known what was going on. He had difficulty accepting that the monks could not make the change they wished, for the foundress of the monastery had declared that she had established it so that it would not be subject to any other religious house. The monks could choose their allegiance to Clairvaux and the Cistercian Order if they so wished. Bernard had been told that the monks of Carrezeda complained that they had been wronged. He left the matter in his correspondent's hands "so that an Order that has been recognized by the Church can have peace, for God's glory and the benefit of your soul." In other words, the monastery of Toldanos should be allowed to choose affiliation with Clairvaux. Bernard revealed that he had sent his brother Nivard as a go-between and had expressed "complete confidence . . . because of your great devotion towards us" as well as a promise Sancia had made to him. It is not clear whether this Nivard was Bernard's youngest brother, but in view of the delicacy of such a mission, it seems conceivable that Bernard would have made use of his own brother. If the king's sister's advice on the matter was not respected, then Bernard suggested the affair be submitted to the two bishops in whose dioceses the monasteries were situated. Finally he asked for Sancia to support another Cistercian foundation, that of Espina, from 1147: "Strengthened by your kindness the brothers may continue unhindered in the service of God and their Order."

Bernard had some decades earlier warned against founding Cistercian houses in Spain because they were so far from the Cistercian heartland of Burgundy and Champagne. But he had clearly changed his mind and seems now to have been doing his best to foster such foundations. In another letter to Sancia he praised her for her devotion, faith, and confidence in the Cistercians. He had heard of her praiseworthy actions from brother Nivard and in return granted her "the brotherhood of our house and our prayers." Here is the idea of a lay confraternity that could also be extended to women. Sancia for her good works would share the spiritual benefits of Cistercian monks.

The opposition of the monastery Carrezeda, however, appeared to be a problem. Bernard said its monks were spreading lies about the Cistercians and their intentions: "We hand over the affair to you so that you can do what is necessary to suppress it." Once again Bernard mentioned the possibility of arbitration by local bishops. Thus, as in the previous letter, Bernard made use of good contacts in order to further a Cistercian foundation. He sent brother Nivard but also offered a royal person a share in the spiritual benefits that came from the monks' prayers.

In such letters it is clear that Bernard had no qualms about appealing to the highest echelons of society in order to make certain that Cistercian foundations were recognized. Bernard was involving himself at a late point in his life. He had been coping for decades with the responsibility not only of furthering the Cistercian Order but also of promoting justice and order in the Church. He rarely in these letters referred to his own fatigue or illness. He simply kept going, more or less to the very end, as if the world could not exist without him.

A Great Betrayal: Nicholas of Montiéramey

Bernard had to solicit the help of several secretaries in order to keep up with his flourishing correspondence. One monk who for a time proved himself invaluable was Nicholas of Montiéramey, so called after the Benedictine monastery near Troyes he entered in 1145 or 1146. Once professed, Nicholas decided to become a Cistercian monk at Clairvaux, and here he quickly made himself indispensable to Bernard as one of his secretaries. At the same time Nicholas maintained close relations with Peter the Venerable of Cluny and became a go-between for the two abbots. This bond is apparent in a letter of November 1149 from Bernard to Peter. Bernard wrote that when a letter from the abbot of Cluny arrived, his duties allowed him to give its contents only a furtive glance. But he nevertheless was able subsequently to absent himself from "all the endless questioning and petitions made by everyone" and instead withdrew into a place of hiding with Nicholas, "to whom you [Peter] are so attached." Bernard was impressed by Peter's letter, but he could not spend long on it because "a huge number of people from almost every nation in the world had come to see me: I had to look after them because for my sins I am born to be taken up in multiple cares."

Bernard's rhetoric can be questioned, and his effusive admiration of Peter may have been more a polite gesture than genuine feeling. But his behavior indicates that Bernard had made Nicholas into a kind of valued private secretary, sharing with him the demands of writing endless letters. Bernard allowed Nicholas to make his own contribution apparent, as in letting him end this letter to Peter the Venerable with the greeting "I your Nicholas greet you for eternity and beyond as well, as that household of yours which adheres to you and your spirit." The language is effusive and differentiates itself from what Bernard would write: he expressed affectivity, while Nicholas tried to convey a hyperbole of devotion.

The honeymoon did not last. Writing to Pope Eugenius at some time between 1149 and 1152, probably closer to 1152, Bernard complained that a scoundrel "without my knowledge" had gotten hold of letters of recommendation supposedly sent by Bernard and obtained through the bishop of Beauvais, whom we saw above was Henry, the brother of King Louis VII. Bernard did not name Nicholas in this letter, nor in another to Eugenius, which can be dated to 1151–52, where he was more specific about what was happening: "I am placed in danger from brothers who are false. A number of forged letters have been sent with my forged seal." Bernard was concerned that such falsifications had even gotten to the pope. He had therefore stopped using his former seal and had adopted a new one. The new one had both his image and his name. Bernard asked Eugenius not to accept any other seal that purported to come from him.

It is remarkable that Bernard did not name Nicholas in these letters. He may have been uncertain about his secretary's culpability, but when he wrote the pope in May or June 1152, there was no longer any doubt: "Nicholas has gone his way because he did not belong to us." Bernard said the man had left behind his foul tracks. For some time Bernard claimed to have known who Nicholas was, but he had waited either for God to convert him to something better or for himself to betray his identity, like some Judas, and this is what took place. After he left Clairvaux, there were found on him books, money, and a great deal of gold, as well as three seals. The one was Bernard's, the other belonged to the prior of Clairvaux, and the third was Nicholas's own. The seal of Bernard's was not his old one but the new one he had made precisely because of fear of misuse. Bernard referred to a previous letter to Eugenius, where he had avoided giving any names, but only stated he was in danger from false brethren. Thus Bernard now indicated that he knew all along Nicholas was deceiving him, but this claim may simplify a complex situation in which Bernard was divided between affection for Nicholas and his talents and fear that the man was exploiting him.

Now Bernard had had enough: "Who can know how many people he has written anything he has wanted, using my seal, but without my having any knowledge of the matter?" Nicholas had apparently confessed that he had written to the pope under a false identity, not once but several times. Bernard reminded Eugenius of the crimes of Arnold of Brescia, and he found Nicholas to be a new Arnold: "No one better deserves to be imprisoned for life, and no one is more deserving to be sentenced to perpetual silence."

It might seem that with such a harsh condemnation by Bernard, Nicholas's career was over for good. But his charms and talents enabled him to elude all the condemnations. After the death of Eugenius and in the papacy of Adrian IV, Nicholas gained an office. He ended up serving the Count of Champagne, Henry the Liberal, the man who apparently had caused such grief for his mother. But Nicholas knew how to convince his surroundings of his usefulness, and Bernard's desire to have him imprisoned came to nothing.

Making Malachy into a Saint

Bernard's *Life of Malachy* is, besides his sermons and letters, one of the few products of his pen that date from his last years. In the wake of the archbishop of Armagh's death at Clairvaux on 2 November 1148, Bernard decided to celebrate a prelate who had chosen to end his days as a Cistercian monk. Geoffrey of Auxerre, ever aware of Bernard's inner life, claimed in a sermon he wrote on the anniversary of Bernard's death that the abbot of Clairvaux had "left his own image in the blessed Malachy, though not on purpose." This is a wise evaluation of what Malachy meant for Bernard: in the Irish prelate Bernard found himself. The Cistercian recognition of this closeness is indicated by the fact that when Bernard was canonized in 1174, the office used for his feast day was partly taken from the one intended for Malachy. Though one was abbot and the other archbishop, in terms of way of life the two men were seen as being close-knit. In writing the *Life of Malachy*, Bernard seems to have arranged his material so that Malachy's life experience conformed to his own. Bernard was especially concerned with the way that Malachy insisted on church reform. He enhanced the episcopal position and brought the Irish Church into line with Rome, just as Bernard himself worked for Rome as the center of the Church.

Bernard's primary hagiographical model was the *Life of Martin of Tours* by Sulpicius Severus, written at the end of the fourth century, a heroic biography of a man known for his miracles. Martin had the virtue of first being a devout monk and abbot before being made to accept election to bishop. Bernard could mirror himself in Martin, except for the fact that Bernard avoided being persuaded or compelled to be made bishop, as had ostensibly been the case with Martin. But Malachy had done something even more praiseworthy: first he had been a zealous bishop, and in his last days he had laid aside the office and become a simple monk. What better recommendation for the Cistercian way of life?

Bernard wrote that he deliberately omitted any description of Malachy's "inner man." He wanted to show how Malachy had made a difference to his surroundings, and so Bernard emphasized the terrible state of the Irish Church. Consequently, he showed no sympathy whatsoever for the fact that Irish Christianity could be different from Roman. For him it was a question of conforming Armagh to Rome, and he seemed to accept without any hesitation Malachy's negative description of the Irish situation. The archbishop had visited Clairvaux three times, the first two in 1139 on his way to and from Rome. Malachy had accepted the papal summons to the Third Lateran Council, the one that Bernard presumably did not attend. The archbishop could only have had a few days at Clairvaux in 1139, but the visits left a lasting impression. He wanted to bring Cistercian monks to Ireland and arranged on his second visit to Clairvaux to have some of his companions remain there so they could prepare for being sent back to Ireland as Cistercian monks. This in fact did happen with the foundation of Mellifont in 1142 under Abbot Christian. The Irish are described in Bernard's *Life of Malachy* as a barbarian people who had not yet seen monks. This characterization is quite amazing in view of the fact that there had been monks in Ireland since the early Christian centuries. But Bernard was thinking of the reformed monasticism of the twelfth century, which he considered to have been completely lacking before Malachy's reform.

In describing Malachy's third and final visit to Clairvaux, Bernard sketched what might be called a personal friendship. Malachy arrived on 18 October and died on 2 November, and thus he and Bernard had only two weeks to be with each other. Bernard moved fast, probably because he saw in Malachy a reflection of his own person and program. He offered Malachy the privilege of being buried at Clairvaux, and as it turned out, very close to the grave that Bernard would have. Thus there took place a *translatio sanctitatis*, a transfer of holiness from Ireland to Clairvaux. Bernard opposed the idea of Ireland as the isle of saints and focused on Clairvaux as the place of rest for spiritual heroes like Malachy. In his Preface to the hagiography he showed gratefulness to the dying Malachy: "He blessed me and I possess this blessing in inheritance."

Time and again Malachy's life parallels Bernard's, as in the way the Irish brethren could be displeased by Malachy's long absences from them. Like Bernard, Malachy often had to leave his community behind. But Malachy is described as having found his true vocation in the Cistercian way of life. This came at a late point, but it was enough for Bernard that his last days were spent at Clairvaux. Dying at Clairvaux was just as important as living there, and surely Bernard intended his work as an incentive for other bishops and church officials to end their days in monastic community. Here he became intimately attached to Malachy. On his death he took the man's tunic and kept it for himself. When he said the Mass in his memory, he read the text for a confessor, thus indicating that in his view Malachy already was a saint. This was an unorthodox step, but Bernard must have considered it carefully.

Bernard's Malachy is also to be seen in the three letters we have from the abbot to the archbishop. In the first, dated to 1140, Bernard responded to Malachy's request that Clairvaux send brothers to found a monastery in Ireland. Bernard required that the Irish brethren "be more fully formed in Christ" at Clairvaux before being brought back to Ireland: "The time is not far away before I with the grace of God will be able to send you men who have been reshaped in the grace of God." The second letter is briefer and announces that Bernard had sent the brothers who had been requested. In the third letter, from 1142 and marking the first Irish Cistercian foundation, Bernard expressed all the affection that he could offer to one who shared the Cistercian life with him. The language is that of romantic friendship: "I am completely yours, even though this be but little."

In interpreting such a letter, it might seem odd that Bernard at this point had known Malachy only for a few days, perhaps only hours: "I ask that our affection, which is not something new, may yet develop each day." But the bond between Bernard and Malachy was the new Cistercian foundation at Mellifont: "I commend my sons to you, for they belong to you also." Bernard was convinced, as he demonstrated in his *Life of Malachy*, that the situation of monasticism in Ireland was not favorable: "There is need for care in a new land with a people that is not used to monastic life and ignorant of it." The Celtic tradition apparently meant nothing to Bernard, and he saw in Mellifont a necessary new establishment of monastic observance. Bernard wrote that he had instructed Christian, who became the first abbot, in the Order's observances. He had sent Christian with other men, but Bernard apologized for their smallness in numbers. He explained that he did not want to force any of his monks to leave Clairvaux against their own desires.

When Malachy died in 1148, Bernard wrote to the Irish brethren and expressed his grief at the loss of his friend. Although it was right to feel a loss, at the same time there was reason to be glad because of the life Malachy had lived. It was fitting to feel sorrow at his death, but also right to celebrate the life into which he had come. Now there was a patron in heaven, for Malachy must now love his sons even more than he did when he was with them. Bernard expressed his compassion for the Irish Church and encouraged the brethren to follow Malachy's example: "May he bring me after him so that I can hasten with eagerness in the fragrance of his virtue." Through Malachy Bernard could see the continuing expansion of the Cistercian Order and especially the Clairvaux line of monasteries. It would be excessive to consider Bernard as being obsessed with a growing Order, but he did think of Clarevallian foundations as a manifestation of God's blessing on the Cistercian way of life. He was grateful to Malachy for sharing that growth, and especially for ending his days at Clairvaux itself.

Malachy thus came to sum up all that Bernard sought, especially in his last years: the expansion of the Cistercian Order, its spread to a part of Europe where reformed monasticism had been unknown, and the incarnation of the new monasticism in a prelate who chose to share that way of life in retirement at Clairvaux itself. Malachy's story of course contradicts the view largely held today about how the Irish "saved civilization" through their monasteries in the early Christian centuries. Bernard had another view, one that saw monasticism as having died out and having to be revived by Malachy and the Cistercians. Malachy became a friend, perhaps not intimate, but certainly important in Bernard's late life.

A Friend from the North, Eskil

Eskil, archbishop of Lund (1137–77), came to take the place that Malachy had occupied in Bernard's consciousness. He is an obscure figure in European history and has often been dismissed as difficult and unattractive in comparison with his successor, Absalon, who became the hero of Saxo's account of Danish expansion in the north, the so-called *Gesta Danorum* (Deeds of the Danes). But Eskil was a central figure in Bernard's last years. In 1143 he helped bring monks to found the first Cistercian houses in Scandinavia, Alvastra and Nydala in the Swedish kingdom. Then in 1150 or 1151, Eskil visited Clairvaux and brought back with him a group of monks to found the Danish Cistercian monastery, Esrum in northern Zealand. At the same time, Eskil turned to Bernard for help in avoiding what at this point seemed almost inevitable: a reversion of the see of Lund to its former status as subject to the metropolitan of Hamburg. Since about 1103 Lund had been an archbishopric directly under Rome, but Hamburg's archbishops were not happy with this status and did their best to subject the North to their domination.

Eskil seems to have found in the Cistercians and especially in Bernard a bulwark against German domination. It was not only the fact that Cîteaux-Clairvaux belonged to the French-speaking world. There was also the hope that by linking Cistercian monasteries in the north with those in the Cistercian heartland, the Danish-Swedish church would find a much-needed identity and independence from German interests. Eskil's precarious position not only toward the ecclesiastical interests of Hamburg but also in a civil

war among various candidates for Danish kingship helps explain his eagerness to turn to Bernard for guidance and encouragement.

Bernard's one surviving letter to Eskil may be from the early summer of
1152 but more likely was written already in the autumn of 1151. Bernard
made use of the same type of affective language he had employed in his
contact with Malachy. Eskil had apparently written Bernard of the difficulties he was having in his position as archbishop, and Bernard replied in kind:
"I can only feel sorrow for your sorrow, dear father, or receive word of your
concerns and troubles with my own concern and care." Bernard felt a bond
with Eskil: "Whatever upsets you also upsets me and whatever oppresses
you also burdens me." Much of Bernard's language could be dismissed as an
expression of humility, the abbot before the great archbishop, and the closeness that came to characterize Bernard's relation to Malachy is not present
here. Bernard used clichés that may have been genuinely meant, but they
are commonplaces in the art of *dictamen* or the writing of letters, such as
how "the living word" is to be preferred to the written one. The speaker's
eyes confirm his words, and the face better expresses affection than does
the pen.

After all this elegant language, Bernard in the last lines of the letter came
to his message. He mentioned a matter of business (*negotium*) and a private
matter (*secretum*). The second is often interpreted as Eskil's desire to leave his
office and withdraw to Clairvaux, something he actually did some decades
later in 1177. But Eskil's secret was more likely his concern about the status
of Lund as an archbishopric and keeping it independent of Hamburg. He
had turned to Bernard with this concern, and now Bernard was offering him
help and consolation, as we can see from Bernard's letter to Eugenius where
he mentioned Eskil. As for the business matter, this was apparently Eskil's
plan to convert the Benedictine foundation at Esrum he had made some
years earlier to a Cistercian monastery. The William mentioned in this letter
as Eskil's envoy would continue to Rome and in December 1151 obtained
a foundation charter from Pope Eugenius. William became Esrum's first
abbot. Bernard was thus facilitating a bond: Lund-Esrum-Clairvaux-Rome.
Bernard was a master at such networking, and Eskil apparently knew that
the abbot could provide the contacts that he himself lacked.

When Bernard died, the first church prelate to whom Geoffrey of Auxerre turned in order to make the fact officially known was Eskil. In the years
afterwards, Eskil maintained his bond with the Cistercians and especially
Clairvaux. After Eskil was taken into captivity in 1156, he wrote to the Danish Church and people about how he looked upon his situation, and he used
a language concerned with the fact of redemption that reflected Bernard's

own theology. Once he gave up his office of archbishop in 1177 and came to Clairvaux to be a simple monk, Eskil became friendly with the monk Herbert and told him stories about his concerns in Denmark and his devotion to the Cistercians. Some of these stories ended up in Herbert's *Book of Miracles*, completed before Eskil's death in 1181 and showing his continuing attachment to the Cistercian way of life.

As a brother of Clairvaux, Eskil came to value the Cistercian desire to share inner life and spirituality. Some of the stories he told Herbert are horrific, assertions of an Old Testament God of vengeance. But the Cistercians and especially Bernard seem to have provided Eskil with a new spirituality, so that in him a revenging God met a loving Lord. The sympathy and understanding Eskil had exchanged with Bernard, he continued to have with other brothers after Bernard's death. The Cistercians had a talent for attracting difficult and complex personalities like Eskil. At the same time Bernard had a talent for bringing figures like Malachy and Eskil to him and to Clairvaux and thus making the Cistercians into a European movement. The monastic reform movement that had begun so modestly in 1098 at the "New Monastery" (Cîteaux) became one of the most dynamic forces in twelfth-century European society.

Last Sermons, a Final Excursion, Illness, and Death

During these final months of his life Bernard poured forth his gospel of love in his final sermons on the Song of Songs. Sermon 80 deals with the relationship between the soul and the Word that comes to it. This comparison continues in Sermon 81: "I am free because I am like God, unhappy because I am in opposition to God." Sermon 82 starts with a description of someone who "in the course of a sermon, kept something back which the Spirit was putting into his mind," for he wanted to save something for use later. But then a voice seemed to come to him: "As long as you hold that back you will receive no more." Bernard was here using the Pauline device of "I know a man" in order to talk about himself (2 Cor 12:2–3). He wanted his audience to know that he on occasion doubted his own gifts and failed to see them as coming from God. Such an anecdote provides a safeguard against a hagiographical treatment of Bernard: he saw and admitted his own imperfections. This sermon turns into a song of praise for the coming of the vision of God, concluding: "The soul will know as it is known and love as it is loved, and the Bridegroom will rejoice over the Bride, knowing and known, loving and loved." Surely in these last sermons, Bernard was summing up his perception of love and indicating that he enjoyed its reception and looked forward to its full revelation. If there ever was a question about Bernard as a visionary, it is answered in these sermons.

Probably in the spring of 1153 Bernard was called upon to leave Clairvaux and come to the aid of the citizens of Metz. Once again, he set out on a relatively long journey, 125 miles northeast of the monastery, this time at the request of Hillin, the archbishop of Trier. Geoffrey of Auxerre in his narrative is rather vague about the cause of the problem. He merely stated that the city was provoked by "neighboring princes" and that the opposing forces were confined to a certain area at Froidmont and on the river Mosel. Here in the course of an hour, more than two thousand are said to have died, "some cut down by the sword and many others drowned in the deep river." The Chronicle of Metz dates this disaster to 28 February 1153, thus six months before Bernard's death on 20 August.

Geoffrey saw Bernard's involvement in the controversy as revitalizing the sick and dying man: "So for a few days [the Lord] relieved him of his bodily sicknesses." For Geoffrey, Bernard had "not been called back from death but to death." Bernard was given a reprieve so he could concentrate on what was needed. For Geoffrey he had a gift so that "as often as a serious necessity came about, he swept aside all his weakness." His mental state overcame bodily weakness, but once the matter at hand seemed settled, then he "returned to himself" and again felt his illness. Bernard nevertheless "seemed to gain strength from his labors."

This description of Bernard's last efforts to mediate peace in a troubled world rings true, for he had on many occasions poured his energy into trying to reconcile warring or conflicted parties. Ever since his tireless travels to the South of France and Italy in the 1130s during the papal schism, Bernard had indeed gained strength from such involvements. What is missing, however, is a sense of how Bernard functioned in his physical environment. Geoffrey says nothing about how it was for the ailing abbot to travel to Metz. It is only indirectly that the narrative reveals that Bernard came to be present in the city. Nor does Geoffrey give his readers a clear picture of what the dispute involved. Neither does he describe the negotiations Bernard may have had with the warring parties. Geoffrey's genre is hagiography, not history, and he did not want to spend time and energy with details that for him were unimportant.

For Geoffrey the military confrontation between two warring parties ended happily, thanks to Bernard. When all were gathered on an island in the middle of the river, they accepted "an agreement devised by Bernard, the faithful arbiter." They shook hands and exchanged the kiss of peace. For Geoffrey the matter was resolved, thanks to Bernard. But a letter from the

bishop of Metz to the abbot of Corbie lamented that the settlement brought
about by Bernard "not only has brought us no remedy but has wounded us
more severely." As so often with hagiography, we are told about the saint's
success, not his failures. Bernard was clearly dealing with forces beyond his
control. He obtained a temporary truce but not a solution to a conflict whose
content Geoffrey did not grasp. What he did record was yet another cure.
Bernard was trying to negotiate with the citizens of Metz when a paralyzed
woman was brought to him. As in the healings described in detail from the
Rhineland journey, Bernard had pity on those in distress. There was also a
blind man who approached Bernard and was healed. Other cures took place
at monastery close to the Mosel River. It is in these moments manifesting
divine power that Bernard seems to have become present to his surroundings. The expectations he created were enormous, and as far as Geoffrey was
concerned, Bernard did not neglect people who came to him in their need.

The historian is at a loss when accounting for medieval miracle stories. It
has been traditional since the nineteenth century to discount such narratives
as wishful thinking or political manipulation. But in trying to enter into the
minds and hearts of the people described in these sources, it is clear that
almost everyone believed in the veracity of divine intervention. Bernard was
the *thaumaturge*, the miracle maker, and he had a European audience from
southern Italy to the north of France. It is likely that in making this last trip
to Metz and meeting the people whom he tried to reconcile, he gathered
strength from his encounters and was also able to respond positively to those
who sought him out for cures from their ills.

In some of his last letters Bernard referred to the state of his health, as
when he wrote Pope Eugenius, probably in early 1151 that he "was more
weak than usual." His life flowed out of him, drop by drop. To King Louis
at the end of 1152 or in early 1153, Bernard wrote that he was slightly better and had "for now been delivered from the danger of death, but I am still
weak, very weak."

In this letter Bernard also told the king that he had been visited by Louis's
brother, Robert. Apparently Robert had participated in a revolt against Louis
before the king returned from the crusade. It had been stopped by Suger, but
after speaking to Bernard, Robert had promised to do his best to please his
brother and to be "guided by the good counsels I provide." Bernard ended
the letter by saying he did not have his seal available to certify the genuineness of the letter. But "anyone who reads this letter will recognize my style
of writing, for I dictated it myself." After the affair with Nicholas, Bernard
had become careful about sending letters, but here he was certain that his
manner of expressing himself would be known and accepted.

The most detailed letter of this final period in Bernard's life is one he composed for his uncle Andrew, a Templar. Andrew of Montbard was the brother of Bernard's mother, Aleth. Through his brother's marriage he was related to Hugh of Payns, the founder of the Knights Templar. Bernard opened by saying that Andrew's letter had come to him when he was lying in bed. It had caused him great pleasure, but his pleasure would be greater if Andrew came to him. Bernard detected Andrew's desire to see him but also his fear because of the difficulties faced by "the land which the Lord blessed with his presence and the city which he graced with his blood." Bernard was thus still concerned with the Holy Land and its status: he saw that the recent crusade had been a failure and that Jerusalem might fall, as it did some decades later. Bernard, however, insisted that the Lord would have the victory and "provide courage for his people." Andrew and his men would be rewarded for their fighting.

After this review of the status of the Holy Land and the vocation of Andrew, Bernard returned to his uncle's desire to see him: "What can I say? I want you to come, and yet I am afraid if you do come." The problem was that Andrew's presence in the Holy Land was necessary, for "a catastrophe might result from your leaving. And so I cannot dare send for you, but I want so much to see you before I die." Bernard speculated that Andrew's presence in the West might be useful, for he would be able to recruit others to go to the East. As before, Bernard was thinking about the Holy Land and its situation: the fiasco of the crusade was a fact that followed him to his grave, and yet he continued to hope that the defeat could be reversed.

Toward the end of the letter Bernard became more practical and told Andrew that if he intended to come to Clairvaux, then he should do so quickly: "Otherwise when you get here, you will not find me." Bernard described how he was getting weaker, and "I am afraid that I do not have a long time left on this earth." He hoped for Andrew's presence and made it clear that he did want him to visit, regardless of what it would mean for his uncle's functions and responsibilities. Bernard ended the letter with greetings to the brothers of the Temple and also those of the Hospital. He had invested himself in the crusading state and its defenders, and he wanted Andrew to know that he remained concerned. But he also conceded at this late date in his life that he wanted Andrew's physical presence. In this way he was returning to the world of his childhood and his mother, though Bernard here did not mention Aleth.

Bernard's last months seem amazingly active, and it is difficult to imagine a sick man dictating letters from his bed and then getting up to travel the long distance to Metz. The historian Beryl Smalley once described Bernard as a sick man living on his nerves [see question 15], and this description seems very much to apply to him especially in the last months of his life. Geoffrey perhaps grasped the source of Bernard's vitality when he wrote that Bernard found new strength in making new commitments. But there remains a quality of wonder in Bernard, as when he said, probably to Geoffrey, that "he could hardly believe that people could trust him as being as useful as they said." How could "true and honest men" be deceived? But Bernard "alone was unable to see the wonders he had done, namely the splendor of his works or of his counsel." Such an observation might be dismissed as pure hagiography, and yet it may reflect the reaction of a basically simple human being who had taken on complicated tasks. Holy naivete (*sancta simplicitas*) is not unknown among spiritual people, but Bernard combined it with a worldly wisdom that meant he was sought out for advice and counsel.

The present biography is not intended to be hagiography. My purpose has been not to celebrate the saint but to begin to understand the inner life of an extraordinary human being. Bernard was unique, but so is every human being who lives in accord with what the twentieth-century monk Jean Leclercq called the love of learning and the desire for God. The literary genre of hagiography, however, can make it difficult to reach the living reality of Bernard. Geoffrey of Auxerre provides little help in visualizing the scene of Bernard's passing. In his last hours, a number of local bishops, abbots, and brothers came to watch over Bernard. He died in the third hour of the day, so at around 9 a.m., on 20 August 1153. His former monk, Pope Eugenius, had preceded him in death by a little more than a month, on 8 July. Thus in the course of 1153 two outstanding Cistercians left this world and thereby ceased the tense dialogue they had carried on with each other.

Jean Leclercq used to say that he looked forward to speaking with Bernard in the beyond and posing all the questions about his life and thought that had been unanswered while he lived. Perhaps it was the same for Bernard and Eugenius, who at last could converse without the frustrations that had characterized their earthly contacts. When Bernard's time came, he could stop caring about matters that previously had been his concern. In Geoffrey's language, "He withdrew his affections and the bonds of his sacred desires, which he had previously showed with such careful attention." But Bernard apparently still had room to think of his brothers at Clairvaux and to console them in facing their approaching loss. At the end of his life Bernard remained what he had been since his youth, a monk sharing his affective life with others.

Bernard in Death

A Cistercian monastery in the twelfth century was off limits to anyone except monks. But an exception was made for those who came to pay their respects to Bernard in death. According to Geoffrey of Auxerre, nobles and others assembled from many places, "so that the whole valley was filled with weeping and wailing." Women, however, were kept from entering the monastery: "The discipline of the monastic order inexorably denied entry to women." This prohibition fitted the kind of monk and person that Bernard had been: all his life since the death of his mother, he had kept women at a distance, and now they were not to have the privilege of mourning in the presence of his body.

For two days Bernard lay in state. On the second day at noon the crowd was so great that it "besieged his body on every side," and so the monks of Clairvaux, almost in a panic, hastened Bernard's burial. He was interred in the abbey church in front of the altar of Mary, and on his breast was placed a container with the relics of the apostle Jude. Bernard himself had ordered that the capsule be placed on his body "so that he might cleave to that apostle on the day of their common resurrection."

Meanwhile the abbot of Cîteaux, Bernard's father abbot, had arrived. We hear of his visit not from Geoffrey but from the account later made describing the first Cistercian century, the *Exordium Magnum Cisterciense*. This was Abbot Goswin (1151–55), whom Bernard had commended in a letter to Pope Eugenius. The abbot was alarmed by the crush of people filing into the church and feared "that their unruliness might endanger the discipline of the Order and that the fervor of holy observance might grow tepid in that place." Abbot Goswin forbade Bernard to work further miracles. Thus the bond of obedience that had existed in life between the abbot of Clairvaux and his father abbot continued after death. The miracles ceased, except for members of the Order: "For it was clear that the abbot of Cîteaux was averse only to those signs which threatened the discipline of the Order by attracting crowds of people."

It is of note that this episode is not included in the *Vita Prima*. One can guess that Geoffrey did not find that it fit his celebration of Bernard in death as in life. For Geoffrey, Bernard was always able to demonstrate spiritual power. He must have deliberately omitted the role of the abbot of Cîteaux in connection with Bernard's death and burial. Geoffrey filled out the legacy of Bernard with a number of miracles and visions, very much in harmony with his narratives from Bernard's lifetime. Most revealing is a story about William, abbot of Grandselve, which had been a Cistercian house since 1145.

On the very night of Bernard's death, William had a dream in which he conversed with Bernard, who told him that they had come to the foot of Mount Lebanon. William was to remain at the base, while Bernard would ascend the mountain. When asked why he wanted to climb the mountain, Bernard answered: "I want to learn." William was amazed, for he considered Bernard to be the most learned man of his time. Bernard explained: "Here there is no knowledge, no true understanding. Up there is the very fullness of knowledge, up there is the true and full knowledge of the Truth."

Geoffrey used this vision to formulate a prayer to Bernard, whom he asked to look down from his high mountain, and "be with those who labor still. . . . Give confidence to us as once you did; do not empty us of it now." Bernard had not left behind a collection of prayers, as other outstanding spiritual figures such as Anselm of Canterbury had done. His prayers have to be extricated from the body of his sermons. But for Geoffrey it was natural to pray to Bernard as a receptacle of divine grace and an inspiration especially to those who shared the monastic life with him.

The Phenomenon of Bernard

There is no doubt that the memory of Bernard was treasured at Clairvaux and reverence shown to his grave. During the French Revolution, however, the monastery was invaded, and the graves of its saints desecrated. Here legend met history, but it seems as if local peasants managed to smuggle out the remains of Bernard as well as those of other monastic figures. His head was eventually brought to the treasury of the cathedral of Troyes. Whatever else remained of Bernard was mixed up with the bones of other saints, and so the glass case in a parish church today that claims the remains of Bernard is unable to tell the observer what belongs to Bernard and what are the bones of other holy men.

Perhaps it does not matter: Bernard of Clairvaux as we have seen him in these pages is more than a relic. He was a central phenomenon in twelfth-century life and spirituality. He inspired many to follow him into the monastery. Wherever he traveled, he left behind new monastic foundations. At the same time, he was a European figure: he cannot be called French or Burgundian or Champenois, for his presence reached far beyond kingdoms, duchies, and counties. In calling him "the first European" in a Danish-language biography, I tried to capture his unique quality of offering to his surroundings a way of life that reached into every corner of Western Europe. Bernard's impact was international in a learned world that recruited wandering scholars and sought to give their life content and meaning in monastic communities that praised God and transformed their physical surroundings.

Charlemagne is more commonly given the title of "the first European." The first emperor in the West after the demise of the Roman Empire, he is celebrated for creating a realm that encompassed much of what would be considered as Europe. In political terms, then, Charlemagne may the first European. In spiritual terms, however, Charlemagne's achievements were limited; he is perhaps best remembered for his forced conversion of the Saxons. Although Bernard encouraged conversions that can hardly be called voluntary (such as when he encouraged German leaders to baptize or "destroy" the Wends), his main concern was to spread Christianity by word and example, founding new monasteries or refounding them, encouraging bishops to participate in the reform of the Church, and stamping out simony with all possible zeal. Bernard made a difference to his surroundings in ways that transcended the political boundaries created by kingdoms, duchies, and counties. In Bernard's time, the term "European" was a purely geographical description, but from our perspective, he was a European figure who began the process of cultural unification that continues into the present, despite conflicts and crises.

For many, Bernard remains the villain who sought to stop Abelard—and to some extent succeeded. Indeed, there is no reason to try to whitewash Bernard or make him politically correct for our age. Bernard believed he possessed the truth, which made him free to pursue his enemies. There will always be an aspect of him that is hard to stomach, as my Oxford thesis supervisor, Sir Richard Southern, knew. This effort to understand Bernard and to account for his inner life has been an exercise in scholarly humility, for I have been able to follow the evidence only as far as it can bring me. In the end Bernard remains an enigma, a stunning success in spreading his vision and a failure in convincing those in later centuries of his seminal contributions to Western European culture.

Bernard was creative in his talent for establishing networks of friends and scholars and in his desire to build up an Order based on a constitution, the Charter of Charity. Its author, Stephen Harding, as abbot of Cîteaux until 1133, must at times have wondered how to control this energetic young man, who combined stomach ailments with brilliant sermons on Mary. Bernard was restless and relentless, and in his passing Europe lost a figure that had managed to unite the Church and reconcile it with lay society. The years to come would show the fragility of Bernard's construction, with disputes between emperor and pope and popular uprisings in Italy and elsewhere. But Bernard had not lived in order to change society, however much he involved himself in affairs of church and state. His life was a contemplative journey, one that time and again became feverishly active. In this difficult combination lies Bernard's enigma: seeking peace and interiority while getting caught up in the concerns of the world. The secret of it all lies perhaps in the Cistercian term *affectus*, not affection or emotion but the search for attachment, both human and divine. In Bernard's affective life are his strength and stamina.

As I write these lines, European unity seems to be dissolving thanks to Brexit, Eastern European refusal to accept Western European democratic practices, and right-wing political movements that demonize immigrants and consider Muslims to be enemies. It might seem odd, then, to attribute the creation of Europe to a figure who was hardly a liberal or a free-thinker. Abelard is seemingly a more persuasive spiritual founder of a tolerant and open Europe. Such a distinction would be unfair, however, for Bernard as much as Abelard contributed to a European culture founded on the discussion of ideas. Both men based their lives on dialogue and debate; both came to find the monastery the best environment for such exchanges. Far from the dark age caricature he has become, the example of Bernard's life and his writings signal an openness to the achievements of the human spirit, guided by Christian revelation, that make possible a love that knows no end.

✿ FIFTEEN QUESTIONS ABOUT BERNARD: THE BACKGROUND FOR MY PORTRAIT

1. What are the primary sources for the life of Bernard?

The most important source for Bernard's life, besides his own writings, is the so-called *Vita Prima* (VP), the "First Life," which has three different authors and a complex history. The first book was written by Bernard's friend, the abbot and theologian William of Saint-Thierry, and was completed before William's own death in 1148, five years before Bernard died. We thus have a fairly rare case of a saint's life, or hagiography, written before the death of the subject. William showed an awareness of his dilemma of describing a life before it was finished, and it remains an open question to what extent Bernard wanted William to complete his project. It seems likely that William did not have much direct contact with Bernard in the last years of their lives, and thus book I of the VP can be looked upon as a nostalgic recollection of the first years when William and Bernard spent time with each other and before Bernard set out on his European mission.[1]

The VP has come to us in two versions, known as A and B. The first was completed soon after Bernard's death in 1153, while the second was composed about a decade later, as part of the effort to get Bernard canonized. The text of the second version is close to the first but is a bit shorter and leaves out, for example, a rather lurid account of how a woman tried to persuade the young Bernard to go to bed with her. Both A and B are partly based on the so-called *Fragmenta*, the brief tales about Bernard collected by his secretary, Geoffrey of Auxerre. But a few come from the monk Raynald of Clairvaux.[2]

In the 1140s William of Saint-Thierry brought together anecdotes about Bernard's family and early life from the *Fragmenta*. To these he added his own account of meetings with Bernard. Thus William was able to draw on a preexistent body of stories about Bernard, but the freshest part of book I is the record of William's eyewitness account of the saint. Most modern biographies of Bernard take their point of departure from William, not only because his narrative reflects a close friendship but also because it contains relatively few accounts of miracles. But Bernard for one reason or another kept William at a distance and did not give way to William's desire to join him as a monk of Clairvaux. Bernard insisted that William continue in his office as abbot of Saint-Thierry. At some point, however, William "jumped ship" and joined another Cistercian house, Signy. A lively tension existed between the two figures and a certain distance, including in William's descriptions of Bernard's ascetic regime, where there is an undertone of criticism.

The VP was continued after Bernard's death, and the task was handed over to a Benedictine abbot, Arnold of Bonneval, a house near Chartres. Arnold had known Bernard but can hardly be called a close friend. A large part of book II of the VP is dedicated to the story of Bernard's intervention in the papal schism that arose after a double election in Rome in 1130. It may be that Geoffrey of Auxerre, who directed the Bernard biography through many stages, deliberately chose a non-Cistercian to continue work on the VP in order to make the account more credible. But Arnold also included information about what happened at Clairvaux, including its building program, about which Bernard at first was skeptical but eventually was persuaded by the brothers that the monastery had to be able to accommodate the many recruits who were coming to it (VP II.29–30). Thus book II is more than church politics. Like William of Saint-Thierry and Geoffrey of Auxerre, Arnold tried to get inside Bernard and understand what it was that made him a saint. All three authors of the VP wrote for a European monastic and clerical audience. They wanted to show how in his way of life Bernard was imitating Christ.

When Bernard died in 1153, papal canonization of saints was still a relatively new phenomenon. Aside from a single canonization of this type in the ninth century, the first figure to be papally recognized as a saint was the Danish king Canute, who in 1086 was murdered before the altar of Saint Albans Church in Odense and then canonized in about 1100.[3] The reformed papacy that emerged from the eleventh century was naturally interested in extending its influence by recognizing outstanding figures as saints, but in Bernard's case there was bound to be opposition. His treatment of Abelard created enemies in the papal chancellery, and the one Cistercian pope who could have canonized Bernard, Eugenius III, died a little more than a month before him.

Thus when Geoffrey of Auxerre, formerly Bernard's secretary, set about writing the last three books of the VP, he was painfully aware of the need to create a Bernard who was convincing not only in terms of his holiness of life but also as a sympathetic human being. In the third book of the VP, he began with a portrait of Bernard as a person, including his physical characteristics and eating habits. Geoffrey saw Bernard as one who "tasted the delight of inward solitude, which he carried around within him, heedless of what was going on around him or what he saw outside himself" (VP III.2). Saintliness and solitude met in Bernard—something we see as a "topos" or common-place. The fact that a virtue or habit is praised, however, does not necessarily mean that it has been made up by the hagiographer or writer of a saint's life.

The above description of Bernard's solitude I have borrowed from a rela-tively new translation of the VP by Hilary Costello, who was a monk at Mount Saint Bernard's Abbey in England. I will make good use of Father Hilary's work, which captures the mood and tone of the source and conveys it in a manner attractive to the modern reader.

The problem with book III of the VP is that it contains everything but the proverbial kitchen sink: Bernard's travels, his conversations with peasants, his total recall of Scripture, preaching the crusade, attacks on Peter Abelard, Gilbert de la Porrée and Henry of Toulouse, some of his miracles, his sorrow at the death of his brother Gerard, and so on. In Geoffrey's efforts we find an explanation for what has become a major problem in presentations of Ber-nard: his feverish activities make it difficult to capture the meaning of his life.

Books IV and V are much easier to characterize than book III: the first is almost exclusively dedicated to descriptions of Bernard's miracles, while the second narrates his last days and death. Thus the five books of the VP live up to what by the twelfth century was becoming the regular pattern of hagiographical literature: first the life, then the miracles, and finally the cir-cumstances around the death and the visions or miracles that occurred soon afterwards (though in Bernard's case there are not many postmortem mir-acles included in VP). Geoffrey of Auxerre was certainly aware of this con-tent, but his task was made greater by the fact that Bernard had a biographer, William of Saint-Thierry, who was much more intimate with Clairvaux's abbot than Geoffrey ever could have been. But Geoffrey clearly wanted Wil-liam to make his contribution, for he handed over to him the brief anecdotes known as the *Fragmenta*. So Geoffrey became not only a contributor to the VP, but also its organizer, the keeper of the Bernard tradition and a primary mover in the attempt to have him canonized.

Geoffrey also compiled what has been called book VI of the VP, even though it is not an integral part of the work itself. It is an account of Bernard's preaching of the Second Crusade in the Rhineland in 1146, an almost day-to-day narrative not of what he said but of the miracles that flowed from his hand and mouth (PL 185:369–416). The Cistercian monks who accompanied

Bernard made a careful record of what he accomplished, and their care and concern enable us to get a firsthand impression of the impact Bernard could have on laypersons.

The existence of this narrative, together with later attempts to capture the person and sanctity of Bernard, points to the fact that contemporary Cistercians wanted more than what they found in the VP. Its contents did not sufficiently capture Bernard as he was remembered. So Alan of Auxerre, first monk of Clairvaux, later abbot of L'Arrivour, and then bishop, gave up his office in 1167 and returned to Clairvaux, where he wrote what is known as *Vita Secunda*, the "Second Life" of Bernard (PL 185:469–524). Although this text starts out with some promise, for Alan had known Bernard, he ends up essentially providing a summary of the VP without providing any new insights.

What is known as the *Vita Tertia*, the "Third Life," in the edition of Bernard materials by Dom Mabillon in the *Patrologia Latina*, vol. 185, is actually the *Fragmenta* collected by Geoffrey of Auxerre. This text follows the A version of the VP, while the newest English translation, by Hilary Costello, follows the B version, on the basis of a precious manuscript kept in his monastery. Differences between the two versions are not great, but it is not always possible to use Costello's translation and compare it with the Latin text as found in the Corpus Christianorum edition.

Finally, we have what is known as the *Vita Quarta*, the "Fourth Life," which is a collection of anecdotes about Bernard, some of which are already found in the VP, and some which are new (PL 185:531–50). Some of these were contributed by Bernard's cousin Robert of Châtillon, who apparently lived to a great age and was able to recall events from decades earlier. This text is not hagiography in the literal sense but more a collection of edifying stories, *exempla*, that reflect credit on Bernard and could be used to encourage Cistercian monks.

There seems to have been a great thirst at Clairvaux for anecdotes revealing various sides of Bernard, and in the 1170s the prior, John, collected some of these in a work that was left unfinished, the *Collectaneum Clarevallense*, indicating that after the canonization of Bernard in 1174 there was still interest in gathering together what could be remembered about him.[4] But elsewhere at Clairvaux the monk Herbert continued to collect miracle stories, including many about other Cistercians than Bernard. His *Liber miraculorum*, dated 1178–81, became the foundation for an ambitious summation of the lives of the first century of Cistercian monks, the *Exordium Magnum Cisterciense* (EM), completed around 1200 and recently translated into English.[5] The EM contains twenty chapters devoted to Bernard alone. These include miracle stories meant to summarize who he was and what he did for the Cistercian Order and the Church. Perhaps the most remarkable story tells how a monk at Clairvaux came upon Bernard in prayer. The figure of Jesus bent down from the cross and embraced Bernard, a moment captured in art as the *amplexus* or "embrace."[6] There is nothing in the VP to prefigure this image, and yet it is very much in harmony with what we find in Bernard's writings about seeking union with God.

The half century after Bernard's death in 1153 witnessed one attempt after another to capture the meaning of his life and demonstrate the impact he had on his surroundings. In spite of these efforts, there arose no "definitive" hagiographical text. The first book of the VP perhaps remains the best source for Bernard as a human being, but we must remember that its purpose, as that of all other accounts, is not to describe Bernard the person but Bernard the saint. Our contemporary search for Bernard conflicts with the interests of the twelfth-century Cistercian hagiographers and collectors of *exemplum* stories. We want to get to know Bernard as a human being, while they revered him as a saint.

It would be a mistake to ignore the saint and to claim that one can get back to the pure person. Bernard as he was remembered by those who knew and loved him is inseparable from Bernard the human being. Sainthood does not disqualify a person from historical treatment, and the one cannot be completely separated from the other. Costello's recent translation of the VP provides a happy combination of critical sense and genuine appreciation of the man.

2. What can previous biographies of Bernard tell us?

When Sir Richard Southern in 1975 encouraged me to write a new biography of Bernard, he said that the last good one was written by Elphège Vacandard and first published in 1895.[7] Today, almost a half century after my conversation with Sir Richard, his evaluation remains in force. Even now, no other modern biography of Bernard meets the standard of the work by Vacandard. Vacandard (1849–1927) was a secular priest and taught at the Lycée Corneille in Rouen. A prolific author of works about doctrine and the sacraments, his most ambitious publication is a study of the Inquisition, which appeared in 1907 and was translated immediately into English, appearing the next year as *A Critical and Historical Study of the Coercive Power of the Church*.

The first pages of Vacandard's *Vie de Saint Bernard, abbé de Clairvaux*, which I own in a copy of its third edition from 1902, contains a letter in Latin from Pope Leo XIII, dated to 1897. The pope expressed his congratulations to Vacandard for his "diligence and learning." Such a recommendation needs to be seen in view of the harsh struggle between advocates of Catholicism in France and those who wanted to secularize society. In 1905 the seculars won out, and schools and other institutions were taken away from the Church. Vacandard wrote his biography of Bernard in the face of those who considered Bernard to have been a representative of a culture that shackled the human spirit. Even today there are those who would accept such an evaluation of Bernard's place in history. For this reason Vacandard remains valuable as a statement of how Bernard could be understood. In his preface Vacandard conceded the difficulty of doing justice to the sources, but his attention to detail made his account the most reliable and complete for many decades. It is noteworthy that the standard edition of Bernard's works, *Sancti Bernardi Opera* (SBO), refers often in its notes to Vacandard's datings of Bernard's letters as the best authority, even though Ferruccio Gastaldelli's more recent annotations to the letters can at times revise Vacandard's datings.

There is no doubt that Vacandard burned the midnight oil examining the sources for Bernard's life, but he remains a Catholic priest who was treating a saint. Awkward moments in Bernard's life are sometimes left out, such as the likelihood, which I deal with in this biography, that he deliberately stayed away from the Second Lateran Council in 1139 because he disagreed with the pope's treatment of his former rivals in the schism. Vacandard clearly loved Bernard and Cistercian culture, and at times the genre of hagiography, the portrait of a saint, almost overtakes biography, the portrait of a human being.

Although Vacandard has pride of place as the author of the central biography of Bernard for our times, he had predecessors. Of some interest is James Cotter Morison's *The Life and Times of Saint Bernard*, first published in 1863. A graduate of Lincoln College, Oxford, Morison had a colorful career and knew how to bring the world of the twelfth century to life. He was generally faithful to the primary sources but had difficulty accepting the content of Bernard's life and his spirituality. He seems to have been both attracted and repelled by Saint Bernard.

The most complete English-language biography of Bernard in the last century is Watkin Williams's *Saint Bernard of Clairvaux*, originally published by the University of Manchester in 1935 and republished in 1952 in the United States by the Newman Press. In his preface, Williams thanked "the late abbé Elphège Vacandard" for his encouragement and insisted that he was just picking up Vacandard's gleanings. He characterized Bernard as "neither a philosopher, nor a theologian, nor a statesman, but a mystic."[8] This assertion somewhat short-circuits the multiplicity of roles played by Bernard over his life. Certainly he was a mystic, as Bernard McGinn has pointed out so convincingly in a recent work.[9] Williams's biography does reveal the many voices with which Bernard spoke. The problem with his treatment is that it is so crowded with information that it is virtually impossible to read. Like many academic publications, it functions best as a reference work, leading the reader back to the sources that cast light on Bernard's thinking and activities. But it is painful to try to sit down and read the story of Bernard's life in Willams's biography.

Just two years after Williams's biography appeared, Ailbe J. Luddy's *Life and Teaching of St. Bernard* was published.[10] Luddy was what is known as a "regular Cistercian." His initials were O.Cist., in contrast with the Trappist-Cistercian Order (O.C.S.O.). The Cistercian Order split into two orders in the 1890s, and for the next decades there was a great distance between the "Cistercians of the Strict Observance" (Trappists) and the Regular Cistercians. The members of the first Order isolated themselves in their monasteries, hardly ever spoke to each other, and in general lived lives of heroic asceticism. The Regular Cistercians were more in contact with the world. Many of their monasteries had schools for boys. In the 1960s the Trappists reformed themselves and opened their monasteries to the world in terms of guests and encouraged some members to participate in academic life. It would be wrong to say there is no longer any difference between the two Orders, but today they are in close contact with each other and appreciate each other.

Luddy's treatment became a textbook for generations of Cistercian monks and nuns; however, in visiting Cistercian monasteries, I have occasionally heard that his more than 700-page book summarizing Bernard's life and writings was not always appreciated. His method was to provide the reader with long quotations from Bernard's writings. There are no footnotes, and learned discussions are placed in the ample appendices, such as the first one, dealing with Bernard and the Immaculate Conception, a painful question in an age where the Catholic Church since 1854 had accepted as doctrine that Mary was conceived without sin.

In visits to Trappist-Cistercian houses, especially in the United States, I have discovered that monks and nuns are not always attached to Saint Bernard. Thanks to Cistercian Publications, which began publishing Bernard's works in English translation in the 1970s, it has become easier to encounter Bernard in a modern language. But this opening has not always been to Bernard's advantage. He is by no means a Cistercian author favored by a majority of the monks I have known. But interest in his theology has been furthered by a seminal work that can still be read with profit today, Étienne Gilson's *La théologie mystique de Saint Bernard*, the first edition of which appeared in

1934. Gilson's book was translated into English as *The Mystical Theology of Saint Bernard* and published in 1940 by Sheed and Ward, and reissued in 1990 by Cistercian Publications.

Gilson did not intend to write an account of Bernard's life, but he managed to provide an intellectual and spiritual biography of the man. His chapters introducing major themes in Bernard's writings became guides for later scholarship. Gilson clearly inspired the man who is probably the finest Bernard scholar of the twentieth century, the Benedictine monk Jean Leclercq, who wrote a preface to the 1990 reprint of Gilson's work. Leclercq's own *Love of Learning and Desire for God* (1957), translated into English in 1974, is a brilliant summation of the development of monastic culture and spirituality, ending with the witness of Saint Bernard.[11] Although we do not yet have a biography, both Gilson and Leclercq have contributed greatly to our understanding of Bernard's inner life and thinking.

Surprisingly Leclercq never came to write the full-scale biography of Bernard that he might have been expected to write. In the 1970s, when he and Henri Rochais completed their critical edition of Bernard's works, he "discovered" North America and traveled from one monastery and university to another, gave talks that often appeared in scholarly journals, but did not choose to compose a standard biography of Saint Bernard. Already in 1966 he had published *Saint Bernard et l'esprit cistercien* in the prestigious Éditions de Seuil series in Paris. It was translated and appeared in 1976 in Cistercian Publications as *Bernard of Clairvaux and the Cistercian Spirit*. This little book of about 160 pages is divided into themes, such as Bernard's message, his later image and influence, Bernard on Bernard, Bernard the biblical preacher, and Bernard's theology. The book is invaluable as an introduction to Bernard's life and thought, but Leclercq did not provide a full biography accounting for the chronology of Bernard's life.

In all fairness it should be added that back in 1948 Leclercq published *Saint Bernard mystique* (Paris: Desclée de Bouwer, 1948), which he dedicated to his own abbot at Clervaux in Luxembourg, Jacques Winandy. This presentation of Bernard is more a series of homilies than an analysis of his thought. It is not an accident that the work was never translated into English. It was only when he gave the lectures that turned into *The Love of Learning* that Leclercq convincingly captured the spirituality of Cistercian life and especially Bernard.

A much more ambitious attempt to capture the facts of Bernard's existence appeared in 1953, in connection with a conference to mark the anniversary of Bernard's death: *Bernard de Clairvaux*, published by the Commission d'Histoire de l'Ordre de Cîteaux (Paris: Éditions Alsatia, 1953); hereafter cited as *Bernard 1953*. The preface was written by Thomas Merton, monk of Gethsemani Abbey in Kentucky, whose writings, especially *The Seven Storey Mountain*, made monasticism visible and attractive for the post–Second World War generation. Merton opened his preface with almost a cry to arms: "Le saint est toujours un signe de Dieu" (The saint is always a manifestation of God). The historian must be skeptical: the saint can very much be the product of human engineering. But the articles that follow are examples of solid, careful craftsmanship, and the product of generations of scholarship; the article by Jean Richard of Dijon on the family background of Bernard is just one example. At first the articles follow the chronology of Bernard's life, but subsequent to Robert Fossier's treatment of the growth of Clairvaux under Bernard, related topics are considered, such as Bernard and Cluny, Bernard and the canons regular, Bernard and the papal schism or the Second Crusade. Although these articles are detailed, they do not provide a continuous narrative of Bernard's life.

The study of history in recent decades has been attentive to anniversaries of the birth or death of the persons being studied. Bernard has been no exception, so in 1990, on the nine-hundredth anniversary of his birth, conferences were held in many places, including Kalamazoo, Michigan, which has become a center of Cistercian studies and is the site of a yearly conference, attended by monks, nuns, and lay scholars. The publication marking the anniversary of Bernard's birth was edited by John R. Sommerfeldt, whose own work on the theology of Bernard has been widely distributed. Entitled *Bernardus Magister* (1992), the book looks especially at the intellectual Bernard. Emero Stiegman, for example, writes about aesthetics in Bernard, while Beverly Mayne Kienzle explores the function of language in one of Bernard's sermons. Perhaps the most surprising article for me was the Benedictine scholar Hugh Feiss's treatment of Bernard and Hugh of St. Victor on baptism. Feiss showed how Bernard's monastic theology in no way differs from the approach of the scholastic theology of his day. Jean Leclercq's use of the term "monastic theology" comes into question.

In France three sites were chosen for a "colloque" on Bernard in 1990: Lyon, Cîteaux, and Dijon. The title of the conference publication, *Bernard de Clairvaux: Histoire, mentalités, spiritualité*, Sources chrétiennes (Paris: Éditions du Cerf, 1992), is an apt summary of the volume's three areas of concentration. Articles in the first section treat "the man and his milieu," providing a general background for Bernard's life. The next section, dedicated to "the monk," considers Bernard and the Bible, as well as the liturgy, with André Louf looking at Bernard as abbot. The next sections cover Bernard the reformer, the thinker, and the saint. Each article is a genuine contribution to Bernard studies, but there is no attempt to review the course of his life. In the case of this volume it seems as if Bernard had become too broad to allow any one scholar to capture the fullness of his existence.

At this time I tried myself to summarize the contribution of Bernard to medieval life and spirituality. My collection of articles, *The Difficult Saint: Bernard of Clairvaux and His Tradition* (1991), made no attempt to recount the life of the saint. Instead I looked at how Bernard was received and interpreted by his heirs. In other words I engaged in the history of Bernard's reception. Reluctant to approach Bernard in his own time, I limited myself to his afterlife. It is only recently, in editing the Brill *Companion to Bernard of Clairvaux* (Brill Companion), that I allowed myself in the initial article to recount the bare facts of Bernard's life. This attempt became a point of departure for the present book. I have already written three books on Bernard, but would insist that they are quite different: *The Difficult Saint* tells how Bernard was remembered after his death; the Brill Companion provides an introduction to Bernard in various aspects of his life and thought; *Den første europæer* (The First European) is a Danish-language introduction to Bernard and his age for a contemporary audience interested in church history, monasticism, and Christianity. The present book is intended to offer insight into Bernard as a person, placing him in the context of his age.

Any biography of Bernard has to take into account Adriaan H. Bredero's *Bernard of Clairvaux: Between Cult and History*, first published in Dutch in 1993 and in English in 1996.[12] This important work is not a traditional biography of Bernard. It is a collection of analyses of the sources for Bernard's life, considering the rocky path to his canonization in 1174, as well as the ways historians have made use of the *Vita Prima* and their views of Bernard as saint. Only in his sixth chapter, "Bernard in His Monastic *Umwelt*" does Bredero come close to composing his own Bernard biography, but here he seems to have been more interested in the place of Clairvaux in monastic history and spirituality than in the specific role of Bernard.

I have returned time and again to Bredero's work for guidance, but I have also felt frustrated by his reluctance to provide the chronological framework for Bernard's life that a biography requires. His expertise relied on a lifelong study of the *Vita Prima*, its composition, and various versions. In the end, Bredero's skepticism about the central source for Bernard's life made it impossible to go further and provide the reader with a satisfying treatment of Bernard. Bredero's concern with how other scholars have seen Bernard meant that he was unwilling or unable to write the biography that his insight and knowledge of the primary sources might have generated.

A final problem I encountered in Bredero, for whom I have the greatest respect, is his distinction between "cult" and "history." Bredero is suspicious of "cult," or the means by which Bernard has been made into a saint, while seeking "history," the truthful record of what really happened. In my own work on Bernard I have found that the stories or legends that grew up around him are just as important as the way he "really" was. A man or woman attains the status of saint because they convince their surroundings that they have spiritual power or intelligence that can be an inspiration to other people. When Bernard was remembered as having been embraced by Christ on the cross, he was known as being especially close to Jesus and able to convey this intimacy to his surroundings.

Another historian who has provided studies of Bernard's life but never wrote the biography he might have is Christopher Holdsworth, who was professor of history at Exeter University. Holdsworth claimed to be working on a biography and certainly produced a number of valuable articles. As editor of the Brill Companion, I asked Christopher to write on how Bernard related to his monks. In my mind there is very little literature about Bernard in terms of how he functioned as abbot at Clairvaux, as most attention has been given to Bernard's involvement in the world outside Clairvaux. Holdsworth produced what I find to be an invaluable study, "Bernard as a Father Abbot," which reviews about a hundred of his letters. Holdsworth concluded that Bernard's letters "show someone able to respond to correspondents in a way that answered their needs in an acceptable manner."[13]

Another of Holdsworth's important contributions to the historical Bernard is his article "The Early Writings of Bernard of Clairvaux,"[14] in which he redated a number of Bernard's works and made sense of them in terms of Bernard's earlier years, until 1126. Scholarly attention is usually given to Bernard after 1130, when he became involved in the papal schism, so with this article Holdsworth provided new material for understanding the young abbot of Clairvaux.

A much more ambitious study of Bernard, but with more questionable results, was made by Jean Leclercq in 1976 and translated into English in 1990 as *A Second Look at Bernard of Clairvaux*. The French subtitle is more revealing, *Approches psycho-historiques*. Leclercq thought of himself as having become a psychohistorian in a period when this window on the past was fashionable. I remember standing with him in the lunch line at the Medieval Congress in Kalamazoo and someone asked him what he studied. He replied with his Gallic accent, "I am a psychohistorian." This gentle and kind man intended to get inside Bernard, and he held regular seminars in Rome with psychologists to consider Bernard's psyche. The book, however, provides no

summary of what was said at these seminars, and however much psychol-
ogy seems to have inspired Leclercq, he concluded by giving his readers a
portrait of Bernard the saint rather than one of Bernard the human being.
Leclercq blamed any expression of aggressivity or anger in Bernard on his
friend and biographer William of Saint-Thierry. Only in reviewing Bernard's
controversy with Peter Abelard did Leclercq concede that the saint may have
gone too far: "May we not also conjecture that he was sorry for having used
strong words in some of his letters"; as a result Bernard tried to avoid the letters being "widely circulated." Leclercq conceded "a certain inflexible rigid-
ity" in Bernard, and even the possibility of "a certain unconscious fear for
his own stability."[15] He concluded, however, that he could not be sure, and
his method of putting his subject on the couch provides a warning against
psychologizing people in the past.

Leclercq also wrote a study of Bernard and women, to which I will return
later. While it is important to consider the signal contribution of this monk
and scholar to the study of Bernard, at the same time I have great reservations about his conclusions. When I succeeded in having him speak at
a medieval conference at Copenhagen University in 1983, Leclercq spent
much of his time sitting politely through the other contributions and writing postcards. He used to send my son drawings of clowns, and I am sure
that Leclercq considered himself to be God's clown. He loved learning and
sought the presence of God, but his contributions to a biography of Bernard
are incomplete.

It must be remembered, however, that, together with Henri Rochais,
Leclercq spent decades editing and publishing Bernard's works in their modern edition, the eight volumes of SBO that appeared in 1957–77. At the same
time Leclercq collected the many articles he composed in preparing the critical edition in the five volumes of his *Recueil d'études sur saint Bernard et ses
écrits*.[16] This labor of love provided Leclercq with a solid foundation for his
understanding of Bernard. There are only very brief annotations, however,
to the letters in the Leclercq-Rochais edition, and here we are indebted to the
Italian scholar Ferruccio Gastaldelli, who provided invaluable commentaries
for all of Bernard's letters, originally in the Italian translation, and later in
volumes 2 and 3 of the German.[17]

The Leclercq-Rochais edition of Bernard's writings invited scholars to
make new evaluations of the saint. One of the most prominent among these
scholars was Peter Dinzelbacher, an Austrian and one of the most prolific
medieval scholars in the German-speaking world. In connection with the
anniversary of the founding of Cîteaux, Dinzelbacher published in 1998,
with the distinguished publisher Wissenschaftliche Buchgesellschaft, an

ambitious work of almost five hundred pages, including notes: *Bernhard von Clairvaux: Leben und Werk des berühmten Ziserziensers*. This work is the closest we can come to a contemporary biography of Bernard. Nevertheless I find it lacks insight at times, such as when the author claims that Bernard became a monk out of fear of going to hell. Dinzelbacher fails to grasp the central role of friendship in leading Bernard to the monastery and his remaining close to the friends of his youth. The work shows solid scholarly achievement, but in human terms it is disappointing. However much I admire Dinzelbacher's learning, I do not think he succeeded in capturing the meaning of Bernard's life.

A much briefer and more accessible biography of Bernard, by Bruno Scott James, was published in 1957 with the modest title *Saint Bernard of Clairvaux: An Essay in Biography*.[18] This work followed James's 1953 translation of Bernard's lettters in *The Letters of Saint Bernard of Clairvaux*. James's careful and fluent translations are often accompanied by supplementary notes that provide valuable information about historical background. Without the detail of Gastaldelli's annotations to the letters, in these notes James managed to provide for the English-speaking world a guide to Bernard's thought and life. In the biography James allowed himself an informal tone and took nothing for granted in terms of what the reader might know. He went into the very mind of Bernard in a way that some historians might find questionable: "After about six months of prayer and solitude at Châtillon Bernard decided that the time had come to set out for Cîteaux." On the way Bernard stopped at Fontaines "to say good-bye to Tescelin," his father. James speculated on what Tescelin might have been thinking at this point. The approach is charming, but at times the biography seems more like a novel than a historical account. Even so, this little book deserves a reprint.

I have not chosen here to review analyses of Bernard's theology, for they do not provide us with anything but a supplement to his biography. I think it necessary, however, to include two scholars who approach Bernard in his role as a writer. In 1994 the Dutch scholar M. B. Pranger published *Bernard of Clairvaux and the Shape of Monastic Thought: Broken Dreams*.[19] The almost melancholy title provides an indication of the tone of the book. We are presented with a man who "rhetorically speaking . . . has reached the nadir of grief in this final display of bitterness."[20] Bernard is seen in the context of death, but Pranger did not want his readers to draw any psychological conclusions. In his article in the Brill Companion he criticized me for what he called a psycho-historical approach. I chose to interpret Bernard's lament for his dead brother Gerard as an expression of human pain. Pranger took me to task for ignoring the "formal and rhetorical aspects of Bernard's text."[21]

A clear inspiration for Pranger was Peter von Moos's monumental work, *Consolatio: Studien zur Mittellateinischen Trostlitteratur*. As Pranger pointed out, Moos's analysis showed how Bernard's lament for his dead brother is heavily dependent on Augustine's *Confessions* and Ambrose's lament for his dead brother. But Pranger refused to accept "the identification of those [natural] impulses with emotions as they figure in literary texts."[22] Ultimately Bernard is read as literature, an approach I accept, but I seek to get beyond this understanding and meet Bernard as a person who lived and experienced more than the creation of texts.

At the same time, however, I find Pranger's approach fruitful and even necessary, for it would be wrong to characterize an inner life without taking into consideration the literary genre this person was using in order to communicate with his surroundings. Pranger's work is an important milestone in Bernard studies, and therefore I asked him to contribute to the Brill Companion. Another literary scholar is Mette B. Bruun, whose contribution to the same volume is entitled "Bernard of Clairvaux and the Landscape of Salvation." Bruun sought what she calls "spiritual topography" in "the route-map of salvation history from Paradise to the celestian Jerusalem."[23] She sees Bernard as a pilgrim (*peregrinus*) seeking out places bringing salvation. Bruun's Bernard is vastly different from my own, for she sees him through texts that provide a journey or what she calls a "topographical register." The richness of Bernard's material and the subtlety of his literary invention are reflected in both Pranger and Bruun.

The study of Bernard has become somewhat esoteric, and biography remains perhaps the one area where old-fashioned narrative based on chronology is still acceptable. But sometimes this "naive" approach is insufficient, as is the case with Pierre Aube's *Saint Bernard de Clairvaux* of 2003.[24] Aube, professor at Rouen for more than thirty years, ends up writing a general history of Western Europe in the second quarter of the twelfth century, when Bernard was so dominant. But he fails to capture the qualities that make Bernard interesting even today: his spirituality, his gift for friendship, his ability to recruit talented people. At times Aube seems more interested in figures such as King Roger II of Sicily than in Bernard, and surely his great knowledge of such secular magnates has contributed to this book. But because of this, his book is more a general medieval European history than a biography of Bernard.

It might seem from this review of treatments of Bernard's life since Vacandard that the literature on him has become so abundant that it is impossible for a single historian to improve on the achievement of the French divine. Certainly the humanities in our time has branched out to such an extent that no one person dominates the field. In the history of medieval spiritualty, the contributions of Caroline Walker Bynum since the 1970s have been renewing the field. Her point of departure was the study *Jesus as Mother*, which also looked at the abbot as a mother figure for his monks.[25] Here Bynum found an important role for Bernard in his self-understanding. Bynum has long since left Clairvaux behind and has ventured into many other areas of medieval life, such as the cult of the Eucharist and the doctrine of the resurrection. She has made Bernard studies richer, but her own scholarly pilgrimage has gone beyond Bernard.

One warning against exaggerating the place of Bernard in his own time was provided in a paper by the Trappist-Cistercian Paschal Phillips at the anniversary conference in 1990: "The Presence—and Absence—of Bernard of Clairvaux in the Twelfth-Century Chronicles."[26] Phillips reviewed the narrative sources that are the point of departure for our knowledge of the age, and he rarely found mentions of Bernard. He concluded by asking whether Bernard would have been so celebrated if he had not been sponsored "by an enormous religious family dedicated to continuing his memory." I was present at the talk that was the basis of this article, and it caused some consternation. But academic articles have a way of disappearing into journals or collections, and I am afraid that Phillips's reassessment of Bernard's place in history has not been given the attention it deserves.

Michael Casey of Australia, another Trappist-Cistercian, contributed to the same volume. Casey's article has the long title "Toward a Methodology for the *Vita Prima*: Translating the First Life into Biography." His thesis is that the *Vita Prima* has to be read as hagiography, not biography. He considers the central contribution of Geoffrey of Auxerre, who saw Bernard as "a serious man without much in the way of lightheartedness or spontaneity."[27] Sometimes it is possible to corroborate Geoffrey's information about Bernard from other sources, but the best confirmation is provided by Bernard's own writings. Here Bernard takes on a vitality that some readers do not find in the *Vita Prima*.

In recent years Casey has become a sought-after interpreter of Bernard, and he has spent time giving conferences at Cistercian abbeys all over the world. For the Brill Companion I asked him to provide a practical article on how Bernard's writings can be approached. His title sounds derivative of Marshal McLuhan's universe: "Reading Saint Bernard: The Man, the Medium, the Message."[28] This treatment builds on Casey's own seminal study: *Athirst for God: Spiritual Desire in Bernard of Clairvaux's Sermons on the Song of Songs.*[29] The article, however, focuses on all of Bernard. Casey starts with Bernard the man in terms of humor and self-deprecation, even admission of mistakes. Casey sees Bernard as showing concern for others and appreciating them. From here he turns to "The Medium," especially the sermons Bernard gave, and finally "The Message" in desire for God, reform and discipline, love and the practice of virtues. Finally comes contemplation, where Casey shows how Bernard's text "illustrates the difficulty of assessing Bernard's mystical status."[30]

As a whole the article aptly sums up how to read Bernard, and Casey's conclusions differ greatly from those of Pranger. I included both articles in the collection I edited precisely because I know how differently Bernard is read and understood in different contexts. But Casey in my mind is close to the experience of Bernard, and he certainly would be eminently qualified to write the definitive biography for which the world has long waited. The fact that he has not yet done so allows the proverbial fool to step in where angels fear to tread. I conjecture that one day a biography of Bernard by Michael Casey will appear, and I am certain that its content and approach will be different from the present biography. "The difficult saint" defies characterization, and so Bernard continues to invite new interpretations.

3. How did Bernard relate to women?

The first Cistercians kept a certain distance from women, but women's studies in the past decades have made it clear that from an early point in time, some female houses took on the Cistercian usages and for all practical purposes were Cistercian. But it was not until some years after the death of Bernard in 1153 that the Order officially recognized women's houses, and its reluctance may well have been connected to the fact that a woman's house required the guidance and support of a male house, something not all abbots were keen to provide.

Where was Bernard in this development? A woodcut from a collection of his sermons translated into Italian and dating from Florence in 1495 provides an indication of the Cistercian tradition about Bernard and women. Here we see nuns either kneeling or bowing to Bernard as he hands over a book, presumably his sermons, which they would be reading in the vernacular instead of Latin. It is an attractive scene and was used for the cover of *Women and St. Bernard of Clairvaux*, the English translation of Jean Leclercq's study *La femme et les femmes dans l'oeuvre de Saint Bernard*.[31] My copy is signed by Leclercq, who added the word "friendship." He was indeed a monastic friend, and I value the guidance his work still gives me.

The idyllic woodcut from the end of the Middle Ages gives the impression that at some time Bernard visited a Cistercian monastery for women.

We know of no such visitation, and we have no idea if the sisters who faithfully followed Cistercian practices were dressed in the habits shown in the woodcut. So far as I can tell, Bernard was not all that interested in monastic women, and here I am afraid I have to challenge Leclercq's work.

Leclercq noted that there are only twenty-three letters to women in the collection of about five hundred of Bernard's letters that have been preserved. Leclercq pointed to an early letter, from 1127, in which Bernard addressed his friend Count Theobald of Champagne.[32] He told of how he recently had passed through the town of Bar and was met by a "poor woman" who told him of her sorrows. Now Bernard was asking the count to look out for her. Her husband had committed a crime and been punished by the count: "Please have pity on this woman, and God will have pity on you."[33]

There is no doubt that Bernard felt sympathy for this person, as he did for many a woman who came to him later, in the 1140s, when he was preaching the crusade. Geoffrey of Auxerre's account of Bernard's travels in the Rhineland makes no distinction between healings of men and women. Outside the monastery and traveling in the lay world, Bernard to a large extent was available to any and all who sought him out.

Leclercq reviewed all the letters to women, and in these letters he found time and again that Bernard contacted powerful women in order to gain favor or protection for a Cistercian monastery. Thus in writing to Mathilda, queen of England and wife of Henry I, Bernard reminded her of a promise she once had made that involved the monastery of La Chapelle. It was a question of a tithe the abbot had requested: "For if I correctly remember, I spoke to you of it at Boulogne."[34] This is hardly a letter of friendship. It was a business matter, and Bernard clearly thought that if he turned to the queen instead of the king, then he might get what he desired.

Bernard can surprise us. There are two letters to one woman that capture the tone and content of his warmest letters of friendship to men. He wrote to Ermengarde, Countess of Brittany, who had been involved in trying to discontinue the building of a monastery at Buzay, near Nantes. Bernard had come on visitation and was upset by what he found, so he threatened to remove his monks. Thanks to his protest the monks were reestablished and the buildings completed. With this trauma behind him Bernard now wrote to Ermengarde what can only be called a letter of spiritual direction: "You have to realize that I am always near you; as for me, I admit, I am never without you and I never abandon you."[35] A second letter is briefer but indicates that Ermengarde had written Bernard to tell him that she had found peace in her new way of life.[36] Bernard added that he was hindered from seeing Ermengarde because of all the duties to which he had to attend. But he

looked forward to the day when he could see her, even though "such possibilities are seldom bestowed on me . . . but it would be better to see you
once in a while rather that not at all." Bernard here made use of the topos
or commonplace of letters of friendship that it is important for friends to
see each other: "How much I would prefer to talk with you in your physical
presence rather than write to you while you are absent."

Leclercq rightly grasped the heartfelt tone of this letter, whose language
seems genuinely affectionate. In his introduction to the first of the letters
Bruno Scott James conceded: "To modern tastes the word of the letter may
seem rather extravagant." But James saw in what Bernard wrote the type of
expressions found in Aelred of Rievaulx on friendship. Thus Bernard was
capable of suggesting intimacy with a woman, but such a correspondence
is an exception that proves the rule that generally Bernard did not offer the
same closeness to women as he did to men. Somehow Ermengarde overcame the barriers that Bernard normally placed between himself and the few
women with whom he exchanged letters.

In his chapter "Bernard and Nuns," Leclercq mentions Bernard's letter to
Hildegard of Bingen. The translation given in Bruno Scott James is of a later
text, dated between 1180 and 1190, where Bernard is very favorable to Hildegard. It is this version that often is used in modern biographies of Hildegard
to indicate that Bernard approved of her visions. But in the much sparser
text that is apparently that of the original letter, Bernard merely wrote that
"we rejoice in the grace of God, which is in you."[37] He praised Hildegard's
"humility and devotion" and spoke of the "interior teaching" and "anointing" that come from above. Certainly according to medieval theology, God's
grace is to be found in every person who is living in the state of grace, so
Bernard was not conceding any special status to Hildegard. In the face of an
effusive letter from her, he was responding not in kind but with caution. He
did not reject her witness, but he certainly did not endorse it.

Jean Leclercq is a bit more generous to Bernard than I am. In analyzing the
letter to Hildegard, he wrote of Bernard: "His style, though restrained, is not
curt." Leclercq's exegesis is all too kind: "The abbot of Clairvaux effectively
defended a woman, to the great joy of many."[38] I prefer to conclude that
Bernard's decision not to attack Hildegard gave her a necessary freedom, but
he by no means embraced her visions. It was Bernard's former monk, Pope
Eugenius III, who championed Hildegard, not Bernard.

In his chapter "Myths about St. Bernard," Leclercq rightly attacked some
of the standard assertions about Bernard being misogynous. But there is one
story that I find hard to reject, even though Leclercq did his best to challenge
its historical basis. This concerns Bernard's sister, Humbeline, who came

with a retinue to Clairvaux and asked to see her brother. She was apparently dressed in her finest, and according to William of Saint-Thierry's narrative, "Bernard utterly refused to go to see her, saying that he despised her appearance."[39] I find this to be a key passage in terms of how Bernard related to women. He preferred keeping women at a distance, even when it was his own sister. The story ends with Bernard coming out to Humbeline, for she appealed to him as a sinner who needed his counsel and guidance. Bernard ordered her to give up her "worldly grandeur in fashionable dress" and to live in the modest fashion that their mother had chosen. Humbeline eventually left her husband and entered the monastery of Jully, perhaps the first women's house that came to follow the Cistercian way of life.

The story thus becomes an *exemplum* of conversion to the monastic life, and Bernard's initial rejection and later embrace of his sister are clearly meant to inspire other women to leave their husbands and get to a monastery! Bernard is described as having been repelled by a woman who was overdressed and tried to play the grande dame, and so his reluctance to meet his sister is seen not as hating her as a woman but being repelled by someone caught up in appearances. Leclercq, however, could not allow Bernard's behavior to be dubious at all but concluded that the story was a commonplace tale invented by William of Saint-Thierry, "who depended on literary tradition."[40] Here Leclercq came close to the practice of Adriaan Bredero, who when he came upon a story that did not fit his view of Bernard dismissed it as derivative or dubious.

It is not my intention to reject out of hand the insights of a scholar who spent decades reading and writing about Bernard. In the end, however, Leclercq has a tendency to make Bernard more attractive for our time than I think he was. He lived in a world where women were on the margins, and he usually dealt with them primarily when they were essential to the founding of a new monastery or its preservation. Other women he would bless and sometimes cure when he traveled the roads of Europe preaching the crusade. But the only women to whom he was utterly beholden were his own mother, whom he lost when he was a teenager, and Mary the mother of Jesus, for whom he wrote some of his most beautiful sermons. He did not hate the female sex, and he seems to have loved a few women, such as Ermengarde. But the central loves of his life were Jesus, his brothers in the flesh, and his other brothers in the monastery.

4. How did Bernard relate to the body?

One of the more remarkable statements by Bernard, as recorded by William of Saint-Thierry, was his order to the novices of Clairvaux that if they intended to enter the monastery, then they must leave their bodies outside: "Only your spirits enter here."[41] The novices are said to have been afraid of "the novelty of these words," and so Bernard comforted them with the explanation that he only required them to leave outside "the desires of the flesh" (1 Jn 2:46). William contrasted Bernard's understanding for his novices with his own strict regime: "He put this continual mortification into practice as was his custom." Asceticism was, of course, nothing new in the monastic life and can be traced back to the Desert Fathers. But Bernard is said to have been wary about experiencing "the sweetness of God's love" because he feared "those bodily expressions." He mortified not only the desires of the flesh, "but even the body itself."

It is possible to read Bernard's life in terms of the undoing of the body, and here William is very specific: "Whatever is left over to nourish his body is not so much to sustain his life as to defer his death."[42] In spite of this regime, or perhaps because of it, Bernard is supposed to have considered others to be far holier than himself. He would require of himself the same discipline as the other brothers experienced, even though he was physically weaker than the others. At the same time he came to realize that he was asking more of his monks than was reasonable: he sought "a degree of perfection that he himself had not yet attained." He came to accept the need to live with his monks "in a more humane fashion" and to "enjoy the fruits of their common conversation."[43]

The lesson of these chapters seems to be that Bernard made extreme demands on himself but came to understand that he could not do the same with his monks. Also, in order to reach them in his preaching, he had to make himself comprehensible in a way they could grasp. Otherwise "his preaching might prove more of a stumbling block to them than a way of building up their interior lives."[44]

In William's view Bernard continued to impose an ascetic regime on himself: "He would not spare his own body but had to add vigor to his spiritual gains." William even tells of a receptacle placed next to Bernard in choir so he could vomit into it. Bernard's "body was undermined by various sicknesses, brought on by his fasting and constant vigils."[45]

The denial of the body that became almost an obsession for Bernard entered into his sermons, as when he told the brothers at Clairvaux that he was afraid of dying, for he was not certain of the fate he would meet: "I shall be the laughing stock of the devils who intercept me."[46] Bernard turned to the experience of Paul, who also had to deal with "the sensuality of the body that he could not possibly avoid while living on earth." Bernard recalled Paul's lament "Who will deliver me from this body of death?" (Rom

7:24). For Bernard, Paul had to endure sensual desire "because it was rooted in the flesh."

Paul was nevertheless saved, and Bernard in preaching to his monks offered them the possibility of heaven. Not by killing the flesh but by transforming it. Here the Clairvaux tradition about Bernard offered an image that we first find in the *Exordium Magnum Cisterciense*, already mentioned in question 1 above, and later found in medieval art: the *amplexus* or "embrace." A brother at Clairvaux is said to have seen Bernard at prayer before a crucifix. The figure of Jesus bent down and embraced Bernard. Thus Jesus has a body and Bernard also a body, and these two bodies meet. There need be nothing sensuous or erotic about this image, but it certainly provides us with an indication that the body was important for the early Cistercians. It was not something to be rejected, only to be fashioned in a manner that allowed the embrace of Christ.

In one of his Sermons on the Song of Songs, Bernard asked his monks not to be obsessed with medicine: "You will be judged not on the quality of your constitution but on your profession."[47] What mattered was that the monk had his "own peace." Some monks apparently thought they required special food or medicine. Bernard had a number of recommendations and warnings, but his main purpose seems to have been to tell his monks that they had to live under a common discipline and avoid demanding individual treatment. He conceded that Paul had allowed drinking wine, but "you should not overlook the word 'little' with which he qualified it."

There is no doubt that Bernard required an ascetic regime of his monks, but the *Vita Prima*, especially the first book, by William of Saint-Thierry, indicates that he had to come to accept that there are human limitations, and the body has certain needs. Bernard's wrestling with such concerns is apparent in the Sermons on the Song of Songs. Even if these literary masterpieces are not necessarily what he preached to his monks, they do hint at what Bernard could have said. He demanded self-discipline but did not deny the body. The novices were allowed to take their bodies inside with them, so long as the needs of the body did not outweigh those of the soul. Cistercian reformed monasticism under Bernard combined self-denial with the embrace of the body of Christ. So the body persisted, and Bernard avoided the extremes of dualism.

One aspect of Bernard's teaching on the body that helps to explain his relatively positive view is his invitation in one of his Sermons on the Song of Songs to embrace the "carnal love of Christ." (SC 20.4) As Bernard McGinn has pointed out, Bernard, together with other early Cistercians, emphasized "that human love of the exemplary human, Jesus Christ," does not mean putting aside "our carnal nature" but could be "the starting point for beginning the path to loving God in a spiritual way."[48] The body that in Augustine is the source of concupiscence is in Bernard the point of departure for the love of God.

5. Can Bernard's sexual identity be defined?

The early Cistercians loved each other's company and considered themselves to be a band of brothers totally loyal to each other. William of Saint-Thierry remembered fondly the Clairvaux he had visited as a "valley full of men, where none was at rest" and whose "love was well ordered."[49] There is in such descriptions an element of eroticism, in which Bernard inspired his monks to share each other's lives in spiritual intimacy. This erotic asceticism is also reflected in Aelred of Rievaulx's *Mirror of Charity*, written at Bernard's request in order to demonstrate that monastic life combines both self-denial and the embrace of one's fellow monk.[50] The word here, as so often in twelfth-century Cistercian spirituality, is *affectus*.

It is my contention that Bernard's leadership was more than that of a military figure doing what he could to gather his troops. There was a reservoir of spiritual friendship that Bernard drew on in his letters time and again and which certainly moved Aelred to write his treatise on precisely this phenomenon. Even though modern terms for medieval phenomena can so easily be misunderstood, I find an element of homoeroticism in the lives of Bernard and Aelred. However Aelred had lived before he became a monk—and his sexuality has been much discussed—he was able once he entered Rievaulx to sublimate his impulses and to create an atmosphere of affectivity that fulfilled his own needs.[51] After his death, however, the silence about him at Rievaulx may indicate a turning away from such an affective climate. We can never know for sure how he was remembered at his monastery, for the silence can be interpreted in many different ways.

As for Bernard, we are on firmer ground. In one of his Sermons on the Song of Songs, where he was excoriating the dualist heretics of Toulouse, he considered those who defended the practice according to which men and women lived together without being married.[52] So far as Bernard was concerned, it was impossible to be with a woman for a long period of time without there being sex: "To be always in a woman's company without having carnal knowledge of her, is this not a greater miracle than raising the dead?" He described how there would be touching, the meeting of eyes, the joining of hands when one was at work: "Do you expect to be thought chaste? It may be that you are, but I have my suspicions."

Bernard here was projecting his own imagination on the men and women of Toulouse. Certainly he was backed up by the Gregorian Reform of the eleventh century and its suspicion of double monasteries, where men and women had lived in separate quarters. But his statement here goes far beyond a rejection of such institutions. He advocated strict separation of men and women, for otherwise there would be sexual contact. Bernard's suspicion of male-female bonds indicates that he felt strongly attracted to women. He was convinced that the only way to avoid intimacy with women was to withdraw into the monastery. At the same time we have rather conventional stories of how Bernard was tempted by women.[53] I do not find them to be very revealing, for in the standard hagiographical narrative, a potential saint is supposed to be tempted. But in Bernard's own words we have a confession that he found women powerfully attractive, and so his solution was to keep them at a physical and emotional distance.

It was an expression of Bernard's genius that in Aelred of Rievaulx he apparently recognized a type of affectivity different from his own. When Aelred visited him at Clairvaux on the way to Rome, Bernard understood that the young monk with his troubled past could express the power and meaning of the affective life in the Cistercian tradition. Such a bond meant that Bernard could turn aside Aelred's arguments about his own inadequacy and insist that the natural world is the best teacher. Aelred was sent back to Yorkshire and encouraged to continue focusing his affectivity on the Cistercian way of life. Bernard asked him to write about how the monk transforms his inner life into a new spirituality without sacrificing his affective bonds to others. The result in the *Mirror of Charity* is perhaps the most complete statement of monastic theology that came out of the twelfth century.

Bernard had a talent for making use of capable, sensitive men like Aelred. At the same time he kept his distance from most women. In medieval culture there was no word for being heterosexual or homosexual, but there was a keen awareness of the power of sexual attraction. For Bernard the danger lay in women, not in men, and so he could celebrate male companionship and foster one daughter house of Clairvaux after another.

6. How did Bernard express his commitment as monk and abbot?

In this book I have asked time and again how it was possible for the abbot of a monastery that sought separation from the world to become so involved in that same world. I have no satisfactory answer. Bernard's self-description as the chimera of his age is interesting but inadequate.[54] He could have been making fun of himself, but even if he was serious, he was not really explaining how he justified being someone who long since had stopped living the life of a monk and had only kept the habit.

It would be natural for us to turn to the moment when everything changed for Bernard and he became involved in the affairs of the Church in connection with the papal schism. We know he attended the Council of Étampes in 1130 and there argued for Innocent as the true pope. We have the account of Abbot Arnold of Bonneval, who described how Bernard was in doubt about how to act. But on the way to the council, he is said to have received a vision of a "great church singing the praises of God in harmony."[55] So he could arrive at Étampes and back Innocent: "Then he opened his mouth and the Holy Spirit filled it."

It would be reassuring if we had a letter from Bernard in which he accounted for his uncertainty and the reassurances he received. But we do not. In fact the first letters from Bernard to Pope Innocent are from 1133, three years after Étampes, and at this point Bernard was unshakable in his devotion to Innocent and deeply entrenched in the affairs of the schism and the Church in general. What seems so obvious in Arnold cannot be substantiated by other sources. Bernard glides into his leading position in the Church, and we are left behind to wonder what it was that convinced him to play such a role.

Once the schism was over and Innocent securely in place, Bernard had to face the fact that there were other issues that forced him to be active and to leave his monastery behind. This was the case with his opposition to Peter Abelard, and here he wrote a letter to Pope Innocent that can be looked upon as a kind of confession: "I am weary of life and I know not whether it would be well for me to die."[56] The saints, he continued, were encouraged by seeking what was better, "while I am forced to plod on only in order to escape what is scandalous and troublesome."

I can hardly imagine a more direct indication that Bernard had come to the point where he experienced his life as a melancholy attempt to avoid scandal! But he seems to have taken it for granted that this was the best he could do. He had succeeded in overcoming the "madness of the lion" (Peter Leone = Pope Anacletus), "so now the Church enjoys peace, but I do not." He continued in this vein: "My sorrow overcomes me and does not end for me." He thus repeated his refrain: "We have escaped from the lion but have become victims to the dragon." This is Peter Abelard, and from here Bernard described his efforts to call Abelard to order at Sens.

Whatever Bernard wrote, it is steeped in the language of the Bible and often also derivative of classical authors. It would be a mistake to interpret his inner life solely on the basis of the surface meaning of his letters. But in contrasting his life with that of the saints, he was expressing self-doubt. It is likely that with the schism over, Bernard thought he could return to Clairvaux and limit himself to his functions as abbot. But this was not to be the case. He was called away, whether it was to Sens for the question of Abelard's theology or later to Vézelay to preach the crusade that in the years after 1146 would capture virtually all his attention.

At Étampes in 1130, Bernard's biographer Arnold claimed that the French king and princes as well as the bishops decided "that the business of God should be handed over to the servant of God."[57] Thus Bernard was asked to say the final word that would recognize Innocent as true pope. This may be an idealized description of what really happened, but the result would be in harmony with what we see Bernard doing later in his life: he allowed the urging and persuasion of others to convince him to leave behind his monastery and involve himself in the larger affairs of the Church. Certainly with the Abelard affair it is apparent that Bernard did not take the initiative by himself. It was his friend William of Saint-Thierry who warned him about Abelard's theology as a danger to orthodoxy. Bernard replied that he accepted William's judgment, even though he had not yet read the little treatise that William had sent him.[58] But it is likely that William's warnings prepared the way for Bernard's view of Abelard as a heretic. Once convinced, he did his utmost to get Abelard's teaching condemned.

In this situation it is apparent that Bernard followed the guidance of a friend. He did not take the initiative himself, but once he had come to share William's concern, there was no limit to his involvement. He could tell Pope Innocent: "A new faith is being made in France. Virtue and vice are being discussed with no morality, while the sacraments are taught falsely."[59] Bernard made use of every rhetorical device to warn the pope and the whole world against this "Peter the Dragon who attacks the faith of Simon Peter [the Apostle]."

Both with the schism and with the attack on Peter Abelard it is possible to establish the following scenario: Bernard was at Clairvaux and was involved in the everyday concerns of a large monastery. Letters arrived, which he read when he had the time. Once he did so, Bernard became more and more concerned about the matter at hand. Eventually he convinced himself that he was morally obliged to deal with the question by attending a meeting, whether at Étampes in 1130 or Sens in 1140 or 1141 (the dating of this council is disputed). He went in fear and trembling, but by the time he arrived at his destination, he had become convinced through prayer and perhaps a vision that all would be well. He then knew how to react, and he dedicated his rhetorical gifts to telling the world what needed to be done in order to save the unity of the Church.

Bernard could act as he did because he had a loyal support group in his Cistercian world. First he had his brothers in the flesh, even though they at times tried to hold Bernard back. According to William of Saint-Thierry they did their best to limit Bernard's first miracles. His uncle Gaudry and eldest brother Guy told the other brothers that they should not encourage Bernard in his matter: "They did not spare him, even abusing him with harsh words."[60] The brothers were so hard on him that they often made him cry because of "their hasty and reproachful speech." The young Bernard was thus not trusted and had to defend his involvement in the needs of other people. When Gaudry himself became ill, he turned to Bernard for help, and so his fever subsided. Thus "he felt within himself the healing he had complained about in other people."[61]

Bernard was unusual in taking with him to the monastery his blood relatives. Once they established Clairvaux, they more or less stayed together. Other recruits to the monastery were often sent out to found daughter houses, but Bernard kept his brothers with him. When he journeyed to Italy during the papal schism, Bernard took his brother Gerard with him. When Gerard became ill on the last Italian journey, Bernard stormed heaven with prayer in order to make it possible for Gerard to return with him to Clairvaux. Once back home, Gerard's illness returned and he died. Bernard's lament for his dead brother is today looked upon as an outstanding display of *consolatio*, the comfort sought and given when a beloved friend or relative dies. Bernard's lament is in my mind a demonstration of his need for his siblings, even though the bonds of monastic life are not supposed to include a need for blood relations. Bernard short-circuited the usual monastic attitudes and insisted that he needed his brothers in the flesh. When Gerard died, he expressed heartfelt sorrow.

In the course of describing his sense of loss at Gerard's death, Bernard made a statement that contradicted centuries of monastic attitudes warning against dependence on other human beings: "It is but human and necessary that we respond to our friends with feeling. . . . Social intercourse, especially between friends, cannot be purposeless." Mutual love is rightly expressed when friends are together, and so it is natural that there is "yearning for each other when separated."[62]

Bernard was merely expressing what already can be found in Cicero's *On Friendship* and which Aelred of Rievaulx would describe more fully in *On Spiritual Friendship*. But Bernard's statement implicitly went against not only the Desert Fathers but to some extent the Gospels themselves, where

Jesus exhorted his disciples to leave family and friends in order to follow him. Bernard took family and friends with him inside the monastery and kept them there with him. By so doing Bernard made sure that he always had individuals whom he knew and trusted nearby, some of whom he had known since childhood. Thus his commitment as monk and abbot took its point of departure from the faith he had in his brothers, even when some of them excoriated him and drove him to tears. Bernard knew that they would be there at Clairvaux for him, wherever he went, and they would look after the needs of the monastery.

There is no reason to idealize the arrangement that Bernard created at Clairvaux so that he could spend more and more time away from his monastery. One can only imagine that there was talk about the absent abbot. The letters Bernard wrote to the brothers of Clairvaux nearly apologized for leaving them behind. In every monastic community there can be fear that an abbot might lose interest in his position and overcommit himself to matters outside the monastery. Bernard was aware of this danger and succeeded in demonstrating his loyalty to Clairvaux. He made sure that he never gave way to any of the several attempts to get him elected bishop or archbishop. As abbot of Clairvaux he had a secure base, and from it he could devote himself to church matters that had nothing to do with monastic life. His excuse was that his involvement was required because of "the needs of the Church."[63]

Bernard profited from several support groups. First of all his brothers in the flesh, secondly the other brothers of Clairvaux, thirdly the friends outside the monastery who were devoted to him. With friends and supporters of this kind, it must have been easy and natural to leave Clairvaux behind and venture out into the world. He could assume that he would return to a monastery where he would be welcomed back. Whatever reservations some of the brothers may have had, Bernard remained their father abbot. Christopher Holdsworth's review of Bernard's letters claims that they "tell us much about Bernard's attempt to care for his monastic family in attracting some men to join it, in getting others to serve as abbots."[64] Bernard was a genius at networking, and this talent enabled him to make sure that his many journeys did not end up alienating his monks at Clairvaux. At least so far as we know!

7. What was Bernard's involvement in the Second Crusade?

Perhaps the best review of Bernard's involvement in what history calls the Second Crusade appeared in the 1953 collection of articles marking the eight-hundredth anniversary of his death. André Seguin succeeded in providing the political and military background for the crusade, while he also highlighed Bernard's role. Seguin's analysis is to some extent dependent on Vacandard, and both emphasize that Bernard committed himself only after he received word from Pope Eugenius III that it was necessary to preach a new crusade. At this point "the abbot of Clairvaux dedicated himself to the task with all his heart (de tout coeur)."[65] Seguin did admit that Bernard might have had some hesitation, and he pointed out that neither Vacandard nor Watkin Williams saw any reservation in Bernard. His fragile health did not hold him back.

Seguin asked what Jerusalem meant to Bernard. Here he managed to penetrate into what I consider to be a central concern in Bernard's life, "the royal path which opened before him," to which he "brought his eloquence, his enthusiasm and the flame of his genius."[66] Seguin's article contains a somewhat old-fashioned hyperbole of style, but he captured Bernard's devotion to Jerusalem as the place "where the Lord walked." This historian was aware of Bernard's loving account of Jerusalem and its surroundings in his celebration of the new knighthood. Bernard would never himself see such places but, in a way, he did not need to do so. They dwelled in his mind, and he came to see it as the duty of the Christian knight to defend them.

Bernard was not interested in the translation of the Koran that Peter the Venerable sent him. For him what mattered was to defend the faith when it was threatened: "For Saint Bernard had no hesitation. It was a pious act."[67] For Seguin, Bernard belonged to the feudal universe, with its "profound sense of discipline and obedience that were his heritage."[68] For Bernard the crusade became a ministry that had been specially handed over to him. In preaching a crusade against the Wends he promised that its participants who confessed their sins would obtain an indulgence for their efforts.[69] He even declared that there would be forgiveness for murderers, thieves, adulterers, and oath breakers who went on crusade.[70]

We find here the traditional French Catholic view of Bernard as a courageous advocate of the crusade and the product of a feudal world. But Seguin also saw his limitations with "an element of naiveté in imagining that even for the most holy conflict men would be disposed to renounce their interests."[71] For Bernard the debacle of the crusade was the result of "moral faults of men, their iniquities and those of the men who commanded, the princes, and were responsible for the disaster."[72] In summing up the result of the Second Crusade, Seguin regretted "so much error and disregard for realities" that brought the failure "of an enterprise, which if it had succeeded would perhaps have definitively consolidated the position of the Frankish State" in the East.[73] In the final analysis he saw Bernard as "this French saint who did not know how to separate the love of his country from that which he harbored for his God." Seguin saw Bernard's involvement as "a worthy endeavor" and "perhaps one of the most beautiful manifestations of the work of Saint Bernard, who in adversity reminded the world that the saints are the greatest of heroes."[74]

Before 2001 it might have been possible to dismiss such a statement as a manifestation of an antiquated worldview, an attempt to capture French glory after the debacle of 1940, in harmony with Charles de Gaulle's fervent belief in his nation and his religion. Seguin concluded in attacking those who "forget this magnificent history and the greatness of their country" and who denigrate it. Today with the return of what can only be called xenophobic nationalism in Europe and the United States, it is no longer so easy to insist that the clash of civilizations is over and we can all live together in harmony. Thus Bernard's engagement in the crusade needs to be seen as more than a past manifestation of a disappeared age. Fundamentalist Islam and fundamentalist Christianity embrace aggression and even war as legitimate means of protecting their interests. Thus Bernard is not an anachronism. He is a sign of the times.

The Benedictine monk and scholar Jean Leclercq, who in his career covered almost every aspect of Bernard's life and thought, chose in one study to look at Bernard in terms of his "attitude toward war."[75] Leclercq began with the assertion that in Bernard's time it was "sometimes easier to learn how to fight than to make progress in the intellectual field."[76] For Bernard, however, the religious vocation was superior to the call to arms. Leclercq saw him as the "greatest non-violent leader of his time" because he attracted youths "toward communities of non-violence."[77] According to Leclercq, Bernard advocated "as few wars as possible," and when they did take place, he "advocated the least possible violence."

Leclercq's assertion is both correct and incorrect. Bernard did not advocate war, but he did accept it as a necessity, as when he supported the new militia of the Knights Templar. Leclercq takes up Bernard's oft-quoted assertion in the meeting of prelates and princes at Frankfurt on 13 March 1147, that it was necessary "to destroy these nations entirely or indeed to convert them."[78] Leclercq concludes that Bernard did not thereby advocate using force in order to convert the Wends. I, however, find the whole tenor of his remarks as supporting the idea that a victory over the Wends would involve their being converted to Christianity by force.

Turning to the Second Crusade, Leclercq makes the important point that the papal summons was meant mainly for France, while Bernard expanded the invitation to all Christian nations. Bernard is seen as never instigating violence, but if others took the initiative, then the Christian knight could make use of it in self-defense. Certainly the preaching of crusade can be looked upon as an exhortation to Christian kings and knights to defend the Latin kingdoms in the East, and not as an aggressive act. But Leclercq, at the end of his important article, admitted that Bernard's political impact was marginal: "We can rightly contest his political sense, but we cannot refuse him the merit of having retained a genuine concern for the individual." For Leclercq, Bernard's writings on war show his religious ideals, as well as "his limitations in the field of politics."[79] Here at the end of Leclercq's article is a necessary admission that Bernard was not able to overcome the political limitations of his environment. However much he looked upon the crusade as a moral imperative, he was not able to persuade its participants to forget their differences and unite in a common cause. The Byzantine emperor, the French and German kings, the Knights Templar, the rulers of the crusading states—all of them harbored different interests, and Bernard could by no means reconcile them.

In a brief article, Giles Constable, one of the outstanding monastic historians of our time, recalled how in *On Consideration* Bernard attributed the failure of the Second Crusade not only to the sins of its participants but also to the incomprehensible "workings of the ways of God." Constable saw what Seguin and Leclercq failed to admit, that Bernard "was deeply troubled by the outcome of the expedition he had done so much to promote."[80] In an *exemplum* story from a century later, Bernard is said to have tried to comfort returning crusaders and to restore their faith. He explained that God had punished their pride because they had depended on their own strength rather than on his help. God had turned them aside here on earth in order to show the crusaders that their salvation was in heaven. This account of Bernard's reaction, as Constable pointed out, is not historical, because it was written down so much later. But like much in the *exemplum* tradition, it contains a moral truth that may correspond to what Bernard in fact believed and advocated. As in the *amplexus* story, this story offers an aspect of Bernard that is not contemporary with his life or to be found in the *Vita Prima*. But the *exemplum* gives the impression that Bernard's own conclusions in *On Consideration* were known and were able to provide material for such a story.

In an introduction to *The Second Crusade and the Cistercians*, a collection of articles edited by Michael Gerver, Giles Constable offers further thoughts on Bernard's role. He finds him to have been more "a catalyst than an initiator." Thus his role was limited, but Constable sees Bernard as contributing "spiritual enthusiasm and charismatic personality" that "raised the expectations for the success of the Crusade." In this way Bernard "contributed to the disappointment at its failure."[81] To my mind Bernard had little sense of what he was creating, and it was a shock for him as well as the crusaders when their efforts ended so tragically. In this vein John G. Rowe in an article in the same collection finds in Bernard "a holy simplicity of his own," so that he failed to be "fully aware of the complexity of certain events." Bernard's "matchless, magical eloquence" meant that he was considered the very cause of the crusade, and so he was "blamed for the ultimate disasters which overtook the expedition."[82]

Only one article in this collection considers Bernard's possible hesitation at involving himself in backing the crusade. George Ferzoco takes Bernard at his word in his stated desire to remain at Clairvaux. Ferzoco criticizes other historians for having failed to understand Bernard's way of thinking. His involvement was not primarily a question of politics. In Ferzoco's view he was following the order given by the pope, but part of him remained at the Clairvaux that he loved.[83]

One of the most helpful articles in the collection is by Brenda Bolton, who examines the attempt to launch a new crusade after the failure of its predecessor. Here Bernard was proposed as the likely leader of such an expedition. But Pope Eugenius expressed his doubts that the abbot of Clairvaux could handle such a burden, considering his bad health. The proposal was finally dropped, probably because of "a concern for the welfare and health of Bernard."[84] Cistercian sources, however, say nothing of the matter. Bolton concludes that it is likely the key person in withholding consent was Pope Eugenius himself. I would disagree and assume that Bernard made his own decision, perhaps realizing that a monk had no business leading a crusade. Eugenius may have involved himself, but Bernard could see that his vocation did not allow him to stand at the head of a crusading army. Even though he was tempted.

If we return to Seguin's analysis and remove its patriotic surface and accept Leclercq's admission that Bernard did not have a keen grasp of secular politics, then the outcome of the Second Crusade in terms of his involvement becomes clear. Bernard had no idea of what was at stake when he committed himself to preaching the crusade. He willingly sent thousands of men to the East, and few of them ever came back. For him Jerusalem was a vision, a biblical series of events, a manifestation of God's grace and glory. The material Jerusalem of intrigue and betrayal did not interest him, but when it came time for accounting for the failures of the crusade, then Bernard had to contemplate its disastrous aftermath. It had not been enough to come from a family of brave knights. Palestine was not Champagne, and Bernard's military idealism could not cope with political and military realities. It is not sufficient to call Bernard naive. He was quite simply ignorant of what lay beneath the surface of the promises made by the rulers who went on crusade. Bernard became a witness to a tragic inability to understand another culture, a failing still present in our own culture and which has seemed even to increase in our time.

8. Did Bernard show tolerance toward the Jews?

I have already provided an overview of Bernard's understanding of the presence of the Jewish people in the history of salvation. He respected them as witnesses to Scripture, its "living words . . . living witnesses of our redemption."[85] These words Bernard wrote to the English people, but also to the clergy and people of Eastern Francia and Bavaria. Bernard's exhortation needs to be seen in the context of a period in Western history when a traditional tolerance toward the Jewish people had given way to suspicion and outright persecution. Here the Gregorian Reform, with its new religious devotion bordering on fanaticism, meant that an earlier respect for Jews, as manifested by Carolingian rulers, had disappeared. Even worse was the preaching of the First Crusade, where Jews were accused of being the killers of Christ, and so liable themselves to being killed.

We have a chronicle for the Jewish community in Mainz written by Solomon Bar Simson and dated after 1140, so almost contemporary with the Second Crusade. According to Solomon, the crusaders reasoned that there was no point in traveling far in order to take revenge on the Jews, for they were present in their midst, the very Jews whose ancestors killed and crucified Christ: "Let us first take revenge on them and stamp them out . . . so that the name of Israel no longer will be remembered."[86] Many Jews chose suicide in order to escape Christian persecution and forced conversion. Solomon noted that bishops and counts did not support such attacks. They did their best to protect "their" Jews.

It was in the Rhineland that the most barbaric attacks on the Jewish population took place in the 1140s, and here Bernard was at the fore in speaking out against a former Cistercian monk, Raoul, and his atttempt to provoke the Christian population of the Rhineland to kill their Jews. Bernard's efforts were noted in the Jewish community, by Ephraim of Bonn, for example, who described how God "sent after the evil priest [Raoul] a decent priest, a great man and the mentor of all the priests, one who knows and understands their faith." Ephraim described Bernard's preaching: "It is fitting that you go forth against the Muslims. However, anyone who attacks a Jew and tries to kill him it is as though he attacks Jesus himself."[87] Bernard is supposed to have referred to the book of Psalms: "Kill them not, lest my people forget" (Ps

59:11). Ephraim recognized that "this priest" was considered by his people to be "one of their saints." He did not think that Bernard had taken a bribe for his support for the Jews, perhaps a reflection of the fact that many Jews during these years tried to save themselves and their families by paying large sums as bribes: "Whatever they requested from us, silver and gold, we did not withhold." For selfless reasons and thanks to God's mercy, the abbot is said to have saved "a remnant or survivor" of the Jewish people.

This is one of the relatively few instances in contemporary sources outside the Cistercian Order that Bernard was mentioned and appreciated. He does seem to have made a difference in protecting the Jews, even though many succumbed to the attacks that Raoul helped provoke. There has been a great deal of research in this area. I will mention just one article, by David Berger, "The Attitude of St. Bernard of Clairvaux toward the Jews."[88] Berger makes the important point that Bernard's atttitude was formed "almost entirely on the basis of theoretical and theological considerations." Aside from knowing about Jews and usury, "his contact with Jews was minimal." Berger points to the fact that Stephen Harding consulted rabbis in dealing with problems in the Scriptures, but there is no evidence that Bernard similarly had personal contacts with Jewish people.

As for Bernard's statements about protecting Jews, Berger makes use of Malcolm Hay's statement that the abbot opposed the massacres not for "humanitarian" but for "theological" reasons. I think this distinction is artificial: Bernard's theology is an expression of his humanitarian ideals, and the two can hardly be distinguished. Good theology is in its very basis humanitarian, for it concerns the ways of God to humankind and the individual's response to it. Berger sees Hay's views as "more a condemnation of medieval anti-Semitism generally than they are of Bernard." Bernard "maintained the most liberal of the views that were possible within the accepted theology." Berger points to how Bernard "firmly believed that the Jews will be saved at the final judgment." For him Jews "retain some special status even after the crucifixion" and "some Biblical promises still apply to them."[89]

In spite of this review of Bernard's relatively positive view of the place of Jews in the history of salvation, Berger considered "the general tenor of Bernard's sermons and letters" to be "strongly anti-Semitic."[90] At several places in his writings and letters he emphasized Jews as a cruel people, and he made use of "anti-Jewish stereotypes." He accused them of being devoted to gain.[91] Perhaps these characterizations merely demonstrate that Bernard belonged to his own time in harboring standard views of the Jews, but, as Berger shows, his language in attacking Anacletus on the basis of his Jewish ancestry was "vicious."[92] Berger concluded that Bernard in his crusade preaching did what he could to protect Jews, but at the same time he was "an equally strong spokesman for anti-Jewish stereotypes and prejudices." Bernard may have been aware of this contradiction, for he could "combine fierce denunciations" of Jewish people "with a description of the incredible mercy shown toward them by Jesus and the Church."[93]

The result of this detailed and careful article is a sense of the duplicity of Bernard's contribution. On the one hand, he insisted that Jews have a right to live in Christian society and that they were to continue to exist until the end of the world, when they would be converted. On the other hand, he accepted the prejudices of his culture that looked upon Jews as grasping people, out for material gain, and not to be trusted. Bernard never reconciled these two opposed views, and so Berger concluded his article with a pessimistic statement: "The hatred which he preached was fanning the flames of violence in lesser men. The great Christian protector of twelfth-century Jewry sowed seeds which would claim the life of many a Jewish martyr."[94] But "lesser men" had no need of Bernard's stereotypes to act violently against the Jewish population. Anti-Semitism was rampant in Christian medieval culture, but it was held back and limited by people such as Bernard. In the words of Ephraim of Bonn, "Were it not for the mercies of our Creator, who sent the aforesaid abbot and his letters, there would not have been a remnant or survivor among the Jews."[95]

9. How did Bernard relate to Cîteaux's abbot and to the Cistercian Order?

How much was Bernard involved with the development of the Cistercian Order and to what extent did he have amicable and collegial relations with his father abbot, Stephen Harding of Cîteaux? Here the decisive event was the General Chapter of 1119, where Stephen presented his Charter of Charity.[96] It is from this moment that we can speak of a Cistercian Order, for Stephen made certain that father abbots would visit daughter houses and abbots of daughter houses would also supervise the houses of their fathers immediate. The bond of charity meant that the daughter houses would be associated with the abbeys that had founded them not because of any financial obligations but on the basis of a freely bestowed act of allegiance. This was a brilliant arrangement and something that had not been anticipated in former congregations of monks, such as that of Cluny.

When the Charter of Charity is read today, its provisions seem so obvious that it is easy to ignore the fact that it was innovative and provided the structure for the first monastic order in Christian Europe. Until 1119 the Rule of

Benedict had been interpreted as providing a great degree of independence for each individual monastery. Formal bonds among monasteries, as in the congregation of Cluny, were mostly concerned with regular payments to the leading monastery. Stephen Harding left such financial considerations aside, and now the Cistercian Order defined itself in terms of a yearly general chapter at Cîteaux and regular visitations of daughter houses by father abbots. The founders felt that they were living up to the Rule of Benedict in a manner that none of their predecessors had done. In fact they were expanding the tenets of that Rule in order to establish regular contacts among the monasteries.

Perhaps the most complete study of the way Bernard involved himself in the fledgling Cistercian Order was provided in 1953 by Jean de la Croix Bouton, who is best known for his edition of the early Cistercian legislative texts. This was for many years the standard edition of these sources but has been replaced by that of Chrysogonus Waddell.[97] In any case, Bouton's article, *"Negotia Ordinis,"* is a thorough review of Bernard's dealings with Stephen Harding and the Order in general.[98] He claims that Bernard was one of the abbots who in the General Chapter of 1119 gave their approbation to the Charter of Charity. Bouton does not specifically assert that Bernard was present, but his description seems to take it for granted. In any case, it is unlikely that Bernard would have been at Cîteaux. The *Vita Prima* describes how it was William of Champeaux who came to the General Chapter on Bernard's behalf. William asked that Bernard for a year be under his supervision, in order to recover from his illness.[99] So the text makes it clear that it was William and not Bernard who came to Cîteaux during that decisive time when the Order as such was formed constitutionally.

It is likely that Bernard did give his assent to the Charter of Charity, but he would have had to do so from his sickbed outside Clairvaux, and not in being present at Cîteaux. Bouton noted that in his *Apology* Bernard may have been attacking the decorated manuscripts of Cîteaux. This would have been a reason for a distance and separation between Bernard and the abbot of Cîteaux, a fact that Bouton concedes. He also admits that it is difficult to detect Bernard's influence in the decisions of the General Chapter, except for the prohibition against painted letters in manuscripts.[100] This came, however, toward the end of the abbacy of Stephen's successor, Rainald around 1150.

Bouton pointed out that Bernard's involvement in the fledgling Cistercian Order is most clearly seen in his reaction to Abbot Arnold of Morimond's desertion of his monastery. Abbot Stephen was in Flanders when Bernard wrote, but the abbot of Cîteaux had previously passed through Clairvaux. Bernard claimed it was good fortune that Stephen could ignore this situation for the longest possible time. Bouton interprets this reaction as a "delicacy of sentiments by Bernard to the father of all the Order." But if we look at what Bernard actually wrote, it can be seen as almost patronizing: "Happy he is for the time being who can ignore such sad rumors."[101]

It is apparent from this context that Stephen on his visitation did not hear about the Morimond abbot's move to take some of his monks to the Holy Land. Bouton failed to point out that Bernard in involving himself in this matter without consulting his father abbot thereby ignored the chain of command in the Cistercian Order. Bernard acted on his own initiative, instead of sending a messenger first to Abbot Stephen and coordinating a response.

Since we have virtually nothing from Stephen's hand, we cannot know how he reacted to Bernard's initiative. There were moments, however, when the abbot of Cîteaux followed Bernard's counsel, as in a dispute between the canons of St. Stephen of Dijon and the monks of Saint-Seine.[102] Bouton described "a common action" but then admitted that "the abbot of Clairvaux speaks very little of the father of all the Order in his many letters, and this fact remains to surprise us." Bouton tried to explain the silence of Bernard toward Stephen as follows: "Bernard did not want to disturb the quiet of the elderly saint in sharing his cares with him."

It is difficult to imagine that Bernard's distance from Stephen was a result of such concern. There was a real separation, as indicated by the fact, noted by Bouton, that the cartulary of Cîteaux does not mention Bernard's name a single time.[103] It is always problematic to argue on the basis of silence in the sources, but it is significant that we have no mention in any of Bernard's letters of the death of Stephen in 1134, while in 1151 he mourned the death of Stephen's successor, Rainald of Bar: "The Lord of Cîteaux has left us. This is a great loss in the order. For me there is a double reason for sorrow, because in one and the same man I lost a father and a son."[104] This is a classic juxtaposition of fact and emotion, which Bernard managed so well. Rainald had been a monk of Clairvaux before he became abbot of Cîteaux, so he was both son and father to Bernard.

In going through the limited evidence for Bernard's relationship with Stephen, Bouton came to a question that is much more important than that of a possible difference of personalities. Did Bernard try to maintain Stephen Harding's ideals, or was he responsible for a certain deviation from them?[105] To put the matter differently, did Bernard have a different brand for what was thought to be Cistercian? Here Bouton has no doubt: Bernard in his treatises and letters affirmed the ideals of Cîteaux, as evidenced in a letter to Adam, the companion of Arnold of Morimond, where Bernard stated:

"I have my religious profession at Cîteaux."[106] He did think of himself as a monk of Cîteaux, but Bouton went further and said that Stephen was the modest source of what became a "great river" in Bernard.[107] Here Bouton underestimated the contribution of Abbot Stephen to the very definition of what the word Cistercian came to mean. However much Bernard became a visible river, he could not have run his course without the contribution and structure that Stephen provided in creating the Order.

Bouton tried to be fair by saying that Bernard realized the work carried out by Cîteaux in the monastic and social spheres. Bernard certainly thought of his writings, both letters and treatises, as defining the boundaries of monastic life. At the same time we simply do not know very much about what Abbot Stephen created or left behind besides the constitutions of the Order, but his valedictory letter to the Benedictine monks of Sherborne, where he had been a monk in his youth, indicates a keen awareness of the meaning of the monastic vocation.[108] In the final analysis Stephen and Bernard were working for the same goal, even though their methods and visibility were quite different.

This detailed treatment of Bernard's relationship to the Cistercian Order ends with an important observation. All the monasteries that came to join the Order had their own particular usages, which they in many cases were allowed to keep.[109] This was "to the great detriment of uniformity." The General Chapter in its decisions sought this uniformity, but Bernard's reputation multiplied requests for foundations and for affiliation within the Cistercian Order. In 1152 the Chapter forbade new foundations, but this decison was not observed. Bernard's successor at Clairvaux could hardly hold annual visitations of all seventy houses that came to have him as their father immediate.

Christopher Holdsworth's "Bernard as a Father Abbot" reviews all that we know about how Bernard functioned in his relations within the Order, as well as the pastoral care he showed to the monasteries under Clairvaux. He took the General Chapter seriously (when he attended, which I think was not often). Holdsworth concludes that Bernard "must have gained much information from personal contacts with abbots at the General Chapter" and during his many journeys. His letters contain "practical advice with spiritual counsel."[110]

Bouton provides us with one anecdote that in my mind tells a great deal about Bernard and the General Chapter, even though the story was only written down more than half a century after his death. It is found, however, in the Chronicle of Alberic of Trois Fontaines, a collection of monastic history that cannot be dismissed out of hand. Bernard one day came to Dijon and stayed the night in the abbey of Saint Benigne, which he had always loved, for here his mother was buried. Before the altar he heard the hymn "Salve Regina" sung by angels. But at first he thought it was the monks who were singing, and the next day he said to the abbot: "Last night you sang the hymn well . . . before the altar of the Virgin." But the abbot told him that the monks had been asleep at that hour. As a result Bernard decided that the hymn be sung before the Virgin Mary's altar at Clairvaux. And in a General Chapter of the Order he received the privilege that this hymn be sung by the entire Order, and "this was done."[111]

The story is valuable because it helps explain that in his lifetime Bernard was associated with the "Salve Regina," but it does not claim, as is often asserted, that he was the author of the hymn. Here he appears as instrumental in spreading the usage of a hymn that became universal in the Cistercian Order and to this day is sung at the end of Compline in all Cistercian houses. However late the story, it is perhaps an invaluable indication of how Bernard was able to transmit his own spirituality and convert it into regular practice not only in his own monastery but in the entire Cistercian Order. And here he made good use of the General Chapter.

One of the most important and well-documented contributions of Bernard to the Cistercian Order is his reform of the Cistercian Antiphonary, the chant followed by the monks in their daily office. Bernard explained in the Prologue to the Cistercian Antiphonary that the abbots were frustrated with the results gleaned from the Antiphonary of Metz, which was supposed to be close to the original Gregorian chant. "Having agreed that the Antiphonary was to be revised and corrected, they put me in charge of the task."[112] Bernard explained that he had gathered together the brothers "who proved to be better instructed and more skillful in the theory and practice of chant." It was his wish that the new Antiphonary be used in all Cistercian monasteries, for it had been approved by the General Chapter, where it was "acccepted and confirmed by all the abbots."

The date of the revised Antiphonary is 1147 or close to that time. Bernard had preached the Second Crusade and traveled through the Rhineland. He was enormously busy, and yet he invested his energy in a project that he clearly thought was important for the Order and its inner life. He did not do so at the request or command of his father abbot at Cîteaux, even though the present abbot, Rainald, must have approved the project. But Bernard cared for uniformity in the life of the Order, and the chants used were part of this concern. For once it is possible to see him fitting into a larger monastic perspective, instead of pursuing his own monastic goal.

A final indication of Bernard's relationship to his father abbot is contained in a story about Stephen Harding found in the *Exordium Magnum Cisterciense* and thus written down about seventy years after Stephen's death in 1134. And yet as with the *exemplum* about the adoption of "Salve Regina" by all Cistercian monasteries, there seems to be a historical basis for the story. As a novice at Cîteaux Bernard would say the seven penitential psalms for the sake of his mother's soul. One day he did so after Compline but left some out, "whether through forgetfulness or sleepiness."[113] He went to bed without realizing his oversight, but Abbot Stephen came to him the next day and questioned him. Bernard blushed and asked himself how his abbot could have known about his promise and how he had failed to keep it: "He understood that he had been caught out by a spiritual man and threw himself at his feet, confessing his negligence and asking pardon." Afterwards he was more careful about carrying out "both private and public observances."

This is a remarkable story because it indicates that there was a tradition at Clairvaux and Cîteaux after Bernard's death that could allow for his having to grow and mature in his vocation. This is a fallible Bernard, far from the perfect human being and monk that is expected in the saint. At the same time there may well be a hint here that there was tension with Stephen, not only when Bernard was a novice, but later on in life, when Stephen similarly could have reminded the abbot of his daughter house that improvements could be made and promises kept. It would be wrong to push such a source too far as a key to understanding the relationship between the two men. It may well reflect merely the fact that Bernard had to develop as a person and a monk while he was a novice, and Stephen was there to encourage and sometimes correct him. But here I find a symbolic indication of what I consider to have been a tense relationship. Stephen had to put up with an abbot who always seemed to know what was best. It could at times have been ennervating.

10. Bernard the monster? Returning to Peter Abelard and Gilbert de la Porrée

In the centuries since his death Bernard's reputation has suffered because of his treatment of Abelard and Gilbert de la Porrée regarding their theological writings. Especially in the case of Abelard, it is easy to look at Bernard as a representative of the dark Middle Ages and see him as persecuting a scion of modern times. Abelard also gains from his affair with Heloise, even though many today would frame his behavior as that of a teacher taking advantage of a young student. But even a sexual predator like Abelard was transformed in the growth of his relationship with Heloise. He looked after her and her sisters when the abbot of Saint Denis made them homeless, and Abelard handed over to the sisters the Paraclete, where he had been teaching students who came to him from Paris. This is a gripping story and one that Bernard cannot match, for as I have already shown, he maintained a distance from most women, even though it is likely that he came at least once to visit Heloise at the Paraclete.

The story of Abelard and Heloise ensured that their bones were preserved during the French Revolution, while Bernard's were cast aside. The difference in treatment is a commentary on how our culture has valued romantic love, while the ascetic love of a monastic life is looked upon with skepticism. The result is that Abelard is a modern hero, while Bernard for many, including some of my medieval history colleagues, remains at best a doubtful figure, at worst a monster. To understand the difference between the two, it is not enough to provide the traditional distinction between monastic and scholastic theology. Although Bernard's *lectio* or meditation on the meaning of Scripture supposedly could not tolerate the analytical approach of Abelard's early scholasticism, in fact, Bernard could express himself in the same logical terms as Abelard. And in his hymns Abelard could reflect the same deeply meditative prayerfulness that we associate with Bernard. Thanks to the careful research of Chrysogonus Waddell it is now possible to understand Abelard as a deeply spiritual figure solidly planted in the Christian Middle Ages.

So why all the dissension? The simple answer is that Bernard followed the warnings of his friend William of Saint-Thierry and came to view Abelard as a heretic. At the same time Abelard never got a fair chance to explain his beliefs, at least not until his final meeting with Bernard. The language of Abelard's Trinitarian theology was novel and could be contrasted unfavorably with the definitions reached so painfully at councils in the early Christian centuries. At the same time Abelard's view of the redemption, in emphasizing Christ's sufferings and death as an act of love, made his offering into something exemplary but not necessary for human salvation. Bernard for his part insisted on the Pauline view that Christ takes away sin, and this act was required for humankind to be saved. There were indeed essential differences between Abelard and Bernard, though it seems unfair to accept Bernard's claim that he was dealing with a heretic.

At the same time, however, Bernard as we find him in his letters does not come across as a vicious pursuer of some intellectual prey. He only gradually got involved in the question of Abelard's orthodoxy and seems at first to have preferred to keep a certain distance. But as I have indicated frequently in this work, Bernard followed the lead of his friends. With Gilbert de la Porrée, however, his approach was different. Gilbert's Trinitarian theology was difficult to understand, but Bernard convinced himself that Gilbert had turned the persons of the Trinity into substances, discrete from each other.

Once he reached this view, Bernard felt it was his solemn duty to get Gilbert condemned. Unfortunately for Bernard, Gilbert had friends in high places, and the Council of Reims in 1148 exonerated him. The council's acquittal of Gilbert took place at a time when Bernard's own position in the Western Church must have been weakened because of the failure of the Second Crusade, which to some degree could be blamed on him.

Bernard could not accept Gilbert's exoneration from any taint of heresy, and in his later writings, especially *On Consideration*, he returned to the matter and repeatedly argued his case. In this instance he could not let go. One can recognize Bernard's dedication to the cause of theological transparency, but at the same time there was a stubbornness in him that refused to accept the verdict of a church council. Bernard knew that such meetings were political events and were not suitable for dealing with complex theological questions. But once the council had come to its verdict, Bernard would have been wise to relent. It took the fair-mindedness of a John of Salisbury to try to balance the books in recognizing Bernard's insights but still praising Gilbert's learning. At such a moment it is apparent that Bernard did in fact belong to a traditional monastic theology, dwelling on words and phrases, mostly biblical, and being skeptical toward abstract definitions.

Was he then a monster? Bernard loved his monastery and its men, in a common search for the presence and love of God. This quest was sincere and deeply felt, and it would be superficial to dismiss it as an illusion. Bernard will always be a difficult saint, but his *affectus*, his attachment to the love of God and his brothers, was genuine. At times his passion led him to exaggerate his criticism of others, but he was no monster.

11. Bernard and Peter the Venerable: Friendship or rivalry?

In the main sections of this biography I have frequently turned to letters to Bernard from the abbot of Cluny, Peter the Venerable. The two figures tower above many of their contemporaries in their insight and the power of their literary style. In tracing the development of their relationship it might seem natural to claim that they did their best to make use of each other in order to further the interests of their own monastic orders. Thus the many and sometimes effusive expressions of what look likes friendship can be dismissed as window dressing, behind which was political necessity.

In his important study, *Bernard of Clairvaux: Between Cult and History*, Adriaan Bredero has reduced the letters of seeming friendship to "commonplaces" in which monks "more or less repeated the expressions of praise that they chanted in their prayers."[114] However much I admire Bredero's lifetime of dedication to Cistercian studies, I have to differ from him. The language of prayer was not the same as that of friendship. Certainly both modes of expression could draw on a common source, especially the Psalms of David, but both Bernard and Peter, as well as other monastic figures of the twelfth century, renewed this language and intensified it by adding that of the classical antiquity. As I described it in my book on friendship, the period was an "age of friendship," and it is necessary to take the language seriously as more than a collection of clichés.[115]

Bredero points out correctly that "medieval letters were far from private" and usually did not contain "concrete information."[116] This was usually provided by the bearer of the letter, and was made up of "pious expressions" taken from Scripture. Bredero refers to the work of Giles Constable, but so far as I can tell Constable dealt primarily with how the letters were carried and delivered, not their content.[117] Although I disagree with Bredero, I do not want to malign a respected colleague. He reads the sources differently than I do, looking for clichés and political manipulation where I find a renewal of an old language of friendship in an attempt to reconcile Cluny and Clairvaux.

Both Bernard and Peter worked to end the papal schism, and here there was "no conflicting monastic interest."[118] While Bernard was still in Italy in the late 1130s, Peter complained about the privilege given the Cistercians by which they were exempt from paying tithes. The letters that emerged from this matter did not reconcile Bernard with Peter, however, and Bredero sees these letters "as an interchange of diplomatic compliments rather than as expressions of genuine, personal friendship that bound them together."[119] Bredero found confirmation of this view in a long-standing conflict about the election of the bishop of Langres, a case that I reviewed in chapter 7. To summarize here, the see was vacant for about two years because the chapter of Langres could not agree on a successor to the bishop. Some of the canons put forward a Cluniac monk as their candidate, while others refused to accept him. The archbishop, himself a product of Cluny, found the man acceptable and recommended him to Pope Innocent, who appointed him in 1138. On returning from Italy, Bernard objected to the person chosen, as well as to the procedure followed. He resisted the choice until Pope Innocent declared it invalid. Peter the Venerable sent Bernard a letter with his side of the story, where he defended the candidate who had been set aside.[120]

Bredero concludes that Bernard never answered the letter, and two years went by with no further contacts.[121] But do we know this for a fact? Does not Bredero argue from silence in the sources, since we know that Bernard wrote many more letters than those that were preserved in what became his collection. In the disputes and misunderstandings between the two Orders,

Bredero sees Peter as reaching out to Bernard for reconciliation. Over a period of about twenty years, the abbot of Cluny had come to alter his view about Cluny's monastic life and was doing what he could to make it stricter. Bernard apparently did not respond to this gesture, but Bredero saw that he had no time to involve himself in Cluny's internal affairs, for by then he was preaching the crusade. Another means for Peter to get Bernard's attention and sympathy was, according to Bredero, through a relationship with Nicholas of Montiéramey, the bright young man who was first a Cluniac and then became a Cistercian. Once Nicholas had joined Clairvaux and become Bernard's main secretary, Peter had to defend his desire to see the gifted young man back at Cluny: "Is it not reason enough to see a person whom one loves?" Peter pleaded with Bernard: "He is yours indeed but is very dear to me."[122]

After this time Nicholas disgraced himself by running away from Clairvaux and taking a number of seals with him, including Bernard's personal one. Bredero surprisingly minimizes the significance of this theft and claims that "the charges against Nicholas by Bernard were rather a pretext than the real reason" that Nicholas left. It was supposedly the relationship that had grown up between Nicholas and Peter the Venerable of which Bernard did not approve. He believed that Peter was using Nicholas as "his intermediary with Bernard in order to get his cooperation in improving the relationship between the Cluniacs and the Cistercians."[123] Bernard's method for bringing to an end to "this undesirable contact" between Peter and Nicholas was "to force Nicholas to leave," and this could be done "by accusing him of fraud."

This explanation for the disappearance of Nicholas from Clairvaux is far-fetched and only functions because it fails to see that the theft of a personal seal was a serious offense in a society where the seal affixed to a letter or other document was one of the few means to establish its genuineness. Bredero concludes that Nicholas of Montiéramey's fate made it possible for Bernard to avoid future "requests to get involved with the internal problems of the Cluniac Order." From this time on there were no more letters between Bernard and Peter the Venerable. Once again, the absence of sources cannot be used as a proof. Bredero claims that the "total absence" of any mention of Peter the Venerable in the *Vita Prima* also provides proof that the relationship of the two abbots was problematic and came to an end after Nicholas disappeared.

In my own work on friendship in the monastic world, I looked at the change from the letter Peter wrote Bernard in the late 1120s defending Cluniac practices to a letter from 1137 where the tone is much warmer. Some of the language can be dismissed as contact between two powerful abbots who were keeping tabs on each other's signs of goodwill and sympathy.[124] Bernard's epistolary language combined Cicero with Saint Paul in a context that cannot be described as pure commonplaces. The fact that a letter was a public document does not detract from the possibility that it could express human warmth and feeling for the person or persons to whom it was addressed. Certainly Peter was attentive to what Bernard wrote to him. He provided in one letter almost an exegesis of Bernard's letter, quoting whole passages.[125] Peter offered an eloquent plea for concord between Cistercians and Cluniacs. Bredero sees Peter's role as basically positive and concerned with the reform of the Cluniacs, while Bernard remained behind as a rather cynical manipulator. But both abbots combined the language of biblical love with that of classical friendship. Both of them knew that every line would be read and absorbed by their communities, but at the same time they wanted to convey to the other abbot an expression of their inner life and spirituality.

Friendship is difficult to define and to locate, especially when we turn to another culture. But however much I admire the accomplishment of Adriaan Bredero in his lifetime's work on the sources for Bernard's life, I have to disagree with his use of Bernard's correspondence with Peter the Venerable in order to characterize their relationship as purely formal and political. I do not deny that Bernard and Peter were concerned with the position and prestige of their monastic orders, and they can be looked upon as rivals. But they were fascinated by each other, and we can turn to Peter almost as a mirror of Bernard. There was a degree of understanding, but it seems to have been in only one direction, from Cluny to Clairvaux. Yet Bernard did try to reconcile himself, and perhaps for the period after he had headhunted Nicholas as his secretary, he was in fruitful, if tense, contact with the abbot of Cluny.

The historian cannot know hearts and minds, but in the relationship of Bernard with Peter the Venerable there were many human elements: attraction, repulsion, anger, frustration, friendship, even love. The two abbots remain elusive, but their correspondence expresses a host of emotions and moves deftly from one level to another. Certainly their declarations of friendship need to be taken in the context of a culture where monastic friendship was a real and important factor, even for powerful abbots. Friendships can be tumultuous, changeable, passionate. I find all these qualities in the relationship of Bernard and Peter the Venerable. Bernard cannot be dismisssed purely as a political manipulator, for he sought in Peter what he also sought in his other friends: understanding and reconciliation. Considering the fact that the two figures came from quite different backgrounds and had experienced monastic life quite differently, it is surprising that at times they managed to meet in agreement and sympathy. However much they could irritate and disappoint each other, Peter and Bernard were able to find common ground in a language of spiritual friendship and in the appreciation of their community lives.

12. How could Bernard praise monk-knights?

How could a leading figure in a contemplative monastic order have written a tract recommending a new order of knights who also were monks? The development of the Knights Templar and Bernard's contribution was treated at the end of chapter 4, but it is worthwhile to consider Bernard and the Templars in terms of his decision to support the new order. It was, indeed, quite new, and the title Bernard gave his treatise, *De laude novae militiae* (In Praise of the New Knighthood), was a bold assertion in a culture that by no means recommended what was new and usually suspected it of some grave fault. But Bernard did not care. He recognized that having fighting monks was something new and different in the history of monasticism, but he turned to the Old Testament to assert that there had been "ancient witnesses" who "foreshadowed the new knighthood."[126] Thus even though the Rule of Saint Benedict by no means anticipated fighting monks, Bernard found that a spiritual interpretation of the Scriptures gave the possibility of fighting and praying. In Scripture he found an "ancient promise": "I will make you the pride of the ages, a joy from generation to generation"(Is 60:16).

With this background, Bernard could describe the discipline and obedience of the new knights, who "seldom wash and never set their hair," which they were to keep short.[127] Bernard had had his fill of knights who dressed as dandies, and believed he could help fashion a new type of knight, dedicated to an ascetic way of life: "I do not know if it would be more appropriate to refer to them as monks or as soldiers, unless perhaps it would be better to recognize them as being both." His enthusiasm knew no bounds: "It is marvelous in our eyes" (Ps 117:23). "These are the picked troops of God."[128]

Surprisingly this treatise is not given a separate chapter in the important publication *Bernard 1953*. There is only a note in one of the appendices.[129] Perhaps the editors thought it sufficient to portray Bernard's role in the Second Crusade, which could be looked upon as the fulfillment of his commitment to what was supposed to be a holy war. But this omission might be a result of the fact that in the immediate post–Second World War period, the idea of a holy war and monastic knights was not exactly attractive. Certainly the generation that grew up in the West in the 1950s and 1960s had a hard time accepting the idea of warfare and contemplative life. Trappist-Cistercian monasteries in the United States and elsewhere were filled with men who either had chosen not to fight or who had seen action and went to the monastery almost as a refuge from the traumas of war.

It is only in the last decades that war has been "rehabilitated" in Western Europe and North America. Crusade studies have become almost an industry, focusing on the anniversary of the Latin conquest of Jerusalem in 1099. Even in the peaceful kingdom of Denmark, a new generation of scholars has dedicated themselves to understanding the reasons for crusade and how it was not just a phenomenon in Palestine but also in the Baltic. Crusading indulgences have been studied, and a spirituality of Christian war has been investigated. In this context Bernard's *In Praise of the New Knighthood* makes sense as a battle cry for a new type of monk and new type of soldier. It is possible to regret such a development as a far cry from what the monastic vocation was supposed to involve, but the fact is that Bernard and his contemporaries considered this new vocation to be a natural and necessary development in a society that needed good knights. Bernard thought he was contributing to a new type of knighthood, which would transform the way knights lived and died.

How can the contemporary observer, having seen the destructive wars taking place in the last decades in the Middle East and the catastrophes of Western involvement, in any way accept Bernard's arguments about the nobility of making war as a monk? There is a huge gap between the ideals he proposed and the loss of human life brought about by the Second Crusade and its aftermath. Fortunately for Bernard, he never went to the Middle East and could dream of Jerusalem as a heavenly city and be oblivious to its earthly reality. In this sense he failed to accept what he soon was forced to face: the brutality and meaninglessness of war.

It is questionable for the historian to treat topics that he or she finds unpalatable, and so I will give the last word on this subject to Watkin Williams, who in his biography of Bernard was less negative about Bernard's involvement in the new knighthood than I tend to be. Williams saw the treatise as being "to some extent of the nature of an apology. Good reasons had to be offered as to why it was right for the Church to give the sanction of a religious order to an organization ostensibly militant."[130] Certainly Bernard did provide many "good reasons," especially in contrasting the old knighthood in all its venality and self-indulgence to the new one he saw with the Templars, with their ascetic way of life. The ironic fact is that once they lost their foothold in Jerusalem, they ended up as the bankers of French and English kings. To this day "The Temple" station on the London Underground is a reminder of the immense riches that were accumulated by the successors of the new knighthood that Bernard praised. He of course could have no idea of what was to come. His own order would be attacked in the later Middle Ages for its wealth and lack of self-discipline. But in the twelfth century the Templars were a new way of living according to the sword and the cross. A noble vision that Bernard shared, for as long as it lasted. He had grown up in a knightly culture, and so it was natural and even inevitable for him to consider how knights could become good Christians. What better way than to fight for the Lord in genuine dedication to a life of prayer? What Benedict never dreamed of, Bernard helped to create.

13. Can Bernard's liturgical sermons be used as sources for his inner life?

In describing Bernard's inner life, I have not given a great deal of attention to his sermons, at least to those he preached in connection with the solemnities of the Church year. I have at times referred to his Sermons on the Song of Songs, the eighty-six sermons from the mid-1130s to the time of his death. They are his literary masterpiece, and it is not by accident that the standard edition of his writings begins with two volumes containing these sermons. Few of the sermons can be dated, however. The *Sermons in Praise of the Virgin Mother* belong to the time of Bernard's illness, 1119–20. Likewise his Sermons on Psalm 90/91, "He who dwells in the shelter of the most high," were given during Lent 1139, after his return from Italy and the death of his brother Gerard. But the sermons for the liturgical year can be placed only in terms of Bernard's abbacy at Clairvaux, to about 1125–30 and 1138–53.

The sermons are commonly used as a guide to Bernard's thinking, but they also deserve to take their place in any study of him as a person. They tell us of his life as he reflected on the meaning of the Christian message in terms of the liturgical year. In the words of Gerhard Winkler, who published the German translation of Bernard, "The texts are naturally also confessions."[131] Winkler was probably thinking in terms of Augustine's *Confessions*, which contain declarations of belief seen through the writer's experience.

As for the perennial question of to what extent the published sermons reflect what Bernard actually said in Clairvaux's chapter house, we will never really know. Certainly the spoken word must have been less demanding and complex than the written one. But the sermons as they were transmitted outside Clairvaux reflect what Bernard wanted the world to witness in terms of his understanding of Christian revelation and the Church year. Bernard loved the written word, even if in some of his letters he said that the spoken word was better. Whatever he allowed to emerge from his literary workshop is what he intended to reflect his own inner life, thought and feeling. In

Bernard's contribution to twelfth-century experience we find both *intellectus* and *affectus*.

As an illusration of how Bernard constructed his sermons and how they cast light on his person, we can take the six sermons preached for the solemnity of the Ascension.[132] The number of sermons is large, compared to the four for Easter, and it seems signifcant that Bernard spent so much time and effort conveying his understanding of Christ's departure from this earth. But it was not only the fact of Jesus's ascent into heaven that concerned Bernard. He was fascinated with the idea of ascent and descent in this life and the next one. He showed awareness of spiritual and physical movement, of moral growth or decay.

Sermon 1 recounts the Gospel reading itself, from Mark 16:14, where Jesus appears to the apostles and exhorts them to preach, promising: "These signs will accompany those who believe." For Bernard what mattered was not the outward signs but the inner ones. Faith operates through love as compunction of the heart removes sins. Thus Bernard provided a spiritual and moral interpretation of Christ's words that they "will place their hands on the sick and they will be well." This grace is seen in terms of the forgiveness of sins. For a Bernard who was sought after for physical cures, especially on his Rhineland trip, this is a surprising moment of exegesis.

Sermon 2 tells how the Ascension brings everything to its fulfillment. It is a joyful feast that is the final proof of Christ's power and might. Bernard asked how the apostles must have felt when Jesus left them. They were afraid and sorrowful. He formulated a prayer, as he regularly did in the course of his sermons, moving from providing his exposition to speaking directly to God or Jesus. "Who will console me, Lord Jesus," Bernard asked, "because I did not see you hanging from a cross? . . . How could you have left me without farewell?[133] This type of direct address recalls the way Anselm in his prayers expressed his pain and longing for Jesus. Bernard described how difficult it is to ascend, how easy to descend. There are hardly any who follow you, Lord Jesus. His sermon ends in the exclamation: "Blessed is he who everywhere has you as his guide." There is a sense of completion or fulfillment here.

Sermon 3 focuses on intellect and affect, where *affectus* means more than "inclination," for the term suggests emotional-spiritual interior life. Both intellect and affect have to be unified. The apostles were used to having Jesus in the flesh and refused to listen to the prospect of his departure. Their intellect was enlightened, but their affect was not yet purified. Bernard addressed his monks and claimed that their understanding was enlightened, but the affect was not pure. Some found the monastic life easy and sweet, while others were rebellious: "They share in our tribulation but not in our consolation." For Bernard the body must be purified so that the Spirit can be received. He looked forward to Pentecost and the coming of the Holy Spirit.

Sermon 4 considers the various ways of ascending, in seeing the Ascension as the culmination of all the Church's solemnities. Bernard made use of Paul (Eph 4:10): "Christ who descended is the very one who ascended." Christ had to descend so that we could be taught how to ascend. The devil is an angel who has fallen from the heights and cannot ascend again. He shows humankind another mountain that we can ascend. We are in danger of repeating the mistake of our first ancestor in trying to ascend a false mountain. Bernard asked his brothers to flee this place. They were not to be burdened with worldly affairs but to continue a spiritual journey on which they ascend another mountain, where they hear Christ preaching. The remainder of the sermon describes further ascents, including §13: it is necessary to follow Christ as he ascends the cross. Bernard expressed a longing for union with Jesus.

Courage, forbearance, and concord are the themes of Sermon 5. The brothers showed courage in their conversion to the monastic life. There should be forbearance to its end and concord in their daily lives. The heavenly Jerusalem is built by those who show such virtues. In the first Christians waiting for the Holy Spirit to descend to them, Bernard saw a model for the community of Clairvaux.

The sixth and final sermon on the Ascension is the pièce de résistance, summing up the themes of the first five sermons and providing a sense of how Bernard perceived the brothers of Clairvaux. Again understanding (*intellectus*) and affect (*affectus*) provide the framework for a sermon. Bernard began with the Transfiguration and Peter's words "Lord, it is good for us to be here" (Mt 17:4). In this life there is an abundance of wickedness, and so it is necessary to lift up hearts to heaven and follow the Lord as he ascends. Bernard sought "peace which surpasses all understanding" (Phil 4:7), found in the celestial Jerusalem, where brothers dwell together in unity. Bernard praised monks "whose encouragement and way of life so fully instruct all." In almost all religious communities there are men filled with consolation, being joyful and cheerful.[134] But there are also those who are weak and remiss. Monastic discipline can hardly keep them back, and so their lives approach hell, for intellect opposes affect and affect intellect: "They share our tribulation but not our consolation."[135] Bernard asked why spiritual gifts are lacking in some monks, while there was an abundance of them for others. Here he continued his contrast between intellect and affect (§§10–11), and then he returned to the Gospel text, "Where I go, you cannot come" (Jn 8:21). He visualized the reaction of the apostles, their fear when they heard these words.[136] At the end of the sermon he anticipated the coming of the Holy Spirit but also made use of the story of Elijah and Elisha as a model for ascension in the Old Testament. The sermon concludes with an exhortation, in almost ecstatic language, to receive the coming of the Holy Spirit. We must empty ourselves and our "wretched delights," so that the Holy Spirit can fill us.[137]

This review of the contents especially of Sermon 6 reveals how Bernard perceived Clairvaux's brethren. The brother who hesitated in the life is considered a doubting Thomas: "Truth has no love for corners. . . . Truth stands in the open and delights in discipline, the common life and common undertakings."[138]Bernard provided a long list of the characteristics of the weak and remiss brother who has "obedience without dedication, their speech imprudent, their prayer lacking the heart's intention, and their reading without edification."[139] But he also saw good monks at Clairvaux, full of joy. The sermon provided a mirror of Clairvaux into which Bernard peered.

So far as I can tell, the Ascension sermons, and especially the final one, indicate that Bernard was positive about the life he experienced at Clairvaux. He saw the monastery as a viable way to eternal salvation, and even though he found in the community monks who did not live up to the requirements of the Rule in terms of intellect and affect, he was hopeful. Thus he functioned as a teacher showing his monks how to live their lives in the right manner. It can be objected, of course, that a sermon expresses hope and exhorts its audience but does not necessarily reflect the way things really are. But Bernard's pattern for life is essentially dynamic. There were ups and downs, ascents and descents, where the monk could combine intellect and affect in seeking the coming of the Holy Spirit and the "consolation and confirmation" the Spirit could provide.

Bernard invested so much in the Ascension because he saw it as a reflection of the life he found around him. There was constant movement up and down in a moral and spiritual universe. Bernard saw change and development in the monastic life, a dynamism of ascents and descents. The mystery of the Ascension of Christ became a central part of the Christian message and an incentive to the good life of the monastery.

Not all of Bernard's sermons can so easily be translated into a description and analysis of monastic life, but it is apparent that most of the sermons were meant for a monastic audience and intended to warn and encourage the monks of Clairvaux. At the same time Bernard knew that his sermons would be copied and appear elsewhere, and he seems to have had no qualms about the distribution of his work in this context. But the sermons are not easy sources for penetrating his inner life and affect, and my own brief review of the Ascension sermons will have to suffice as a hint of the riches to be found in this literature. Even though Bernard's writings are not overwhelming in number, as, for example, those of Aquinas are, each page is filled with both thought and feeling, and one could spend a lifetime in a monastic *lectio*, slow meditative reading of Bernard. However useful such an exercise might be, I have to leave the reader with just a taste of what Bernard offers. This introduction at least demonstrates how he expressed himself to his monks, appealed to their inner lives, and reflected on their everyday existences. He was very much the father abbot, giving his monks words of consolation, encouragement, and criticism that he believed they needed.

14. Did Bernard contribute to "the persecuting society"?

In the 1970s, when medieval studies was to some extent dominated by Marxist interpretations of history, there appeared two books by the English historian R. I. Moore that made a sober contribution to the debate about power and ideology. Moore's main interest was heresy, how it was identified as such by the Church and how it was opposed and sometimes rooted out in society.[140] Taking as his foundation the fact of heresy and the reaction to it, Moore published a much broader study in 1987, *The Formation of a Persecuting Society: Power and Deviance in Western Europe, 950–1250*.[141] Here he again focused on heresy, but his main interest now was not the heretics but the society that came to persecute them.

It would have been easy for Moore to classify Bernard of Clairvaux as one of the representatives of this persecuting society, but in point of fact Bernard does not get included in this company. In Moore's analysis, Bernard opposed heresy but did not contribute to the inquisitorial methods that were first set in place after his death. Moore saw Bernard as mainly a preacher against heretics, such as Henry of Lausanne: "It took a fullscale preaching mission complete with a battery of miracles from Saint Bernard of Clairvaux in 1145 to shake Henry's command over popular affection."[142] It was the bishop of Toulouse who apparently took Henry captive and imprisoned him, and here Bernard was not directly involved. But in Toulouse Bernard did establish that "the heretics, their supporters and all who gave them any help would not be eligible to give evidence or seek redress in the courts."[143] Heretics would be outcasts in society, a measure that was to be confirmed later in church councils and via the papal inquisition. Thus Bernard is seen at the beginning of a process that would become more and more restrictive, casting known heretics outside the functions of normal society. But it was, according to Moore, the Council of Reims in 1148 (which Bernard attended) that confirmed the end of a long-standing prohibition against the secular power's involvement in the punishment of heretics. It was not until 1178, however, that a papal mission to Toulouse, headed by a successor of Bernard's as abbot of Clairvaux, Henry de Marcy, "put the last major element of inquisitorial procedure in place."[144]

Cistercian abbots were used by the papacy in the last decades of the twelfth century to root out and preach against heresy in what today is the South of France. The last such figure was the papal delegate who was murdered in 1208, opening the way for the crusade against the Albigensians. Moore does not see Bernard as responsible for the central position of the Cistercian Order in the fight against heresy that took place after his death. He credits Bernard for his treatment of the Jews endangered by the fanaticism that arose with the Second Crusade: "Jewish chroniclers believed . . . that in 1146 only the intervention of Bernard of Clairvaux averted a repetition of the events of 1096 when the enthusiasm of the monk Ralph . . . led him to call for the killing of Jews in Europe."[145]

Moore saw Bernard's mission in the Languedoc as "the first occasion upon which opinion was really mobilized to identify the region as being in particular need of attention." But "the decisive turning point" did not come until 1178, after Count Raymond V's appeal to the pope and the French king. Moore thus looked upon Bernard as trying to awaken his surroundings to the fact of heresy in Languedoc but not as initiating the persecution that came only after his death. "It is little more than speculation that Bernard's mission involved the declaration of a concerted boycott in Toulouse," while "it is well established that these [Albi and Carcassonne] were the principal targets of the 1178 mission and its successors."[146]

Bernard emerges from Moore's analysis as a point of departure for the Church's response to heretical movements but not as a contributor to what he calls the persecuting society. The abbot of Clairvaux is seen mainly as a preacher, trying to oppose heretical movements with his own words and those of the Gospel. The *Vita Prima* makes it seem as though Bernard succeeded in wiping out heresy in Languedoc by seeing to it that the heretic Henry was "captured, brought in chains and handed over to the bishop."[147] Who carried out this action? Bernard does not seem to have reverted to force but left it to others.

Moore ends his book with a relatively moderate statement, that "the formation of what we have called the persecuting society was only one aspect . . . of some of the profound and spectacular innovations which made this period a turning point in European society."[148] He added that there was also "challenge or hesitation" about the methods leading to the persecuting society. In a conversation some years ago, he pointed out to me that his book is entitled *The Formation of a Persecuting Society,* not *the Persecuting Church.* He did not see the medieval Christian Church as a relentless organ of persecution of all those in society who were different. As in his treatment of Bernard, Moore saw figures who preferred to preach rather than to persecute.

A later study by Moore, *The First European Revolution,* provides an overview of the development of Western European church and society from about 970 to 1215.[149] Here he points out that Bernard was far harsher in his criticism of the papal court than the heretics Tanchelm of Antwerp and Arnold of Brescia. Moore contrasted Bernard's "celebrated but only partially successful preaching mission against heresy" in Languedoc with that of the abbot of Clairvaux Henry de Marcy: "Henry and his order continued to spearhead both the collection and editing of evidence of heretical activity in the region and the campaign against it." This took place, of course, decades after Bernard's death.[150]

Moore, not surprisingly, spends time on Abelard and Bernard and claims that "Abelard's career was ended by the western equivalent of Koranic literalism, as represented by Bernard of Clairvaux, but the memory of his fall saved other scholars from similar persecution."[151] This is the one time Moore makes use of the term "persecution" in connection with Bernard, and in my mind he exaggerates. Bernard's method of reading the Bible cannot be called "Koranic literalism." He encouraged his brothers to read the text meditatively and to allow themselves many different levels of textual comprehension. Bernard certainly did go after Abelard and got his theology condemned, but in the end, as we have seen, the abbots of Cîteaux and Cluny brought about a reconciliation.

The First European Revolution devotes attention to the failed condemnation of the theology of Gilbert de la Porrée in 1148. Moore sees this result as "the last of these great gladiatorial contests between the champions of the clerks and their monastic or episcopal rivals."[152] Moore found that "the clerks were mounting a collective defence of the interests which they would continue to advance so effectively." He thus advocates a distinction between traditional monastic theology and the new scholasticism, a separation that goes back to the work of Jean Leclercq. I find this view misleading, for Bernard's opposition to Abelard and Gilbert de la Porrée was based not on their methods but on their results. Bernard could provide a "scholastic" analysis of a question, such as with baptism. Every part of his theological analysis is based on the penetration of texts through comparisons and contrasts. In the end, monastic *lectio* is not all that far from scholastic *disputatio*.

R. I. Moore has provided a critical approach to the process that helped bring about the European society that became so dominant in modern times. In considering "the first European revolution," he has included Bernard of Clairvaux. The abbot of Clairvaux has received a relatively gentle treatment as a preacher, even though his Cistercian successors initiated the persecutions of heretics. My purpose here has not been to "whitewash" Bernard, nor to implicate him in what might be called the age of persecution that began in the thirteenth century. Bernard did involve himself and did his best to root out heretical views, but his commitment was limited. With Abelard he can of course be accused of creating a situation where the accused never had a chance to defend himself. Here Bernard was fanatical, but thanks to his own father abbot of Cîteaux, he was convinced to give Abelard a second chance.

15. Was Bernard "a sick man living on his nerves"?

In a detailed review of Jean Leclercq's *Monks and Love in Twelfth-Century France:Psycho-Historical Essays*, in the *Journal of Ecclesiastical History* (1980), the Oxford historian Beryl Smalley concluded with the following assertion:

> Rashly, indeed, I suggest that the psycho-historians might switch their attention from sex and aggression to food. Bernard's revulsion from eating, his indigestion described in the *Vita Prima*, his disgusted fascination with the menus of relaxed monasteries, expressed in his *Apologia ad Guillelmum,* the fact that his health improved when he left Clairvaux on Church business, unwillingly he said, but zestfully, are these psycho-somatic symptoms?
>
> All would agree that Bernard was "a poet, a genius and an innovator." Such men are generally maladjusted and difficult by reason of their sensitivity. I doubt whether Bernard was so exceptional. In any case, it adds to our wonder at his achievement to see him as a sick man living on his nerves.[153]

Beryl Smalley (1905–84) is best known for her pioneering work, *The Study of the Bible in the Middle Ages*. She became a central figure in Oxford medieval history and wrote this review late in life, possibly after she had been diagnosed with stomach cancer. She was told by doctors that she would last longer by eating less. My recollection of her is how she came to lunch in the summer of 1983 and ate nothing but a few peas and crusts of bread. Certainly she was fascinated by food. I recall another occasion when she described with great relish being invited to a fine Italian restaurant in North Oxford.

I became quite fond of Smalley's sharp tongue and incisive analytical instincts, and it is good to think that in her last years she developed a friendship with my Oxford supervisor, Sir Richard Southern. These were the days of psycho-history, and Jean Leclercq in the late 1970s had given a course of lectures at Oxford that became *Monks and Love*. Beryl Smalley was perceptive in trying to shift the historian's focus from what we would call genital sexuality to food. As I have previously indicated, Bernard's sexual temptations in the *Vita Prima* are the stuff of conventional hagiography, and we can learn almost nothing about sexual concerns from his Sermons on the Song of Songs, while William of Saint-Thierry's book I of the *Vita Prima* tells us a great deal about Bernard and his eating or not eating.

At the risk of returning to material already covered, I would like now to go back to William of Saint-Thierry and his view of Bernard's food consumption. From there I will consider some aspects of Bernard's own description of himself. Then I will conclude with Bernard as I see him. For readers who are looking for Bernard the saint, I may be a disappointment. Likewise for anyone who wants to see Bernard exposed as a phony, I will also fail to deliver the goods. I can only offer a unique human being whose life continues to fascinate, attract, and repel.

William described how Bernard ate not "for enjoyment but only because he was afraid of collapsing."[154] The intake of food for him was "like torture." William provided graphic detail: "His ruined stomach would immediaely vomit, undigested, whatever he had compelled to go down his throat. . . . Only with the greatest amount of pain" could the lower parts of the body "rid themselves of anything."[155] The Latin is graphic: *nonnisi cum gravi tormento . . .*

The Bernard that William described kept careful track of whatever he ate: "If he ever found that he exceeded the usual measure in the slightest amount, he would not let it remain unpunished." But William added that even if Bernard wanted to eat more, he would have been incapable of doing so: "His habit of frugality became second nature for him." William did not consider the possibility that Bernard was incapable of consuming more food. In spite of these problems, the young Bernard was sent to found Clairvaux in 1115, but there his digestive problems increased, and his friend Bishop William of Châlons intervened on his behalf at the General Chapter, probably in 1119, and got permission for Bernard to be removed from the monastery and to be excused from all forms of austerity. William was concerned about the care given Bernard, who was dissatisfied with his caretaker.[156]

On returning to Clairvaux, Bernard lived in utmost frugality. William narrated how he vomited in choir and bothered the brothers nearby, so he had placed a container there into which he could empty his discharge.[157] Apparently this solution did not last long: "He was finally forced to quit the gatherings" and to remain apart from the community. A significant number of chapters in the first book of the *Vita Prima* are dedicated to Bernard's asceticism and especially his relationship to food and digestion. William admired Bernard's self-discipline but also admitted that his habits became a problem for members of his community. His description can of course be dismissed as hagiographical convention, but the amount of detail indicates that he was presenting more than a literary cliché. He was telling his audience of the Bernard he knew and admired but also toward whom he harbored reservations about the extremity of his friend's self-denial.

How did Bernard himself interpret his way of life and reconcile extreme asceticism with his obligation as an abbot to look after the needs of his community? We have only a few hints from him, but they are worth considering. Bernard made use of his enforced absence from the community in about 1119 to write his *Homilies in Praise of the Blessed Virgin Mary*. In his Preface he indicated that he had long wanted to compose the work but had been too busy. Now "sickness prevents me from joining the brothers in community," so he could devote himself to the task. Thus for Bernard, illness provided a welcome respite from business and so an opportunity for creativity. We cannot be certain whether Bernard wrote this Preface while he was ill or if he added it after his return to Clairvaux. He admitted that his brothers at Clairvaux did not necessarily require this work, but he did so in order "to satisfy my own devotion."[158] Thus physical illness and artistic creatvity could coexist for Bernard.

Bernard's sermons to Mary were original. He was one of the first medieval writers to consider the role of Joseph in the economy of salvation: "To him it was given not only to see and to hear what many kings and prophets had longed to see and did not see, to hear and did not hear, but even to carry him, to take him by the hand, to hug and kiss him, to feed him and to keep him safe."[159] There was a new emphasis here on the humanity of Christ but also on the meaning of fatherhood. It can be asked whether Bernard's enforced isolation from his community actually gave him the necessary room to consider such matters in a new way.

Late in the 1130s, Bernard looked back on this early period of his monastic life and spoke of how he then could feel "coldness and hardness of heart."[160] In seeking relief he looked for a friend to help him out. When he found such a person, he was grateful but also "embarrassed and humiliated." Bernard claimed to have been bothered that the presence of a human person had a greater impact on him than the experience of God's presence: "I feel ashamed that the remembrance of human goodness should affect me more powerfully than the thought of God." Bernard concluded that it had to be this way. Here he used, appropriately, the image of food and nourishment: "One and the same food is medicine for the sick and nourishment for the convalescent. It gives strength to the weak and pleasure to the strong. One and the same food cures sickness, preserves health, builds up the body, titillates the palate." Here the food of human kindness became a necessary form of nurture. Bernard admitted that he needed other people, even though he was driven by a corresponding need to separate himself from others.

As I see him, Bernard was indeed a sick man living on his nerves. But physically and psychologically he was able to restore himself in spite of his illness, whatever we choose to call it: anorexia, nervous breakdown, existential youth crisis? He had the support of his biological brothers, as well as that presumably of his father abbot Stephen and probably also many of the brothers of Clairvaux. His greatness may lie in the fact that he reconciled his creativity with his asceticism. Bernard learned to live with and on his nerves. He experienced a crisis of identity, physical collapse, and the gradual recreation of the self. Here the medieval term *conversio* is the best indication of what took place in Bernard, the turning of self away from inward obsessions toward an outward embrace of his community and his search for God.

It was not easy to be Bernard, but his surroundings did what they could to help him pull through. He seems to have grown in insight and self-understanding as he reached out for his friends, and they for him. Such a conclusion is not intended to be hagiographical. Bernard was a human being with talents and limitations. His genius lay in his writings and to some extent in his human bonding. He managed to overcome the crisis of his youth and achieve self-integration. Here we meet Bernard's spirituality and special Cistercian charism: a sense of identification with his brethen sharing in the life and sufferings of Christ. Thanks to his brothers, Bernard could to some extent get over his illnesses and stop living on his nerves. He became Bernard: father, brother, friend, churchman, writer, polemicist, and many more roles. In these roles he transcended his own time and transmitted himself to the centuries to come as a representative of Christian spirituality and monastic life.

❧ NOTES

Fifteen Questions about Bernard: The Background for My Portrait

1. E. Rozanne Elder, "The Influence of Clairvaux: The Experience of William of Saint-Thierry," *Cistercian Studies Quarterly* 51 (2016): 55–75.

2. See Corpus Christianorum: Continuatio Mediaevalis 89B (Turnhout: Brepols, 2010), ed. Paul Verdeyen. The *Fragmenta* are edited by Christine Vande Veire.

3. See "Canute," in David Hugh Farmer, *The Oxford Dictionary of Saints* (Oxford: Oxford University Press, 1992), 84. His *vita* or hagiography is found in M. Cl. Gertz, *Vitae Sanctorum Danorum* (Copenhagen: G.E.C. Gad, 1908–12).

4. *Collectaneum Clarevallense*, ed. Olivier Legendre, Corpus Christianorum: Continuatio Mediaevalis 208 (Turnhout: Brepols, 2005).

5. The Latin text, *Exordium Magnum Cisterciense*, was edited by Bruno Griesser (Rome: Editiones Cistercienses, 1961). EM = the translation: *The Great Beginning of Cîteaux*, trans. Benedicta Ward and Paul Savage (Collegeville MN: Liturgical Press and Cistercian Publications, 2012).

6. EM II.7.

7. Elphège Vacandard, *Vie de Saint Bernard, abbé de Clairvaux*, 2 vols. (Paris: Victor Lecoffre, 1895, 1897).

8. Watkin Williams, *Saint Bernard of Clairvaux* (1935; repr., Westminster, MD: Newman Press, 1952), x (hereafter Williams).

9. Bernard McGinn, *The Great Cistercian Mystics: A History* (New York: Crossroad, 2019), ch. 1, "Bernard of Clairvaux: The Great Contemplative."

10. Ailbe J. Luddy, *Life and Teaching of St. Bernard* (Dublin: M.H.Gill & Son, 1937).

11. Jean Leclercq, *L'amour des lettres et le désir de Dieu: Initiation aux auteurs monastiques du moyen age* (Paris: Éditions du Cerf, 1957).

12. Adriaan H. Bredero, *Bernard of Clairvaux: Between Cult and History* (Grand Rapids, MI: Eerdmans, 1996).

13. Christopher Holdsworth, "Bernard as a Father Abbot," in Brill Companion, 169–219, quote on 215.

14. Christopher Holdsworth, "The Early Writings of Bernard of Clairvaux," *Cîteaux: Commentarii Cistercienses* 45 (1994): 21–60.

15. Jean Leclercq, *A Second Look at Saint Bernard* (Kalamazoo, MI: Cistercian Publications, 1990), 101.

16. Jean Leclercq, *Recueil d'études sur saint Bernard et ses écrits*, vols. 1–5 (Rome: Edizioni di Storia et Letteratura, 1962–92).

17. *Bernhard von Clairvaux: Sämtliche Werke*, ed. Gerhard B. Winkler, vols. 1–10 (Innsbruck: Tyrolia Verlag, 1990–99).

18. Bruno Scott James, *Saint Bernard of Clairvaux: An Essay in Biography* (London: Hodder & Stoughton, 1957).

19. M. B. Pranger, *Bernard of Clairvaux and the Shape of Monastic Thought: Broken Dreams* (Leiden: Brill, 1994).

20. Pranger, *Shape of Monastic Thought*, 173.

21. M. B. Pranger, "Bernard the Writer," in *A Companion to Bernard of Clairvaux*, ed. Brian Patrick McGuire (Leiden: Brill, 2011), 239.

22. Pranger, Brill Companion, 241.

23. Mette B. Bruun, "Bernard of Clairvaux and the Landscape of Salvation," in Brill Companion, 253.

24. Pierre Aube, *Saint Bernard de Clairvaux* (Paris: Fayard, 2003).

25. Caroline Walker Bynum, *Jesus as Mother: Studies in the Spirituality of the High Middle Ages* (Berkeley: University of California Press, 1982).

26. Paschal Phillips, "The Presence—and Absence—of Bernard of Clairvaux in the Twelfth-Century Chronicles," in *Bernardus Magister*, ed. John R. Sommerfeldt, Cîteaux: Texts and Documents 42 (Kalamazoo, MI: Cistercian Publications, 1992), 35–53.

27. Michael Casey, "Toward a Methodology for the *Vita Prima*: Translating the First Life into Biography," in *Bernardus Magister*, 55–70, reference to Geoffrey on 61.

28. Michael Casey, "Reading Saint Bernard: The Man, the Medium, the Message," in Brill Companion, 62–107.

29. Michael Casey, *Athirst for God: Spiritual Desire in Bernard of Clairvaux's Sermons on the Song of Songs* (Kalamazoo, MI: Cistercian Publications, 1988).

30. Casey, "Reading Saint Bernard," 106.

31. Jean Leclercq, *Women and St. Bernard of Clairvaux* (Kalamazoo, MI: Cistercian Publications, 1989); Leclercq, *La femme et les femmes dans l'oeuvre de Saint Bernard* (Paris: Téqui, 1982).

32. SBO 7, no. 39; James, no. 41.

33. See Leclercq, *Women and St. Bernard*, 15–16.

34. SBO 8, no. 315; James, no. 376.

35. SBO 7, no. 116; James, no. 119.

36. SBO 8, no. 117; James, no. 120.

37. SBO 8, no. 366; James, no. 390.

38. Leclercq, *Women and St. Bernard*, 67.

39. VP I.30, trans. p. 34.

40. Leclercq, *Women and St. Bernard*, 123.

41. VP I.20, trans. p. 23.

42. VP I.22, trans. p. 25.

43. VP I.29 and 30, trans. p. 33.

44. VP I.29, trans. p. 33.

45. VP I.38–39, trans. pp. 43–45.

46. SC 56.5.

47. SC 30.12.

48. Bernard McGinn, "The Spiritual Teaching of the Early Cistercians," in *The Cambridge Companion to the Cistercian Order*, ed. Mette Birkedal Bruun (Cambridge: Cambridge University Press, 2013), 223.

49. VP I.35, trans. p. 40. Reference to Song of Songs 2:4.

50. Bernard's letter to Aelred is SBO 8, no. 523; James, no. 177. Aelred of Rievaulx, *Mirror of Charity*, trans. Elizabeth Connor (Kalamazoo, MI: Cistercian Publications, 1990).

51. See my *Brother and Lover: Aelred of Rievaulx* (New York: Crossroad, 1994).

52. SC 65.4.

53. VP I.6–7, trans. pp. 9–10.

54. SBO 8, no. 250; James, no. 326.

55. VP II.3, trans. p. 82.

56. SBO 8, no. 189; James, no. 239.

57. VP II.3, trans. p. 82.

58. SBO 8, no. 327; James, no. 236.

59. SBO 8, no. 330; James, no. 242.

60. VP I.45, trans. p. 51.

61. VP I.46, trans. p. 52.

62. SC 26.10.

63. SBO 7, no. 143; James, no. 144.

64. Holdsworth, "Bernard as a Father Abbot," Brill Companion, 215.

65. André Seguin, "Bernard et la seconde croisade," in *Bernard 1953*, 394.

66. Seguin, 396.

67. Seguin, 397.

68. Seguin, 400.

69. SBO 8, no. 457; James, no. 458.

70. SBO 8, no. 363; not translated in James.

71. Seguin, 406.

72. SBO 8, no. 288; James, no. 410.

73. Seguin, 409.

74. Seguin, 409: *une des plus beaux fleurons, le plus beau peut-être, de l'oeuvre de saint Bernard, qui dans l'adversité rappele au monde que les saints sont les plus grands des héros.*

75. Jean Leclercq, "Saint Bernard's Attitude toward War," in *Studies in Medieval Cistercian History II*, ed. John R. Sommerfeldt (Kalamazoo, MI: Cistercian Publications, 1976), 1–39.

76. Leclercq, "Attitude toward War," 6.

77. Leclercq, 12.

78. Leclercq, 20–21.

79. Leclercq, 39.

80. Giles Constable, "A Report of a Lost Sermon by St Bernard on the Failure of the Second Crusade," *Studies in Medieval Cistercian History* (Shannon: Irish University Press, 1971), 49–54, at 51.

81. Giles Constable, introduction to *The Second Crusade and the Cistercians*, ed. Michael Gerver (New York: Palgrave Macmillan, 1992), xx.

82. John G. Rowe, "The Origins of the Second Crusade: Pope Eugenius III, Bernard, and Louis VII," in Gerver, *The Cistercians and the Second Crusade*, 79–90, at 87.

83. George Ferzoco, "The Origin of the Second Crusade," in Gerver, *The Cistercians and the Second Crusade*, 91–100.

84. Brenda Bolton, "The Cistercians in the Aftermath of the Second Crusade," in Gerver, *The Cistercians and the Second Crusade*, 131–40, at 138.

85. James, no. 391. Corresponds to SBO 8, no. 363.

86. "The Chronicle of Solomon Bar Simson," in *The Jews and the Crusaders: Hebrew Chronicles of the First and Second Crusades* (1969; repr., Hoboken NJ: KTAV, 1996), 17–72.

87. Robert Chazan, "The Report of Ephraim of Bonn," *Church, State, and Jew in the Middle Ages* (West Orange, NJ: Behrman House, 1980), 107–8. I am grateful to Jamie Griffin for pointing this reference in my direction.

88. David Berger, "The Attitude of St. Bernard of Clairvaux toward the Jews," *Proceedings of the American Academy for Jewish Research* 40 (1972): 89–108.

89. Berger, 95, 97, 99.

90. Berger, 100.

91. Bernard's phrase is *affectus in lucris totus erat*, SC 60.3.

92. Berger, 105.

93. Berger, 107.

94. Berger, 108.

95. Berger, 108.

96. For background, see my chapter "Constitutions and the General Chapter," in Bruun, *The Cambridge Companion to the Cistercian Order*, 87–99.

97. Chrysogonus Waddell, ed., *Narrative and Legislative Texts from Early Cîteaux* (Cîteaux: Commentarii Cistercienses, 1999).

98. Jean de la Croix Bouton, "*Negotia Ordinis*," in *Bernard 1953*, 147–82.

99. VP I.32, trans. p. 37.

100. Bouton, "*Negotia Ordinis*," 152.

101. SBO 7, no. 4; James, no. 4.

102. Bouton, 174–75.

103. Bouton, 173.

104. SBO 8, no. 270; James, no. 340.

105. Bouton, 176.

106. SBO 7, no. 7, §16; James, no. 8, p. 35.

107. Bouton, 178.

108. Chrysogonus Waddell, "Notes towards the Exegesis of a Letter by Saint Stephen Harding," in *Noble Piety and Reformed Monasticism*, ed. E. Rozanne Elder, Studies in Medieval Cistercian History (Kalamazoo, MI: Cistercian Publications, 1981), 10–39.

109. Bouton, 181–82.

110. Holdsworth, "Bernard as a Father Abbot," 215.

111. "Chronica Alberici Monachi Trium Fontium," in *Monumenta Germaniae Historica: Scriptores* 23, ed. G. H. Pertz (Leipzig, 1925), 828.

112. "Prologue to the Cistercian Antiphonary," introduction by Chrysogonus Waddell, in *The Works of Bernard of Clairvaux*, vol. 1, *Treatises I* (Shannon: Irish University Press, 1970), 161. SBO 3, pp. 515–16.

113. EM I.23.

114. Bredero, 227.

115. Brian Patrick McGuire, *Friendship and Community: The Monastic Experience, 350–1250* (Ithaca: Cornell University Press, 2010), 231–95.

116. Bredero, 228.

117. Giles Constable, *The Letters of Peter the Venerable* (Cambridge, MA: Harvard University Press, 1967), vol. 2, pp. 23–28.

118. Bredero, 231.

119. Bredero, 233.

120. Constable, *Letters of Peter the Venerable*, vol. 1, no. 29.

121. Bredero, 234–35.

122. Bredero, 244; Constable, *Letters of Peter the Venerable*, vol. 1, no. 181, p. 423.

123. Bredero, 247.

124. McGuire, *Friendship and Community*, 251–52.

125. McGuire, 256–57; Constable, *Letters of Peter the Venerable*, vol. 1, no. 111, pp. 276–77.

126. Bernard de Clairvaux, *In Praise of the New Knighthood*, trans. Conrad Greenia, in *The Works of Bernard of Clairvaux: Treatises III* (Kalamazoo, MI: Cistercian Publications, 1977), ch. 3.6; SBO 3, p. 218.

127. *In Praise* 4.7, trans. p. 139.

128. *In Praise* 4.8, trans. p. 141.

129. *Bernard 1953*, 673.

130. Williams, 238.

131. Winkler, *Bernhard von Clairvaux*, vol. 28, p. 28: "Die Texte sind natürlich auch Bekenntnisse."

132. SBO 5, pp. 123–60; Bernard of Clairvaux, *Sermons for the Summer Season*, trans. Beverly Mayne Kienzle (Kalamazoo, MI: Cistercian Publications, 1991), 29–68.

133. Sermon 2.4, trans. p. 34.

134. Sermon 6.5–7, trans. pp. 59–60.

135. Sermon 6, SBO 5, p. 154. The Latin is so elegant that it deserves citation: *Socii plane tribulationis sed non consolationis.*

136. Sermon 6.12.

137. Sermon 6.15, trans. p. 67.

138. Sermon 6.13, trans. p. 65.

139. Sermon 6.7, trans. p. 61.

140. R. I. Moore, *The Origins of European Dissent* (London: Allen Lane, 1977).

141. R. I. Moore, *The Formation of a Persecuting Society: Power and Deviance in Western Europe, 950–1250* (Oxford: Blackwell, 1990).

142. Moore, *Formation of a Persecuting Society*, 20.

143. Moore, *Formation*, 25.

144. Moore, *Formation*, 26.

145. Moore, *Formation*, 117.

146. Moore, *Formation*, 145.

147. VP III.17.

148. Moore, *Formation*, 152.

149. R. I. Moore, *The First European Revolution* (Oxford: Blackwell, 2000).

150. Moore, *First European Revolution*, 142.

151. Moore, *Revolution*, 170.

152. Moore, *Revolution*, 126.

153. Beryl Smalley, review of *Monks and Love in Twelfth-Century France*, by Jean Leclercq, *Journal of Ecclesiastical History* 31 (1980): 108–10.

154. VP I.22, trans. p. 25.

155. Corpus Christianorum: Continuatio Mediaevalis 89B, p. 50.

156. VP I.33, trans. pp. 38–39.

157. VP I.40, trans. pp. 45–46.

158. Bernard of Clairvaux, *Homilies in Praise of the Virgin Mary*, trans. Marie-Bernard Saïd (Kalamazoo, MI: Cistercian Publications, 1993), 3.

159. Homily 2.16, trans. p. 29.

160. SC 14.6.

❧ Sources and References

English translations of the works of Bernard of Clairvaux, as well as the *Vita Prima*, appear courtesy of Cistercian Publications, Inc. © 2008 and © 2015, by Order of Saint Benedict, Collegeville, Minnesota. Used with permission.

Major Primary Sources

EM = *Exordium Magnum Cisterciense*, ed. Bruno Griesser (Rome: Editiones Cistercienses, 1961). The great collection of stories from the first century of Cistercian life. I provide book and chapter numbers: thus I.23 = book I, chapter 23. Translated by Benedicta Ward and Paul Savage and edited by E. Rozanne Elder as *The Great Beginning of Cîteaux* (Collegeville, MN: Cistercian Publications and Liturgical Press, 2012). A new and important edition of Herbert of Clairvaux's *Liber Miraculorum* is found in Giancarlo Zichi, Graziano Fois, and Stefano Mula, eds., Corpus Christianorum Continuatio Mediaevalis: Exempla Medii Aevi 8 (Turnhout: Brepols, 2017).

Fragmenta = Notes made by Bernard's secretary, Geoffrey of Auxerre, on his life, with an addition by Raynald of Clairvaux, now published together with VP (see below).

James = Bruno Scott James, trans., *The Letters of St. Bernard of Clairvaux* (Kalamazoo, MI: Cistercian Publications, 1998; originally published by Burns and Oates, 1953), with a helpful new introduction by Beverley Mayne Kienzle. For the letters I have made my own translations, but much helped by James. His numbering can differ from that of SBO, so I often give both.

PL = J. P. Migne, *Patrologia Latina*, vol. 182–185. Volume 185 contains materials for Bernard's biography, for the most part replaced by modern editions, but the *Vita Quarta* can be found here. Other references to Migne will be to volume and column.

SBO = The writings of Bernard of Clairvaux are almost all to be found in the critical edition published between 1957 and 1977 by Jean Leclercq and Henri Rochais: *Sancti Bernardi Opera*, vols. 1–8 (Rome: Editiones Cistercienses). My references are to volume and page, except for the letters of Bernard, found in volumes 7 and 8, which are cited by the number of the letter.

SC = Bernard's Sermons on the Song of Songs, contained in SBO 1 and 2. These are cited by sermon and paragraph number: thus, SC (= *Sermones in Cantica*) 2.3. The English translations in Cistercian Publications appear in four volumes.

VP = The *Vita Prima* of Bernard, now available in a critical edition edited by Paul Verdeyen in the series Corpus Christianorum: Continuatio Mediaevalis 89B, under the works of William of Saint-Thierry (Turnhout: Brepols, 2010). My references are to book and chapter: thus I.23 = book I, chapter 23. Translated by Hilary Costello as *The First Life of Bernard of Clairvaux* (Collegeville, MN: Cistercian Publications and Liturgical Press, 2015).

Major Secondary Sources

Bernard 1953 = *Bernard de Clairvaux*, Commission d'Histoire de l'Ordre de Cîteaux 3 (Paris: Éditions Alsatia, 1953).

Bredero = Adriaan H. Bredero, *Bernard of Clairvaux: Between Cult and History* (Grand Rapids, MI: Eerdmans, 1996). Translation of the original Dutch version (1993).

Brill Companion = *A Companion to Bernard of Clairvaux*, ed. Brian Patrick McGuire (Leiden: Brill, 2011).

Gastaldelli = Ferruccio Gastaldelli, "Anmerkungen und historischer Kommentar," in *Bernhard von Clairvaux: Sämtliche Werke*, ed. Gerhard B. Winkler (Innsbruck: Tyrolia Verlag, 1992). See especially volumes 2 and 3, Bernard's letters, where Gastaldelli's datings are invaluable.

Vacandard = Elphège Vacandard, *Vie de Saint Bernard, abbé de Clairvaux*, 2 vols. (Paris: V. Lecoffre, 1895, 1897). The most authoritative of Bernard biographies to date.

Williams = Watkin Williams, *Saint Bernard of Clairvaux* (1935; repr., Westminster, MD: Newman Press, 1952).

References by Chapter

Introduction: In Pursuit of a Difficult Saint

For the relics of Saint Bernard, see the account by the Comte de Montalembert from 1846, *Sur les reliques de S. Bernard et de S. Malchie,* in PL 185:1661–1714, esp. 1699–1700.

For the grave of Abelard and Heloise at Père Lachaise, see https://www.solosophie.com/heloise-and-abelard/. See also M. T. Clanchy's outstanding biography, *Abelard: A Medieval Life* (Oxford: Blackwell, 1997, 1999), 328.

I was told about Umberto Eco's view of Bernard by a Dutch colleague who had been in contact with him in order to make a translation of *The Name of the Rose*, though I have been unable to find the assertion in Eco's own works.

R. W. Southern's contributions to medieval studies in the twentieth century were immense. He published a classic biography of Saint Anselm in 1966 (*Saint Anselm and His Biographer*) but always claimed to be dissatisfied with it. When the publisher encouraged him to bring the work up to date, Southern published a completely new biography in 1990: *Saint Anselm: A Portrait in a Landscape* (Cambridge: Cambridge University Press, 1990).

Stories about Bernard's being tempted by women: VP I.7.

Bernard's lament for his brother Gerard: SC 26.3–13.

For medieval letters, see Giles Constable, *Letters and Letter-Collections* (Turnhout: Brepols, 1976).

1. A Time of Hope and Change

A standard treatment of the period is Giles Constable, *The Reformation of the Twelfth Century* (Cambridge: Cambridge University Press, 1996). Constable's title has inspired me to use the term "reformation" to describe the Church's evolution at this time.

Another classic is R. W. Southern, *Western Society and the Church in the Middle Ages* (Harmondsworth, Eng.: Penguin, 1970). Southern linked the development of the Church with that of society in general.

Southern's *Medieval Humanism and Other Studies* (Oxford: Blackwell, 1970) provides insightful introductions to the world of the twelfth century. It contributes greatly to our understanding of the period in which Bernard lived.

Perhaps the most comprehensive and insightful introduction to Western monasticism is Gert Melville's *The World of Medieval Monasticism: Its History and Forms of Life* (Collegeville, MN: Liturgical Press and Cistercian Publications, 2016).

Publications on the First Crusade are legion. Still useful is Steven Runciman, *A History of the Crusades,* vol. 1, *The First Crusade* (Cambridge: Cambridge University Press, 1962).

For John of Fécamp, see my "John of Fécamp and Anselm of Bec: A New Language of Prayer," in *Prayer and Thought in Monastic Tradition: Essays in Honour of Benedicta Ward*, ed. Santha Bhattacharji, Rowan William, and Dominic Mattos (London: Bloomsbury, 2014), 153–66.

Treatments of the Vikings are legion and have a tendency to heroize these pirates. Seeing them in the context of European civilization, Christopher Dawson in 1932 provided an introduction in *The Making of Europe: An Introduction to the History of European Unity* (Washington, DC: Catholic University of America Press, 2003).

2. A Saint's Origins

FONTAINES-LÈS-DIJON

For Bernard's family, see Jean Richard, "Le milieu familial," in *Bernard 1953*, 3–15. Perhaps the most complete study of Bernard's youth is Ferruccio Gastaldelli, "I primi vent'anni di San Bernardo: Problemi e interpretazioni," in *Studi su San Bernardo e Goffredo di Auxerre* (Florence: Sismel, 2001), 3–41.

Vita Quarta on Aleth: PL 185:535D.

William of Saint-Thierry on Aleth: VP I.5. Gerard as a knight: VP I.11.

The knights whom Bernard regaled with ale: VP I.55.

The knights became students who drank wine, not beer, in the account of Bernard's life by Jacobus de Voragine, in *The Golden Legend* (for August 20), trans. Granger Ryan and Helmut Ripperger (New York: Arno Press, 1969), 476.

Aleth's dream: VP I.2. Her nursing her own children: VP I.1.

Bernard's headache and the soothsayer: VP I.4.

CHÂTILLON-SUR-SEINE

For Bernard's education, see Jean Marilier, "Les premières années: Les études à Châtillon," in *Bernard 1953*, 20–25.

See also Jacques Berlioz, *Un saint dans la ville: Bernard de Clairvaux à Châtillon-sur-Seine* (Saint-Julien-du-Sault: Éditions de l'Armancon, 1998). Berlioz has been a perennial inspiration in his study of medieval traditions about Bernard.

Bernard's devotion to his studies: VP I.3.

His dream of the birth of Jesus: VP I.4. Raynald's version: *Fragmenta*, p. 307.

The *Homilies in Praise of the Blessed Virgin Mary* are found in SBO 4, pp. 13–58. Translated by Marie-Bernard Saïd (Kalamazoo, MI: Cistercian Publications, 1979 and later).

The death of Aleth: *Vita Quarta* 1.6, PL 185:538. William's description of Aleth: VP I.5.

Bernard's age at his mother's death: Williams, 7; Vacandard, vol. 1, pp. 16–17.

The lactation: "Bernard and Mary's Milk: A Northern Contribution," in Brian Patrick McGuire, *The Difficult Saint: Bernard of Clairvaux and His Tradition* (Kalamazoo, MI: Cistercian Publications, 1991), esp. 196–204.

UNCERTAIN YEARS (1107–1111)

William on the attractiveness of Bernard: VP I.6.

His female temptresses: VP I.7.

Michael Casey was a plenary speaker at the 1990 Congress on Medieval Studies in Kalamazoo, marking the anniversary of Bernard's birth. I have not found this assertion in his published writings.

Berengar's invective: PL 178:1357.

This is not the place for a prolonged discussion, but I profited from a fruitful exchange of points of view with the Yale historian John Boswell. Prior to the publication of his landmark work on medieval homosexuality I had published an article on Anselm's sexuality, based on his letters, and concluded that Anselm expressed homoerotic attachments, without being homosexual, if that word even can be used about a medieval person. Boswell disagreed, and we tried to find some consensus about the vocabulary of medieval sexuality. We never came to full agreement, but I am grateful to Professor Boswell for having taken the time to respond to an obscure colleague. See my "Love, Friendship, and Sex in the Eleventh Century: The Experience of Anselm," *Studia Theologica* (Oslo) 28 (1974): 122–50; and John Boswell, *Christianity, Social Tolerance, and Homosexuality* (Chicago: University of Chicago Press, 1980).

PLAYING MONKS (1111–1112)

The moment of Bernard's conversion: VP I.9. Here as elsewhere I use the translation of Hilary Costello.

The house at Châtillon: VP I.15.

Leclercq's assertion about Bernard's early leadership is found in "La paternité de S. Bernard et les débuts de l'ordre cistercien," *Revue bénédictine* 103 (1993): 445–81. My response is in "Who Founded the Order of Cîteaux?," in *The Joy of Learning and the Love of God*, ed. E. Rozanne Elder (Kalamazoo, MI: Cistercian Publications, 1995), 389–413, esp. 405–8.

Brother Andrew's conversion: VP I.10.

For Leclercq's view of Bernard and women, see his *Women and St. Bernard of Clairvaux* (Kalamazoo, MI: Cistercian Publications, 1989). I will return to this matter in the Fifteen Questions about Bernard: The Background for My Portrait section.

Heloise's denigration of marriage is recounted by Abelard in his so-called *Historia Calamitatum*, the first letter in his collection.

Hugh of Macon: VP I.14.

The miserable brother: VP I.16. The *Fragmenta* do not contain this story.

Nivard: VP I.17. For Nivard in the *Fragmenta*, see ch. 11, p. 279.

The story of Humbeline, which I consider to be central in revealing Bernard's view of women, is found in VP I.30.

For the Cistercian official opening to women after Bernard's death, see Brigitte Degler-Spengler, "The Incorporation of Cistercian Nuns into the Order in the Twelfth and Thirteenth Century," in *Hidden Springs: Cistercian Monastic Women*, ed. John A. Nicholas and Lillian Thomas Shank, Medieval Religious Women 3 (Kalamazoo, MI: Cistercian Publications 1995), 85–134.

The monopoly on salvation to a favored few began to end with the Cistercians. They offered to their lay brothers "a full assurance of salvation to illiterate men," "virtually for the first time in the history of medieval western Christendom," as pointed out by R. W. Southern, *Western Society and the Church in the Middle Ages* (Harmondsworth, Eng.: Penguin, 1970), 259.

Geoffrey of Auxerre's physical description of Bernard: VP 3.1.

ENTERING CÎTEAUX (1113)

For the historical context in which Cîteaux was founded, the literature is rich, but a good point of departure remains Bede K. Lackner, *The Eleventh-Century Background of Cîteaux* (Washington, DC: Cistercian Publications, 1972).

For early Cîteaux, see Jane Burton and Julie Kerr, "The 'desert-place called Cîteaux'" in their *The Cistercians in the Middle Ages* (Woodbridge, Eng.: The Boydell Press, 2011).

William's claim that Cîteaux suffered from few vocations before Bernard's entrance: VP I.18.

The *Exordium Parvum* can be found in Latin and English translation in Chrysogonus Waddell, ed., *Narrative and Legislative Texts from Early Cîteaux* (Cîteaux: Commentarii Cistercienses, 1999), esp. xvi and xvii, 436–39 on the sorrow of the monks under Alberic because of lack of recruitment and their joy under Stephen because the monastery began to grow. This text is more readily available in Pauline Matarasso's superb translation, *The Cistercian World: Monastic Writings of the Twelfth Century* (London: Penguin, 1993), 7–9.

See Bredero, pp. 201–2.

I have heard Michael Casey using the term "Cistercian propaganda machine," but I cannot find it in his writings. The expression has become fairly common, as in Frederic L. Cheyette, *Ermengard of Narbonne and the World of the Troubadours* (Ithaca: Cornell University Press, 2001), 329.

For Abbot Stephen of Cîteaux, see my "Who Founded the Order of Cîteaux," cited above under "Playing Monks."

Bernard's desire to "disappear": VP I.19. The order to leave bodies outside: VP I.20. Michael Casey has considered Bernard's seeming lack of awareness of his surroundings, in "Bernard the Observer," *Goad and Nail*, ed. E. Rozanne Elder, Studies in Medieval Cistercian History 10 (Kalamazoo, MI: Cistercian Publications, 1986), 1–20.

Bernard and sleep: VP I.21. His attitude toward food: VP I.22. Geoffrey of Auxerre provides further detail about his problematic digestion in VP III.2.

Beryl Smalley's remark is found in her review of *Monks and Love in Twelfth-Century France*, by Jean Leclercq, in *Journal of Ecclesiastical History* 31 (1980): 109.

Bernard's conviction that others were much more perfect than himself: VP I.22.

The assertion that oaks and beeches were Bernard's teachers: VP I.23. See his letter to Aelred of Rievaulx: SBO 8, no. 523; James, no. 177. Also SBO 7, no. 106; James, no. 107.

Bernard's solitude: VP I.24. Such passages are of course the stuff of hagiography, and even modern Cistercian monks have confided in me that they have difficulty believing such stories. But their source is William, who knew Bernard intimately, and so it would be too facile to reject out of hand such a description.

Abbot Stephen's correction of Bernard when he was a novice: EM I.23. For Stephen and the making of the Cistercian Order, see my "Who Founded the Order of Cîteaux?," cited above under "Playing Monks." Today the Cistercian Order has a solemnity or feast for all three founders of Cîteaux: Robert of Molesme, Alberic, and Stephen. In this way no one is left out!

Bernard's absorption of the word and meaning of Scripture described by William: VP I.24. Geoffrey's description of Bernard in this regard: VP III.6.

The description of coldness when Bernard was in his early period as monk: SC 14.6. Here, as in so much else from medieval literature, it has been modern practice to dismiss what seems to be personal and consider it literary filling. I read such a passage as an expression of a common Cistercian practice: using one's own experience as a way to encourage one's listeners or readers. Thus the self became an *exemplum*, and the speaker/writer was indeed making use of personal experience.

Bernard on community: SC 29.4. William on Bernard as a preacher: VP I.24.

3. From the New Monastery to the Valley Of Light, 1115–1124

Founding Clairvaux

Abbot Stephen's apparently surprising choice of Bernard: VP I.25.

Clairvaux's foundation charter: Williams, 19.

In describing the early history of the Danish Cistercian monastery of Esrum
(founded 1151), I wrote: "When we read that the Cistercians came to
desolate and isolated places it does not necessarily mean that no one had
been living there before them." Brian Patrick McGuire, *The Cistercians in
Denmark* (Kalamazoo, MI: Cistercian Publications, 1982), 55.

William's claim that Bernard was not concerned with the physical environment of
Clairvaux: VP I.26.

For Caroline Walker Bynum's interpretation of Cistercian and especially
Bernardine language, see her *Jesus as Mother: Studies in the Spirituality of the
High Middle Ages* (Berkeley: University of California Press, 1982), 110–69.

William's description of Bernard's extremes of dejection and elation: VP I.26.
William naturally saw Bernard as mastering his feelings and reconciling
himself with the result, but behind the hagiographical language there is a
hint that Bernard could become discouraged and then "his burning ardor
makes him forget himself."

EARLY DAYS

According to the *Instituta Generalis Capituli* XII, "Twelve monks together with the
abbot as the thirteenth are to be sent to new monasteries." Chrysogonus
Waddell, ed., *Narrative and Legislative Texts from Early Cîteaux* (Cîteaux:
Commentarii Cistercienses, 1999), 461.

Lament for Gerard: SC 26. Bernard's description of Gerard's abilities as cellarer: SC
26.7–8.

Bernard's apparent first miracle of healing: VP I.27. His terrifying his monks: VP
I.28.

The vision of the boy: VP I.29, trans. p. 33. His ability to participate in "ordinary
conversation": VP I.30. The Latin is very revealing: *inter homines conversari et
humana agere et tolerare*.

Tescelin's coming to Clairvaux: VP I.30.

The foundation of Trois Fontaines: VP I.64.

The letter to the monks of the Grande Chartreuse: SBO 7, no. 11. The new dating:
Gastaldelli, vol. 2, p. 1053. The translation: James, pp. 41–48, esp. p. 46.

ILLNESS AND TREATMENT (1119–1120)

Bernard's ordination to the priesthood: VP I.31. William of Champeaux's
attendance at the Cistercian General Chapter on behalf of Bernard: VP I.32.

William of Saint-Thierry's graphic description of Bernard's stomach ailments
and its consequences: VP I.39. William's summary of Bernard's
accomplishments: VP I.40 (so, immediately after the account of his illnesses).
William's point seems to be that in spite of physical suffering, Bernard could
be very productive.

William's idyllic account of his meeting with Bernard: VP I.33. Bernard's vision of
Clairvaux's future status: VP I.34.

The earlier vision: VP I.26. Bernard's hesitancy about expanding the monastery: VP II.29.

William's idealized description of the Clairvaux he remembered from his first
   visits: VP I.35. See also E. Rozanne Elder, "The Influence of Clairvaux:
   The Experience of William of Saint-Thierry," *Cistercian Studies Quarterly* 51
   (2016): 55–75, a seminal article that helps explain much about William and
   Bernard.

William's account of the silence at Clairvaux: VP I.35, p. 41.

William's insightful lament that Bernard should have had the same concern for
   himself that he showed for others: VP I.38.

First Literary Productions

Homilies in Praise of the Blessed Virgin Mary, trans. Marie-Bernard Saïd
   (Kalamazoo, MI: Cistercian Publications, 1993). The Latin: SBO 4,
   pp. 13–58. Mention of Joseph: Homily 2.16. As far as I can tell, Bernard
   was one of the first spiritual writers to emphasize the place of Joseph in
   the economy of salvation. See my "Becoming a Father and a Husband:
   St. Joseph in Bernard of Clairvaux and Jean Gerson," in *Joseph of Nazareth
   through the Centuries*, ed. Joseph F. Chorpenning (Philadelphia: St. Joseph's
   University Press, 2011), 49–62, esp. 51–52.

Bernard's address to Mary for the "word which earth and hell and heaven . . . are
   waiting for": Homily 4.8.

The Steps of Humility and Pride, trans. M. Ambrose Conway, in *The Works of Bernard
   of Clairvaux: Treatises II* (Washington, DC: Cistercian Publications, 1974). The
   Latin text: SBO 3, pp. 13–59.

The warning against singularity is the fifth step of pride and is found in 14.42,
   pp. 70–71 of the translation. The description of revolt: 19.48, pp. 75–76.

For lay brother revolts, see Brian Noelle, "Expectation and Unrest among Cistercian
   Lay Brothers in the Twelfth and Thirteenth Centuries," *Journal of Medieval
   History* 32 (2006): 253–74.

A Distant Daughter: Foigny (1121)

Foigny's foundation: Williams, 31.

Bernard's first letter to Rainald: SBO 7, no. 72; trans. James, no. 75, pp. 103–6. The
   second letter: SBO 7, no. 73; James, no. 75, pp. 106–7. The third letter: SBO
   7, no. 74; James, no. 77, p. 108. The fourth letter: SBO 8, no. 413, James,
   no. 444. Christopher Holdsworth has provided an excellent analysis of
   how Bernard functioned in his duties as father abbot to daughter houses:
   "Bernard as a Father Abbot," in Brill Companion, 169–219.

Letters to Errant Relatives (Early 1120s)

The letter to Robert: SBO 7, no. 1; James, no. 1, pp. 1–10. For background, see the
   invaluable comments of Gastaldelli, vol. 2, pp. 1046–47.

For the oblate system and the Cistercian response, see my "Children and
Youth in Monastic Life: Western Europe, 400–1250," in *Childhood in
History: Perceptions of Children in the Ancient and Medieval Worlds*, ed.
Reidar Aasgaard and Cornelia Horn (Abingdon, Eng.: Routledge, 2018),
157–73.

Bernard's claim that he had prostrated himself at Robert's feet: Letter 1.3 (the third
section).

His assertion that the grand prior of Cluny was the guilty one: 1.4. Robert's change
from the plain Cistercian habit to the attractive Cluniac one: 1.5. Bernard's
appeal to divine judgment: 1.7.

His responsibility for his choice: 1.8. "Rendering account" is a term Benedict
used in his Rule especially for the abbot's situation on Judgment Day
(§2), but Bernard extended responsibility to every single monk who had
taken his vow of stability. There are numerous editions and translations
of the Rule.

Bernard as a father grieved for his lost son: 1.10. The military image: 1.13.

In claiming that he had given birth to Robert in his religious vocation and that
in losing him, half of his own being disappeared (1.10), Bernard used a
vocabulary that soon was to appear in the new chivalric literature of love.
For Étienne Gilson's claim that there was no connection between Bernardine
spirituality and the new romanticism, see *The Mystical Theology of Saint
Bernard* (1940; Kalamazoo, MI: Cistercian Publications, 1990), 186–97
("Courtly Love and Christian Mysticism: Hypothesis of Influence"). See
Jean Leclercq's response in *Monks and Love in Twelfth-Century France* (Oxford:
Clarendon Press, 1979), esp. ch. 6.

The attack on the uncle: Letter 2.7. The contrast between the world and the
cloister: 2.11. For background, see Gastaldelli, vol. 2, pp. 1047–48.

An Apology Attacking Cluny (1122)

The work is found in SBO 2, pp. 81–108. In English translation by Michael Casey, in
The Works of Bernard of Clairvaux, vol. 1, *Treatises I* (Shannon: Irish University
Press, 1970), 33–69.

Bernard's insistence on his good relations with Cluny: *Apologia* II.4, trans. p. 37. The
"stomachs with beans and . . . minds with pride," so quintessentially Bernard
in turn of phrase: *Apologia* VI.12, trans. p. 48.

The monks who are not sick but have the comforts of the infirmary: *Apologia* IX.22,
trans. pp. 57–59. At the end of this section Bernard mentioned the founders of
Cluny. Bernard's caricature of monastic architectural decoration (*Apologia* XII.29,
trans. p. 66) is the best-known part of this treatise, but it only comes after his
concession of the virtues of Cluny. Conrad Rudolph's study of the Cistercians
and art: *"The Things of Greater Importance": Bernard of Clairvaux's "Apologia" and
the Medieval Attitude toward Art* (Philadelphia: University of Pennsylvania Press,
1990).

Bernard's contrast between Cluny's wealth and the Church's poor: *Apologia* XII.28,
trans. p. 65.

The Boundaries of Friendship: Abbot William

The letter to William: SBO 7, no. 84bis. It is not translated in James. Bernard's phrase is *et ut valeam quod vis, eo modo quo vis, ora instantius.*

Bernard's response to William's complaint about unequal love between them: SBO 7, no. 85; James, no. 87. His next letter to William: SBO 7, no. 86; James, no. 88.

The final letter: SBO 7, no. 506; James, no. 89. I presented these letters at a conference on William of Saint-Thierry at Reims in 2018, and it was pointed out that the final letter is in the "vous" form of formal address, which makes it unlikely that it was in fact sent to William, who in the other letters is addressed as "tu." But I think the matter is unresolved. This presentation is now published as "The Friendship of William and Bernard: The Development of Human Feeling," in "Guillaume de Saint-Thierry, de Liège au Mont-Dieu," ed. Laurence Mellerin, *Cîteaux: Commentarii Cistercienses* 69 (2018): 101–8.

For the adage about true friendships (*verae amicitiae non veterascunt, aut verae non fuerunt*), see Jerome's Letter 3, in my *Friendship and Community: The Monastic Experience, 350–1250* (Ithaca: Cornell University Press, 2010), 58–59.

Disciplining a Wayward Abbot (1124)

The first letter of Bernard to Abbot Arnold of Morimond: SBO 7, no. 4; James, no. 4. For the assertion that the Cistercian Order as such did not exist before the middle of the twelfth century, see Constance Berman, *The Cistercian Evolution: The Invention of a Religious Order in Twelfth-Century Europe* (Philadelphia: University of Pennsylvania Press, 2000). See my response in "Bernard's Concept of a Cistercian Order: Vocabulary and Context," *Cîteaux: Commentarii Cistercienses* 54 (2003): 225–49.

Bernard's letter to Pope Calixtus about the Morimond affair: SBO 8, no. 359; James, no. 5.

Bernard's letter-treatise on obedience to the monk Adam: SBO 7, no. 7; James, no. 8.

Discussion about papal compliance: Letter 7.9. Limitations on obedience: 7.16 and 17.

How Could He?

For Carolingian expressions of friendship, see my *Friendship and Community*, 116–33, cited above under "An Apology Attacking Cluny." See also the important work of C. Stephen Jaeger, *Ennobling Love: In Search of a Lost Sensibility* (Philadelphia: University of Pennsylvania Press, 1999), 36–41 and 43–50.

The letter to Bruno: SBO 7, no. 6; James, no. 7. For the development and distribution of Bernard's writings, Jean Leclercq remains the master. Besides his introductions to the individual works of Bernard in SBO 1–7, there are the studies found in *Recueil d'études sur saint Bernard et ses écrits*, vols. 1–5 (Rome: Edizioni de Storia et Letteratura, 1962–92).

For Stephen's remarkable letter to the monks of Sherborne, see the brilliant
analysis of its language by Chrysogonus Waddell, "Notes towards the
Exegesis of a Letter by Saint Stephen Harding," in *Noble Piety and Reformed
Monasticism*, ed. E. Rozanne Elder, Studies in Medieval Cistercian History 7
(Kalamazoo, MI: Cistercian Publications, 1981), 10–39.

Bernard's description of being discouraged: SC 54.8 and 9.

4. Monastic Commitment and Church Politics, 1124–1129

Looking outside Clairvaux

The letter to Jorannus: SBO 7, no. 32; James, no. 33.

The letter to Hugh, abbot of Pontigny: SBO 7, no. 33. James, no. 34. The Latin is
ipsa vos melius pietas docebit. Abbot Hugh in his youth as Bernard's friend: VP
I.13–14. The letter to Drogo: SBO 7, no. 34; James, no. 35. Drogo's return to
Reims: James, p. 65.

The letter to Count Theobald: SBO 7, no. 37; James, no. 39. Humbert: SBO 7, no.
38; James, no. 39. Also SBO 7, no. 39; James, no. 40.

The later letter to Count Theobald listing all those who needed his help: SBO 7, no.
39; James, no. 41.

The other letters to Theobald: SBO 7, nos. 40 and 41; James, nos. 42 and 43.

The Duties of Bishops—and Abbots

The letter-treatise for bishops: SBO 7, no. 42, pp. 100–131. It is not translated in
James, but can be found in *Bernard of Clairvaux: On Baptism and the Office of
Bishops*, trans. Pauline Matarasso (Kalamazoo, MI: Cistercian Publications,
2004).

For the medieval reformation, see Brenda Bolton, *The Medieval Reformation*
(London: Edward Arnold, 1983). In my Danish publications, I have used
the term "reformation" in reference to three medieval reformations of the
Church: the clerical reformation of 1050–1150, the pastoral reformation
of 1150–1250, and the conciliar reformation of 1350–1450. The dates are
approximate.

For the development of the letter collection, see Jean Leclercq, "Recherches sur la
collection des épitres de S. Bernard," *Cahiers de civilisation médiévale* 14 (1971):
217–19; and SBO 7, pp. xv-xvi. See also Martha G. Newman's preface to the
translation of *Office of Bishops*, 22–23. The remark on humility: IX.33, trans.
p. 77. Irresponsible and ambitious youths: VII.27, trans. p. 69. Cistercian
abbots who infringed on humility, IX.33, p. 77.

The letters on behalf of Molesme: SBO 7, nos. 43 and 44; James, nos. 47 and 48.
For the original foundation at Cîteaux from Molesme, see the foundation
documents of the Cistercian Order, such as the *Exordium Parvum*, in
Chrysogonus Waddell, ed., *Narrative and Legislative Texts from Early Cîteaux*
(Cîteaux: Commentarii Cistercienses, 1999), chs. 3–8, pp. 421–26.

The third letter for Molesme: SBO 7, no. 60; James, no. 63.

The letter to Bishop Geoffrey about the renegade hermit: SBO 7, no. 55; James, no. 58. Concerning Norben of Xanten: SBO 7, no. 56; James, no. 59.

The letter to Bishop Ricuin: SBO 7, no. 61; James, no. 64.

Henry, bishop of Verdun: SBO 7, no. 62; James, no. 65. For background, see Michael C. Voigts, *Letters of Ascent: Spiritual Direction in the Letters of Bernard of Clairvaux* (Eugene, OR: Pickwick Publications, 2013), esp. 110–12.

The letter to Alexander, bishop of Lincoln: SBO 7, no. 64; James, no. 67.

The letter to Suger: SBO 7, no. 78; James, no. 80. For background on Suger, see John F. Benton, "Suger's Life and Personality," in *Culture, Power, and Personality in Medieval France*, ed. Thomas N. Bisson (London: Hambledon Press, 1991), 387–408. The phrase *pristinae conversationis insolentia* is found in Letter 78.10. Stephen of Garland: Gastaldelli, vol. 2, p. 1090.

Seeking a New Consensus

The letter-treatise on baptism: SBO 7, no. 77. Translated by Matarasso, in *Bernard of Clairvaux: On Baptism and the Office of Bishops*, cited above under "The Duties of Bishops—Abbots." Bernard's terms are "verbal contests" (*pugnas verborum*) and "novelties of expression" (*novitates . . . vocum*) (SBO 7, p. 184).

Bernard's attack on his opponent: *On Baptism*, §11; trans. p. 164.

Hugh Feiss's study *"Bernardus scholasticus*: The Correspondence of Bernard of Clairvaux and Hugh of Saint Victor on Baptism," is found in *Bernardus Magister*, ed. John R. Sommerfeldt (Kalamazoo, MI: Cistercian Publications, 1992), 349–78.

On Grace and Free Choice, trans. Daniel O'Donovan, in *The Works of Bernard of Clairvaux: Treatises III* (Kalamazoo, MI: Cistercian Publications, 1977), with an introduction by Bernard McGinn, esp. pp. 49–50. Latin text: SBO 3, pp. 165–203. Voluntary consent: *On Grace and Free Choice*: §2; trans. p. 55. Reason and freedom of choice: §15; trans. p. 71. The restoration of the divine image: §32; trans. p. 88.

In Praise of the New Knighthood, trans. Conrad Greenia, in *Bernard of Clairvaux: Treatises III*. Latin text: SBO 3, pp. 213–39. For background, see SBO 3, p. 207; and the introduction to the trans., pp. 115–23. "Rejoice, brave athlete . . .": ch. 1; trans. p. 130. For worldly knighthood: ch. 2; trans. p. 132. The knight of Christ: ch. 3; trans. p. 134.

The Templars' virtuous lives: ch. 4; trans. pp. 139–40. The knights as a family with no personal property: ch. 4; pp. 138–39. "What can we say of this . . .": ch. 4; trans. pp. 140–41.

5. Toward Reformation of Church and Monastery

Addressing the Church's Place in Society

An excellent overview of this period is provided by Uta-Renate Blumenthal, *The Investiture Controversy: Church and Monarchy from the Ninth to the Twelfth Century* (Philadelphia: University of Pennsylvania Press, 1988, 1995).

SBO 7, no. 45 (not translated in James): *Stephanus abbas Cisterciensis, totusque conventus abbatum et fratrum Cisterciensium.*

The letter of Abbots Hugh of Pontigny and Bernard of Clairvaux: SBO 7, no. 46; James, no. 49. The letter in the name of the bishop of Chartres: SBO 7, no. 47; James, no. 50. Bernard for the archbishop of Sens: SBO 7, no. 50; James, no. 53. The letter to Haimeric: SBO 7, no. 48; James, no. 51. Bernard "off in a corner": SBO 7, no. 48.3.

Bernard's more conciliatory letter to Haimeric: SBO 7, no. 53; James, no. 56. He wrote of *vis amicitiae*, the "bond of friendship." His Latin is both concise and and powerful, in speaking of the unity of love: *unitatem dilectionis.*

MONASTIC DISCIPLINE AND COMMITMENTS

The letter to Abbot Simon: SBO 7, no. 83; James, no. 85. For background, see Gastaldelli, vol. 2, p. 1092.

The second letter to Simon: SBO 7, no. 84; James, no. 86.

The letter to the monks of Flay: SBO 7, no. 67; James, no. 70. The second letter: SBO 7, no. 68; James, no. 71. The question of monks with medical knowledge was controversial, but a story in EM IV.1 about Alquirin, monk of Clairvaux, probably reveals the general attitude. He was skilled but used his knowledge for the sake of the poor and kept his distance from the rich and noble.

The letter to Guy of Trois Fontaines: SBO 7, no. 69; James, no. 72. The second letter to Guy: SBO 7, no. 70; James, no. 73. The third letter, to the monks and one monk in particular: SBO 7, no. 71; James, no. 74.

The letter to Abbot Artald of Preuilly: SBO 7, no. 75; James, no. 78. For the elements of a formal letter, see Giles Constable, *Letters and Letter-Collections* (Turnhout: Brepols, 1976).

Abbot Stephen of St. John at Chartres: SBO 7, no. 82; James, no. 84.

The letters to Oger: SBO 7, nos. 87–90; James, nos. 90–93. In Letter 88.3 Bernard mentioned how he had lent his *Apology* to Oger, who had had it copied. For Bernard to Oger about silence and speech, see SBO 7, no. 89; James, no. 92, a masterpiece of rhetoric. The monk is not to teach, but to mourn: SBO 7, no. 89.2: *officium non est docere sed lugere.*

The letter to Oger about how to demonstrate friendship: SBO 7, no. 90; James, no. 93.

6. Healing a Divided Church, 1130–1135

A EUROPEAN FIGURE

Bernard's absent-mindedness in nature: VP III.4.

The Rule of St Benedict's provision for guests is §53.

For Arnold of Bonneval, Adriaan H. Bredero provides a full study in his *Bernard of Clairvaux: Between Cult and History* (Grand Rapids, MI: Eerdmans, 1996), 102–18.

Explaining His Absences to the Brethren

The first letter to the brethren of Clairvaux: SBO 7, no. 143; James, no. 144.
The second letter: SBO 7, no. 144; James, no. 146.
Bernard's return to Clairvaux in the spirit: EM II.12, trans. p. 142.

Beginnings of the Schism

See the account in Williams, 96–113. Even more detailed is Vacandard, vol. 1,
    pp. 280–316.
The claim that Bernard made the decisive difference at the Council of Étampes:
    VP II.3. For Suger's version, see his *The Deeds of Louis the Fat*, trans. Richard
    C. Cusimano and John Moorhead (Washington, DC: Catholic University of
    America Press, 1992), ch. 32, p. 147.
Arnold's description of Bernard's vision and his decisive role at Étampes: VP II.3.
    Bernard's vision of Clairvaux: VP I.26.
Bernard's willingness to take on King Henry I of England's "sin": VP II.4.
    Bernard's taking on responsibility for another man's conscience: EM II.6. For
    background, see my "Taking Responsibility: Medieval Cistercian Abbots and
    Monks as Their Brother's Keepers," in *Friendship and Faith: Cistercian Men,
    Women, and Their Stories, 1100–1250* (Burlington, VT: Ashgate, 2002), 249–68.
The Catholic Encyclopedia entry on the Council of Étampes can be accessed at
    newadvent.org/cathen/08012a.htm.

Liège and Clairvaux: Making a Difference

Again, it is Arnold who tells us about Bernard's central role: VP II.5. Bernard's
    letter about Lothair was to Pope Innocent: SBO 7, no. 150; James, no. 155.
Innocent's visit to Clairvaux: VP II.6. The disturbed brother is in VP II.7, but this
    chapter concludes with Arnold's assertion about the spread of Clairvaux
    monasticism.
For the "propaganda machine," see above, chapter 2, under "Entering Cîteaux."

Taming Aquitaine

The chronology of this period: Williams, esp.114–20; Vacandard, vol. 1, pp. 317–27.
Bernard and Count William: VP II.37–38. Bernard's letter to the bishops of
    Aquitaine: SBO 7, no. 126; James, no. 129. The attack on ambition is in §5.
    The defense of the legitimacy of Innocent is summarized in Letter 126.13.
    The follow-up letter to William: SBO 7, no. 128; James, no. 130.
The new foundations: Vacandard, vol. 1, pp. 398–411; Williams, 46–49.

Descent into Italy

Bernard's letter to the people of Genoa: SBO 7, no. 129; James, no. 131. To the
    Pisans: SBO 7, no. 130; James, no. 132.

The situation in Rome in 1133: Williams, 122–23.

Bernard's presence in Italy as seen by Arnold of Bonneval: VP II.26. The mention of herdsmen seeking his blessing: VP II.28.

Back at Clairvaux: The Challenge of Growth

The reception of Bernard back at Clairvaux, according to Arnold: VP II.28. The brothers' insistence on expanding the monastery: VP II.29. This controversy shows that Arnold had firsthand knowledge of the situation at Clairvaux.

The incident already mentioned (in chapter 5, under "Monastic Discipline") is described in SBO 7, no. 69; James, no. 72.

The expansion of Clairvaux: VP II.31.

a Double Election and Two Murders

Bernard's response to Philip as "intruded" archbishop of Tours: SBO 7, no. 151; James, no. 157.

The letter to Innocent: SBO 8, no. 431; James, no. 156. The later letter on behalf of Philip, now a monk at Clairvaux: SBO 8, no. 257; James, no. 330.

The letter to Innocent about the murder of Thomas, prior of Saint Victor in Paris: SBO 7, no. 158; James, no. 164. For background, see Williams, 127–28, 131.

Bernard's letter concerning the second murder: SBO 7, no. 161; James, no. 165. The meeting at the abbey of Jouarre: Williams, 130; Vacandard, vol. 2, pp. 355–56. The letter to Innocent about the state of the church of Orléans: SBO 7, no. 156; James, no. 162.

Peace in Bamberg and Riots in Milan

Geoffrey of Auxerre's description: VP IV.14.

Bernard's letter to King Louis: SBO 8, no. 255; James, no. 133.

Arnold of Bonneval's reference to Bernard at the Council of Pisa: VP II.8. Bernard's reception at Milan: VP II.9.

Bernard's letter to the people of Milan: SBO 7, no. 133; James, no. 138.

The reference to him as an angel in his support of Pope Innocent is in *Monumenta Germaniae Historica: Scriptores*, vol. 8, ed. G. H. Pertz (Hannover, 1848): Landulfus de Sancto Paulo, *Historia Mediolanensis*, ch. 60, p. 46: *papa adeo ydoneum angelum habuit, sicut Bernardus abbas Claraevalensis fuit*. Landulf's mention of the new asceticism in Milan is in ch. 61, p. 46.

Bernard's letter to novices converted at Milan: SBO 7, no. 134; James, no. 135. For background on the abbey of Chiaravalle Milanese, see Williams, 50–51. His warning to the people of Milan: SBO 7, no. 131; James, no. 140.

Bernard's letter to Innocent about opposition from Cremona and Milanese arrogance: SBO 8, no. 314; James, no. 137.

Letter to Lothair's wife: SBO 7, no. 139; James, no. 137.

AN EXPANDING ORDER: YORKSHIRE AND POITOU

The letter to King Henry I of England for the foundation of Rievaulx: SBO 7, no. 92; James, no. 95.

For the early history of Fountains Abbey, see R. Gilyard-Beer, *Fountains Abbey* (London: Her Majesty's Stationery Office, 1970), 4–5. See also "Houses of Cistercian Monks: Fountains," in *A History of the County of York*, vol. 3, ed. William Page (London: Victoria County History, Institute of Historical Research, 1974), 134–38; *British History Online*, http://www.british-history.ac.uk/vch/yorks/vol3/pp134-138.

Bernard's answer to the abbot of Saint Mary's, York: SBO 7, no. 94; James, no. 168. He was using Gregory the Great's *Pastoral Rule* I.27 (PL 77:104) and the quote about the son being the glory of the father comes from Proverbs 10:1. As always, Bernard had the Bible and the Fathers at his fingertips.

The second letter to the abbot of Saint Mary's, York: SBO 8, no. 313; James, no. 169. The letter to Archbishop Thurstan: SBO 7, no. 170; James, no. 170. The letter to Abbot Richard of Fountains and his brothers: SBO 7, no. 96; James, no. 171.

The letter to King David of Scotland: SBO 8, no. 519; James, no. 172.

The monks of Grace-Dieu: SBO 8, no. 507; James, no. 176.

PREACHING WITH THE MILK OF LOVE

There is a wealth of literature concerning Bernard's Sermons on the Song of Songs. The most accessible introduction is probably Michael Casey, *A Thirst for God: Spiritual Desire in Bernard of Clairvaux's Sermons on the Song of Songs* (Kalamazoo, MI: Cistercian Publications, 1988). Jean Leclercq has considered the possible oral dimension of these sermons in his "Les Sermons sur les Cantiques: Ont-ils été prononcés?," in *Recueil d'études sur saint Bernard et ses écrits* (Rome: Edizioni de Storia et Letteratura, 1962), vol. 1, pp. 193–212.

The Sermons are contained in SBO 1 and 2. Translations are available from Cistercian Publications (now part of Liturgical Press). See the translation of Sermon 1 by Kilian Walsh, *On the Song of Songs 1* (Kalamazoo, MI: Cistercian Publications, 1977), 1–7.

Bernard as seeker: SC 1.4. Endless union with God: 1.7. The renewal of life: 1.9.

"The touch of the Spirit teaches" (*sola unctio docet*) and "Personal experience informs" (*sola addiscit experientia*) = SC 1.10. SC 3.1: "Today we read in the book of experience." (*Hodie legimus in libro experientiae.*)

Augustine, *Soliliquorum* 2.1: *noverim me, noverim te.*

Nuptial union: SC 1.12: *facta nuptiis caelestis sponsi idonea.*

A twelfth-century manuscript containing the Sermons on the Song of Songs in French translation, from modern-day Wallonia, is Nantes, Bibliothèque du Musée, Dobrée 5, mentioned by Wybren Scheepsma, *The Limburg Sermons: Preaching in the Medieval Low Countries at the Turn of the Fourteenth Century* (Leiden: Brill, 2008), 34 n. 117.

7. Victory and Defeat: A Conflicted Church, 1136–1140

A Third Mission in Italy (1136–1137)

The first letter to Lothair: SBO 7, no. 139; James, no. 142. The reference to Anacletus's Jewish ancestry is the following: *iudaicam subolem sedem Petri in Christo occupasse iniuriam.*

"I am faithful to you": *fidelis tamen vester* (Letter 139.2).

Bishop Ambose of Milan barred the emperor Theodosius and his men from entering his church in Milan after a massacre ordered by the emperor; Theodoret, *Ecclesiastical History* 5.17–18. The incident was remembered and used as a precedent for churchmen to challenge actions by secular authorities that were considered wrongful.

The second letter to Lothair: SBO 7, no. 140; James, no. 143.

The annalist is named Saxo, not to be confused with the Danish historian: *Annalista Saxo*, ed. G. Waitz, Monumenta Germaniae Historica: Scriptores (Hannover, 1844), 6:773: *sed mediantibus quibusdam episcopis et abbate Clarevallensi, data magna pecunia ducem placaverunt.* Vacandard's version is in vol. 2, p. 4. See also *Bernard 1953,* Tables chronologiques, p. 591.

The passage is from *On the Song of Songs II*, trans. Kilian Walsh, SC 26.14 (Kalamazoo, MI: Cistercian Publications, 1976), 73.

The Last Months of the Schism (May 1137–January 1138)

The letter to the monks of Clairvaux: SBO 7, no. 144; James, no. 146. Arnold's description of Bernard's actions: VP II.43. Bernard at prayer during battle: VP II.44. Bernard's exhortation to Emperor Lothair: SBO 7, no. 139; James, no. 142. Vacandard's rare criticism of Bernard is in vol. 2, p. 9.

The account of events at Monte Cassino is in the *Chronicon Casinense*, PL 173, esp. cols. 964–65, ch. 122. Vacandard's version is vol. 2, p. 12. See also *Bernard 1953*, "Tables chronologiques," p. 591.

Bernard's sermon: *post peractum ab abbate Clarevallensi sermonem . . .*; Peter the Deacon, PL 173:964.

Bernard to the Cistercian General Chapter: SBO 7, no. 145; James, no. 145. He described himself in human terms as *humanum autem dico proper infirmitatem nostram.* James's comment on Bernard's relative longevity is on p. 213.

The defeat of Roger of Sicily: VP II.44. Bernard's speech to Peter of Pisa: VP II:45.

Bernard's celebratory letter to Abbot Peter the Venerable of Cluny: SBO 7, no. 147; James, no. 147. The key statement is *Nam si socii fuimus laboris, erimus et consolationis.*

In my *Friendship and Community*, 253–58, I see the relationship as one of friendship, even though it could be strained at times. Bredero, 227–48, interprets the correspondence quite differently and does not find friendship at all.

ONE POPE IN A DIVIDED CHURCH

Bernard to the prior of Clairvaux: SBO 8, no. 317; James, no. 148.

James provides a good summary of the Langres affair, p. 249. The letter to Pope Innocent: SBO 7, no. 164; James, no. 179. Bernard's charge about investiture by the French king is in §5 of this letter.

The letter to the church officials at Lyon: SBO 7, no. 165; James, no. 180.

The second letter to Pope Innocent: SBO 7, no. 166; James, no. 181. The third letter to Innocent: SBO 7, no. 167; James, no. 182. To the bishops and cardinals of the Curia: SBO 7, no. 168; James, no. 183.

The letter to Cardinal Umbald: SBO 8, no. 501; James, no. 184. The final letter to Pope Innocent on the matter: SBO 7, no. 169; James, no. 185.

The letter to King Louis VII: SBO 7, no. 170; James, no. 186.

Peter the Venerable's letter to Bernard is no. 29 in his collection: Giles Constable, *The Letters of Peter the Venerable* (Cambridge, MA: Harvard University Press, 1967), vol. 1, pp. 101–4.

Bernard's brief letter to Pope Innocent about the state of the church of Reims: SBO 8, no. 318; James, no. 209. The letter to the French king: SBO 8, no. 449; James, no. 210.

William of Saint-Thierry's description of Bernard in Reims: VP I.67. James's assertion that he preached in the marketplace is on p. 282. Vacandard's description of events here is from vol. 2, p. 45.

SEEKING CONSOLATION FOR A DEAD BROTHER

For a purely literary reading of Bernard's lament, see Peter von Moos, *Consolatio: Studien zur mittelalterlichen Trostliteratur* (Munich: Vilhelm Fink Verlag, 1971). See also M. B. Pranger, "Bernard the Writer," in Brill Companion, 238–43, where he criticizes my interpretation of the lament.

For Cicero's use of the word *consolatio*, see *Tusc.* 3.32.77: *Erit igitur in consolationibus.*

The description of consolation: SC 26.5, trans. p. 62. Bernard's vain attempt at self-control: SC 26.3–4, trans. pp. 60–61. Bernard's complaint against death: SC 26.4, trans. pp. 61–62.

The EM borrowing from Bernard's lament: EM III.1, trans. pp. 211–14. The compiler includes much of SC 26.4–12. The claim "in every emergency I look to Gerard for help": SC 26.6, trans. p. 64. Gerard in the maintenance of discipline: SC 26.7, trans. p. 66. The loss of Gerard meant "drudgery and pain": SC 26.8, trans. p. 67. The Latin here is *ego merear consolari*, literally "I shall deserve to be consoled." Bernard's questioning of his weeping: SC 26.8, trans. p. 68.

Bernard's acceptance of a carnal bond of love to Gerard: SC 26.9, trans. p. 69. The need of friends to enjoy each other's company: SC 26.10, trans. p. 69.

Bernard's letter to Aelred: SBO 8, no. 523; James, no. 177. See my *Brother and Lover: Aelred of Rievaulx* (New York: Crossroad, 1994).

"The sufferings that are shared equally by lovers when compelled to remain apart": SC 26.10, trans. p. 70. "The loss this house has suffered": SC 26.12, trans. p. 71.

Our weeping is not a sign of lack of faith: SC 26.13. The Latin is *Sic nec fletus utique noster infidelitatis est signum, sed conditionis indicium.*

Bernard's narrative of Gerard's illness at Viterbo and his reaction: SC 26.14, trans. p. 73.

LOVING GOD AND LOSING YOURSELF: *DE DEO DILIGENDO*

I use the translation of Robert Walton: *On Loving God,* trans. Robert Walton, in *The Works of Bernard of Clairvaux: Treatises II* (Washington, DC: Cistercian Publications, 1974), 93–132. Latin text: SBO 3, pp. 119–154.

The question of consolation: §11, trans. pp. 102–3.

No limits in loving God: §16, trans. p. 109. The pursuit of fulfillment of mind and will: §17, trans. p. 111.

The fourth degree of love: §27, trans. p. 119. "The evil of the day" is mentioned here (p. 119).

For Bernard's mystical theology, there is the classic study by Étienne Gilson, *The Mystical Theology of Saint Bernard* (1940; Kalamazoo, MI: Cistercian Publications, 1990), but now also Bernard McGinn, *The Great Cistercian Mystics: A History* (New York: Crossroad, 2019), ch. 1, "Bernard of Clairvaux: The Great Contemplative."

Delight in seeing God's will done / All human feelings melt: *On Loving God,* §28, trans. p. 120.

FACING A VINDICTIVE POPE AND COPING WITH ROGER OF SICILY (1139–1140)

The Life and Death of Saint Malachy the Irishman, trans. Robert T. Meyer (SBO 3, pp. 307–78), §37, trans. pp. 51–52. The pope's refusal is §38, trans. p. 52. Meyer's explanation: note p. 140 n. 115.

The decrees of the Second Lateran Council are contained in *Conciliorum oecumenicorum decreta,* ed. Joseph Alberigo (Basel: Herder, 1962), p. 179, no. 30: *Ad haec ordinationes factas a Petro Leonis et aliis schismaticis haereticis evacuamus et irritas esse censemus.*

Bernard's letter to Innocent in protest against being called a traitor: SBO 8, no. 213; James, no. 283.

Vacandard's comment is in vol. 2, p. 58. The disappearance of Peter of Pisa's name from pontifical documents: Vacandard, vol. 2, p. 59 n. 3. The campaign against Roger of Sicily: Vacandard, vol. 2, pp. 61–64; Williams, 157–58.

Vacandard's language can almost be called magisterial: "Quels furent les sentiments de l'abbé de Clairvaux, quand il apprit cette désolante nouvelle?" (vol. 2, p. 63).

Bernard's letter to King Conrad of the Romans: SBO 8, no. 183; James, no. 225. The letter to Roger about a Cistercian foundation in his realm: SBO 8, no. 208; James, no. 277. To Roger on the "need of the brethren": SBO 8, no. 207; James, no. 276. The letter mentioning Master Bruno: SBO 8, no. 209; James, no. 278.

Farfa: VP III.24. For background, see Williams, 67–69.

SEEKING THE LORD'S PROTECTION: SERMONS IN THE SHELTER
OF THE MOST HIGH

These sermons are in SBO 4, pp. 383–492. Translated by Marie-Bernard Saïd,
 Sermons on Conversion (Kalamazoo, MI: Cistercian Publications, 1981),
 113–261.
Bernard's assurance of comfort: *abundat tribulatio vestra . . . abundabit consolatio
 vestra*; SBO 4, p. 383; trans. p. 115. "Consolation in God's word": Preface §2,
 trans. p. 116. The brothers who think they can stop their service: Sermon 1.1,
 trans. p. 120.
The brothers hiding in cloisters and forests: Sermon 4.3, trans. p. 137. To be
 "hidden . . . from other people's eyes": Sermon 4.3, trans. p. 138.
The "vain pursuits" of those who pursue church offices: Sermon 6.7, trans. p. 149.
 The brother who had terrifying visions: Sermon 7.8, trans. p. 158. The
 Paraclete's comfort: Sermon 7.9, trans. p. 159.
The prayer to Jesus woven into the text: Sermon 7.12, trans. p. 163. The open city
 of refuge: Sermon 9.7, trans. p. 189. The consolations that cheer the soul
 (*consolationes eius laetificabunt animam tuam*): Sermon 7.6, trans. p. 188.
Being freed from dangers: Sermon 10.1, trans. p. 193. Bernard's address as contrary
 to Cistercian usages: Sermon 10.6, trans. p. 198. His exemption from manual
 labor: VP I.23–24.
Psalm 91 as encouragement: Sermon 12.3, trans. p. 215. The angels as guardians:
 12.6, trans. p. 217. Monastic good behavior: Sermon 15.4, trans. p. 243. It
 is good to be troubled: Sermon 17.4, trans p. 257. The showing of Jesus:
 Sermon 17.7, trans. p. 260.

CONVERTING CLERICS AND ATTACKING THE CLERGY

The *Ad clericos de conversione* is in SBO 4, pp. 69–116. Translated by Marie-Bernard
 Saïd in the same volume, *Sermons on Conversion*, as those based on Psalm 91
 above (Kalamazoo, MI: Cistercian Publications, 1981), 31–79. Geoffrey of
 Auxerre's description of Bernard's giving the sermon: VP IV.10. The turn
 from empty studies to that of wisdom is phrased elegantly: *ab inanibus studiis
 ad versae sapientiae cultum.*
"No one can be converted . . ." is the heading of §1, trans. p. 31.
Proprio disces experimento: §4, trans. p. 35.
The tongue's complaint: §9, trans. p. 42. Bernard uses the term *respiratio
 consolationis* (§12, trans., p. 45) for the breeze of consolation, one of
 his favored terms. The swollen belly: §13, trans. pp. 47–48. The empty
 consolation of curiosity: §14, trans. p. 48. The goad of the flesh: §22, trans.
 p. 57.
After the struggle there will be comfort: §23, trans. pp. 57–58.
"Delight and learning" (*delectandum et erudiendum*): §24, trans. p. 59. "Not learning
 but anointing teaches" (*non illud eruditio sed unctio docet*); "not knowledge but
 conscience grasps it" (*nec scientia sed conscientia comprehendit*): §25,
 trans. p. 61.

Men sated with money: §26, trans. p. 62. The peace that comes from reconciliation with God: §29, trans. p. 65. Men who usurp the dignity of peacemakers: §33, trans. p. 71. Looking for money, not justice: §33, trans. pp. 71–72. The impure and holy orders: §34, trans. p. 72. Better for the clergy to marry than to live impure lives: §36, trans. pp. 74–75. Bernard's exhortation: §37, trans. p. 75.

A CHAMPION OF REFORM RETURNS TO THE CLOISTER—AND YET . . .

Bernard's letter to Pope Innocent where he claimed to have at first refused the summons to the meeting about Abelard at Sens: SBO 8, no. 189.4; James, no. 239.4.

8. The World after the Schism: One Thing after Another, 1140–1145

THE ABELARD CONTROVERSY

Bernard's letter to William of Saint-Thierry about Abelard: SBO 8, no. 327; James, no. 236. The letter-treatise: SBO 8, no. 190. The translation by Samuel Eales is now available online in the Christian Classics Ethereal Library, https://www.ccel.org/ccel/bernard/letters.i.html.

I follow for the most part this translation. I merely skim the surface of a profound argument, but now Anthony N. S. Lane's *Bernard of Clairvaux: Theologian of the Cross* (Collegeville, MN: Liturgical Press and Cistercian Publications, 2013) provides a valuable study.

Bernard's charges against Abelard are found already in §1 of Letter 190. The review of Abelard on the Trinity begins in §2. The question of consubstantiality: §3. No inequality or dissimilarity: §4. Power and wisdom in the Trinity: §5. Questions long ago settled: §7.

The meaning of faith for Abelard as private judgment (*fidem diffinit aestimationem*): §9.

The devil's power: §11. For Anselm's abrogation of the devil's rights, see R. W. Southern, *Saint Anselm: A Portrait in a Landscape* (Cambridge: Cambridge University Press, 1990), 207–11.

The necessity of satisfaction: Letter190 §15. In Anselm's *Cur Deus Homo*, ch. 11.

Bernard's contention that the Redemption took place "merely that he might give man by his life and teaching a rule of life": Letter 190 §17.

The question of necessity: §19. Illumination and enkindling to love as compared to redemption and liberation, *Illuminatio et provocatio ad amorem* (Abelard) vs. *redemptio et liberatio* (Bernard): §23.

"The sacrament of our redemption": §25. Our restoration by grace: §23.

Letter 190.1 starts out with Bernard's contention that Abelard used to play with dialectics and now has played with the holy Scriptures. The verb *lusit* is used twice.

For the dating of the Council of Sens to 1141, see Constant J. Mews, "The Council of Sens (1141): Abelard, Bernard, and the Fear of Social Upheaval," *Speculum* 77 (2002): 342–82. For a fine study of the confrontation between Bernard and Abelard, see Mews, "Bernard of Clairvaux and Peter Abelard," in Brill Companion, 133–68.

The letter to the bishops of the Sens archdiocese: SBO 8, no. 187; James, no. 237. To the Curia in Rome: SBO 8, no.188; James, no. 238. Bernard to Pope Innocent: SBO 8, no. 189; James, no. 239. "A new gospel": SBO 8, no. 189.2; James, no. 239.2. Bernard's initial refusal to meet Abelard: SBO 8, no. 189.4; James, no. 239.4.

"God has brought forth heretics": SBO 8, no. 189.5; James, no. 239.5.

Bernard's letter to Cardinal Guy of Castello: SBO 8, no. 192; James, no. 240. To Cardinal Ivo: SBO 8, no. 193; James, no. 241. To Pope Innocent: SBO 8, no. 330; James, no. 242. All these letters are dated to 1140 in James but have to be redated to 1141.

To Cardinal Stephen: SBO 8, no. 331; James, no. 243; to a Cardinal G.: SBO 8, no. 332; James, no. 244.

For a partial translation of Pope Innocent's condemnation, see Edward Peters, *Heresy and Authority in Medieval Europe* (Philadelphia: University of Pennsylvania Press, 1980), 82. For the full text, SBO 8, no. 194. For background, see M. T. Clanchy, *Abelard: A Medieval Life* (Oxford: Blackwell, 1997), 317–19.

Bernard's letter to Cardinal Haimeric: SBO 8, no. 338; James, no. 249.

Rainald of Bar appears as the probable author of the *Exordium Parvum*, according to Chrysogonus Waddell, ed., *Narrative and Legislative Texts from Early Cîteaux* (Cîteaux: Commentarii Cistercienses, 1999), 231. He appears in EM I.34.

For the decisive role of Peter the Venerable of Cluny and the Abbot of Cîteaux Rainald, see Giles Constable, *The Letters of Peter the Venerable* (Cambridge, MA: Harvard University Press, 1967), vol. 1, Letter 98, p. 259 and the notes in vol. 2, pp. 164–65. Peter's reference is brief but clear about what happened to Abelard: *Ivit, rediit, cum domino Clarevallensi, mediante Cysterciensi sopitis prioribus querulis se pacifice convenisse.*

Peter the Venerable's remark about Abelard giving up the confusion of the schools: Letter 98, p. 259: *dismissis scolarum et studiorum tumultibus, in Cluniaco vestra sibi perpetuam mansionem elegit.*

APPEALING TO POPE INNOCENT

To Pope Innocent, on behalf of Arnulf of Lisieux: SBO 8, no. 348; James, no. 252.

The letter warning Peter, dean of Besancon: SBO 8, no. 197; James, no. 253. To Pope Innocent on behalf of Abbot Guy of Cherlieu: SBO 8, no.198; James, no. 254. Further letter to the pope: SBO 8, no. 199; James, no. 255.

For the great increase in papal business in the twelfth century, see R. W. Southern, *Western Society and the Church in the Middle Ages* (Harmondsworth, Eng.: Penguin, 1970), esp. 109–25; Southern provides a still valuable overview.

For the Fontevrault case, see Bernard's letter to Bishop Ulger: SBO 8, no. 200; James, no. 256. Bernard to Pope Innocent on behalf of Ulder: SBO 8, no. 340; James, no. 258. The later letter to Ulger: SBO 8, no. 524; James, no. 257.

INTERVENING IN THE AFFAIRS OF BISHOPRICS

Letter to the clergy of Sens: SBO 8, no. 202; James, no. 260.
Letter to the bishop and clergy of Troyes: SBO 8, no. 203; James, no. 262.
   Criticizing Bishop Atto of Troyes: SBO 8, no. 427; James, no. 263. To Pope Innocent on behalf of Bishop Atto: SBO 8, no. 432. Atto as "our friend": SBO 8, no. 467; James, no. 268. "A friend to me and so your friend" (*Homo ipse amici vestri amicus est*): SBO 8, no. 469; James, no. 269.
Bernard's letter of reproach to Pope Innocent: SBO 8, no. 218; James, no. 292.

CONFRONTING THE FRENCH KING

Bernard's letter to the three bishops in the Curia: SBO 8, no. 219; James, no. 293. For background, see James's introduction to the letter, p. 359. See also Williams, 307–8.
The letter to King Louis: SBO 8, no. 220; James, no. 296. To Pope Innocent: SBO 8, no. 216; James, no. 294, whose introduction provides background. Also Williams, 210–13. Williams calls Ralph Raoul.
The best overview of the conflict between Louis VII and Thibaut of Champagne is still Vacandard, vol. 2, ch. xxiv, pp. 182–208.
Bernard's complaint to Pope Innocent: SBO 8, no. 217; James, no. 295. Bernard to King Louis on his missive to the pope: SBO 8, no. 220; James, no. 296. The second letter to King Louis: SBO 8, no. 221; James, no. 297.
Letter to Jocelin, bishop of Soissons, and Suger of Saint Denis: SBO 8, no. 222; James, no. 298.
The story in EM II.6 concerns a brother who could not believe in the real presence of Christ in the Eucharist. Bernard ordered the monk to receive the Eucharist "on my faith." King Henry I of England: VP II.4.
To Bishop Jocelin: SBO 8, no. 223; James, no. 299. Bernard called the king a boy, a real insult: *puerum regem.*
Bernard's letter to Stephen of Palestrina: SBO 8, no. 224; James, no. 300. Letter to Jocelin asking for his attendance at Saint Denis: SBO 8, no. 225; James, no. 301.
The story of Queen Eleanor and Bernard is in *Fragmenta Gaufridi*, no. 50, Corpus Christianorum: Continuatio Mediaevalis 89B, ed. Christine Vande Veire (Turnhout: Brepols, 2011), 300.
Bernard's lament to the king about leaving everyday life at Clairvaux in his work for peace: SBO 8, no. 226; James, no. 302. His phrase about leaving Clairvaux for this purpose is *egressi de domibus nostris.*
Hugh of Macon's conversion to the Cistercian Order: VP I.13.
Letter to Jocelin, bishop of Soisson, in what looks like a personal appeal: SBO 8, no. 227; James, no. 303.
Letter to Pope Celestine for Count Theobald: SBO 8, no. 358; James, no. 304.

TRYING TO STAY AT HOME BUT GETTING INVOLVED ANYWAY

Letter to Peter the Venerable: SBO 8, no. 228; James, no. 305.
Besides Bredero, Gillian R. Knight's *The Correspondence of Peter the Venerable and Bernard of Clairvaux: A Semantic and Structural Analysis* (Burlington, VT: Ashgate, 2002) looks at the letters as literature and not as reflections of inner lives.
Bernard's reference to his broken strength is *Fractus sum viribus*. His promise to keep to himself in peace: *Sedebo et silebo*.
Bernard to three bishops in the Curia: SBO 8, no. 231; James, no. 310.
The letter to John, the abbot of Buzay: SBO 8, no. 233; James, no. 312. For background, see Williams, 51–52. See the comments of Christopher Holdsworth in his important article "Bernard as a Father Abbot," in Brill Companion, 213.

THE YORK ELECTION

For the complicated case of the election of the archbishop of York, the classic study remains David Knowles, "The Case of St. William of York," *Cambridge Historical Journal* 2 (1936): 162–77 and 212–14. See also Williams, 168–76. James, 259–61, provides a brief and helpful summary of events.
Bernard's first letter in the York affairs: SBO 8, no. 346; James, no. 187. His letter of introduction to the emissaries to Pope Innocent: SBO 8, no. 347; James, no. 188. The letter to Cardinal Gerard: SBO 8, no. 525; James, no. 189. The letter to Cardinal Stephen of Palestrina: SBO 8, no. 528; James, no. 192.
Letter to Bishop Henry of Winchester: SBO 8, no. 531; James, no. 195.
To King Stephen: SBO 8, no. 533; James, no. 197.
To Stephen's queen, Matilda (and not the empress Matilda, Stephen's rival for the throne): SBO 8, no. 534; James, no. 198.
To the abbots of Rievaulx and Fountains: SBO 8, no. 535; James, no. 201. "Listen, as if he were myself" is *quem tamquam meipsum audietis*.
Letter to the newly elected Pope Celestine II: SBO 8, no. 235; James, no. 202. To the Curia at Rome: SBO 8, no. 236; James, no. 203.
To Pope Lucius II: SBO 8, no. 520; James, no. 204.
On Precept and Dispensation in SBO 3, pp. 253–94. The work was one of the first to be translated and published in the Cistercian Father Series: *The Works of Bernard of Clairvaux*, vol. 1, *Treatises I* (Shannon: Irish University Press, 1970), with an introduction by Jean Leclercq.
The abbot is not above the Rule: §9, trans. p. 111.
Superiors are to hold their subjects to what they have promised: §11, trans. p. 113.
Superiors are normally to be obeyed, as God's commands: §21, trans. p. 121.
We obey our superior as we would God: §34, trans. p. 131.
Accepting the discipline of regular penance: §33, trans. p. 131.
For Gerson's use of Bernard here, see my *Jean Gerson and the Last Medieval Reformation* (University Park: Pennsylvania State University Press, 2005), 156.

A Cistercian Pope and Great Expectations

For background on the election of Eugenius III, see I. S. Robinson, *The Papacy 1073–1198: Continuity and Innovation* (Cambridge: Cambridge University Press, 1993), 58, 78. There is a good article about Eugenius in the Catholic Encyclopedia, http://www.newadvent.org/cathen/05599a.htm.

Bernard's first letter to Bernardo as Pope Eugenius: SBO 8, no. 238; James, no. 205. His remark about the brevity of life remaining: *residuum vitae meae.*

"How terrible, how awful is the place you hold": SBO 8, no. 238.4, James, p. 278.

The letter to the Roman Curia: SBO 8, no. 237; James, no. 315.

To Eugenius about the brothers who came from him to Bernard: SBO 8, no. 508; James, no. 314.

To Cardinal Robert Pullen: SBO 8, no. 362; James, no. 316. The simplicity of the dove and the wisdom of the serpent come from Mt 10:16, but Bernard added "the cunning of the ancient serpent" (the devil).

To Pope Eugenius concerning the deposition of the archbishop of York: SBO 8, no. 239; James, no. 206.

To Pope Eugenius again about York but also initiative for crusade: SBO 8, no. 240; James, no. 207.

Bernard to Eugenius after the raid on Fountains Abbey: SBO 8, no. 252; James, no. 208.

The outcome of the dispute, and the reputation of William Fitzherbert: James, pp. 260–61.

David Knowles summarizes the time of Henry Murdac as archbishop with this terse sentence: "Nor is it surprising that the experiment of seeking an archbishop of York from among the Cistercians was not repeated." David Knowles, *The Monastic Order in England, 940–1216* (Cambridge: Cambridge University Press, 1966), 257.

The letter to Aelred of Rievaulx: SBO 8, no. 523; James, no. 177. The *Mirror of Charity* has been given an excellent translation by Elizabeth Connor, with a fine introduction by Charles Dumont (Kalamazoo, MI: Cistercian Publications, 1990). See my chapter "Making Love's Mirror," in *Brother and Lover: Aelred of Rievaulx* (New York: Crossroad, 1994), 78–91.

In Pursuit of Heretics: One More Tired Voyage

For Arnold of Brescia's career, which is well documented, though we lack his own writings, see Malcolm Lambert, *Medieval Heresy: Popular Movements from Bogomil to Hus* (London: Edward Arnold, 1977), 57–59.

Bernard's letter to the bishop of Constance warning against Arnold: SBO 8, no. 195; James, no. 250.

To Cardinal Guy: SBO 8, no. 196; James, no. 251.

Bernard's preaching against Henry: VP III.16–17. Vacandard (vol. 2, pp. 226–44) has a chapter on Bernard and Henry that is still useful.

Bernard's letter against Henry to the Count of Toulouse: SBO 8, no. 241; James, no. 317.

To the people of Toulouse: SBO 8, no. 242; James, no. 318.

There is a great deal of literature about the Cathars, much of which heroizes
them as "freedom fighters" against the oppression of the medieval Church.
In point of fact they were dualists who separated the world into absolute
good and absolute evil and thus were the most radical heretics that medieval
Europe came to know. A superb study of the Cathars in their historical
development is Malcolm Lambert, *The Cathars* (Oxford: Blackwell, 1998).

Bernard's claim about the danger in the company of women: SC 65.4. His defense
of the sanctity of marriage, against the Cathars: SC 66.2.

Geoffrey of Auxerre's letter to the monks of Clairvaux is printed as part of book
6 of the *Vita Prima* in PL 185:410–16 but is not included in Hilary Costello's
translation of the VP, which ends with book 5. It is found translated in R. I.
Moore, *The Birth of Popular Heresy* (London: Edward Arnold, 1975), 41–46;
the reference to Bernard's teaching is on p. 43.

Endless Involvements

Letter to canons of Lyon: SBO 7, no. 174; James, no. 215.

R. W. Southern has shown the important role played by the early twelfth-century
Canterbury monk Eadmer in devotion to the Immaculate Conception and its
observance in England: *Saint Anselm and His Biographer: A Study of Monastic
Life and Thought, 1059–c. 1130* (Cambridge: Cambridge University Press,
1966), 290–98.

Bruno Scott James in his introduction to this letter claims that Bernard used the
term "conception" in a different way than the Roman Catholic Church does
today (p. 289). I cannot follow his logic.

Bernard to Pope Eugenius for the bishop of Orléans: SBO 8, no. 245; James,
no. 321.

Bernard's intention of not leaving his monastery is stated here: *Propositum meum
monasterium non egrediendi credo non latere vos.*

Baldwin of Pisa: EM III.26. Gunnar or Gonario: EM III.29. The letter to the Roman
people: SBO 8, no. 243; James, no. 319.

9. Preaching a Crusade and Leaving Miracles Behind, 1146–1150

See Geoffrey of Auxerre's rather unenthusiastic description of what happened,
VP III.9, emphasizing that Bernard did not become involved until the pope
had asked him to preach the crusade. Williams's chapter 12, "The Second
Crusade," provides a good overview, based on primary sources. A complete
treatment is found in Jonathan Phillips, *The Second Crusade: Extending the
Frontiers of Christendom* (New Haven: Yale University Press, 2007).

Odo of Deuil, *De profectione Ludovici vii in orientem: The Journey of Louis VII to the
East,* ed. Virginia Gingerick Berry (New York: W.W. Norton, 1948), with the
Latin text facing an English translation. Bernard's role: 9–11.

Otto of Freising, *The Deeds of Frederick Barbarossa,* trans. Charles Christopher
Mierow (New York: W.W. Norton, 1953), 1.xxxvi.

Bernard's travels after leaving Vézelay are accounted for in Williams, 269, but the primary source for his journey through Germany in October 1146 and until February 1147 is known as *Liber miraculorum*. Geoffrey of Auxerre provided a summary in VP IV.30–39, but the record of daily events, mostly concerned with miracles, but also mentioning Bernard's sermons seeking support for the crusade, is found in PL 185:369–416.

BERNARD'S LANGUAGE OF CRUSADE

Bernard's letter to the clergy of Eastern France and Bavaria: SBO 8, no. 363. It is not translated in James, but his letter to the English people (James, no. 391) is close in tone and content. The sentence about the Jews provides the key to understanding why Bernard wanted them to be protected: they were considered witnesses in the process of salvation (Letter 363.7). For further background, see question 8 about Bernard and the Jews.

Bernard to the archbishop of Mainz against the fanatic Raoul: SBO 8, no. 365; James, no. 393.

His letter to the English people, James, no. 391, is not included in SBO.

His letter to brother abbots about renegade monks: SBO 8, no. 544; James, no. 396.

Letter to all the faithful for a Wendish crusade: SBO 8, no. 457; James, no. 394.

FRANKFURT-CONSTANCE-SPEYER

André Picard has provided a sober and detailed attempt to bring together the evidence for miracles in Bernard's life. It was published in connection with his obtaining the MA in medieval studies at the University of Montreal and can be accessed on the internet at ResearchGate: *La thaumaturgie de Bernard de Clairvaux d'après les Vitae* (1991).

The list of eyewitnesses: PL 185:373, ch. 1. Bernard's complaint about it being nearly a year since he was separated from his loved ones at Clairvaux is also here. Bishop Herman's witness to what others saw: col. 374, ch. 2. Bernard's prayer for the rich: col. 375, ch. 3. Bernard at Basel: col. 376, ch. 5.

The brothers could not see much of what was done because of the crowds: *Multa ea maxime die facta sunt, quae prae tumultu scire nequivimus.*

Geoffrey of Auxerre admitted that so much happened that it could not be remembered: col. 377, ch. 7. The knights had to protect Bermard from the crowd: col. 377, ch. 8.

Abbot Baldwin's witness, *quem ego vidi*: col. 378, ch. 9. In the same chapter, the healing of a knight's son: col. 378. Geoffrey's witness: col. 378, ch. 10. Philip's witness, *et hanc ego vidi*: col. 379, ch. 11. The deaf girl at Winterthur: col. 379, ch. 11. Bernard's sermon and the lame boy: col. 380, ch. 14. Bernard at Speyer at the Christmas court of the emperor: col. 381, ch. 15.

King Conrad's words were to have been (col. 382, ch. 15) *Agnosco prorsus divina munera gratiae, nec deinceps, ipso praestante, ingratus inveniar; partus sum servire ei, quandoquidem ex parte ejus submoneor.*

Bernard's speaking in the Romance language (Old French) (col. 382, ch. 16): *Cujus verba cum minus intellexissem, quod romana lingua loqueretur.*
Conrad's summoning of the princes and Bernard's sermon: col. 383, ch. 17.
Bishop Anselm of Havelberg's cure: col. 384, ch. 19. Bernard's conviction that one person can substitute for another, to make up for his faith, as in the EM story (II.6) about Bernard ordering a monk to take communion on the basis of Bernard's faith.
The lost record of events in Speyer: col. 384, ch. 19.
Bishop Herman of Constance's praise for Bernard: col. 386, ch. 20.

ON THE ROAD FROM SPEYER TO COLOGNE AND LIÈGE

Criterion for writing down miracles (PL 185:387, ch. 22): *Nec dubitamus multo plura et apud vos, et in itinere miracula claruisse, quam tunc potuerimus nosse, aut possimus nunc recordari. Sed certissima tantum et probatissima scripsimus.*
Brother Wolkemar's addition to the narrative: cols. 387–88, ch. 23.
The lame man who did not understand Bernard's language: col. 388, ch. 24.
Bernard in Cologne: cols. 389–90, ch. 25. "We neglected to note them down" (Bernard's cures): *sed quia annotare negleximus superveniente multitudine caeterorum, nobis jam penitus exciderunt.*
Bernard's sermon to the clergy: cols. 389–90, with quotations from Psalms and Isaiah.
His Mass presumably in the cathedral and the cures that followed: col. 390, ch. 26.
Bernard in the hospice window receiving sick people handed over to him: cols. 390–91, ch. 27.
Abbot of Altenkamp's witness: col. 391, ch. 27.
Brother Gerard unable to enter the house because of the crowds: col. 391, ch. 28.
Brother Philip's remark that the greater miracle was how Bernard escaped unharmed: col. 391, ch. 28.
The chanting of the sick and those cured: col. 391, ch. 28.
Abbot of Altenkamp's observation about crowding: col. 391, ch. 29.
The monastery of Brunweiler: col. 392, ch. 30.
Because of the narrow space and crowd, many things happened that we ignore: col. 393, ch. 32.
Geoffrey's letter to Bishop Herman: col. 395, ch. 34, *nihil me scripsisse nisi quod aut vidi oculis meis, aut fratrum nostrorum qui praesentes fuerunt certissima relatione cognovi.*
Villers: col. 397, ch. 36, *Voluit ergo plantationem novellam vel in transit visitare, et peregrinantes filios consolari.* Vaucelles: col. 399, ch. 41, *nolens fraudare filios visitatione et consolatione paterna.*
Bernard the new Martin: *Novo temporis nostri Martino* (col. 399, ch. 41).
The meeting with King Louis: col. 400, ch. 42.
Bar-sur-Aube: col. 401, ch. 44. At Clairvaux, Bernard the happy man: *Felix nimirum . . . tam salubris tactus, sermo tam vivus et efficax invenitur.* Providing for quiet for the brothers: col. 402, ch. 45, *fratrum quieti providens.*

Troyes: col. 403, ch. 47.

Étampes: cols. 404–5, ch. 50.

Molesme: col. 406, ch. 52, *quod est monasterium unde egressi sunt olim patres nostri, a quibus Cisterciensis ecclesia sumpsit exordium.*

Returning to Clairvaux: col. 407, ch. 53.

Trier: col. 407, ch. 54.

Geoffrey's conclusion: col. 410, ch. 59, *ubi plurima quoque miracula claruisse non dubito,* sed *haec coram me facta novi certius, fiducialiusque scripsi.*

THE MEANING OF MIRACLES

Bernard's reflection: VP III.20. A former Cistercian abbot once expressed surprise that I make use of VP, which for him is more a fairy tale than history. But such passages reveal that the authors of the VP did reflect carefully on the meaning and veracity of what they conveyed.

Bernard's early cures and his brothers resistance to them: VP I.43, 45.

Bernard as a prophet recognized in his own country: PL 185:400, ch. 42, *et ipse, multiplicata sunt miracula manifesta, ut plus quam propheta probaretur, propheticus honor non deerat, ne ipsa quidem in patria sua.*

Walter Map, *De nugis curialium: Courtiers' Trifles*, ed. M. R. James, rev. C. N. L. Brooke and R. A. B. Mynors (Oxford: Clarendon Press, 1983). For Walter Map's treatment of Bernard, see his dist. 1, ch. 24, pp. 78–83.

A sober and helpful introduction to miracles in this period is Benedicta Ward, *Miracles and the Medieval Mind* (London: Scolar Press, 1982).

REACTING TO THE CRUSADE'S FAILURE

The Deeds of Frederick Barbarossa, trans. Charles Christopher Mierow (New York: W. W. Norton, 1966), bk. 1, ch. 35 (36), p. 70. Latin text in *Die Taten Friderichs oder richtiger Cronica*, ed. Franz-Joeph Schmale (Darmstadt: Wissenschaftliche Buchgesellschaft, 1965), ch. 36, p. 200.

For the course of the crusade, see Jonathan Phillips, *The Second Crusade* (New Haven: Yale University Press, 2007), esp. 207–27.

Bernard to Peter the Venerable: SBO 8, no. 364; James, no. 398. To Suger: SBO 8, no. 380; James, no. 408. This letter, however, may have been written already before the launching of the Second Crusade.

To Pope Eugenius: SBO 8, no. 256; James, no. 399. Bernard quoted from Seneca's letter 22.7 to Lucilius. This collection was immensely popular in the twelfth century, which I have called the age of friendship (see my *Friendship and Community*, ch. 6).

To Peter the Venerable, that he come to a second crusade meeting: SBO 8, no. 521; James, no. 400.

Five Books on Consideration: Advice to a Pope, trans. John D. Anderson and Elizabeth T. Kennan (Kalamazoo, MI: Cistercian Publications, 1976). Latin edition: SBO

3, pp. 393–493. The passage about the sons of the Church lying prostrate in the desert is 2.1, trans. p. 47. The Old Testament comparison is in 2.2, trans. pp. 48–49.

Looking for victory on a third try: 2.3, trans. p. 50. Seeking a consolation for conscience: 2.4, trans. p. 51.

Arnold of Brescia and Gilbert de la Porrée: Two Enemies

John of Salisbury, *Historia Pontificalis: Memoirs of the Papal Court*, trans. Marjorie Chibnall (London: Thomas Nelson, 1956), ch. 31, p. 63.

There is something insightful in Arnold's characterization of Bernard as someone who only recognized learning when it was found "in his own disciples." Is this John of Salisbury's criticism also?

John's description of Arnold's disciples: *Memoirs*, p. 64.

John on Bernard and Gilbert de la Porrée: *Memoirs*, ch. 8, pp. 15–16. Bernard telling churchmen it was their duty to correct scandals: *Memoirs*, pp. 17–18.

Bernard's attempt to persuade Pope Eugenius: *Memoirs*, ch. 9, p. 20. John's conclusion about Bernard as inspired by charity: *Memoirs*, ch. 11, p. 25. Bernard spoke with the words of prophets and apostles: *Memoirs*, ch. 12, p. 26.

Bernard's own perception of the whole of Scripture before him: VP III.7.

Bernard as more effective in transacting business: *Memoirs*, ch. 12, p. 27.

John on the question of the divorce of Ralph of Vermandois: *Memoirs*, ch. 6, pp. 12–13.

Bernard's prediction about the offspring of Ralph: *Memoirs*, ch. 7, pp. 14–15.

A Semblance of Business as Usual

Bernard to Suger in praise of restoration of the abbey of Sainte Geneviève: SBO 8, no. 369; James, no. 402.

Further on this abbey to Suger: SBO 8, no. 370; James, no. 403.

To Suger so he would attend the Council of Chartres: SBO 8, no. 377; James, no. 404.

To Suger against tournaments: SBO 8, no. 376; James, no. 405.

Telling Suger what to do in a food shortage: SBO 8, no. 379; James, no. 407.

Sending an impoverished abbot to wealthy Suger: SBO 8, no. 379; James, no. 380.

Sermon on the Passing of Saint Malachy, trans. Robert T. Meyer, in *The Life and Death of Saint Malachy the Irishman* (Kalamazoo, MI: Cistercian Publications, 1978), 97–104. Latin text: SBO 5, pp. 417–23.

Malachy "from the ends of the earth": §1, trans. p. 97. Rejoicing in his life: §5, p. 101. The transfer of the bones of the first brothers of Clairvaux: §2, p. 98.

Bernard's Testament: *On Consideration*

For Luther and *De consideratione*, see Franz Posset, "Recommendations by Martin Luther of St. Bernhard's *On Consideration*," *Cistercian Studies* 25 (1990): 175–87.

Five Books on Consideration (cited above under "Reacting to the Crusade's Failure"): Preface, trans. p. 24.

For the chronology of its composition, see the introduction, SBO 3, p. 381.

The demands of litigants, so that the pope's "poor body" can never rest: 1.4, trans. p. 29.

When are we to pray or to teach? 1.5, trans. p. 31.

Apply your experiences . . . nothing for consideration: 1.6, trans. p. 33.

Pope Gregory the Great's consideration: 1.12, trans. p. 43.

Listening to lawyers' subversion of the truth: 1.13, trans. p. 44.

The types of consideration: 2.6, trans. pp. 52–53.

Consider what type of man you are: 2.19, trans. p. 71.

Ambition and Italian greed: 3.5, trans. p. 84.

The abuse of appeals: 3.9, trans. p. 89.

Hand the appeals over to others: 3.12, p. 93.

Neglected decisions from the Council of Reims: 3.19, p. 104.

Characterization of the Roman people: 4.2, p. 111.

Everything given to honor, nothing to sanctity: 4.5, p. 115.

Unique career of the Cistercian cardinal: 4.13, p. 126.

How can this happen, Eugenius? 4.15, p. 128.

Popes' daily review of expenses: 4.20, p. 134.

Avoiding foppish young men: 4.21, p. 135.

See canon 4 of the Second Lateran Council: *et nec in superfluitate, scissura aut colore vestium nec in tonsure, intuentium . . . offendant aspectum. Conciliorum oecumenicorum decreta*, ed. Joseph Alberigo (Basel: Herder, 1962), 173.

Moderation: 4.22, p. 135. The pope as brother: 4.23, p. 137.

Renewed attack on Gilbert de la Porrée's Trinitarian teaching: 5.18, p. 162.

Anticipating the vision of God: 5.27, p. 174.

God still to be sought: 5.32, p. 179.

SAYING GOODBYE TO SUGER

Letter to the dying Suger: SBO 8, no. 266; James, no. 411.

Suger's brief reply: Gastaldelli, vol. 3, p. 1135.

To Ida, Countess of Nevers: SBO 8, no. 375; James, no. 418.

10. Business as Usual in Preparing for Death

DEFINING HIS IDENTITY

Letter to Pope Eugenius, mentioning illness: SBO 8, no. 270. James, no. 340. VP V.2.

SBO 8, no. 310; James, no. 469. See Adriaan Bredero, "Études sur la *Vita Prima* de saint Bernard," *Analecta Cisterciensia* 17 (1961): 254–56. Gastaldelli, whom I consider to be a master of Bernard's letters, has a full analysis of the text in vol. 2, pp. 1160–62. He writes (p. 1161): "Der Brief ist in reinsten Stil Bernhards verfasst." See also Richard Upsher Smith, "Arnold of Bonneval, Bernard of Clairvaux, and Bernard's Epistle 310," *Analecta Cisterciensia* 49 (1993): 273–318.

Bernard's inability to digest his food: VP I.22.
Bernard at Metz: VP V.3–4.
Letter to the prior at Portes: SBO 8, no. 250; James, no. 326

Defending His Record with Carthusians and Premonstratensians

Letter to the abbot of Prémontré: SBO 8, no. 253; James, no. 328. "I wish that before you accused me . . .": §6. The burning of the hut: §8. Villers and the church of St. Follian: §9.
The agreement between Cistercians and Premonstratensians to which Bernard referred is from 1142. See "Les actes de confraternité de 1142 et de 1153 entre Cîteaux et Prémontré," *Analecta Praemonstratensia* 40 (1964): 193–205.
Bernard's insistence on loving deserves quotation from Letter 250.10: *Ego autem, fratres, quidquid vos faciatis, decrevi semper diligere vos, etiam non dilectus.*

Pleading with the Pope: One Appeal after Another

To Eugenius on behalf of brother Philip: SBO 8, no. 257; James, no. 330.
Brother Rualene: SBO 8, nos. 258–60; James, nos. 331–33.
The letter to Rualene himself: SBO 8, no. 260; James, no. 333.
A knight of the Temple: SBO 8, no. 261; James, no. 334.
Appeal for monks of St. Marie-sur-Meuse: SBO 8, no. 262; James, no. 335.
The prior of the Grande Chartreuse: SBO 8, no. 270; James, no. 340.
Bernard's response to Pope Eugenius's confirmation of the Charter of Charity: SBO 8, no. 273; James, no. 343. The text of the papal bull can be found in Chrysogonus Waddell, ed., *Narrative and Legislative Texts from Early Cîteaux* (Cîteaux: Commentarii Cistercienses, 1999), 390–94. The pope's review of the development of the Cistercian Order: PL 182:476–78.
Bernard to Abbot Hugh in Rome: SBO 8, no. 274; James, no. 344.

Contested Episcopal Elections and Conflicted Bishops

To Pope Eugenius, concerning the bishopric of Auxerre after the death of Bernard's friend of youth, Hugh: SBO 8, no. 276; James, no. 345.
On the same matter to Eugenius: SBO 8, no. 275; James, no. 346.
A third letter about the episcopal election, to Eugenius: SBO 8, no. 280; James, no. 347.
Bernard's letter to King Louis about the Auxerre election: SBO 8, no. 282; James, no. 348. The royal prerogative: *licentia elegendi.*
James's summary of the Auxerre election, p. 422. See also Williams, 187–89.
To Pope Eugenius, on behalf of the bishop of Beauvais: SBO 8, no. 305; James, no. 371.
To Cardinal Hugh, for the bishop of Beauvais: SBO 8, no. 307; James, no. 372.

CLUNY AND THE MONKS OF MIROIR

To Pope Eugenius for the monks of Miroir: SBO 8, no. 283; James, no. 353.
Bernard's characterization of Peter the Venerable's intervention: *affectuosius quam efficacius.*
To Eugenius for Peter the Venerable: SBO 8, no. 277; James, no. 349. Bernard expressed his affection: *affectui.* Peter was his friend on pilgrimage: *amicum perigrinantem.*

TELLING OFF LAY LORDS, PROTECTING PIGS, AND ADVISING WOMEN

Letter to Henry the Liberal, Count of Champagne: SBO 8, no. 279; James, no. 351. For background, see the superb study by Theodore Evergates, *Henry the Liberal, Count of Champagne, 1127–1181* (Philadelphia: University of Pennsylvania Press, 2016).
Bernard to the Count of Angoulême: SBO 8, no. 299; James, no. 364.
To the Countess of Blois, regarding Count Henry: SBO 8, no. 300; James, no. 365. "Spirit of gentleness": *spiritu lenitatis.*
There are many translations of the Rule of St. Benedict, including that by Justin McCann (London: Sheed and Ward, 1976).
For Evergates's interpretation of this letter, see *Henry the Liberal*, 28–29.
Letter to Sancia of Spain: SBO 8, no. 301; James, no. 366.
Letter to the aunt of the emperor of Spain: SBO 8, no. 455; James, no. 367.
Bernard's warning against founding Cistercian houses in distant places is discussed in chapter 5 above.

A GREAT BETRAYAL: NICHOLAS OF MONTIÉRAMEY

Bernard's letter to Peter the Venerable: SBO 8, no. 389, James, no. 309, ending with a greeting from Nicholas to Peter: *Ego Nicolaus vester saluto vos in aeternum, et ultra, et domesticam illam familiam, quae lateri et spiritui vestro adhaeret.*
Bernard to Pope Eugenius, he had been deceived: SBO 8, no. 269; James, no. 339.
To Eugenius, forged letters and seal: SBO 8, no. 284; James, no. 354.
To Eugenius, Nicholas has gone away: SBO 8, no. 298; James, no. 363. The previous letter to which Bernard referred was no. 284.
"Sentenced to perpetual silence" is the ending of Letter 298.

MAKING MALACHY INTO A SAINT

Jean Leclercq, "Études sur saint Bernard et le texte de ses écrits," *Analecta Sacri Ordinis Cisterciensis* 9 (1953): 164: *suam expressit imaginen non advertens.*
For the Cistercian recycling of Bernard's description of Malachy into the office for Bernard as saint, see my "Bernard and Malachy Reconsidered," in Brian Patrick McGuire, *The Difficult Saint: Bernard of Clairvaux and His Tradition* (Kalamazoo, MI: Cistercian Publications, 1991), 75–106, esp. 80–82.

Malachy's *interiorem hominem* is in ch. 43 of *Vita sancti Malachiae*, in SBO 3,
    pp. 307–78. Trans. Robert T. Meyer, in *The Life and Death of Saint Malachy the
    Irishman* (Kalamazoo, MI: Cistercian Publications, 1978), 57.

Preface, p. 309: *benedixit mihi, et benedictionem hereditate possideo.*

First letter to Malachy: SBO 8, no. 341; James, no. 383. The next letters: SBO 8, nos.
    356 and 357; James, nos. 384 and 385.

"I am completely yours" (SBO 8, no. 357): *tuum esse modicum id quod sumus.*

Bernard's letter to the Irish brethren on Malachy's death: SBO 8, no. 374; James,
    no. 386.

A FRIEND FROM THE NORTH, ESKIL

For background, see my *The Cistercians in Denmark* (Kalamazoo, MI: Cistercian
    Publications, 1982), ch. 2; and James France, *The Cistercians in Scandinavia*
    (Kalamazoo, MI: Cistercian Publications, 1992), esp. ch. 1.

For Eskil in his relationship to Bernard, see my "Bernard and Eskil: Friendship
    and Confraternity," in Brian Patrick McGuire, *The Difficult Saint: Bernard of
    Clairvaux and His Tradition* (Kalamazoo, MI: Cistercian Publications, 1991),
    107–32.

Letter to Eskil: SBO 8, no. 390; James, no. 424.

Bernard's letter to Eugenius where Eskil is named, as mentioned above: SBO 8,
    no. 280.

Geoffrey of Auxerre's letter to Eskil on the death of Bernard is found at the
    opening of book 5 of VP but is not included in most modern editions of the
    work. This omission is probably a reflection of the fact that the PL edition
    of the VP does not include the letter. For its text it is necessary to go back
    further in time, to the edition of Bernard by Johannis Mabillon, *Sancti
    Bernardi . . . Opera omnia*, vol. 2 (Paris, 1719), 1130–31.

For Eskil and Bernard on the Redemption, see my "Bernard and Eskil," 118–19. For
    his storytelling, pp. 125–26.

LAST SERMONS, A FINAL EXCURSION, ILLNESS, AND DEATH

Geoffrey of Auxerre: Bernard at Metz, VP V.3.

For the date, see Williams, 358.

Bernard's "gaining strength from his labors": VP V.4, trans. p. 236.

The agreement "devised by Bernard, the faithful arbiter": VP V.4, trans. p. 237.

The peace did not last: Williams, 359.

Bernard's cures in the area of Metz: VP V.5–7.

To Pope Eugenius, on his weakness: SBO 8, no. 270; James, no. 340.

To the French king: SBO 8, no. 304; James, no. 370.

Letter to his uncle Andrew: SBO 8, no. 288; James, no. 410.

Bernard's amazement that people so trusted him to be useful to them: VP V.12,
    trans. p. 245.

Bernard's death: VP V.13.

Geoffrey's description of how he withdrew his affections: VP V.8, trans. p. 241.

BERNARD IN DEATH

The entrance of non-monks to Clairvaux: VP V.14, trans. p. 247.

Bernard's burial: VP V.15.

The abbot of Cîteaux's command that the dead Bernard cease his miracles: EM I.20.

Abbot Goswin of Bonneval, then Cîteaux: SBO 8, no. 270; James, no. 340.

Vision of Bernard climbing the mountain: VP V.22.

🐚 INDEX

Abelard, Peter, 2, 18, 63, 74, 140–50, 176, 203–4, 213, 248–49, 252, 262, 274–75, 289–91, 303–4
Adrian IV (pope), 236
Aelred of Rievaulx, 26, 102, 125, 165, 168, 174–75, 209, 268, 272–73, 276
affectus, 5, 81–83, 125, 127, 249, 272, 291, 298–300
Alan of Regny, 226–27
Alberic (abbot), 24, 287
Aleth of Montbard (Bernard's mother), 13–15, 17–18, 20, 244, 269
Altenkamp, 192–94
Ambrose (bishop of Milan), 111, 264
Amplexus (embrace by Christ), ii, 3, 255, 261, 271, 280
Anacletus II (pope), 84, 87, 89–91, 94–95, 98, 100, 110–11, 114, 116–18, 129–30, 132, 147, 221, 274, 283
Andrew (Bernard's brother), 20, 23
Andrew (procurator), 161
Andrew of Montbard (Bernard's uncle), 244
Anselm (abbot and archbishop), 7–8, 135, 144, 247, 298
Anselm (archbishop of Milan), 98
antipope, 111, 114, 130, 132. *See also* Anacletus II (pope)
anti-Semitism, 184–85, 282–84. *See also* Jews
Apulia, 82, 95, 114, 131
Aquitaine, 87–90, 182, 211
Arius, 143, 147–48
Armagh, Ireland, 129, 208, 236–39
armed pilgrimage, 9–10, 182. *See also* Crusades
Arnold of Bonneval, 6, 80–81, 84, 86–88, 91–92, 94, 97–98, 114, 116, 215, 252, 274
Arnold of Brescia, 146, 175–76, 202–3, 235, 303
Arnold of Morimond, 49–50, 52, 285–86
Arnulf (bishop-elect of Lisieux), 150
Artald, abbot of Preuilly, 76

Ascension, 298–301
asceticism, 24–26, 36, 125–26, 138, 169, 216, 252, 257, 270, 290, 305–7. *See also* monastic discipline
Augustine of Hippo, 107, 126, 128, 205, 264, 272, 297
Auxerre, 195, 207, 213, 226–27

balance of power, 9, 86, 88, 129–31, 160, 227
baptism, 8, 63–64, 66, 176, 186, 259, 303
Bar-sur-Aube, 56, 195, 219
Bartholomew (Bernard's brother), 20
Bartholomew (monk), 75, 93
Becket, Thomas, 198
Benedict, Saint, 37, 39, 114, 163
Benedictine monasteries, 55, 80, 102–5, 132, 168–70, 181, 222–23, 234, 240
Benedict of Flay, 72–73
Bernard of Clairvaux: as "a difficult saint," 1–6, 12, 214, 291; biographies of, 2, 251–66; birth of, 13; bodily issues, eating and sleeping habits, 25–26, 36, 79–80, 109, 216, 253, 269–72, 289, 304–7 (*see also* asceticism); canonization, 254; childhood, 13–18; chronology of life and times, xi–xii; as church reformer, 2, 51–53, 134, 217–18, 236 (*see also* ecclesiastical politics; papal schism; reformation, first medieval); death of, 240, 245–47; desecration of grave, 1, 247, 290; family background, 10–11, 13–18, 31; health and illnesses, 35–38, 47, 114–16, 120–21, 163, 170, 215–16, 229, 242–45, 304–7; inner life, 3–6, 45, 47, 54, 109, 118, 196–99, 208–12, 216–17, 236, 245, 248–49, 258, 274–75, 297–301, 307; male companionship and friendships, 4–5, 35–38, 43, 46–49 (*see also* friendship; love); map of immediate world of, xvi; as monk and abbot, 1–6,

Bernard of Clairvaux (*continued*)
19–29, 217, 221–22, 273–77 (*see also*
Clairvaux Abbey); as mother figure,
31–32, 42, 75–76, 221–22, 265; personality,
23–24, 31–33, 41–42, 51–53; phenomenon
of, 247–49; as political figure, 1–6,
199–202, 217, 242–43, 247–49, 273–75 (*see
also* Crusades; secular politics); primary
sources on, 112–13, 251–55; sexuality
and sexual identity, 4, 18–19, 272–73, 305;
as "the first European," 2, 160, 247–49,
260; travels, 79–80, 84, 90–92, 97, 110,
124, 151, 165–66, 181–96, 208, 216, 230,
242–43; women, relations with, 20–21,
213, 262, 266–69, 272–73, 290. *See also*
sermons; theology; writings by
Bernard
Bernard of Montbard, 13
Bernard of Portes, 216–18
Bernardo Paganelli, 169–71, 180. *See also*
Eugenius III (pope)
biblical quotations. *See* Scriptures
bishoprics, 134, 152–62, 226–29
Blois, Countess of, 232–33
Boniface VIII (pope), 211–12
Boswell, John, 19
Bourges, 154–56, 158, 207
Bouton, Jean de la Croix, 285–87
Bredero, Adriaan, 24–25, 81, 260–61, 269,
291–94
Brill Companion (*Companion to Bernard of
Clairvaux*), 260–61, 263–65
Bruun, Mette B., 264
Burgundy, 14–17, 19, 39, 119, 229–31
Bynum, Caroline Walker, 31, 265

Caesar, 111–12
Canterbury, 135, 172–73, 198, 247
Carthusians, 217–18, 223
Casey, Michael, 18, 24, 265–66
Cathars, 177–78
cathedral schools, 63–64
Celestine II (pope), 130, 159, 162, 166–67
celibacy, 139. *See also* sexuality and sexual
identity
Châlons-en-Champagne, 194
Châlons-sur-Marne, 35, 45, 156, 159, 223
Champagne, 11, 39, 156–57, 162, 195, 236
charity, 169, 174, 284. *See also* Charter of
Charity
Charlemagne, 68, 183, 186, 248
Charter of Charity, 29, 35, 248, 284–85
Chartres, 59–60, 84–85, 200, 207

Châtillon-sur-Seine, 15–18, 20–22, 32, 42,
231, 263
children, 9, 42–43, 45
Chrétien de Troyes, 43, 83
Church: politics in (*see* ecclesiastical politics);
power of (*see* ecclesiastical power); reform
in (*see* reformation, first medieval); unity
of, 116–17
Cicero, 51, 123, 125, 276, 294
Cistercian Order: asceticism, 169 (*see also*
asceticism); development of, Bernard's
role in, 284–89; expansion of, xvii, 2,
39, 76, 86–87, 132, 233–34, 237–40,
248; founding of, 25, 28–29, 35, 49–50,
104, 196, 284 (*see also* Cîteaux (The
New Monastery)); liturgy, 133; Marian
devotion, 18; recruiting of monks, 9,
19–24, 42, 55–56, 99, 195; spirituality, 3,
174; statutes, 32, 50, 224; women and,
20–21, 23. *See also* Charter of Charity;
General Chapter; Regular Cistercians
(O.Cist.); Trappist-Cistercian Order
(O.C.S.O.)
Cîteaux (The New Monastery), 49–51, 104,
220, 259; Bernard's entrance into, 19–29;
Clairvaux and, 32; influence of, 241
Clairvaux Abbey: admission of monks
from other monasteries, 72–73, 208,
219–20; Bernard's absences from, 81–83,
140, 160, 273–77 (*see also* ecclesiastical
politics; papal schism; secular politics);
converts, 61; daughter houses, 29–32, 90,
101–5, 133, 151, 177, 224, 276; expansion
of, 92–94, 110, 252; founding of, 30–35;
golden age, 37; Innocent II at, 86–87;
Malachy's death at, 237–39; Sicily and,
132. *See also* Bernard of Clairvaux;
Cistercian Order
Cluny Abbey/Cluniac Order, 13, 42–43,
45–46, 55, 71, 80, 84, 86, 119–21, 148–50,
169, 229–31, 284–85. *See also* Abelard,
Peter; Peter the Venerable (abbot)
Cologne, 191–93
Conrad (king), 98, 101, 131, 186, 189–91,
194, 199
consanguinity, 155, 159–60, 205–6
consolation, 122–27, 133–36, 138, 172,
213, 276
Constable, Giles, 280, 292
Constance, 187, 189
Constantine, 68, 115, 211
conversion, 21, 137, 140
Corbeil, 160–61, 163

Costello, Hilary, 23, 33, 183, 253–55
Crusades, 9–10; Bernard's language of,
    183–86; failure of, 199–202, 244, 291;
    First, 10, 184, 282; Second, 10, 66, 111,
    175, 180–96, 199–202, 253, 277–82, 291,
    295–96, 302; Third, 202. See also Holy
    Land; Jerusalem; Wends
Curia, 120, 145–48, 151, 154, 159, 163, 167,
    171, 173

Dark Ages, 2, 150, 249, 289
daughter houses, 29–32, 90, 101–5, 133, 151,
    177, 224, 276
David (king of Scotland), 104, 174
death, 120, 122–27, 129, 212–14
Denmark, 227, 239, 296
Desert Fathers, 22, 25, 32, 34, 270, 276
Dijon, 13, 230, 259, 287
Dinzelbacher, Peter, 262–63
Drogo (monk), 55–56

Eales, Samuel, 143
Eastern Church, 184, 199–200. See also
    Crusades
Eberhard (chaplain), 187–88, 190, 192, 194
Eberwin of Steinfeld, 177
ecclesiastical politics, 54–67, 79, 94–96, 99,
    115, 134, 150–52, 162–64, 215–21, 229–31;
    criticism of clerics, 139–40, 192, 210–11;
    elections, 118–19, 121, 164–69, 225–29;
    investiture of bishops, 86, 91, 119. See also
    heretics; papal schism
ecclesiastical power, 9, 24, 68–71, 86; abuse
    of, 58, 95, 139. See also papal authority
Edessa, 175, 181, 199
Elbodo of Cîteaux, 35
Elder, E. Rozanne, 37
Eleanor (queen), 155–56, 158–60, 175, 205
English Church, 179
English civil war, 185
Ephraim of Bonn, 282–84
Ermengarde, Countess of Brittany, 267–69
Eskil, archbishop of Lund, 239–41
Espec, Walter, 102
Esrum Abbey, 239–40
Étampes, Council of, 84–85, 112, 195,
    274–75
Eugenius III (pope), 95, 133, 166, 169–76,
    179–80, 182–83, 199–204, 206, 208–11,
    215, 218, 221–28, 230, 235–36, 240, 243,
    245–46, 252, 268, 278, 281
Europe: creation of, 2, 160, 247–49, 260;
    everyday life in, 11; maps of, xvi–xvii

excommunication, 103, 130, 156, 179, 186
exemplum stories, 21, 254–55, 269, 280
Exordium Magnum Cisterciense, 27, 83, 85,
    123–24, 148, 158, 179–80, 246, 254, 271, 288
Exordium Parvum, 196
experience, 107–8, 137–39

faith, 126, 143–44, 298
Farfa Abbey, 132–33, 170, 175
Feiss, Hugh, 63, 259
Ferzoco, George, 281
feudal society, 101–2, 122, 278. See also
    secular politics
Fitzherbert, William, 164–68, 173–74
Flay Abbey, 72–73
Foigny Abbey, 39–41
Fontaines-lès-Dijon, 13–15
Fontenay Abbey, 38, 195
Fontevrault, 151–52
forgiveness, 101, 130, 140, 220
Fossier, Robert, 259
Fountains Abbey, 102–5, 164–65, 167–68,
    173–74
Fragmenta, 15–16, 21–22, 25, 27, 33, 251,
    253–54
Franciscan Order, 80
Francis of Assisi, 16
Frankfurt, 186–87, 189, 196
Frederick, Duke, 190
free choice, 9, 42, 64–67
freedom of expression, 70, 161
friendship, 51, 162–63; church politics and,
    71, 73–74, 153, 157; between monks, 4–5,
    35–38, 43, 46–49, 77–78, 102, 125–27,
    213, 220–21, 237–38, 272; with Peter the
    Venerable, 291–95; truth and, 62. See also
    affectus; love
Fulk (canon), 44

Gallican Church, 97
Gastaldelli, Ferruccio, 256, 262–63
Gaudry (Bernard's uncle), 20, 197, 276
General Chapter, 29, 35, 50, 163, 173,
    222–23, 284–85, 287–88, 305
Genoa, 90–91
Geoffrey (abbot), 102–4
Geoffrey, bishop of Chartres, 59–60, 69, 87, 95
Geoffrey, prior of Clairvaux, 118, 121
Geoffrey of Auxerre, 6, 14–15, 21–23, 39,
    80–81, 96, 132–33, 137, 160, 177, 183,
    187–89, 191–92, 194–96, 205, 215–16,
    236, 240, 242–43, 245–47, 251–52, 254,
    265, 267

Geoffrey of Chartres, 176, 211

Geoffrey of Langres (Bernard's cousin), 195

Gerard (Bernard's brother), 5, 14, 32, 82, 110, 113–14, 197; conversion story, 21; death of, 120, 122–27, 129, 136, 142, 276

Gerard (cardinal), 166

Gerard (monk), 187–88, 193

Gerard of Angoulême, 87–90, 117

Germany, 96–97

Gerson, Jean, 169

Gerver, Michael, 280

Gethsemani Abbey, 22, 93, 259

Gilbert de la Porrée, 203–6, 212–13, 289–91, 303

Gilson, Étienne, 44, 257–58

God: fear of, 53; presence of, 10; protection provided by, 133–36; will of, 123, 128, 214. See also Holy Spirit; Jesus Christ

goodwill, 76, 155, 163, 294

Gospels, 8, 25, 34, 80, 100–101, 193, 197, 276, 298–99. See also Scriptures

Goswin of Bonneval, 223

Goswin of Cîteaux, 246

Gottschalk, Abbot, 219

grace, 64–67, 129, 139, 147, 247, 268

Gregorian Reform, 8–9, 86, 161, 273, 282. See also reformation, first medieval

Gregorio Papareschi, 84. See also Innocent II (pope)

Gregory the Great, 102, 205, 209

Gregory VII (pope), 8, 68, 100, 161

Guilencus of Langres, 59

Gunnar/Gonario of Sardinia, 179–80

Guy (Bernard's brother), 20–21, 276

Guy, abbot of Cherlieu, 151

Guy, abbot of La Grande Chartreuse, 34

Guy, abbot of Trois Fontaines, 73–75

Guy, cardinal in Bohemia, 176

Guy of Castello (cardinal), 147, 166. See also Celestine II (pope)

Hadrian IV, 176

hagiography, 6, 18, 25, 32–33, 80–81, 188, 237, 242–43, 245, 253, 255–56

Haimeric (cardinal), 70–71, 127, 148, 154

Hamburg, 239–40

Hay, Malcolm, 283

Heloise, 2, 21, 142, 289–90

Henry (heretical monk), 176–78, 301

Henry (monk of Clairvaux), 96, 191

Henry, archbishop of Sens, 57, 59

Henry, bishop of Beauvais, 228, 235

Henry, bishop of Sens, 152

Henry, Duke of Bavaria, 112, 114

Henry de Marcy, 302–3

Henry I (king), 84–85, 101, 158, 267

Henry II (king), 57, 160, 197

Henry IV (emperor), 8, 68, 161

Henry of Blois (legate), 165, 168

Henry of Verdun (bishop), 60

Henry of Winchester (bishop), 166, 171

Henry the Liberal (count), 231–32, 236

Herbert of Clairvaux, 3, 27, 241, 254

heretics, 147, 175–78, 210, 290–91; persecution of, 301–4

Herman of Constance (bishop), 187, 191–92, 194

Hervin of Steinfeld (abbot), 192

Hildebert (bishop), 94

Hildegard, abbot of Flay, 73

Hildegard of Bingen, 268

Hillin, archbishop of Trier, 242

Hincmar (cardinal), 172

Holdsworth, Christopher, 261, 277, 287

Holy Land, 10, 244; Knights Templar and, 65–66; Morimond monks in, 49. See also Crusades; Jerusalem

Holy Roman Empire, 91, 98, 110–12, 114–18

Holy Spirit, 108, 143, 299–300

homoeroticism, 19, 272–73. See also sexuality and sexual identity

Honorius II (pope), 69, 83, 85

Hugh (abbot of Trois Fontaines, later cardinal), 224–25, 228–29

Hugh (bishop of Lincoln), 198

Hugh (candidate for bishop), 94

Hugh of Macon, abbot, later bishop, 21–22, 55–56, 69, 161, 225–26

Hugh of Payens, 65, 244

Hugh of Prémontré, 218–20

Hugh of Saint Victor, 63

Humbeline (Bernard's sister), 22–23, 268–69

Humbert, 56, 60

humility, 38–39, 58–59, 75, 98, 111, 240

Ida, Countess of Nevers, 213

Igny Abbey, 219

Immaculate Conception, 178–79, 257

Innocent II (pope), 229, 292; Abelard controversy and, 141–43, 145–49; appeals to, 150–54, 156; Bernardo and, 170; death of, 159, 167; papal schism and, 83–91, 94–97, 99–101, 104, 110–20, 129–33, 274–75; York election and, 165

Innocent III (pope), 100

interiority, 8, 208. *See also* Bernard of Clairvaux: inner life
Irish Church, 237–38
Islam and Muslim states, 199, 202, 279, 282. *See also* Crusades
Italy, 79, 97, 124; papal schism and, 90–92, 110–11, 114–18
Ivo (cardinal), 147, 153–55

James, Bruno Scott, 116, 143, 161, 168, 179, 227, 263, 268
Jerome, 27, 48, 205
Jerusalem, 10, 60, 66, 76, 278, 281, 296; fall of, 202, 210, 244. *See also* Crusades; Holy Land
Jesus Christ, 3, 8, 16, 25, 126, 144–45, 178, 197–98, 252, 306–7. *See also Amplexus* (embrace by Christ)
Jews, 84, 111, 184–87, 282–84, 302
Jocelin of Soissons, 158–61
John of Buzay, 163–64
John of Fécamp, 8
John of Salisbury, 203–6, 291
Jorannus of Saint Nicaise, 55
Josbert de la Ferté, 13, 30, 197
justice, 139, 155, 165, 206, 209–10, 231–32, 234

Kamp, 192
Kienzle, Beverly Mayne, 259
Kirkham, 164
knighthood, 10–11, 14, 21, 44, 65–66
Knights Templar, 3, 181, 222–23, 244, 279–80; founding of, 50, 65–66, 295–97
Knowles, David, 1
Koblenz, 191

"Lactation of Saint Bernard," 3, 17–18
La Ferté Abbey, 24–25
Lagny, 163
La Grâce-Dieu Abbey, 105
La Grande Chartreuse Abbey, 34, 215, 218, 223–24
Landulf of Saint Paul, 98
Lane, Anthony, 145
Lanfranc, 7
Langres, 57, 59, 118–21, 134, 195, 292
Languedoc, 303
Laon, 39, 71, 194
L'Arrivour Abbey, 226
Lateran Councils, 139; First (1123), 58; Second (1139), 100, 129–30, 211, 256; Third, 237

La Torre, 179
Lazarus, 126
learning *(eruditio)*, 138
Leclercq, Jean, 19–20, 26, 43–44, 49, 245, 258–59, 261–62, 266–69, 279–81, 303–5
Lent, 133–34, 136, 141, 228
Leo XIII (pope), 255–56
Liber miraculorum, 27, 254
Liège, 86–87, 183
Life of Martin of Tours, 236
Longpont Abbey, 90
Lothair (king/emperor), 84, 86, 91, 96, 98, 110–12, 116
Louf, André, 259
Louis VI (king), 57, 69–70, 84–85, 97
Louis VII (king), 62, 120–21, 154–62, 168, 175, 182, 191, 194, 199–200, 205, 207, 227–28, 243
love, 34–35, 51, 241; between brothers, 113, 122–27, 276; church politics and, 71; courtly, 126; for God, 106–9, 127–29; God's, for humankind, 144–45; limits of, 47; in monastic life, 73, 213; romantic, 43–44, 48–49, 290. *See also affectus;* friendship
loyalty, 111, 118, 162, 276
Lucca, 112–13
Lucius II (pope), 166, 168, 170
Luddy, Ailbe J., 257
Lund, 239–41
Lund, bishop of, 227
Luther, Martin, 209
Lyon, 119, 178, 229, 259

Mainz, 96, 183–84
Malachy of Armagh, 1, 129, 208, 236–39
manual labor, 26–27, 136, 171
marriage, 21, 139, 155, 159–60, 177, 205–6, 272
Martin, Saint, 8, 211, 236
Mary, Virgin, 3, 17–18, 38, 178–79, 194, 257, 269, 288
Mathilda (queen), 267
Matilda (empress), 165
Matilda (queen), 167
McGinn, Bernard, 64, 257, 271
medicine, 73, 197, 271
meditative reading *(lectio),* 27
Mellifont Abbey, 237–38
mental illness, 86–87
Merton, Thomas, 22, 93, 259
Metz, 216, 242–43
Mews, Constant, 145

Milan, 91, 97–101
miracles, 3–4, 32, 80–81, 91, 98, 109, 122, 243, 246, 253–54, 276; meaning of, 196–99; preaching the crusade and, 186–96
Miroir, monks of, 229–31
Mirror of Charity, 174–75, 209, 272–73
modernity, 2, 150
Molesme Abbey, 24, 58, 104, 195–96
monastic discipline, 71–75, 125; obedience, 50–51, 168–69, 246; poverty and, 86; strictness of, 19, 24, 44–45, 55, 71–73, 102–5, 169, 222–23, 232, 270, 273, 293. *See also* asceticism
monastic institutions: attachment and community in, 5, 28, 71, 81–83, 92, 249 (*see also affectus*; friendship; love); episcopal authority and, 58–59; everyday life, 5, 45; expansion of, 93; revolts against abbots, 39; structure of, 284–85
monastic vow: abandonment for crusades, 185–86; as lifetime choice, 10, 22
Monte Cassino, 114–15, 130
Moore, R. I., 301–4
Moos, Peter von, 264
moralizing literature, 53, 137–38. *See also exemplum* stories
Moreruela Abbey, 90
Morimond Abbey, 49–50, 52, 76, 285–86
Morison, James Cotter, 256
mother figure: Bernard as, 31–32, 42, 75–76, 221–22, 265; Western Church as, 11
mourning, 120, 122–27, 138
Murdac, Henry, 165–68, 174
mystical life, 108, 128, 256–57

Nativity, 16, 38, 47
Nestorius, 147–48
New Monastery. *See* Cîteaux (The New Monastery)
Nicholas (monk), 72
Nicholas II (pope), 83
Nicholas of Montiéramey, 148, 201, 234–36, 243, 293–94
Nicodemus, 63
Nivard (Bernard's brother), 22, 164, 233
Norbert of Xanten, 56, 60
Notre Dame (Paris), 69, 85, 95
nuns, 20, 142, 266–67, 269

obedience, 50–51, 168–69, 246
oblation, 42–43, 45
Odo of Deuil, 182
Old Testament, 8, 31, 201, 241, 295, 300. *See also* Scriptures

Orléans, 84, 95–96, 179
Otto (priest), 187
Otto of Freising, 182, 199
Otto the Great, 186

paganism, 16–17, 146, 186, 210
pantheism, 128
papal authority, 51, 167–68, 172; extent of, 114–15, 151, 212; plenitude of power, 24, 99–101, 211
papal canonization of saints, 252
papal envoy, 95
papal office, 209–12
papal schism, 70, 80–92, 94–101, 109–18, 130, 132, 155, 182, 221, 242, 252, 274–76, 292
Paraclete, 289–90
Paris, 137, 156, 163
pastoral care, 60–61, 74, 287
Patrologia Latina, 183
Paul, Saint, 21, 65, 106, 116, 124, 128, 139–40, 144–45, 185, 270–71, 294, 299
Pelagius, 147
persecuting society, 301–4. *See also* heretics
Peter, cardinal of Pisa, 116–17, 130, 142
Peter, Saint, 171, 211
Peter de la Châtre, 154–55
Peter the Hermit, 184
Peter the Venerable (abbot), 96, 117–19, 121, 148–50, 162–63, 199–201, 209, 213, 229–30, 234, 278, 291–95
Philip (archdeacon), 187, 189
Philip (bishop), 94–95
Philip (monk), 193
Philip (monk at Clairvaux), 61, 221
Phillips, Paschal, 265
Pietro Leone/Pietro Pierleoni, 117, 129, 147. *See also* Anacletus II (pope)
pilgrimage (*peregrinatio*), 181. *See also* armed pilgrimage; Crusades
Pisa, 91, 97–98; Council of, 97–98
Planeta, John, 198
Poitiers, 18, 87–90, 177, 203
Pontigny, 55–56, 76, 161
Portes Abbey, 216–18
Pranger, M. B., 263–64, 266
prayers, 8, 135, 247
Premonstratensians, 23, 60, 177, 217–21
psychohistory, 261–62, 304–7

Rainald of Bar, abbot of Cîteaux, 148–50, 223, 285–86, 288
Rainald of Foigny (abbot), 39–41
Ralph, Count of Vermandois, 155–57, 159, 162, 205–6

Raoul (monk), 184–85, 282–83
Raymond V, Count, 302
Raynald of Clairvaux, 16, 251
rebellion, 81, 101, 104, 298
Redemption, 141, 144–46, 290
reformation, first medieval, 8–9, 58, 68, 86, 88, 91, 129, 139, 161. *See also* ecclesiastical politics
Reginald of Monte Cassino, 114–15
Regular Cistercians (O.Cist.), 6, 257
Reims, 55, 90, 134, 194, 207; Bernard's election as archbishop of, 121–22; Council of, 204–5, 210, 291, 301
Rhineland, 111, 186, 188–96, 253, 282
Richard, Jean, 259
Richenza (Lothair's wife), 101
Ricuin, bishop of Toul, 60
Rievaulx Abbey, 90, 101–2, 104, 164, 167
Robert (abbot), 24
Robert (abbot of Molesme), 24, 59, 196
Robert (brother of Louis VII), 243
Robert (Premonstratensian monk), 219
Robert of Capua, 131
Robert of Châtillon (Bernard's cousin), 13–14, 17, 41–44, 46, 55, 254
Robert Pullen (cardinal), 172
Rochais, Henri, 258, 262
Roger, king of Sicily, 83, 90–91, 101, 111, 114, 116, 129–32, 140
Roman Catholic Church, 139, 179, 257
Roman Church, 43, 97, 99, 130
Roman Empire (Germany), 91, 98, 101
romantic love. *See* love
Rome, 91, 202–3. *See also* Italy
Rowe, John G., 281
Rualene of St. Anastasius, 221–22
Rudolph, Conrad, 46
Rudolph, Count, 207
Rule of Saint Augustine, 44–45
Rule of Saint Benedict, 22, 31, 38, 43, 45, 50–51, 58, 60, 73, 75, 92, 102–4, 124, 168–69, 232, 284–85, 295

Saint Anastasius Abbey, 133, 179, 221–22
Saint-Benoît-sur-Loire Abbey, 84
Saint Denis Abbey, 62, 142, 163, 168, 289
Sainte Geneviève Abbey, 206
Saint Follian Abbey, 219–20
Saint Mary Magdalene church, 181
Saint Mary of Mouzon Abbey, 223
Saint Nicaise Abbey, 55
saints, 14–15, 198, 252, 261. *See also* individual saints
Saint Urban Abbey, 223
Saint Victor Abbey, 206

Saint Vorles church, 16–17
salvation, 11, 63, 65, 136–37, 185, 280, 283, 290, 306
"Salve Regina" (hymn), 18, 288–89
Samson of Reims, 223
Saxo, 112–13, 239
Scandinavia, 227, 239
scholastic theology, 63–64, 143, 290, 303
Scriptures, 27–28, 31, 205; biblical quotations, 3, 8, 21, 34, 53–54, 65, 67, 71, 92–93, 100, 106, 111, 116, 118, 124–25, 127–28, 133, 135–36, 138, 140, 144, 184, 192, 209, 212, 220, 224, 241, 282–83, 292, 297–99. *See also* Gospels; Old Testament; Sermons on the Song of Songs
secular politics, 56–60, 79, 98, 111–12, 121, 154–62, 207–8, 216, 231–32, 242–43, 256. *See also* feudal society
secular power, 24, 68–71, 111, 231
Seguin, André, 277–81
Seneca, 51, 200
Sens, 57, 59, 69–70, 146, 152–53, 195, 207, 275
sermons, 105–9; on conversion, 137–40; criticizing clergy, 192; on God's protection, 133–36; liturgical, 297–301; *Sermon on the Passing of Saint Malachy*, 208. *See also* writings by Bernard
Sermons on the Song of Songs, 3, 5, 28, 34, 53, 105–10, 113, 122, 177, 241, 271–72, 297
sexuality and sexual identity, 139, 177, 198, 272–73, 305. *See also* homoeroticism; love
Sicily, 91, 131. *See also* Roger, king of Sicily
Signy Abbey, 48, 252
Simon of Saint Nicholas, 71–72
simony, 9, 71, 129, 165, 248
Simson, Solomon Bar, 282
singularity, 39
Smalley, Beryl, 26, 244, 304–5
socialis conversatio, 125
Soissons, 207
solitude, 27, 31–32, 141–42, 164, 171, 185–86, 208, 253, 263
Sommerfeldt, John R., 259
Song of Songs, 36. *See also* Sermons on the Song of Songs
Southern, Richard, 2–3, 248, 255, 305
Spain, 90, 233
Speyer, 189, 191
Steinfeld, 192
Stephen (king), 164–67, 173
Stephen Harding of Cîteaux, 24–25, 27–30, 46, 52, 58, 69, 248, 283–89, 307
Stephen of Garland, 62
Stephen of Palestrina, 147, 159, 166

358   **INDEX**

Stephen of Saint John at Chartres, 76
Stephen of Senlis, 69, 95, 137
Suger of Saint Denis, 62–63, 84–85, 158–59, 200, 206–7, 212–14, 243
Sulpicius Severus, 236
Swedish kingdom, 239

Taranto, 95, 221
temptation, 4, 18, 33, 55, 65, 136, 138, 208, 305
Tescelin Sorus (Bernard's father), 13, 33–34, 263
Theobald (nephew of archdeacon of Paris), 95–96
Theobald, Count, 56–57, 59–60, 94, 155–62, 168, 205–7, 231–32, 267
theology, 73–74, 141–50, 212–13, 263, 268, 283, 291, 303; monastic, 63; orthodox, 178–79. See also faith; grace; Redemption; scholastic theology; Trinitarian theology
Thomas (prior of Saint Victor), 95
Thurstan, archbishop of York, 103, 164
Toldanos Abbey, 233
Toul, 111, 196
Toulouse, 177, 179, 301–2
Tours, 94–95
Trappist-Cistercian Order (O.C.S.O.), 6, 93, 257, 295
Tre Fontane Abbey, 169–70, 179
Trier, 196
Trinitarian theology, 141, 143–47, 203–5, 212, 290
Trois Fontaines Abbey, 34, 73–75, 224–25, 287
troubadours, 44
Troyes, 195; bishop of, 153; Council of, 65; court at, 49, 60
Turks, 199

Ulger, bishop of Angers, 151–52
Umbald (cardinal), 120
University of Paris, 143
Urban II (pope), 9–10, 184

Vacandard, Elphège, 2, 112–15, 122, 129–30, 255–56, 278
Vaucelles Abbey, 90
Vauclair Abbey, 167
Vauluisant Abbey, 76
Vézelay, 180–82, 186, 202, 213, 275
Vibald of Monte Cassino, 115
Victor IV (pope), 117
Vikings, 7, 11
Villers, 183, 219–20
Ville-sous-la-Ferté, 1, 30

Vita Prima, 6, 14–17, 27, 37, 80, 83, 86, 93, 96, 122, 132, 137, 158, 160, 183, 197, 216, 246, 251–55, 260, 265, 271, 285, 293, 302, 305
Vita Quarta, 13–14, 17, 254
Vita Secunda, 254
Vita Tertia, 254
Viterbo, 113, 127, 170
Vitry, 156–57
Vitry-le-Brulé, 11
Vulgate (Latin translation of Bible), 4, 27, 67

Waddell, Chrysogonus, 285, 290
Waldef of Kirkham, 165
Walter Map, 197–98
Walter of London, 165, 167
Walter of Nevers, 198
Wends, 186, 248, 278–79
William, abbot of Esrum, 240
William, abbot of Grandselve, 246–47
William, Count, Duke, 87–90, 213
William, Count of Nevers, 226
William of Châlons, 305
William of Champeaux, 35, 37, 45, 285
William of Normandy, 7
William of Rievaulx, 102
William of Saint Barbe, 165, 168
William of Saint-Thierry, 6, 14–22, 24–26, 28, 30, 33, 35, 45, 53, 64, 67, 77, 122, 136, 141–42, 216, 253, 262, 269, 271, 275–76, 290, 305; friendship with Bernard, 36–38, 46–49, 251–52
Williams, Watkin, 17, 84, 183, 256–57, 278, 296
William X, Count of Poitiers, 87–90
Winkler, Gerhard, 297
women, 266–69; Cistercian Order and, 20–21, 23; illicit relations with, 177, 272–73; pastoral care for, 60–61; prohibited from entering Clairvaux, 246; societal attitudes toward, 23. See also nuns
Worms, 86, 91, 183, 191
writings by Bernard, 3–6, 256; Apology, 45–46, 77, 285; On the Conduct and Office of Bishops, 57; On Consideration, 58, 171, 175, 201, 203–4, 208–12, 280, 291; De laude novae militiae (In Praise of the New Knighthood), 65, 295–96; On Grace and Free Choice, 63–64; Homilies in Praise of the Blessed Virgin Mary, 16, 38, 306; Life of Malachy, 236–39; On Loving God, 35, 127–29; On Precept and Dispensation, 168–69; Steps of Humility and Pride, 38–39, 77. See also sermons

York/Yorkshire, 90, 101–4, 164–69, 171–74, 226–27